To Their Own Soil

Books in the **Henry A. Wallace Series on Agricultural History and Rural Studies**
Richard S. Kirkendall, Series Editor

The American Farmer and the New Deal, *by Theodore Saloutos*

Roswell Garst: A Biography, *by Harold Lee*

Railroad Development Programs in the Twentieth Century, *by Roy V. Scott*

Agricultural Science and the Quest for Legitimacy: Farmers, Agricultural Colleges, and Experiment Stations, 1870–1890, *by Alan I Marcus*

To Their Own Soil: Agriculture in the Antebellum North, *by Jeremy Atack and Fred Bateman*

To Their Own Soil

Agriculture in the Antebellum North

JEREMY ATACK
FRED BATEMAN

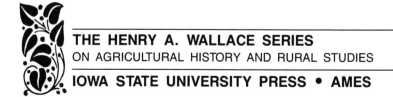

THE HENRY A. WALLACE SERIES
ON AGRICULTURAL HISTORY AND RURAL STUDIES

IOWA STATE UNIVERSITY PRESS • AMES

To
Fred and Emma
Frank and Doreen

Jeremy Atack is Professor of Economics, University of Illinois; Fred Bateman is Chairman and Professor, Business Economics and Public Policy, School of Business, Indiana University.

 Printed by Iowa State University Press from microcomputer diskettes provided by the authors.

First edition, 1987

Library of Congress Cataloging-in-Publication Data

Atack, Jeremy.
To their own soil.

(Henry A. Wallace series on agricultural history and rural studies)
Bibliography: p.
Includes index.
1. Agriculture—Economic aspects—United States—History—19th century. 2. United States—Rural conditions. I. Bateman, Fred, 1937- . II. Title. III. Series.
HD1773.A4A86 1987 338.1′0974 86-21349
ISBN 0-8138-0086-2

CONTENTS

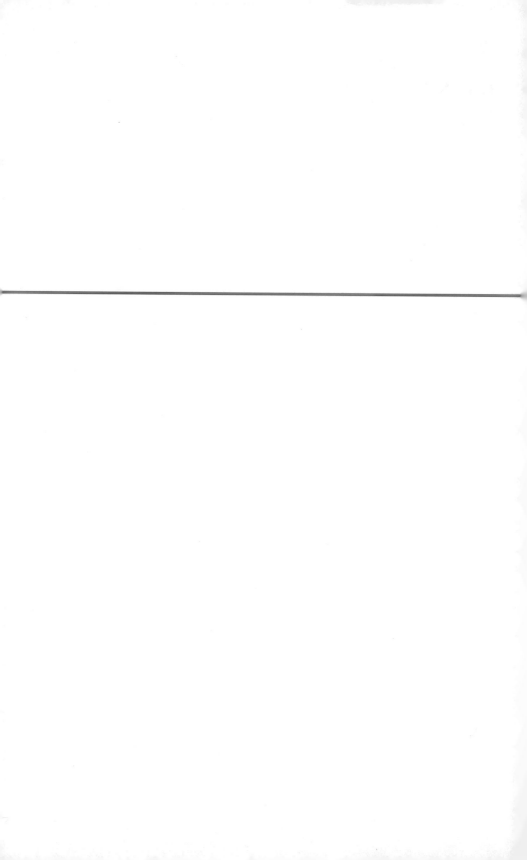

EDITOR'S INTRODUCTION

THE HENRY A. WALLACE SERIES on Agricultural History and Rural Studies is designed to enlarge publishing opportunities in agricultural history and thereby to expand public understanding of the development of agriculture and rural society. The Series will be composed of volumes that explore the many aspects of agriculture and rural life within historical perspectives. It will evolve as the field evolves. The press and the editor will solicit and welcome the submission of manuscripts that illustrate, in good and fresh ways, that evolution. Our interests are broad. They do not stop with Iowa and U.S. agriculture but extend to all other parts of the world. They encompass the social, intellectual, scientific, and technological aspects of the subject as well as the economic and political. The emphasis of the Series is on the scholarly monograph, but historically significant memoirs of people involved in and with agriculture and rural life and major sources for research in the field will also be included.

Most appropriately, this Iowa-based Series is dedicated to a highly significant agriculturist who began in Iowa, developed a large, well-informed interest in its rural life, and expanded the scope of his interests beyond the state to the nation and the world. An Iowa native and son of an agricultural scientist, journalist, and secretary of agriculture, Henry A. Wallace was a 1910 graduate of Iowa State College, a frequent participant in its scientific activities, editor of *Wallaces' Farmer* from 1921 to 1933, founder in 1926 of the Hi-Bred Corn Company (now Pioneer Hi-Bred International, Inc.), secretary of agriculture from 1933 to 1940, and vice president of the United States from 1941 to 1945. In the agricultural phases of his wide-ranging career, he was both a person of large importance in the development of America's agriculture and the leading policymaker during the most creative period in the history of American farm policy.

This volume takes the Wallace Series in new directions. The four earlier ones emphasized policy, science, and technology; this one focuses on farming itself. The earlier books employed long-established historical methods; this one uses the quantitative techniques that have taken on large importance in historical work only during the past two decades. One participant in that development, Robert P. Swierenga, points out that this new book "rests upon a massive data base and the most complex and sophisticated econometric techniques." And Allan G. Bogue, himself a pioneer, defines the work as "the first attempt to do a baseline analysis of a rigorously quantitative nature that is solidly grounded in the individual census returns at a pivotal point in national economic growth."

In agricultural history, quantitative methods have been employed significantly in studies of the South, but Atack and Bateman examine northern agriculture. They look at a time and a place when and where farming conformed rather closely to the Jeffersonian model. Studying family-type farming just before the United States became a highly industrialized nation, they reach important conclusions. They demonstrate, for example, that most northern farmers produced for markets as well as for their own families but were not influenced solely by business considerations. Agrarian ideals also affected their behavior.

RICHARD S. KIRKENDALL
Henry A. Wallace Professor of
Agricultural History and Rural Studies
Iowa State University

PREFACE

WITH A QUARTER-CENTURY OF HINDSIGHT, the major influence of the "New Economic History" has become apparent in the way we view American economic development. By first offering the negative contribution of bringing existing explanations into serious question and ultimately providing new ones to replace them, practitioners using the new methodology virtually revolutionized historical interpretations of some issues. Even where they did not, their sometimes awkward incursions into traditional realms of inquiry stimulated debate and produced a healthy rekindling of interest in the study of our economic past. Scholars today cannot perceive such areas as slavery, transportation, international trade, banking, or manufacturing in the same context as they did twenty-five years ago, not only because of the natural evolution of academic investigation, but also because a radically new framework has been created. New answers were provided but, more importantly, new questions were posed.

Curiously, one major area of U.S. economic life remained virtually untouched by the new approach. Indeed, it was the single most important economic activity practiced by Americans throughout most of the nineteenth century: Agriculture. The neglect has not been total. Agriculture as it related to the institution of slavery has been examined in nearly microscopic detail, but the concern lay more with the "Peculiar Institution" than with the economics of farming itself. The great scholarly void in the Cliometric Revolution oddly has been northern agriculture.

Our purpose in this book is to begin filling this gap by investigating the northern farm economy, a system that was fundamental to the Jeffersonian concept of America. Our approach reflects, we believe, the current methodological state in U.S. economic history. The field is less combative, less confrontational, and more tolerant of alternative approaches than it was even a decade ago. It has matured into an eclectic blend of history and economics that integrates scientific method, empirical substance, and historical narrative. In it, we found all three components valuable; without any one of them the story that we relate would have been different and to the detriment of understanding this subject. And despite our invocation of econometric models and economic analysis, we have tried hard to prevent the techniques from obstructing readers' understanding of the substantive results.

Underlying this study is an enormous data base collected from the manuscripts of the agricultural and population censuses by Fred Bateman and James Foust. Its creation was prompted by two pioneers in the new methodology, Robert Fogel and Stanley Engerman. When they were beginning their analysis of slavery, they believed that a data sample for antebellum northern agriculture would provide a benchmark against which to compare the southern experience. The result was this sample, funded by the National Science Foundation and completed in the early 1970s, which we exploit for our study. Beyond relatively limited use for specific research projects, its massive amount of quantitative information has never been fully utilized until the present work. Although it has been supplemented for our purposes by an extensive amount of additional research materials, quantitative and otherwise, this sample of nearly 12,000 farms, 21,000 rural households, and 108,000 persons formed the foundation for our work. As we hope this book will reveal, it has proven to be a powerful empirical resource. We also owe an intellectual debt to William Parker and Robert Gallman, whose sample of southern agriculture pioneered in providing data bases for our profession. Parker's work on agriculture further provided a continuing stimulus for our own research efforts.

Typical of academic researchers, we have published articles along the way while writing this monograph. Many individuals commented on our work privately and at professional meetings. When the full copy for the book was first drafted, we further imposed on friends to read all or portions of it. Throughout this process none was more helpful than Stanley Engerman, who commented on several papers and chapters with his usual generosity of insights. Our research benefited enormously from his counsel. We also owe our gratitude to James Foust for his efforts in originally helping to develop the sample. Among the many others who discussed this work with us were Clarence Danhof, Richard Easterlin, Robert Fogel, David Galenson, Robert Gallman, Judith Klein, Larry Neal, Alan Olmstead, William Parker, Winifred Rothenberg, Richard Steckel, Paul Uselding, Thomas Weiss, Jeffrey Williamson, and Gavin Wright. Papers on several topics were presented at workshops at the University of Illinois, Indiana University, the Newberry Library, Northwestern University, the University of Toronto, and the University of Chicago as well as at the annual meetings of the Agricultural History Society, the Cliometrics Society, the Economic History Association, and the Social

Science History Association. In 1984, a presentation outlining much of this book was presented at a conference in Montreal sponsored by the Interuniversity Centre for European Studies. Some research that has been incorporated into this manuscript has appeared previously in *Agricultural History*, *Agricultural History Review*, *Economics Letters*, *Historical Methods Newsletter*, *Journal of Economic History*, *Research in Economic History*, *Review of Economics and Statistics*, and *Social Science History*. To editors of these journals, we are grateful for permission to reprint portions of this work. We also thank the Lilly Library of Indiana University for providing the copy of a first edition of Thomas Jefferson, *Notes on the State of Virginia* (Paris, 1782) from which our title is taken. Suzanne Lowitt of the Iowa State University Press was particularly helpful during the preparation of the final copy.

Our writing was underwritten by sabbatical leave support from our institutions, the University of Illinois and Indiana University, the Bureau of Economic and Business Research of the College of Commerce and Business Administration at the University of Illinois, and the Illinois Investors in a Business Education. Research assistance and computer funding has been provided by the University of Illinois Research Board and by the Indiana University School of Business. We are grateful to them for this assistance, and for the able research assistance provided by Robert C. Graham, Susan Hotopp, and David W. Martin. Finally, but clearly not last in importance, the National Science Foundation deserves recognition for its financial support for the costly process of gathering the enormous data collection that underlies this study. Without their support we could not have amassed this information; without this information we could not have written this book.

JEREMY ATACK
FRED BATEMAN

Corruption of morals in the mass of cultivators is a phenomenon of which no age nor nation has furnished an example. It is the mark set on those, who not looking up to heaven, to their own soil and industry, as does the husbandman, for their subsistance, depend for it on the casualties and caprice of customers.

—THOMAS JEFFERSON
Notes on the State of Virginia

To Their Own Soil

CHAPTER ONE

Northern Agriculture before the Civil War

BY THE MIDDLE OF THE NINETEENTH CENTURY, the American Industrial Revolution was well underway. Within a comparatively brief time span, manufacturing had gained a sound foothold in a few eastern states. Over the remaining years of the century, it would advance westward across the northern states toward the Great Lakes to form the industrial heartland of the New World. When it came, the industrial transformation was swift and it altered the shape, pace, and conduct of American life in irrevocable ways. At midcentury though, most Americans still lived and worked as farmers and rural life remained the dominant ethos. This study is a detailed, quantitative historical examination of that economy and the farmer's role within it on the eve of its transformation.

Even those who no longer farmed were often only one step removed as workers in the agricultural processing activities that dominated the manufacturing sector or the service sector serving a rural population and the needs of farmers. In the West, South, and Middle Atlantic states, flour milling was the largest industry by value of product and tobacco manufacturing, liquor distilling, and sugar refining were among the top five in one or more regions. Even in New England, where manufacturing was comparatively advanced, flour and grist milling was the fifth largest industry.[1] Of the major industries, only textile production had progressed very far beyond the processing stage to a point where the product bore little resemblance to the agricultural commodity from which it was made.

Although growing in relative importance, manufacturing in 1860 employed far fewer workers, used much less capital, and produced a substantially smaller value-added than agriculture.[2] The inclusion of inputs of family labor that are not reported in official records and the value of land only further increases the relative dominance of agriculture in the late antebellum economy (see Table 1.1). Moreover, the population remained overwhelmingly rural. Only in Massachusetts and Rhode Island did the urban population exceed the rural. In the industrializing northeastern region as a whole, however, the rural population outnumbered city dwellers by almost two to one and further west the ratio was much higher.[3] On the eve of the Civil War, the economy remained based on agriculture as it had been since colonial days. In the South, where manufacturing and overland transportation development lagged behind that of the North, a contemporary observer would have had little difficulty identifying it as an agrarian economy. The plantation, the small self-sufficient farm, the slave system, the urban areas with their emphasis on commerce, export trade, and financial services all signaled the dominance of agriculture. Even in the North, there could have been no doubt for, excepting southern New England and portions of New York, Pennsylvania, and Delaware, the structure and composition of the economic system was clearly agrarian. While in some eastern cities private businesses and the government were building infrastructures to support industrialization, in most areas activities were directed to serving the needs of the agricultural sector. A short distance outside major urban and industrial centers such as New York or Philadelphia were dairies and truck farms that supplied these markets with perishables. Even after the Civil War, farming maintained its preeminence until during the 1880s industrial value-added finally exceeded that from agriculture. Manufacturing employment, however, only surpassed that in agriculture after the First World War.[4] Industrial activity before the Civil War retained close supply linkages with agriculture. An examination of most manufacturing establishments even in the northeastern states at this time would have convinced an observer that the economy had only taken its first, often hesitant, steps away from the farm toward specialized agricultural processing. Manufacturers also depended upon rural and farm buyers for many of their sales. Furthermore, agriculture played a critical role in America's foreign trade. Even excluding raw cotton exports, the export value of agricultural commodities exceeded that of semimanufactured and finished goods until the twentieth century.[5] Agriculture thus stood at the center of the economic system as a major source of demand, a principal supplier of inputs to manufacturers, and as the nation's largest single labor employer.

Farming has not escaped scholarly inquiry. Agriculture in the southern states during the antebellum era has received generous attention from historians and social scientists because of its distinctive personality. Slavery, its most infamous characteristic, was but one component of a

TABLE 1.1. Agriculture and Manufacturing in the United States in 1860

	Agriculture	Manufacturing
Employment (000s)[a]		
Farmers & Planters	2,509	
Farm Laborers	796	
TOTAL	3,305	1,311
Capital		
Land Value (billions)[b]	$6.645	
Farm Implements Value (billions)	$0.246	
TOTAL	$6.891	$1.010
Value Added (billions)	$1.50	$0.82

Sources: U.S. Census Office, Eighth Census, *Population of the United States in 1860* (Washington, D.C., 1864), 662–80; U.S. Census Office, Eighth Census, *Agriculture in the United States in 1860* (Washington, D.C., 1864), 184; U.S. Census Office, Eighth Census, *Manufacturers,* 742. Value-added data from U.S. Department of Commerce, *Historical Statistics of the United States,* Series F239 and F241.

[a]Employment figures for agriculture include only those reporting occupations as farmer, planter, or farm laborer. Manufacturing employment is for wage earners.

[b]Includes the value of improvements to the land.

complex social arrangement that was aristocratic—even autocratic—agrarian and paternalistic. Nevertheless, the South's economic orientation was interregional and international. In that society, land and slaves conferred social status and represented economic wealth. Land also represented wealth in the northern states, but there the individual parcels were smaller and more widely distributed among the population, making the social and political systems decidedly more democratic and less obviously paternalistic. Furthermore, immigration created a more heterogeneous and less parochial society.

Largely because the North lacked the South's forced labor system, there is an imbalance in our knowledge of southern and northern agriculture before the Civil War. Against the rich historical analysis and description of the slave South must be compared the relative paucity of quantitative analysis and even description of antebellum northern agriculture. Although it lacks the emotional impact of the plantation South's economic structure, northern agricultural development is more important for understanding the subsequent long-run economic development of the United States, both agriculturally and industrially.

Our study attempts to rectify this situation. Its use of econometric methods sets it apart from others on northern agriculture. It supplements such descriptive statistical works as Allan Bogue's *From Prairie to Cornbelt,* Merle Curti's *The Making of an American Community,* Clarence Danhof's *Change in Agriculture,* and Robert Swierenga's *Pioneers and Profits: Land Speculation on the Iowa Frontier* but does not try to replace them, and it obviously differs from Bidwell and Falconer's classic study.

Our interests extend beyond the confines of a single community or thesis such as in Curti's study, we transcend the state or regional focus of Bogue or Swierenga, and this study is less encyclopedic than that of Bidwell and Falconer.

The work is organized around a large sample of quantitative data drawn from the manuscripts of the federal census for 1860 for 102 townships across the northern tier of the United States from New Hampshire to Kansas and as far southward as Maryland and Missouri. Our temporal coverage is the second half of the nineteenth century with the primary emphasis on the late antebellum period. What emerges is a detailed quantitative description and analysis of northern agriculture as reflected in that massive economic-demographic survey, the Eighth Census of the United States, but one that could not be duplicated from the published sources.[6] It is, we think, a compelling picture providing not merely a statistical profile but, somewhat to our surprise, a revealing insight into American behavior and attitudes in the nineteenth century.

Farming acted as a magnet drawing people, capital, and natural resources into its productive processes. Land, although not free until after the passage of the Homestead Act in 1862, was readily and cheaply available throughout most of the nineteenth century in the less densely settled areas of the United States and especially on the frontier. It promised economic and personal independence and proved an irresistible attraction to millions. Public land at the margins of settlement offered one entry level. This land could be bought at public auction for as little as $1.25 per acre, or even less if purchased under the Graduation Act or with depreciated military land warrants. It could also be bought at a premium from land speculators and land-grant recipients. Paradoxically, the public land sales made large-scale land speculation feasible. However, the ability of private sellers to reap monopoly profits beyond those accruing to the unique characteristics of the plot of land in question was constrained by the vastness of the public domain and the frequency of its sale. There was also an active resale market in farmland both in the East and West, which offered an alternate entry level.

Between 1850 and 1859, the federal government sold almost 50 million acres of public land, or an area approximately one and a half times larger than New York State.[7] This land and more was turned into farms. Over the same period farmland increased by over 100 million acres, of which about half was cultivable, and almost 600,000 new farms were created. The most rapid expansion took place on the frontier. Farmland in Texas expanded by 12 million acres, that in Illinois by 9 million, while in Iowa farmland increased by over 7 million acres. In Massachusetts and Rhode Island, by contrast, the land in farms was beginning to decrease.[8]

Public land policy thus played a major role in the growth and development of American agriculture and, while its effects were most pronounced on the frontier, its influence was pervasive. Midwestern agricultural progress in particular had important ramifications for the agricultural sector in the Northeast. Similar tensions were also felt between the Old South and the New. As a result the spatial distribution of the population was radically altered, economic activities changed, and the size and composition of national income differed from what they would have been in the absence of this public land policy.

Among agricultural historians, land policy has commanded considerable attention, notably in the works of Paul Gates. Cliometricans have not been so attentive, choosing to focus primarily upon the speculator's role or efficiency effects of land disposal policy. In an important but sometimes overlooked cliometric analysis, Robert Fogel and Jack Rutner developed a model relevant to broader issues, many of which are investigated later in this book.[9] They considered the case in which land and labor are needed to produce agricultural goods in two geographically separate but contiguous regions, the East and the West. The land is of variable quality and the farmers may or may not be equally competent. Under these circumstances, the marginal product of labor will be declining in both regions; that is, each additional new farmer contributes less to total output than his predecessor because the land-labor ratio falls. Moreover, the best land is farmed first and newcomers squeezed onto more marginal lands. This situation is graphed in Figure 1.1. The horizontal axis OO′ represents the total available farm labor supply. This is a function of the size of the population, some given fraction of which are farmers and farm laborers. The marginal product of western labor is represented by the line WX and is read against the left, and the marginal product of eastern labor (EF) against the right, axis. In the absence of transport costs, the distribution of labor (and population) and national income, with its component parts of wages and rents, is then determined by the intersection of these two curves at N. At this point the marginal products of eastern and western labor are equal. Consequently, labor in both regions is paid the same real wage and there is no economic incentive for labor to migrate. If marginal products differed between the regions, then labor would move from the low- to the high-wage area, reducing the marginal product in the latter and raising it in the former until equilibrium is restored. If we admit the possibility of transport costs (including implicit and explicit dislocation and information costs) then wages in one region could exceed those in the other, but only by the capitalized value of moving costs. National income is represented by the area OWNEO′ in Figure 1.1, of which OabO′ is labor's share, with cNbO′ going to eastern labor (that is, O′c of labor employed in the East at a wage rate of O′b) and cNaO goes to

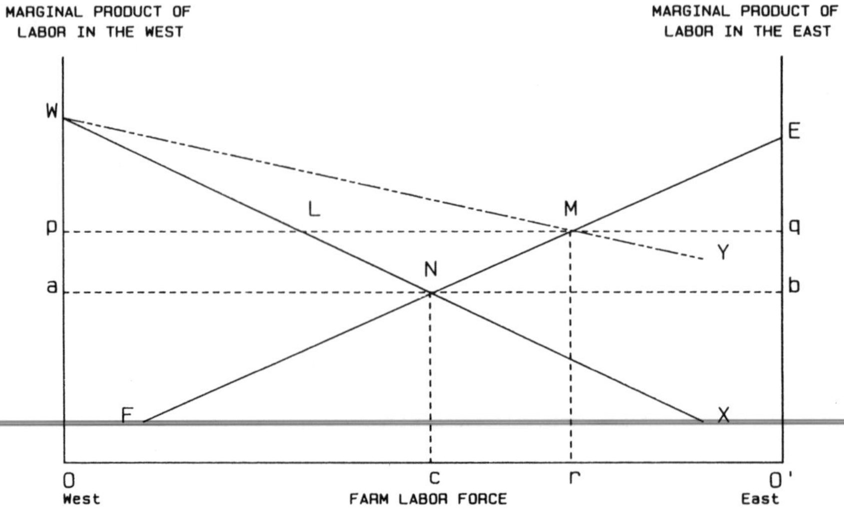

FIG. 1.1. Impact of public land policy on national income, wages, and the geographic distribution of labor.

western labor. Land in the West earns a rental income of aWN, while that in the East earns bEN.

To return to the issue of land policy, suppose now that the government releases new public lands for settlement located in the West. If it has the same distribution of fertility as that already settled in the region, then the western marginal product of labor curve, WX, would pivot around W to a new location such as WY.[10] As a result, national income would increase by WNM to OWMEO′. Eastern national income would be reduced by cNMr to rMEO′ of which rMqO′ goes to rO′ of labor at the prevailing (higher) wage rate, O′q and MEq accrues to eastern landowners as rents. The eastern loss of income is a transfer to the West associated with the migration of cr of its labor force from eastern to western lands. Loss of this labor also reduces the scarcity value of eastern land and accounts for the decline in rents in that region. Wages are increased to Op = O′q.

Provided that at least some of the newly released western lands are more fertile than the land used by the marginal farmer in the East or West, then this public policy of releasing lands from the public domain has a number of unequivocal economic consequences:[11]

1. Rise in national income
2. Higher wage rate

3. Increased labor share in national income
4. Migration of some portion of eastern labor to the West
5. Decrease in eastern rental income
6. Decrease in the East's share of national income

Whatever the dynamic validity of this particular model, it is clear that people were drawn westward by the sale of public land. There is also evidence that population growth was not independent of land policy. As we will show in Chapter 4, everything else equal, midwestern women produced more children than eastern women and land availability offers the best explanation for this phenomenon. Moreover, immigrants flooded into this country. Whether this was a direct response to offers of cheap land or a result of the higher American wages that it engendered is irrelevant because both were consequences of public land policy.

Within this model, population growth and the consequential increase in the labor force may be represented by the extension of the horizontal axis of Figure 1.1. This is shown in Figure 1.2. The labor force is increased by O′O″. As a consequence, national income rises by the difference between EE′O″O′ and MEE′M′. Wages are reduced from Op to Op′ because labor is relatively less scarce, while rents rise as land becomes relatively scarcer. Although it is conceivable that the labor supply

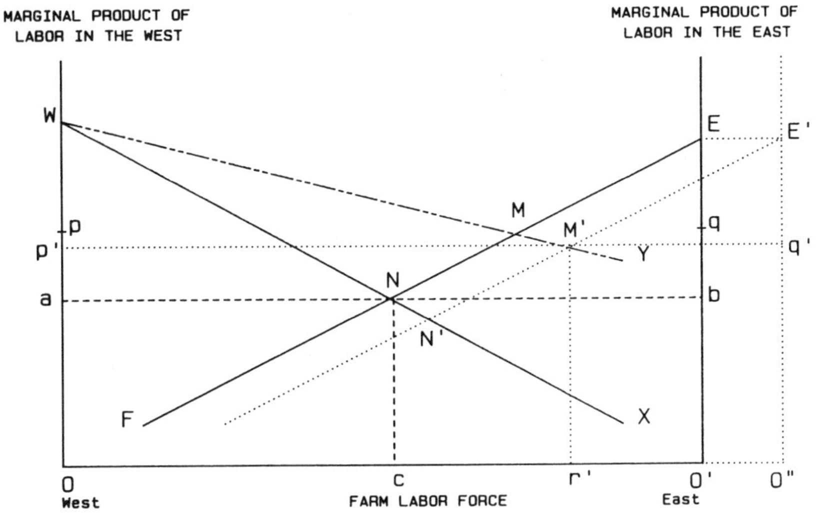

FIG. 1.2. Interaction between public land policy and population growth.

response could be so great as to wipe out the initial rise in wages produced by the release of land, there is no evidence that this was the case. Of the increased national income, WNM is due to the land policy and NMM′N′ to the interaction of this policy with population.

This new population is then also redistributed between East and West. Most of the people born in the West stayed there, being joined by many from the East who migrated to that region. Furthermore, almost 5 million immigrants landed after 1820, mostly on the East Coast. Some of them also moved westward, but of 4.1 million immigrants alive in 1860, 1.4 million resided in just two states: New York and Pennsylvania. In these states, they may have had the effect of displacing native residents who in turn moved westward.

Continued eastern population growth also led to a westward displacement of farm families to provide working farms for sons under a partitive inheritance system. Rather than scatter the family through the migration of younger sons to western lands, break up the eastern family farm into uneconomic units, or try to buy sufficient land in the immediate area to satisfy family inheritances, the entire family would move westward to a location where the proceeds from the sale of an eastern farm would buy a substantially larger one.

With few exceptions, suitable farmlands did not exist in the East by this time. In Rhode Island cropland was already decreasing, and in Massachusetts unimproved lands were removed from farms faster than land was improved.[12] Elsewhere in the East, competition from western producers forced the adoption of a different crop mix, one that relied upon more intensive cultivation to raise the marginal product of labor. Truck crops and dairy products were substituted for corn and wheat and marginal lands converted to hay to supply the burgeoning urban demand for horse fodder. These produced higher income levels but demanded more work from the farmer and would not produce the accustomed level of income with less work-effort.[13]

At midcentury, America remained an agrarian nation where the lure of the land was strong. Once land was secured in some minimally useful acreage through purchase or family succession, ofttimes it could only be reached by traveling long distances. In thousands of cases such a domestic migration had been preceded by a transoceanic one. If new, this land needed clearing and other investments before it could be cultivated. These costs were inescapable. They were embodied in the price of existing farmland and borne by new settlers only if their implicit wage was less than or equal to the capitalized value of existing improvements on old land.

After settlement, the next order of business was to provide at least a basic subsistence for the family, which of course was typically an intrinsic element of American agricultural life. To feed, clothe, and shelter these individuals—who were not only loved ones but the primary or total labor supply as well as the creators of much of the enterprise's real capital—was the first priority.

Self-sufficient subsistence farming, however, was not the sole ambition of the small, independent farmers of the North. While it may have been a necessary short-term goal, for most it was not a sufficient long-range one. The peasant's instinctive drive for biological survival was soon superseded by the entrepreneur's quest for financial growth. Perhaps the northern farmer did not possess an acquisitive motive equal to that exhibited by the new manufacturers or the older trading interests, but the desire for profit existed nonetheless. Commercialism beckoned, and the northern yeomanry sought participation, often only haltingly, in the developing commercial markets. There was a strong drive to produce "marketable surpluses," a pursuit which depended upon raising the productivity of land, labor, and capital. The desire to improve productivity led northern farmers to mechanize, expand onto more fertile soils, and to experiment with what was to become "scientific farming." Not only did it drive innovation toward improved farm practices and implements, it encouraged the diffusion and acceptance of novel techniques among a generally conservative farm community.

The availability of various alternative machines, implements, plant varieties, animal breeds, and agricultural practices compelled the commercially oriented farmers to make economic decisions regarding input usage and output levels. Growing market opportunities strengthened the importance of rational decision making by raising the cost of bad decisions. Expanding debt levels resulting from land, equipment, and other purchases inexorably drew farmers into the market economy by further increasing their needs for the cash flow generated by marketable output. Yet through all these changing circumstances, the dual nature of American farming endured; although increasingly a market-oriented enterprise, the family farm still possessed noneconomic attributes that shaped the economic choices in ways not characteristic of manufacturing, transport, or other economic activities.

Like manufacturers, farmers were driven to use labor-saving techniques. On the farm this encouraged cultivation of land-extensive crops, livestock grazing, neglect of crops once planted until harvest, and adoption of implements requiring comparatively more animal or steam power with less human effort. On the frontier these pressures also took an additional turn. The difficulties of obtaining hired help at an economically justifiable price given productivity levels seems to have been an important determinant of family size.

To the commercially oriented farmers, profit became an inescapable pursuit. Given their noneconomic constraints, most probably found a goal of profit maximization unattainable; but subject to those constraints, it seems that they aimed in that direction. Consequently, most earned a positive rate of return even though they may not have calculated it as consciously as their industrial contemporaries or as their twentieth-century agricultural successors.

With individually owned small farms in a lightly populated country, early self-sufficiency had become a way of life, a complete arrangement of family and a social organization. This differed in fundamental ways both from earlier agrarian relationships and the new urban-industrial ones emerging in Western Europe and the eastern United States. However, the intrusion of commercial pressures through such forces as changing tastes favoring a greater variety of consumption goods or a desire to provide one's children with a comparable or superior standard of living, made profitability an increasingly important goal. What had been a way of life increasingly took on the characteristics of a business, but the transition was incomplete.

This dual nature of the nineteenth-century American agrarian experience intrigues yet bedevils scholars; agriculture was simultaneously a complex, successful economic activity as well as an engine of family and social organization with strong noneconomic motivations. This emerged as an unexpectedly strong theme in this study. Consequently, both the constraints and the trade-offs in the economic model of the farm differ from those in other purely economic activities such as manufacturing or transportation. Thus nineteenth-century American agriculture does not lend itself as completely to economic analysis as do these other endeavors.

The intermingling of economic and noneconomic influences in northern agriculture clouds certain issues. As economists we do not propose a detailed examination of the sociological or psychological components of the nineteenth-century family farm and yet to overlook them entirely would risk presenting erroneous, or certainly misleading, interpretations to a far greater extent than such an omission would in the manufacturing, service, or transport sectors. Our approach is therefore a compromise. Most of our analytical work focuses on purely economic aspects; the remainder deals with demographic characteristics of the rural population. Whenever the analysis produces results that seem implausible from a strictly economic standpoint, we explore the noneconomic attributes that may underlie them, though, of course, noneconomic influences may still be at work even when the results make sense by the standards of economic theory. Most such characteristics, even those that are noneconomic or seem irrational by traditional theoretical economic standards, can be integrated into an economic explanation through their effects on costs or benefits.

To illustrate, farm labor supply conditions during this period do not always lend themselves fully to conventional microeconomic analysis. On a farm where family members provide most or all of the work force, allocation decisions sometimes seem irrational unless the low opportunity costs of fixed components of the labor supply such as children or the elderly are considered. The existence of such components is not totally the result of economic decisions, but to a degree, once the noneconomic element is recognized, its influence can sometimes be given an economic dimension. This labor made a widely diversified product mix economical. Furthermore, ostensibly surplus (that is, nonproductive) labor could produce capital on the farm through land improvements such as fencing and ditching or new structures whose value appeared on the capital account more than the current income account of the farm and was therefore often overlooked.

Similarly, maximizing short-run profit was not necessarily the overriding goal of the individual nineteenth-century farmer. The land, the farm capital, and the labor of the family members provided a degree of economic security to the farm household that was unavailable to urban, nonfarm workers. When times were hard, farmers could live off their capital, much of which they had created and which was embodied in their farm, longer than industrial producers. Even commercially oriented farmers could hope that their personal survival would be guaranteed during years when surplus production was too small to produce a high rate of return on their investment. Moreover, those who tilled a family farm seem to have placed greater emphasis on potential capital gains than did investors in nonagricultural pursuits.

The recurrent conflict between economic and noneconomic goals created tensions within the farm sector, particularly after midcentury as the industrialization and urbanization accelerated. This often led to actions that in retrospect appear perverse when perceived within an economically rational context. American farmers as a group clearly wanted their farms to be prosperous, profit-making enterprises, but they also regarded their occupation as a way of life, as an independent, psychically rewarding endeavor. Inevitably, industrialization and the rise of giant corporate enterprises heightened these tensions among the farm population and eventually induced the intense political agitation that began in the last third of the nineteenth century.

Although it lacks the unifying theme of slavery, northern agriculture poses a complex set of questions equal to those of the South, yet it has attracted little attention from the more theoretical, quantitative scholars. For the slave South, abundant quantitative, analytic studies supplement the plentiful narrative histories of southern farming, but there are no comparable analyses of northern agriculture.

In the following chapters we investigate some of the issues cited above. Using a sizable amount of economic and demographic data drawn from the federal censuses of 1860, economic theory, econometric analyses, and, where appropriate, interpretations based on noneconomic considerations, we reconstruct the rural economy and the agricultural system that supported it in the years before the Civil War. We think that this provides a reasonably complete picture of the status of northern agriculture at a time when the dream of a pastoral, agrarian America still seemed possible. The first part of this book examines the family and the rural community of which it was a part; the second focuses on the economic aspects of farming in the mid-nineteenth-century North.

PART ONE

The Rural Community: A Way of Life

AS LATE AS 1860, many Americans and a large percentage of the potential immigrants still dreamed of becoming independent landowning farmers. This was particularly true in the western states of the northern region where, free of the institution of forced labor, the grip of large landholders, and the burden of traditions, the Jeffersonian dream could seem realistically attainable. In that lightly industrialized economy, being a small, secure, and independent yeoman still seemed possible and the financial and other impediments to attaining that goal decreased the farther west one went.

However, their dream was never a purely economic one. Read Jefferson's writings and it becomes clear that American agrarianism incorporated a moral dimension:

> Those who labor in the earth are the chosen people of God, if ever He had a chosen people, whose breast He has made His peculiar deposit for substantial and genuine virtue. It is the focus in which He keeps alive that sacred fire, which otherwise must escape from the earth. Corruption of morals in the mass of cultivators is a phenomenon of which no age nor nation has furnished an example.[1]

and

> Cultivators of the earth are the most valuable citizens. They are the most vigorous, the most independent, the most virtuous, and they are tied to their country, and wedded to its liberty and interests, by the most lasting bonds.[2]

Of the alternative, manufacturing, Jefferson wrote "I consider the class of artificers as the panderers of vice, and the instruments by which the liberties of a country are generally overturned."[3] Consequently, "[m]anufacture must therefore be resorted to of necessity not of choice."[4] Urban life in comparison with rural fared equally poorly in Jefferson's estimation:

> A city life offers you indeed more means of dissipating time, but more frequent, also, and more painful objects of vice and wretchedness. New York, for example, like London, seems to be a Cloacina [i.e., sewer] of all the depravities of human nature. Philadelphia doubtless has its share. Here [at Monticello], on the contrary, crime is scarcely heard of, breaches of order rare, and our societies, if not refined, are rational, moral, and affectionate at least.[5]

The individual and his family thus gained in moral rectitude when part of a farm unit settled in the countryside and lost important values when transferred to an industrial and urban environment.

Once the commitment to the family farm was made, economic decisions became intertwined with social and moral issues. The economic unit, the farm, was inseparable from the social unit, the family. Each influenced and constrained the other. Ultimately, this pastoral paradise fit neatly with the belief in the virtues of an egalitarian society, one in which there was equal access to social and economic opportunity, unfettered by existing large concentrations of power or vested interest. The nonslave areas of the interior region provided a laboratory for this noble experiment, or, at least, appeared to offer the best hope for its realization in the antebellum years.

Using data from a sample of 102 rural townships in the North, which is described in the following chapter, we are able to examine the characteristics of the farm family in the North across a wide range of age, economic, and geographic categories. However, because the sample also included the nonfarm rural population in these townships, we are able to go beyond the agricultural population to analyze the larger rural community of which it was a part. This enables us to investigate the agrarian ideal within the broader nonurban context in which it was set.

CHAPTER TWO

A Sample of Households from the 1860 Federal Census

THE CONSTITUTION REQUIRED a decennial census of population as the means of apportioning representation among the people. To temper any enthusiasm for gaining political advantage and to encourage accuracy, the Founding Fathers also specified that the count should serve as the basis for apportioning direct taxation.[1] Although an enumeration was all that was needed to fulfill the Constitutional provision, from its inception the census was also used as a vehicle for gathering additional information about the population. The first census in 1790 went beyond the basic count by distinguishing the sex and color of free persons and the number of free males, 16 and older. Subsequent censuses went much further. At the Second Census, the number of age categories was increased. By the time of the Third Census in 1810, the threat to American welfare from the Embargo of 1807 prompted the addition of inquiries regarding manufactures. However, there was no formal schedule for those inquiries until the Fourth Census in 1820. Agriculture, despite its importance in the economy, was neglected until 1840 when it was included on a combined schedule for "Mines, Agriculture, Commerce, Manufactures, etc." Beginning with the Seventh Census in 1850, however, agriculture had its own separate schedule and this practice was continued at subsequent censuses.[2]

Our data come from the manuscripts of the Eighth Census of the United States, which was taken in 1860. Compared with subsequent censuses such as the Tenth, which asked 13,010 questions on 215 separate schedules, the Eighth Census was a modest undertaking. Nevertheless, it was the most elaborate one to date, consisting of 142 questions on six separate schedules.[3] In this study we use the information contained in the free and slave schedules and those for agriculture. Discussion of the agricultural schedules is deferred to Chapter 7.

The household was the primary sampling unit for the free population, and assistant marshals, who served as census enumerators, were directed to ask twenty-four questions of the head of each household they visited.[4] Slave owners answered an additional nine. The questions, without elaboration, appeared across the top of a printed form that was supposed to be filled out on the spot (Fig. 2.1). Enumerators were provided with folios in which to keep these papers on their daily rounds, however, the general neatness and condition of the manuscripts makes it likely that they were recopied from notes.[5] They may therefore contain transcription errors.

The manuscript census page reproduced as Figure 2.1 is for the sample township of Honey Creek in Adams County, Illinois. Consider the household headed by Apollo Shriver that appears on line 15. Mr. Shriver gave his occupation as farmer and reported ownership of $4,000 of real estate and $900 in personal property.[6] Born in Pennsylvania and aged 42, he was probably married to Mary, age 44, who was listed on the next line. She was also born in Pennsylvania. The next six persons listed in the schedule could be their children: John, age 19, and Elizabeth, age 13, were born in Pennsylvania, while Martin, age 8, Hester, age 7, Amanda, age 5, and Stephen, age 1, were all born in Illinois. Their relationship to Mary and Apollo Shriver is deduced from the descending age ordering and because the difference between Mary's age and that of the eldest and youngest yields plausible maternal ages for first birth and last birth. We cannot infer from the data that these are all the children ever born to Mary. Some may have died or be living away from home. Furthermore, the family's fertility history may not necessarily have ended with the birth of Stephen, although further successful pregnancies are unlikely.

Explicit information on relationships between household members was not collected until the Tenth Census in 1880.[7] We can only imperfectly reconstruct it from the 1860 data. Indeed, any interpretation is possible only because enumerators were instructed to begin "with the father and mother, or, if either or both be dead, begin with some other ostensible head of the family, to be followed, as far as practicable, with

---

FIG. 2.1. Copy of population manuscript form used and data collected by census enumerators for the Eighth Census, 1860.

Page No. ~~1001~~ 1001

SCHEDULE 1.—Free Inhabitants in Honey Creek **in the County of** Adams **State of** Illinois **enumerated by me, on the** 15th **day of** Sept **1860.** B F Grover **Ass't Marshal.**

Post Office Mendon

	Dwelling-houses—numbered in the order of visitation	Families numbered in the order of visitation	The name of every person whose usual place of abode on the first day of June, 1860, was in this family	Description: Age	Description: Sex	Description: Color, (White, black, or mulatto)	Profession, Occupation, or Trade of each person, male and female, over 15 years of age	Value of Estate Owned: Value of Real Estate	Value of Estate Owned: Value of Personal Estate	Place of Birth, Naming the State, Territory, or Country	Married within the year	Attended School within the year	Persons over 20 y'rs of age who cannot read & write	Whether deaf and dumb, blind, insane, idiotic, pauper, or convict
	1	2	3	4	5	6	7	8	9	10	11	12	13	14
1	3456	3484	Joseph Fletcher	27	m		Miller		1600	O				
2			Elizabeth	28	f					Ills				
3			Mary	5	f					"				
4			George	3	m					"				
5			Joseph	1	m					"				
6	3457	3485	B F Simon	22	m		Laborer		100	Pa				
7			Malinda	18	f					Ills				
8			Nancy E Robertson	8	f					"				
9	3458	3486	Louis Frederick	42	m		Farmer		100	O				
10			Mary	36	f					"				
11			Charles	8	m					Iowa		1		
12			Louis	6	m					"		1		
13			Electa	3	f					"				
14			Darius	1	m					"				
15	3459	3487	Apollo Shriver	42	m		Farmer	4000	900	Pa				
16			Mary	44	f					"				
17			John	19	m					"		1		
18			Elizabeth	13	f					"		1		
19			Martin	8	m					Ills		1		
20			Hester	7	f					Ills		1		
21			Amanda	5	f					"				
22			Stephen	1	m					"				
23	3460	3488	Jacob Sweney	25	m		Farmer		50	O				
24			Mary	22	f					Ills				
25			Adelia	4	f					"				
26			Alice	2	f					"				
27	3461	3489	William Stout	45	m		Farmer	2000	600	Ky				
28			Lorenza	42	f					O				
29			Anderson	20	m					Ind		1		
30			John	18	m					"		1		
31			Julia	16	f					"		1		
32			Perry	14	m					"		1		
33			Permelia	13	f					"		1		
34			William	12	m					"		1		
35			Lyson	11	m					Ills		1		
36			Catharine	10	f					"		1		
37			Nancy	8	f					"		1		
38			Elias	6	m					"		1		
39			Malinda	4	f					"				
40			Benjamin	2	m					"				
			No. white males, 24 No. white females, 19				No. colored males, ___ No. colored females, ___ No. foreign born, ___ No. deaf and dumb, ___ No. blind, ___ No. insane, ___	6.000	9.400	No. idiotic, ___ No. paupers, ___				No. convicts, ___

the name of the oldest child residing at home, then the next oldest, and so on to the youngest, then the other inmates, lodgers, and boarders, laborers, domestics, and servants."[8] We rely upon these instructions plus some deductive and inductive reasoning to establish a set of rules for determining interpersonal relationships within the households. These are described below. The accuracy of our deductions, however, is limited by the extent to which enumerators faithfully executed their instructions.

Some inferences can also be made about the family's migratory experience from the data that the census collected. From the birthplaces and ages of Elizabeth and Martin, we can infer that the family migrated from Pennsylvania to Illinois sometime between 1847 and 1852. We cannot, however, be sure that they had lived in the same place in Illinois since then. An examination of the 1850 federal census manuscripts and the 1855 Illinois census records could help resolve some of these uncertainties.[9] John, Elizabeth, Martin, and Hester attended school during the previous year and none reported an occupation, though presumably they assisted on the family farm, especially at harvest time.

The Stout family from Adams County, Illinois (Fig. 2.1, line 27), consisted of William, age 45, and wife, Lovinia, age 42, both born in Kentucky. They had twelve children living with them: Anderson, 20; John, 18; Julia, 16; Perry, 14; Amelia, 13; and William, 12, were born in Indiana, and Logan, 11; Catherine, 10; Henry, 8; Elias, 6; Melinda, 4; and Benjamin, 2, were born in Illinois. Since it is plausible that a 42-year-old woman should have borne her first child at age 22 and her last child at age 40, we attribute all these children to the issue of William and Lovinia Stout. Even by the standards of the day, this was a big family. Less than 0.1 percent of the sampled husband-wife households were as large. None was larger. From the places of birth, we deduce that the family migrated to Illinois from Indiana between 1848 and 1849. All the children, including 20-year-old Anderson and 18-year-old John, but excepting Melinda and Benjamin who were too young, were reported as attending school. This family was making a more significant investment in their children's education than most.

The first household listed in Figure 2.1, that headed by Joseph Fletcher, was a nonfarm family. Mr. Fletcher gave his occupation as miller and the value of his personal estate, $1,600, was sufficient to be the capital invested in a rural flour mill in 1860.

Completed schedules were subsequently forwarded to Washington for tabulation and summary. They were eventually returned to the states and it is from these that our sample is drawn. Except for the information on names and the implicit evidence contained in the manuscripts about family structure, fertility, and mobility, all the data were aggregated and published in the census compendia.[10] Some of the data, such as the number of dwellings, were only published by state, while age data were only published by age group. In the process of this tabulation, errors were introduced. Officials in Washington often amended returns unilaterally and made repeated simple arithmetic errors. Printer errors further compound the problems with these published summaries.

One advantage of returning to the original schedules is that we are able to correct arithmetic errors and make independent judgments about the validity of amended figures. More importantly, however, we can derive more detailed distributional statistics and recover the implicit evidence embodied in the responses to the enumerators' questions. This is a major contribution of our study.

Some of the census inquiries such as those regarding sex and state or country of birth were fairly straightforward. Others, however, were elaborated at length in the instructions given to each enumerator in an effort to ensure uniform responses. Since these questions and the responses they elicited are fundamental to this study, the instructions to enumerators for the population (free and slave) and agricultural schedules are reproduced in an Appendix to this chapter. Carroll Wright in his history of the U.S. Census thought that all copies of the 1860 instructions to enumerators had been lost and claimed that they simply repeated those for 1850 instructions.[11] They did not, as recently discovered copies show.[12] Additional instructions were added to cover the new questions on the value of personal estate and slave housing that were included in the 1860 census. Perhaps more importantly though, the instructions for some of the questions that were thought to have been improperly or incompletely answered at the 1850 census, such as place of birth, were revised.[13] We can thus see the efforts that the Census Bureau made to eliminate ambiguities and response bias.

Even seemingly simple and unambiguous questions, such as age, were clearly defined. A person's age was to be that (in years) at their last birthday for everybody over 1 year old, while the age of infants under 1 was to be reported in months. However, an analysis of the data shows that respondents were incapable of answering as unambiguous a question as this accurately. Ages are heaped at five- and, particularly, ten-year intervals. For example, 1.5 percent of the rural population gave their age as 35 compared with only 1.0 and 1.1 percent who reported their age as 34 and 36 respectively. Moreover, 1.6 percent said they were 40 years old compared with 0.9 who gave their age as 39 and 0.6 who claimed to be 41 years old. The problem was most acute among the elderly and nonexistent among children and teenagers, possibly because people did not keep careful track of their age or else the arithmetic involved was beyond their skills. With a response error as high as this on a simple and unambiguous question, one must wonder about the answers to more complex questions, especially those relating to wealth. However, by the judicious selection of intervals and rounding, these problems can be mitigated.

Our data are a two-stage, variable-cluster sample from the manuscript censuses of agriculture and population for 1860 collected by James Foust and Fred Bateman under National Science Foundation sponsorship.[14] The primary sampling unit was the county, from which one nonurban township (the cluster) was selected. All the data from the population and agricultural returns in the sampled townships were recorded, matched, and coded. Farms were linked where possible to households in the population manuscripts using the name of the farm operator as the key. A similar procedure was used by William N. Parker and Robert E. Gallman for their sample of 5,230 farms from the major cotton counties of the South, but the basic sample designs differ. The random elements in our sample design were in the selection of counties and townships, whereas in the Parker-Gallman sample the random element was the selection of a cluster of 5 farms in every 280.[15]

There were some farms for which no match could be found between the name of the farm operator and names in the population schedules for the township (see Chap. 7). There were also people who reported their occupation as farmer but for whom no farm could be found. These "farmers without farms" are discussed in more detail in Chapter 3. No data, however, were discarded.

The universe from which the sample was chosen comprised the 956 counties in twenty northern states: Connecticut, Delaware, Illinois, Indiana, Iowa, Kansas, Maine, Maryland, Massachusetts, Michigan, Minnesota, Missouri, New Hampshire, New Jersey, New York, Ohio, Pennsylvania, Rhode Island, Vermont, and Wisconsin. From them, 102 nonurban counties were drawn at random.[16] By chance, no counties in Delaware, Maine, Massachusetts, or Rhode Island were selected. One nonurban township was then selected at random within each county.[17] The locations of the sampled counties are shown in Figure 2.2, and the names of the sample counties and townships are given in the key. Although the sampling units were townships, we have chosen to refer to the township samples by the names of the counties from which they were drawn because of the lack of familiarity with township names.

The sample, which includes all of the available social and demographic information for the members of 21,118 households except their names, preserves the original census ordering of household members that was supposed to be the head, followed by spouse, children by birth order, other related family members, and last, unrelated household members. Linked with these households on the basis of the name of the farm owner

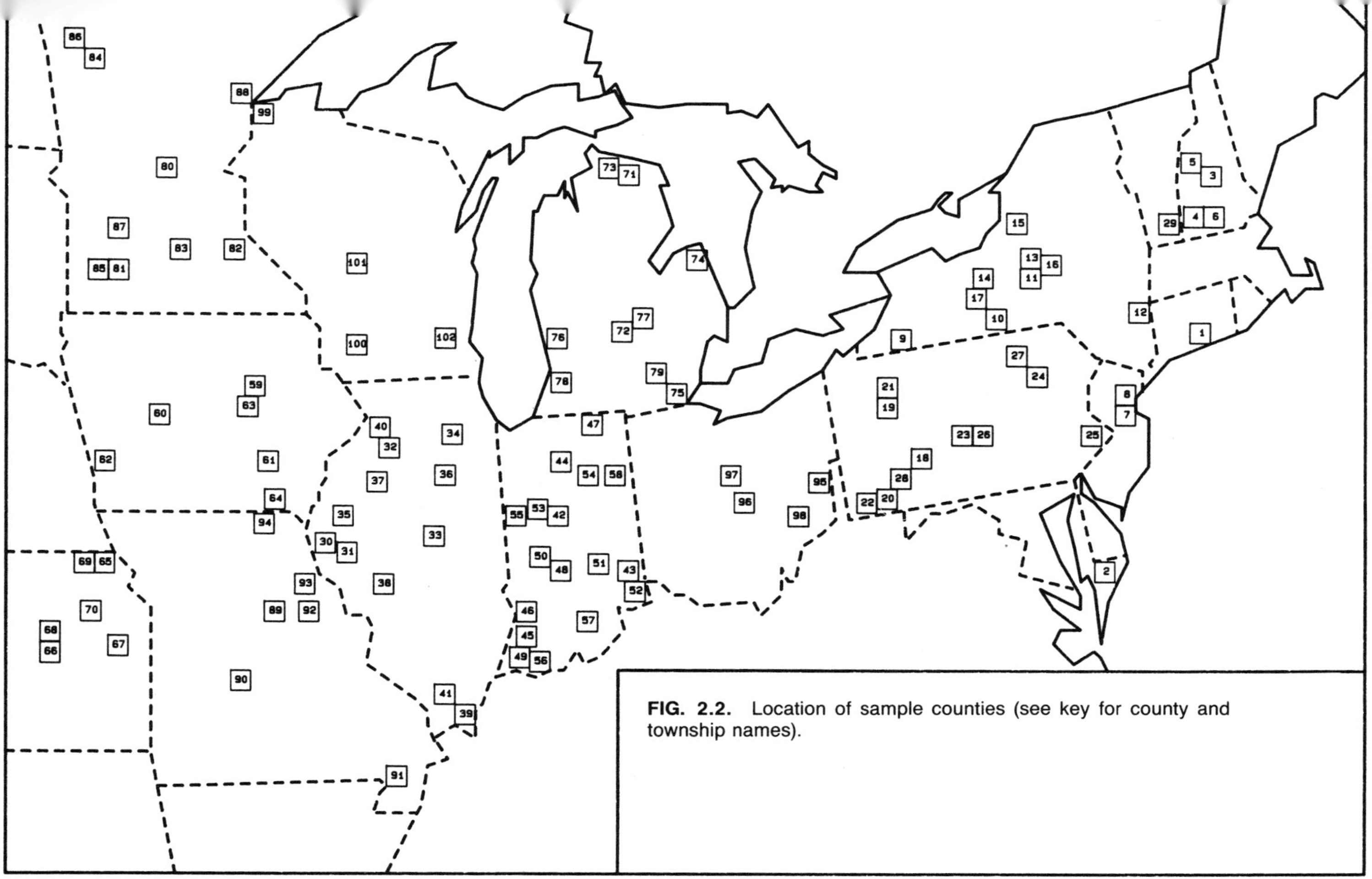

FIG. 2.2. Location of sample counties (see key for county and township names).

KEY TO FIGURE 2.2. LIST OF SAMPLE TOWNSHIPS

Key	State	County	Township
		Eastern Region	
1	**Connecticut**	Middlesex	Durham
2	**Maryland**	Worcester	Costin
3	**New Hampshire**	Belknap	Center Harbor
4		Cheshire	Sullivan
5		Grafton	Canaan
6		Hillsboro	Lyndeborough
7	**New Jersey**	Middlesex	North Brunswick
8		Union	Springfield
9	**New York**	Cattaraugus	Ashford
10		Chemung	Erin
11		Chenango	Smyrna
12		Dutchess	Clinton
13		Madison	Eaton
14		Ontario	Richmond
15		Oswego	Sandy Creek
16		Otsego	Laurens
17		Yates	Jerusalem
18	**Pennsylvania**	Cambria	Richland
19		Clarion	Salem
20		Fayette	Washington
21		Forest	Barnett
22		Greene	Jefferson
23		Huntingdon	Cromwell
24		Luzerne	Abingdon
25		Montgomery	Norriton
26		Perry	Miller
27		Sullivan	Fox
28		Westmoreland	Penn
29	**Vermont**	Windham	Vernon
		Western Region	
30	**Illinois**	Adams	Honey Creek
31		Brown	Ripley
32		Bureau	Fairfield
33		Dewitt	Barnett
34		Kendall	Seward
35		Knox	Persifer
36		Livingston	Nevada
37		McDonough	Macomb
38		Macoupin	T10,R6[a]
39		Massac	T16, R5[b]
40		Whiteside	Union Grove
41		Williamson	T10,R4[c]
42	**Indiana**	Clinton	Perry
43		Franklin	Highland
44		Fulton	Aubbeenaubbee
45		Gibson	Johnson
46		Knox	Washington
47		LaGrange	Newbury
48		Morgan	Gregg
49		Posey	Harmony
50		Putnam	Mill Creek
51		Shelby	Moral
52		Switzerland	Cotton
53		Tippecanoe	Wea
54		Wabash	LaGro

KEY TO FIGURE 2.2. *(continued)*

Key	State	County	Township
55		Warren	Warren
56		Warrick	Boon
57		Washington	Washington
58		Wells	Harrison
59	**Iowa**	Black Hawk	East Waterloo
60		Greene	Kendrick
61		Keokuk	Liberty
62		Pottawatomie	Silver Creek
63		Tama	Toledo
64		Van Buren	Village
65	**Kansas**	Brown	Irving
66		Chase	Bazaar
67		Franklin	Peoria
68		Morris	Council Grove
69		Nemeha	Clear Creek
70		Shawnee	Topeka
71	**Michigan**	Cheboygan	Inverness
72		Clinton	Bingham
73		Emmet	La Croix
74		Huron	Rubicon
75		Monroe	Summerfield
76		Ottawa	Holland
77		Shiawassee	Fairfield
78		Van Buren	Waverly
79		Washtenaw	Augusta
80	**Minnesota**	Benton	Princeton
81		Cottonwood	All
82		Goodhue	Vasa
83		Le Sueur	Waterville
84		Mahnomen	All
85		Murray	All
86		Polk	All
87		Renville	Birch Cooley
88		St. Louis	Fon Du Lac
89	**Missouri**	Boone	Rocky Fork
90		Camden	Jackson
91		Dunklin	Freeborn
92		Montgomery	Prairie
93		Ralls	Salt River
94		Scotland	Mt. Pleasant
95	**Ohio**	Harrison	North
96		Licking	St. Albans
97		Morrow	Perry
98		Noble	Beaver
99	**Wisconsin**	Douglas	Nemadjo
100		Iowa	Waldwick
101		Juneau	Clearfield
102		Waukesha	Oconomowoc

[a]Now known as Shaw's Point (T = township and R = range, designations given under the Land Ordinances of 1785).

[b]Now known as Brookport.

[c]Now known as Grassy.

or operator are the data from the agricultural schedules. In Maryland and Missouri, these data are also linked with the slave schedules.

There were 20,661 households in the 102 sample townships for which demographic data were recorded.[18] Of these, 11,485 were linked to the agricultural schedules and we refer to these as the farm households.[19] The balance, 9,176 households, could not be linked, although 3,374 people in them claimed that they were farmers. We refer to them as the nonfarm households (see Table 2.1). More than 17,000 of the households were headed by people born in the United States but there were few farm households headed by immigrant females in the Northeast. Fortunately this was not a category of special interest to us; in much of the demographic analysis that follows, attention is focused upon the husband-wife households. The basis of the classification into husband-wife, other-male-headed, and female-headed households is described below. Where analysis was based upon individuals rather than households, the number of observations increased dramatically. For example, 42,315 free persons lived in the nonfarm households, while 65,575 people lived on farms. There were also 658 slaves in the Maryland and Missouri townships.

None of the households in Figure 2.1 presents any complications in determining family relationships. Problems did arise, however, with others. In some, children were not listed in strict descending order of age;

TABLE 2.1. Sample Sizes by Household Type and Geographic Location

Household Type	Midwest		Northeast	
Husband-Wife		10,080		6,990
Nonfarm	3,990		3,411	
Natives	3,058		2,877	
Immigrants	932		534	
Farm	6,090		3,579	
Natives	4,939		3,368	
Immigrants	1,151		211	
Other-Male-Headed		1,414		895
Nonfarm	599		365	
Natives	421		316	
Immigrants	178		49	
Farm	815		530	
Natives	603		504	
Immigrants	212		26	
Female-Headed		668		614
Nonfarm	361		450	
Natives	316		423	
Immigrants	45		27	
Farm	307		164	
Natives	257		153	
Immigrants	50		11	

in others, the second person listed was too old to be considered the spouse of the head, while the third member of the household, a woman, would be both old enough and young enough to be the spouse and the mother of the children listed in the household. As a result rules were devised as a basis for determining familial relationships. These covered exceptions to the instructions given enumerators and established the margins of error that we were willing to tolerate in our analysis. For much of our demographic analysis, it is crucial that we associate children with their mothers and we selected rules for this that err on the conservative side—that is, we would prefer to exclude some own children for a woman rather than include too many. As a result we believe that our demographic results, strong as they are, understate our case.

Households were divided into two broad groups: those headed by husbands and wives, which are our primary focus, and those headed by other males or females. We also compare East and West, where western states are defined as those lying to the west and north of the Ohio River, and farm and nonfarm households. Classification was complicated because the only name taken from the census manuscripts was that of the head for use as a key to match against the agricultural schedules and this was not preserved once the matches were made.

Our methodology was essentially the same as that used by Richard Easterlin, George Alter, and Gretchen Condran, with some minor variations.[20] The differences between our results are inconsequential and reflect different interests and judgments. Easterlin's primary interest, for example, was farm fertility. While we share that concern, we are also interested in how farm family fertility differed from that of nonfarm families in the same community and in the influence of such factors as land availability, ethnic origin, and migratory experience.[21] It was not our intention to replicate their results.

The census enumerators invariably credited headship to a male whenever a suitable one was present in a household. Only 4 percent of the farm households had a woman listed first (therefore classified as heads of household), while 8.8 percent of nonfarm households were female headed. To qualify as a husband-wife household, an eligible male (15 or older) had to be the first person listed, followed by a female 15 or older who was not more than nineteen years younger than the "husband" nor more than nine years older than he. Households with a male listed first but violating one or more of these conditions were classified as "other-male-headed."

For husband-wife households, we also attempted to identify own and stepchildren and also nonnuclear members of the household. Own children were classified as being more than fourteen years and less than fifty years younger than the "wife" (i.e., "mother") and following a wife or grandparent or stepchildren, if present, in descending age order.[22] Some deviations in birth order, however, were permitted to accommodate minor variations made by enumerators. We also allowed a deviation that was introduced when the data were keypunched. When there were more than six people in a household, the data were split across two or more punch cards. In these instances we often found that the keypunch operators had entered the data in columns rather than rows. If a head of household with children had been widowed (or divorced, an unlikely occurrence) and remarried, his children should be listed before children of his current wife. These stepchildren are nuclear family members; but if one is interested in specific marital fertility, such children must not be linked to the current wife. Stepchildren were defined as following the wife (or grandparent if present) and less than fifteen years younger than the wife but more than nineteen years younger than the head. They were found in 461 families. Although children generally followed immediately after the wife, occasionally a parent of either the head or wife was listed before the children of the head. To qualify as a grandparent, the person had to be the third person listed and at least fourteen years older than either the head or wife. According to this rule, 213 households were judged to be extended families containing a grandparent. All children under 10 were counted as nuclear children unless they followed a woman who was old enough to be their mother but not young enough to be a daughter of the wife. Someone not meeting these criteria and too old to be a child was classified as nonnuclear. All persons regardless of age following someone classified as nonnuclear were also classified as nonnuclear. If the last person in a household could have qualified as an own child but was out of order, they were also designated as nonnuclear.

The effects of these decision rules may be illustrated by reference to some of the sample data. Consider, for example, the following household in Brown County, Kansas:

Listed Order	Sex	Age	Born	Reorder
1	Male	38	New York	1
2	Female	35	Ohio	2
3	Male	6	Illinois	5
4	Female	14	Illinois	3
5	Female	4	Illinois	6
6	Female	8	Illinois	4
7	Male	0	Kansas	7
8	Male	10	New York	8
9	Female	12	Ohio	9

It was reordered as shown. The 10-year-old boy and 12-year-old girl could qualify as own children on the basis of their age and the resultant birth intervals but were classified as nonnuclear by the program. When we look at their places of birth, this decision seems correct. Maybe they were nephew and niece, but they were almost certainly not nuclear children.

A household from Kendall County, Illinois, illustrates a different set of problems and how our decision rules handled it:

Listed Order	Sex	Age	Born	Reorder
1	Male	38	England	1
2	Female	44	England	2
3	Female	20	New York	4
4	Female	14	New York	5
5	Female	12	New York	6
6	Male	8	New York	7
7	Female	24	New York	3
8	Female	5	New York	8
9	Female	3	New York	9
10	Male	13	Illinois	10

According to our criteria, this was a husband-wife household with seven own children, the eldest of whom was a 24-year-old woman and the youngest a 3-year-old girl. There was also one nonnuclear family member, a 13-year-old boy born in Illinois. One could argue whether the 5-year-old and the 3-year-old (listed eighth and ninth) are own children of the 44-year-old wife, or children of the 24-year-old daughter. We suspect the latter as no eligible male (i.e., "husband") is present in the household for this woman. If these children are those of the 24-year-old daughter, then the last surviving birth for the wife was eight years earlier at age 36. This implies either high infant mortality rates or some deliberate and successful family limitation. On balance, therefore, we counted them as own children of the 44-year-old woman. This decision is also supported by sample evidence that a married woman aged 36–44 was more likely to be having children than a woman was to be married at age 18 or 19.

The data for the husband-wife households are much richer because of the relationships they imply than those for other headship groups. From them, for example, we can calculate fertility rates, deduce levels of investment in the education of children, and trace the patterns of national and international migration. In the following four chapters we concentrate much of our attention on the social aspects of the Jeffersonian vision of a rural farm democracy, relying heavily upon evidence drawn from the husband-wife households in the sample.

APPENDIX TO CHAPTER TWO

SPECIAL INSTRUCTIONS

Schedule No. 1—Free Inhabitants

In filling up this schedule, first enter on a sheet the pages, then fill up the blanks in the heading in their proper order, commencing with the less division, as town, townships, ward, or borough; then the name of the county and State, with the date of taking; after that enter your own name and record the name of the post office of the vicinage. Every day you will change the date and on every page write your name. All the other entries are to be repeated so long as the returns apply, but the moment you enter upon another town, township, ward, borough, or county, you must change the heading to correspond. (Inasmuch as these directions are equally applicable to other schedules, as will appear on their face, they need not be repeated, although to be observed as if they were reiterated.)

1. *Dwelling houses numbered.*—Under heading 1, insert in numerical order the number of dwelling houses occupied by free inhabitants, as they are visited. The first house you enter is to be No. 1, the second No. 2, and so on to the last house in your subdivision. The numbering of houses is to be continuously maintained, without regard to minor divisions, from the first to the last house included in your work, so that your last entry will express the whole number of dwelling houses in your subdivision. By "dwelling house" is meant a separate tenement, inhabited or uninhabited, and may contain one or more families under one roof. Where several tenements are in one block with walls to separate them, having different entrances, they are each to be numbered separately, but where not so divided they are to be enumerated as one house. Houses which are tenantable but without inhabitants, are to be returned and numbered, but represented as unoccupied, in column 3, while no number is to be entered in column No. 2. If a house is used partly for a store or other purpose and partly for a dwelling, it is to be numbered as a dwelling house. Hotels, poor houses, garrisons, hospitals, asylums, jails, penitentiaries, and establishments of kindred character, are to be numbered, and if they consist of a group of several houses, each is to be numbered separately, while you will use particular care to write longitudinally in the column the designation or description of the house, and specify particularly and clearly whether it or they be poor house, hotel, hospital, &c.

2. *Families.*—Under heading 2, entitled "*Families numbered in the order of visitation,*" insert the number of families of free persons as they are visited. By the term "family" is meant either one person living separately and alone in a house, or a part of a house, and providing for him or herself, or several persons living together in a house, or part of a house, upon one common means of support and separately from others in similar circumstances. A widow living alone and separately providing for herself, or two hundred individuals living together and pro-

vided for by a common head, should each be numbered as one family. The resident inmates of a hotel, jail, garrison, hospital, or other similar institution, should be recorded as one family, unless there be several tenements or distinct families, in which case they should be separated. There may be several families in a garrison, in which case they should be recorded distinct, but should all, by a marginal note, be embraced as of or belonging to such garrison.

3. *Individual Names.*–Under heading 3, entitled "*The name of every person whose usual place of abode on the 1st day of June, 1860, was in this family,*" insert the name of every free person in each family of every age, including the names of those temporarily absent on a journey, visit, or for the purposes of education, as well as those that were at home on that day. The name of any member of a family who may have died *since the 1st day of June* is to be entered and the person described as if living, but the name of any person born since the 1st day of June is to be omitted. The names are to be written beginning with the father and mother, or, if either or both be dead, begin with some other ostensible head of the family, to be followed, as far as practicable, with the name of the oldest child residing at home, then the next oldest, and so on to the youngest, then the other inmates, lodgers, and boarders, laborers, domestics, and servants.

All landlords, jailors, superintendents of poor-houses, garrisons, hospitals, asylums, and other similar institutions, are to be considered as heads of their respective families, and the inmates under their care to be registered as members thereof, and the details concerning each, designated in their proper columns, so distinctly as to preclude any doubt as to who form the family proper and who the guests, prisoners, or other inmates, carefully omitting all transient persons.

4. By "place of abode" is meant the house or usual lodging place of persons. Any one who is temporarily absent on a visit or journey, or for purposes, with the intention of again returning, is to be considered a member of the family to which he belongs, and not of that where he may be temporarily sojourning; and care should be exercised to make full inquiry for such absentees, that none may be omitted on your lists whose names should properly appear there.

5. *Indians.*–Indians *not taxed* are not to be enumerated. The families of Indians who have renounced tribal rule, and who under State or Territorial laws exercise the rights of citizens, are to be enumerated. In all such cases write "Ind." opposite their names, in column 6, under heading "Color."

6. *Eating-houses, Stores, Shops, &c.*–You will make inquiry at all stores, shops, eating-houses, and all similar places, and take the name and description of every free person who usually slept there previous to or about the 1st day of June, provided such person be not otherwise enumerated.
Ships and Vessels.–Persons on board any description of ships or vessels accidentally or temporarily in port; those who are temporarily boarding at a sailor's boarding or lodging-house, if they belong to other places, are not to be enumerated in your district. All seafaring people are to be enumerated at their land homes, or usual place of abode, whether they be present or at sea; and if any free person live on vessels or boats, acknowledging no other home, they are to be enumerated as belonging to the place where they have been engaged, shipped, or hired; and Assistants should make inquiry respecting all vessels employed in the

internal navigation of the United States, and thus enumerate all who are not recorded as belonging to some family on shore; and all persons of such description, in any one vessel, are to be considered as belonging to one family and the vessel as their place of abode.

7. *Ages.* – Under heading 4, entitled "*Age,*" insert in figures what was the specific age of each person at his or her last birth day previous to the 1st day of June, opposite the name of such person. Where the exact age cannot be ascertained insert a number which shall be the nearest approximation thereto. The exact or estimated age of every individual is to be recorded. If the person be a child under one year old, born previous to the 1st day of June, the entry is to be made by the fractional parts of a year, thus: one month, 1/12; two months, 2/12; and so on to eleven months, 11/12. Omit months in all cases where the person is of one year and upwards.

8. *Sex.* – Under heading 5, entitled "*Sex,*" insert the letter "m" for male, and "f" for female, opposite the name, in all cases, as the fact may be.

9. *Color.* – Under heading 6, entitled "*Color,*" in all cases where the person is white leave the space blank; in all cases where the person is black without admixture insert the letter "B;" if a mulatto, or of mixed blood, write "M;" if an Indian, write "Ind." It is very desirable to have these directions carefully observed.

10. *Profession, Trade, and Occupation.* – Under heading 7, entitled "*Profession, occupation, or trade of each person over fifteen years of age,*" insert the specific profession, occupations, or trade the individual being enumerated is reputed to follow. The proprietor of a farm for the time being, who pursues agriculture professionally or practically, is to be recorded as a farmer; the men who are employed for wages by him are to be termed farm laborers. The members, or inmates of a family employed in domestic duties at wages you will record as "servants," or "serving," or "domestic," according to the custom of the vicinage.

A mechanic who employs others under him is to be termed differently from the one employed. The first is a master mechanic, and should be termed "master mason," "master carpenter," &c., as the case may be, and you should be very particular in designating the employers or master mechanics from the workmen or employed. Where persons (over 15) are learning trades or serving apprenticeship, they should be recorded as "apprentices," with the name of the trade whereunto they are apprenticed. The employment of every person over 15, having an occupation, should be asked and recorded. In *every case* insert the kind of labor and nature of apprenticeship.

When the individual is a clergyman, insert the initials of the denomination to which he belongs – as Meth. for Methodist; R.C. for Roman Catholic; O.S.P., Old School Presbyterian; P.E., Protestant Episcopal; or other appropriate designation, as the case may require. If a person follows several occupations, insert the name of the most prominent. If the person should be a teacher or professor, state the character of the occupation, as teacher of French, of common school; professor of mathematics, of languages, of Philosophy, &c. In fine, record the occupation of every human being, male and female, (over 15) who has an occupation or means of living, and let your record be so clear as to leave no doubt on the subject.

12. *Value of Real Estate.*—Under heading 8, insert the value of real estate owned by each individual enumerated. You are to obtain this information by personal inquiry of each head of a family, and are to insert the amount in dollars, be the estate located where it may. You are not to consider any question of lien or encumbrance; it is simply your duty to enter the value as given by the respondent.

13. *Value of Personal Estate.*—Under heading 9, insert (in dollars) the value of personal property or estate. Here you are to include the value of all the property, possessions, or wealth of each individual which is not embraced in the column previous, consist of what it may; the value of bonds, mortgages, notes, slaves, live stock, plate, jewels, or furniture; in fine, the value of whatever constitutes the personal wealth of individuals. Exact accuracy may not be arrived at, but all persons should be encouraged to give a near and prompt estimate for your information. Should any respondent manifest hesitation or unwillingness to make a free reply on this or any other subject, you will direct attention to Nos. 6 and 13 of your general instructions and the 15th section of the law.

14. *Birth Place.*—Under heading 10, you are to insert the place of birth of every individual whose name you record. If born in the State or Territory of their present residence, insert the name, abbreviation, or initials of such State or Territory. If born out of the United States, insert the name of the country of birth. To insert simply Germany would not be deemed a sufficiently specific localization of birth place, unless no better can be had. The particular German State should be given—as Baden, Bavaria, Hanover. Where the birth place cannot be ascertained, write "unknown" in the proper column; but it must be of rare occurrence that the place of birth may not be understood. You should ascertain the exact birth place of children as well as of parents, and not infer because parents were born in Baden that so also were the children.

15. *Married during the Year.*—Under heading 11, you are to make a dash (1) opposite the name of each person, male and female, married within the year previous to June 1; that is, of all persons who are residents, and whose names are entered on the schedule.

16. *At School.*—Under heading 12, entitled *"At school within the year,"* you should insert a (1) opposite the names of all those, whether male or female, who are or have been in educational institutions, or who have been receiving stated instruction in any manner within the year; those whose education has been limited to Sunday schools are not to be included.

17. *Number who cannot Read and Write.*—Under heading 13, entitled *"Persons over 20 years who cannot read and write,"* you should be careful to designate every person in the family of this description; and it will be your duty to inquire whether any inmate of the family, being a free person over 20 years of age, is unable to read and write, and opposite the names of all such you will make a mark thus (1). If the person can read and write in a foreign or in our own language, the space is to be left blank.

18. *Deaf and Dumb, Blind, Insane, Idiotic, Pauper, Convict.*—It will be your duty to inquire whether there be any persons of the above description in the family you are enumerating, and if any, you must under heading 14, indicate opposite the

name of such person, the fact as it may be. A person is to be noted deaf and dumb who was born deaf, or who lost the faculty of hearing before acquiring the use of speech. If a person be *blind* from a known cause, it would be well to insert the cause in the column or on the margin. Partial blindness should not be noted. The various degrees of *insanity* often create a doubt as to the propriety of thus classifying individuals, and demands the exercise of discretion. A person may be reputed erratic on some subject, but if competent to manage his or her business affairs without manifesting any symptoms of insanity to an ordinary observer, such person should not be recorded as insane. Where persons are in institutions for safety or restoration, there can exist no doubt as to how you should classify them. As a general rule, the term Insanity applies to individuals who have once possessed mental faculties which have become impaired; whereas Idiocy applies to persons who have never possessed vigorous mental faculties, but from their birth have manifested aberration. The cases wherein it may be difficult to distinguish between insanity and idiocy are not numerous; should such occur, however, you may rely on the opinion of any physician to whom the case is known. It is to be hoped you will not fail to make record respecting all these classes of persons who may be in your subdivision. In all cases of insane persons, you will write in the space where you enter the word "Insane," the *cause* of such insanity; and you will in every case inquire into the cause or origin thereof, and write the word—as intemperance, spiritualism, grief, affliction, hereditary, misfortune, &c. As nearly every case of insanity may be traced to some known cause, it is earnestly desired that you will not fail to make your return in this respect as perfect as possible. If any person whose name you record be at the time, or within the year, so indigent or destitute of the means of support as to require the support of the community, obtained either by alms-begging or public maintenance, by taxation or poor fund, you are to write the word "pauper" in column 14, on a line with the name of such person. When persons who have been convicted of crime within the year resided, on the 1st of June, in any family you enumerate, the fact should be stated by giving in column 14, on a line with the name, the character of the crime; but as such an interrogatory might give offense you had better, where you can do so, refer to the county records for the information, but use care in applying the crime to the proper individual on the schedule. Of course, you are not to insert the name (or crime) of any person who died previous to the 1st day of June on this schedule, but may do so on the schedule of mortality. With the county or parish record, and your own knowledge, you will be able to make this return very correctly without occasioning offense by personal inquiry of individuals. Respecting persons in confinement you will experience no difficulty.

Should a poor-house, asylum for the blind, insane, idiotic, or other charitable institution, or penitentiary, jail, house of refuge or reformation, or other place of punishment be visited, you must number such building or buildings in their regular order, and write in perpendicular column No. 1, the nature of such institution, and in column 14, opposite the name of each inmate, you must state the character of the infirmity or misfortune, in the one case, and in the other the nature of the crime for which each inmate is confined and of which the party stands convicted, and in the column with the name give the year when convicted.

The remaining columns, respecting age, sex, color &c., you must fill with as much care as in other cases. The prison records of these institutions will generally supply the facts required, and, where they do, may be relied on.

The foregoing schedule will serve as your guide for nearly all the entries you will be required to make on the population sheet, and you are requested to study it carefully.

SCHEDULE NO. 2–SLAVE INHABITANTS

This schedule is to be filled up in the following manner: The heading is to be filled up in all respects after the manner of Schedule No. 1, omitting only the name of post office.

1. *Owners of Slaves.*–Under heading No. 1 insert, in proper consecutive order, the names of all owners of slaves. When slaves are the property of a corporation enter the name of the corporation. If held in trust for persons who have attained to their majority, whose names as owners do not elsewhere appear, the names of such persons may be entered, or their number, as "John Smith and two others;" always provided that the "others" do not appear as owners in other places. If held in trust for minors, give the number of such minors. The desire is to obtain a true return of the number of owners.

2. *Number of Slaves.*–Under heading 2, entitled "*Number of slaves,*" insert, in regular numerical order, the number of all the slaves, of both sexes, and of every age, belonging to the owner whose name you have recorded. In the case of slaves, numbers are to be substituted for names. The description of every slave, as numbered, is to be recorded, and you are to enumerate such slaves as may be temporarily absent, provided they are usually held to service in your subdivision. The slaves of each owner are to be numbered separately, beginning with the older at No. 1. The person in whose charge, or on whose plantation the slave is found to be employed may return all slaves in his charge, (although they may be owned by other persons,) provided they are not returned by their proper owner. The name of the *bona fide* owner should be returned as proprietor, and the name of the person having them in charge as employer.

3. *Ages.*–Under heading 3, entitled "*Age,*" insert, in figures, the specific age of each slave opposite the number of such slave. If the exact age cannot be ascertained insert a number which shall be the nearest approximation thereto. The exact or estimated age of every slave is to be inserted. If the slave be a child which on the 1st day of June was less than one year old the entry is to be made by fractional parts of a year, as directed in Rule 7, Schedule 1. Slaves who (born previously) have died since the 1st day of June are to be entered as living, and all details respecting them to be given with as much care as if the slave were living. You are desired to give the names of all slaves whose age reaches or exceeds 100 years.

4. *Sex.*–Under heading 4, opposite each number, insert "m" for male, and "f" for female, in all cases, as the fact may be. In the case of slaves it is very essential that the sex be specified, because of the entire omission of name. The compensation for all returns where this fact is omitted will be reduced.

5. *Color.*–Under heading 5, entitled "*Color,*" insert, in all cases where the slave is black, the letter "B." When he or she is a mulatto, insert "M." You are to note the color of every slave. Those who are in any degree of mixed blood are to be termed mulatto, "M."

6. *Fugitives.*–Under heading 6 insert, in figures, opposite the name of the owner, a mark or number designating the fugitives who, having escaped within the year, have *not been returned* to their owners. Such fugitives are to be described as fully as if in possession of their masters. No allusion is to be made respecting such as may have absconded subsequent to the 1st day of June; they are to be recorded as if in possession of their proper owners.

7. *No. Manumitted.*–In column No. 7, insert opposite the name of the former owner thereof the number of slaves manumitted within the year ending on the 1st day of June. The name of the person is to be given although at the time of enumeration, or on the 1st day of June, such person may have held no slaves. The description of all the slaves manumitted may or may not be given at your pleasure, but the number manumitted must be clearly expressed. If you describe them separately, write "*manumitted*" under the name of the former owner in a line with each one described. If the former owner of slaves manumitted within the year should have died or removed, such circumstance is not to obviate the necessity of their enumeration as directed.

8. *Deaf and Dumb, Blind, Insane, Idiotic.*–You should be particular in every instance to inquire whether any slave comes within the above description, and if so insert the fact in column 8, opposite the number and general description of such slave. If slaves be found imprisoned convicts, mention the crime in column 8, and the date of conviction in the vacant space No. 1. By carefully observing the following schedule, you will experience no difficulty in making proper returns: . . .

9. *Number of Slave Houses.*–In column 9 you will insert the number of slave tenements or dwellings on every farm and plantation, and in every family where slaves are held you will inquire what number of separate tenements are occupied by slaves, and you will insert the number in every instance on a line with the last slave described as belonging to the person or estate whereof you are instituting inquiry. We wish by this column to learn the number of occupied houses, the abode of slaves, belonging to each slaveholder.

CHAPTER THREE

The Structure of the Rural Population

THE SAMPLE WITH DATA on almost 108,000 individuals in over 20,000 households provides a unique opportunity for a detailed study of the structure of the rural population in the Northeast and Midwest on the eve of the Civil War. Perhaps the most surprising aspect of the sample is apparent in the data in Table 2.1. Despite the deliberate selection of rural townships, a large percentage of households in both the Northeast and the Midwest did not operate farms. Only 58 percent of midwesterners lived on farms in rural areas. In the Northeast, 50 percent of the rural households operated farms. Even more remarkable is that in the frontier states such as Kansas and Minnesota the percentage of farm households was below the midwestern average. Indeed, in Iowa, Kansas, and Michigan less than half of the households held farms. On the other hand, two-thirds of Missouri and Wisconsin households had farms. Connecticut, where only two out of five households operated farms, had the lowest proportion of farmers among the northeastern sample states, while Vermont, with 56.5 percent of households living on farms, had the highest rate in the region.

It is clear from just this one statistic that population characteristics varied from state to state. However, rather than document these, we have elected to focus upon the differences between the Northeast and the Midwest and farm versus nonfarm. Among husband-wife headed households, for example, whether on or off the farm, northeastern heads of household and their spouses were older, had higher literacy rates, married later, and produced fewer children than the comparable group in the

Midwest. Indeed, these populations differed significantly from one another in virtually every characteristic. There were similar differences between farm and nonfarm populations within each region. Farmers and farmers' wives tended to be older, more literate, and marry later than their nonfarm counterparts. Farmers, however, tended to have larger families.

The regional differences might be simply explained. Two-thirds or more of northeastern families were living in the state in which the head of household had been born; three-quarters or more of midwestern heads of household had been born elsewhere. The Northeast was therefore a more stable and settled society in which long-standing traditions and customs dictated some of the norms of behavior and determined social status. In the Midwest, where in some states almost everybody was from somewhere else, these forces must have been much weaker. We would expect, therefore, social and economic status to be more fluid and more equal. Moreover, the northeastern population was older, richer, more literate, and more homogeneous than that in the Midwest. As a result we would expect tastes and preferences to differ between the regions and this should be reflected in behavior patterns and reactions to external circumstances.

Age also seems to be the principal characteristic in these rural communities that differentiates farm from nonfarm households. Among the husband-wife households, farm husbands on average were much older than nonfarm. This is consistent with a life cycle of wealth accumulation where farm ownership was the major source of wealth in rural communities. Farm wives were also significantly older than nonfarm spouses. The age differential between husband and wife, however, was virtually the same between farm and nonfarm households. There were also substantial differences between husband and wife households, on and off the farm, between the Northeast and the Midwest. Eastern farm couples were the oldest; nonfarm couples in the Midwest, the youngest.

Age thus figures prominently in our explanation of regional and group differences. It is a major factor influencing such diverse attributes as economic status, tastes, philosophical beliefs, and patterns of behavior. And the age structures of the midwestern and northeastern populations were fundamentally different. Moreover, neither was quite what we expected a priori. Because of the role played by migration in the rapid settlement and economic development of the Midwest, we expected to find its age and sex distribution skewed towards the young adult males who generally make up migrant streams. Instead, what we found was a structure that shows the classic profile of a young and rapidly growing population (Fig. 3.1) and no evidence of a sex ratio imbalance. Infants under 1, for example, represented almost 3.6 percent of the population

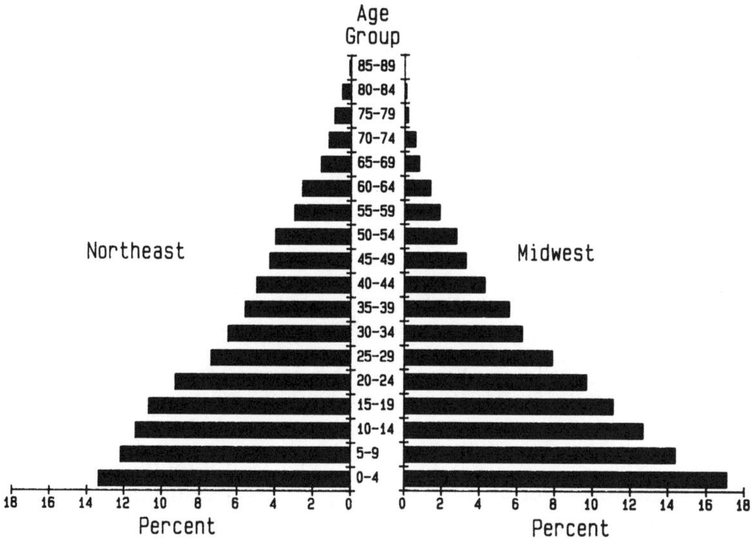

FIG. 3.1. Age distribution of the rural population in the Northeast and Midwest, 1860.

and children aged 1–4 constituted another 13.5 percent.[1] Children under age 10 were almost one-third of the midwestern rural population. Only 0.3 percent of the population was 75 or older. This age structure is almost identical to that in Mexico between 1959 and 1961, where infants represented 3.3 percent of that population; children 1–4, 13.3 percent; and children under 10, 31.9 percent.[2] The Mexican population has since become the fastest growing population in the world.

In the Northeast, individuals appear to have experienced greater longevity. Beyond age 70, the Northeast had at least double the proportion of elderly that were in the Midwest. In part, this reflects the relative youth of all settlement in the Midwest, but it probably also results from the greater rigors of life on the frontier and their effects upon life expectancy. The northeastern population was also growing less rapidly. Children under 1 constituted slightly less than 2.8 percent of the population; about a quarter of the population was under 10 years old. At the opposite extreme, 1.5 percent of the population was older than 75. The fractions for the young are slightly higher than in the United States during the post–World War II "baby boom," while greater life expectancy in the twentieth century has led to much higher fractions of the population being 75 and over.

The differences in the shapes of the population age structures are also noteworthy.[3] That for the Midwest is a smooth, parabolic trace with no pronounced irregularities. This is the characteristic pattern for a population that is growing rapidly through natural increase. The traditional assumption, however, held that the midwestern population was growing rapidly because of in-migration. If this were the case, then we would expect to observe a bulge in the age distribution for the 20- and 30-year-olds, who were most likely to make up the migrant stream, except in the unlikely event that they all went to midwestern cities. We would also expect a sex imbalance favoring men because they were more likely to migrate in search of economic opportunity than women. There were slightly more men than women in the Midwest, but the same pattern also prevailed in the Northeast and does not account for the difference.

Age structure in the Northeast corresponds neither to that of a young and rapidly growing population nor of an aging, stable one with comparatively favorable life expectancies. Rather, there are elements of both extremes visible for different ranges of ages. Succeeding quinquennia age cohorts between 0 and 19, for example, were only slightly smaller than the preceding ones, suggesting comparatively slow rates of net population growth over the previous nineteen years (between 1841 and 1860). There was then a sharp break in cohort sizes between that of 15–19 and that of 20–24, with another sharp break between the 20–24 age cohort and those 25–29. A similar break occurs between ages 50–54 and 55–59, and again between 60–64 and 65–69.

There are two alternate hypotheses that may explain these patterns. The first is that the rate of natural increase of the population fluctuated quite sharply in the period between the Revolution and the 1850s. Compare the slope of the parabolic trace across the age cohorts 20–50 with that for 0–19. Successive cohorts of the 20- to 54-year-olds decreased much more sharply than those 0–19. This implies that population growth had been accelerating during the period when these cohorts were born, which was between 1806 and 1840. In particular, growth seems to have been especially rapid during the 1830s and very slow between 1806 and 1815. This slow rate of growth during the Embargo period and the War of 1812 is especially marked against the more rapid pace of population expansion that both preceded and followed it. Population also grew rapidly between about 1801 and 1806 following a period of slow growth in the late 1790s that came on the heels of a sharp population spurt after the Revolution. These patterns correspond quite closely with what we know about economic conditions during the first half-century or so of American independence. Moreover, depending upon precisely where one locates the breaks between slow and rapid population growth, it is possible to interpret the more stable, slower growing cohorts as the offspring of the more rapidly growing, older ones.

The alternate hypothesis is that out-migration in specific periods altered the rate of overall population growth in the region. Certainly, the irregularities in the age distribution among northeasterners are consistent with what we know about out-migration from that region.[4] The sharp break between the 20–24 and the 25–29 age cohorts, for example, suggests out-migration by those who would be 25–29, which presumably occurred sometime during the preceding decade. Similarly, there are breaks between the 50–54 and the 55–59 cohorts and the 60–64 and 65–69 groupings. If out-migrations in these groups had also occurred when members were in their early to middle twenties, then the migrations would have taken place in the 1810s, the late 1820s, and the early 1830s. These dates coincide with the mass settlement of Indiana, Illinois, and Michigan, and the establishment of the Iowa and Wisconsin territories. The effects on the northeastern population would have been reinforced by lower fertility rates and low nuptuality rates in that region that resulted thereby (see Chap. 4).

It is possible to discriminate between these competing hypotheses with the data that are available. In the former case, we would expect a fairly even sex ratio in each cohort, allowing for the slightly higher rate of male to female births and the effects of high maternal mortality to favor men. In the latter case, we would expect the reverse. There is, however, no evidence of out-migration by males from the Northeast in the age-sex distribution of that population. Men and women bore reasonable proportions to one another in each period, with men outnumbering women by a small margin in each of the "deficient" cohorts.[5] It therefore seems likely that the natural rate of population growth was slow during these periods, not that out-migration reduced the rate of population increase.

On the frontier, however, the age-sex distribution was skewed in favor of young adult males who migrated there. In Minnesota and Kansas, for example, there were more individuals aged 20–24 than 15–19 and even more males aged 25–29 (Fig. 3.2). These are the prime ages at which people migrated and the migrants were predominantly single males. Men in these age groups accounted for almost 14 percent of the population, while women were only 9 percent. Moreover, few people were old, nobody being over 75. Migration skewed the overall sex distribution in favor of men. About 56 percent of the population was male, and nuptuality was consequently lower among this population than among the northern rural population as a whole. There was no such distortion in the sex ratio among the children, but among young adults (25–29 years old) there was an acute shortage of women, with only 188 women to 326 men.

In-migration was not the only source of population growth in these states. They were also growing rapidly through natural increase. About 4 percent of the population was under 1 year old; a third were less than 10.

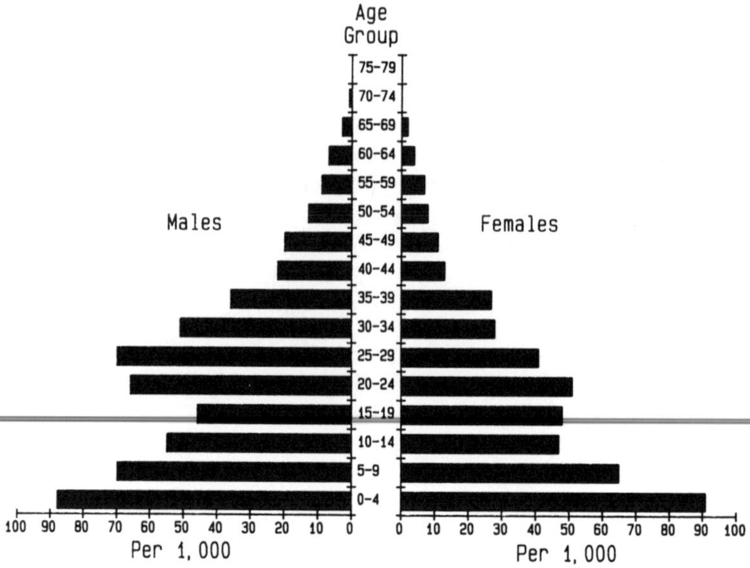

FIG. 3.2. Age distribution of the rural population of Kansas and Minnesota by sex, 1860.

As these children reached maturity, beginning about 1870 and continuing to the end of the century, this population would have grown explosively if each had the same number of children as his or her parents. This did not occur because in the intervening period the region passed through a demographic transition.[6]

On the frontier, therefore, we can conclude that young adult males were the principal migrants. Where married, they exhibited fertility rates akin to those for the midwestern rural population as a whole. Elsewhere in the Midwest, to the extent that there had been recent in-migration, families, not individuals, seem to have made the decision to migrate. Because the arrival of these migrant families in the Midwest did not distort the age structure of the population, they must have had fertility rates similar to those of the existing midwestern population. Moreover, since many were quite recent arrivals, it seems likely that their fertility patterns were established before their migration.

Significant differences existed between the average characteristics of the different headship groups. Husband-wife households were usually considerably younger than either other-male- or female-headed households. Women-headed households had the highest average age; nonfarm husband-wife households the lowest. Among the other-male- and female-headed households there were almost certainly many widowers and widows. These aside, however, the average age of those in households not containing spouses is inconsistent with an argument that this status simply reflects an early stage in their life cycle. They were single by choice. There were also other differences between them that we consider below.

Female-headed households frequently contained children. This, and the high average age of the woman, suggests that they were probably widows. There was no significant difference in the average age between farm and nonfarm households; those living on farms averaged 49.6 years old; those not had a mean age of 49.8 years. Nor was there much difference in this group between East and West. Few of them, however, were to be found operating farms. There were more than twice as many nonfarm female-headed households as farm households. For social or other reasons, widowed farm wives may have found it difficult to keep up the family farm without a man to assist or they may have relinquished nominal headship (if only in the eyes of the census enumerators) to the eldest son; more likely though, a widow with a farm was an attractive marriage prospect.

Young men were more likely to be single heads of household than young women and therefore may be considered eligible bachelors. The proportion of young single male heads of household was also much higher in the West than in the East, consistent with their playing an important role in the migrant stream. However, other-male heads as a group were much older than the male heads in husband-wife households, both on and off the farm. Some of these were almost certainly widowers as suggested by the presence of young children in a few of the households. Other-male heads who were farmers were older (46.6 years) than the nonfarmers (44.3 years).

Farming dominated rural occupations in both regions. The data suggest a greater variety of occupations in the Northeast but the differences are marginal (Fig. 3.3). Indeed, it is surprising to find these rural areas, particularly in the West, with such diversified local economies. They supported the agricultural sector and were dependent upon it, but between a quarter and two-thirds of the gainfully employed population had nonagricultural jobs. Of the 129 separately identified occupations pursued by one or more of the rural inhabitants in the sample, northeasterners followed 114 and midwesterners, 112. Furthermore, whereas 20 occupations in the Northeast employed 0.5 percent or more of the working population, 14 activities engaged 0.5 percent or more of the midwestern population.

The most pronounced differences between the regions are in the fractions of the working population listing their occupation as "farmer" and those who listed themselves as "laborer." Fifty-five percent of midwest-

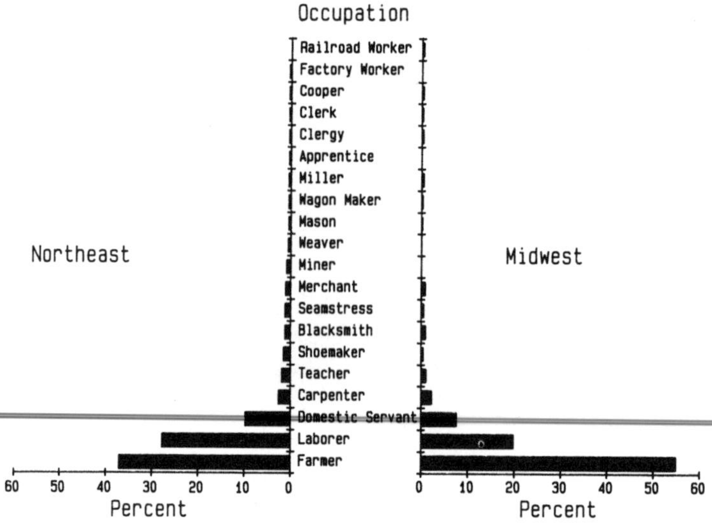

FIG. 3.3. Distribution of rural heads of household by occupation by region, 1860.

erners were described as farmers, while 20 percent were laborers. In the East, the percentage of farmers was considerably lower (37 percent) and of laborers, higher (28 percent). In part, this reflects a life cycle phenomenon—what Merle Curti has referred to as the "agricultural ladder" with laborers on its bottom-most rung.[7] Farmers, as a group, were much older (averaging 40.4 years) than laborers (who averaged only 26.8 years). In the East, however, both laborers and farmers were older than their midwestern counterparts.

In both regions there were substantial numbers of "farmers without farms." Both Bogue and Curti argue that for the most part these were optimists, aspiring would-be farmers, perhaps one step removed from farm laborer on the agricultural ladder. Our sample provides additional evidence of this. There were proportionately far more farmers without farms on the western frontier than in the East or even the more settled western states. In Michigan and Kansas, for example, there were more than 80 percent as many farmers without farms as there were farms.[8] In Illinois, the fraction was 0.57 and in Ohio, 0.27. In the East, it was everywhere below 50 percent. There were few optimists in the slave-holding states. The fraction of farmers without farms in Missouri was 0.29. In Maryland, it was less than 10 percent.

Some of the farmers without farms lived on farms. These were often the sons of farmers and there was some basis to their expectations. Because they may also have shared in the decision making, they considered themselves to be a farmer with some justification. Nowhere, however, did this group make up a majority of the farmers without farms.

There was a notable curiosity about the data: sixty-nine midwesterners gave their occupations as part-time farmers while only fourteen northeasterners did. Since smaller farms were more characteristic of the Northeast than than the Midwest, we would have expected this relationship to be reversed. We have no information about their other jobs, and the evidence from the census manuscripts is ambiguous. On the one hand, since none of these part-time farmers lived on a farm, it could be argued that they may be more accurately described as farm laborers. As a group, however, they reported real estate holdings averaging almost $3,000. This, as we will show subsequently, was more than adequate for a viable farm anywhere.

Among white-collar service workers, there were relatively more teachers in rural areas of the Northeast than in the Midwest. This difference becomes more pronounced when the greater proportion of children in the Midwest is considered. In that region, there was one teacher to every 68 children aged 6–14, while in the Northeast the teacher-student ratio was 1:34. In most other white-collar occupations, the regions compare quite favorably. There were marginally fewer merchants in the Midwest, which is consistent with estimates of regional per capita income, but in the other important white-collar occupations – doctors, lawyers, and clergy – the proportions of the population in these professions were virtually identical between these regions.

The relative proportions of skilled artisans – blacksmiths, carpenters, coopers, masons, for example – are not too dissimilar between the regions, although the Midwest had slightly lower densities in each occupation, much to its disadvantage. Blacksmithing, for example, was a critically important occupation in rural areas, especially those lacking a ready supply of factory-made products or spare parts, yet 1.3 percent of gainfully employed rural northeasterners listed this as their occupation, compared with only 1.1 percent in the Midwest, where a priori one would expect that demand for their services would have been greater. A midwestern farmer as a consequence probably had to be much more a "Jack-of-all-trades," especially as farrier and in the maintenance and repair of farm equipment. One puzzling aspect of the occupational data for skilled crafts is the comparatively low incidence of apprenticeship in the Midwest. Despite approximately equal proportions of skilled tradesmen in each region, the apprenticeship rate in the Northeast was two and a half times greater than in the Midwest.

The most marked difference between East and Midwest in the occupational structure, aside from that for farmers, laborers, and teachers, is in the proportions of the rural populations engaged in manufacturing activities. Shoemakers, for example, made up 1.6 percent of the rural northeastern population but only 0.6 percent of the midwestern. Collectively, certain manufacturing activities, carder, factory worker, harness maker, manufacturer, miller, seamstress, shoemaker, and weaver employed 5.4 percent of the population in the Northeast, compared with 2.2 percent in the Midwest. We have counted seamstresses and weavers in this category because the small volume of home manufactures reported suggests that these people were employed outside the home.

Few women reported occupations at the 1860 Census. The published figures give no breakdown of occupations by sex except for the industrial classification in the *Census of Manufactures*. In our sample from the population schedules, almost a half of the female heads of household on farms reported no occupation, yet it seems highly probable that they did much of the farm management, if not the heavy manual work. Even more surprising is the denial of an occupation by almost three-quarters of the single women living off farms. Among those women reporting occupations, farming dominated (43.5 percent among those on farms; 6.4 percent among the nonfarm females), followed by domestic service (4.4 percent and 6.3 percent respectively), seamstress (0.7 percent and 4.2 percent). Nonfarm female heads of household also reported employment as weavers and laundresses.

The sample data also let us examine occupation by age. We have done this only for males because of the limited number of females who reported jobs. We distinguish only between an occupation and no occupation. Estimates of the percentage of males with an occupation by quinquennia are shown in Figure 3.4. It is tempting to interpret the shortfall in these data from 100 percent as unemployment rates, but the census enumerators were directed to report "the specific profession, occupations, or trade the individual being enumerated is reputed to follow" rather than whether or not they were currently engaged in that activity.[9] Consequently, these data show participation rates.

Participation rates were higher in the Midwest among adults, but somewhat lower among teenagers. No rates are reported for juveniles under 15 since the enumerators were only directed to collect occupational data for those 15 and older, except for apprentices. In both regions, participation rates began to decline noticeably among males in their late sixties. We interpret this as retirement, but it is also obvious that this was not a universal privilege or choice. More than 70 percent of men in their seventies still had occupations. While the percentage declined with increasing age in the Midwest, in the Northeast it was higher among those in their late seventies than those in their early seventies and remained high for those in their eighties. Greater life expectancy and longevity in the Northeast were accompanied by a longer working life, which may

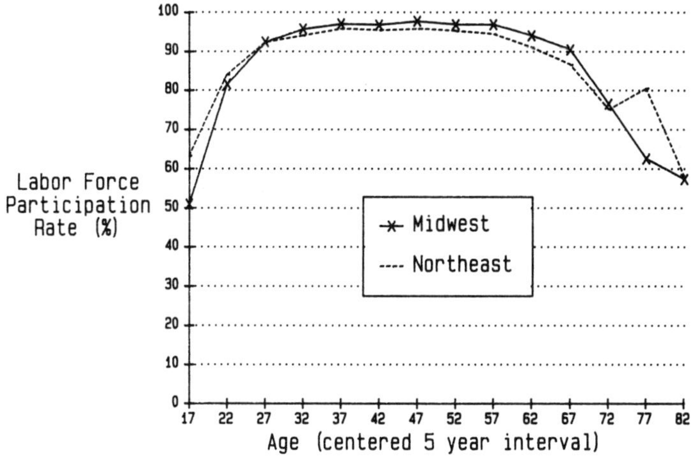

FIG. 3.4. Labor force participation rates for adult males by quinquennia in the Northeast and Midwest, 1860.

have encouraged younger children to give up on the prospects of an early inheritance and migrate instead to the West.

Data on school attendance by age shows a similar pattern between Northeast and Midwest. Attendance rates rose through about age 10 before reaching a plateau and declining for those aged 14 and older (Fig. 3.5). Proportionately more children under 15 were in school in the Northeast. Nevertheless, in both regions more than 70 percent of all children aged 8–14 attended school in the preceding year. This seems a quite high level of educational commitment in a rural society without compulsory schooling.

Although a greater proportion of younger children were in school in the Northeast, the Midwest had proportionately more children aged 15–19 attending. Two conflicting interpretations are possible. Either the level of long-term educational commitment in the Midwest was higher, which seems unlikely, or else the quality and quantity of schooling there was such that students needed to attend longer to master the basics. This would be consistent with heavy labor demands, especially at planting and harvesttime, in the relatively more agrarian Midwest.

In both regions, school attendance rates were approximately the same for boys and girls up to age 14. Thereafter, attendance by girls fell sharply. Among 15-year-olds, attendance rates were 4 or 5 percentage points lower for girls than for boys and by age 17 attendance rates for boys were one- to two-thirds higher than for girls.

Between farm and nonfarm populations, farmers seem to have invested much more in the education of their children. As a group they had

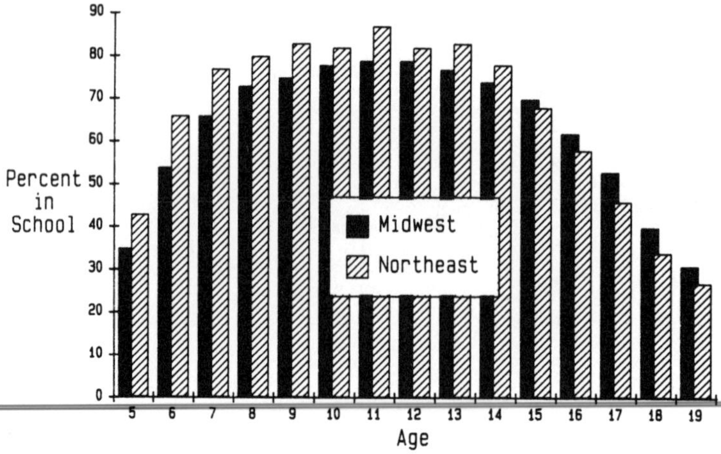

FIG. 3.5. Percentage of children attending school during the year by region and age, 1859–1860.

substantially higher attendance rates at each age group and in each region. The differences between the groups were especially marked among older children where rates often differed by 20 percentage points or more. One can interpret these data pessimistically in low educational attainment for years of attendance among farm children because of other demands upon their time and energies. However, since farmers were among the top wealth holders, a relatively high level of investment in education by this group would not be out of place. Proportionately more children of native Americans attended school in each region and in each age group than the children of immigrants. To the extent that immigrant offspring had greater obstacles to overcome, this would perpetuate their relative disadvantage.

Among adults the only quantifiable impact of the educational system from the available data was whether or not individuals could read and write. The only discernible trends parallel those among the children, namely illiteracy was higher among women, nonfarm workers, and immigrants but with higher literacy rates among these populations in the Northeast. Literacy rates in each population declined somewhat with age, but the differences were fairly minor.

Some important descriptive elements of the rural population such as the age of marriage, the average number of children, and place of birth have not been dealt with here. They form crucial elements in the next two chapters on fertility and migration. In these we will concentrate our attention on the husband-wife households in the sample for an analysis of some of the social aspects of Jefferson's vision of a rural farm democracy.

CHAPTER FOUR

Family Formation: The Pattern of Fertility

THE DATA THAT WE PRESENTED in Chapter 3 on the age structures of the northeastern and midwestern rural populations implied markedly different rates of population growth in the two regions. The Midwest was growing more rapidly and had a young population; in the Northeast population growth was slower and the population older. These same differences are to be found among the husband-wife households in our sample. Male heads of household in the East were, on average, 43 years old, with a wife of 39. Heads and their wives in the West were four years younger. Despite their relative youth, however, midwestern wives had an average of 3 surviving children compared with only 2.1 children per northeastern mother. Such differences predated the Eighth Census. Ezra Seaman, for example, in his analysis of the data collected at the Sixth Census in 1840 drew attention to the diverse proportions of children under the age of 10 among the regions and the different rates of population growth that they implied.[1] Since then, this phenomenon has been exhaustively documented and analyzed with attention focused especially on the differences between East and West, rather than on those North and South.[2]

Measuring fertility by the child-woman ratio, which is defined as the ratio of children under 10 per 1,000 women of childbearing age (assumed to be 16–44), our sample data also reveal a marked difference between East and West among the rural population. Whereas the child-woman ratio in the East was 1,110, that in the West was more than one-third higher, 1,519. However, our data also reveal a hitherto unremarked difference between farm and nonfarm households within the same geographic location (Figs. 4.1 and 4.2). In the Northeast, farm-women fertility was lower than nonfarm, sometimes substantially so. In Vermont, for example, the child-woman ratio for farm residents was only 55 percent of that among nonfarm residents within the same community (Table 4.1). In the Midwest, by contrast, farm-women fertility was generally higher than nonfarm-women fertility, but nonfarm-women fertility was not substantially different between the regions. These differentials were unobservable to earlier researchers such as Yasuba and Forster and Tucker, who relied upon aggregate data; others, such as Easterlin and Leet, though using data for individuals were focusing on the wider issues raised by Yasuba as explanations for the East-West differences.[3] In this chapter, in addition to providing new demographic evidence on the sources and reasons for the East-West fertility difference, we also extend these earlier studies by examining those variations between farm and nonfarm households. Moreover, our data provide a unique opportunity to investigate fertility differences between immigrants and native-born.

The mean number of own surviving children per woman peaked in the Northeast at 2.78 children for the cohort of women aged 35–39 and decreased to 2.74 children for the 40- to 44-year-old cohort. In the Midwest, it peaked at 4.13 for women 40–44. Concentrating on the mean number of children, however, disguises the radical differences between the two regions in the distribution of family sizes (Fig. 4.3). In the West, less than 10 percent of married women aged 35–44 remained childless. The modal number of children was 5, and over 15 percent of these women had 7 or more children. In the East, by contrast, almost 14 percent remained childless; the modal number of children was 1, and less than 6 percent of families had 7 or more children. Among farm families, the differences were even more marked.[4]

The decline in the family size of women in their forties is interpreted as the oldest children leaving home to establish their own households. This occurred earlier in the Northeast than the Midwest despite the later marriage of northeastern women. We therefore conclude that children left home at a younger age in that region. Moreover, since northeasterners married later and yet the proportions of unmarried household heads were similar between East and West, we conclude that the children who left home in the East moved to urban areas. This is consistent with the relative demand for farm labor between the Northeast and Midwest and the availability of nonfarm urban employment in the East. Furthermore, as shown in Chapter 3, the age difference between female-headed households in the two regions was slight, while other-male-headed households were younger in the West.

Other things equal, it is expected that women who marry younger

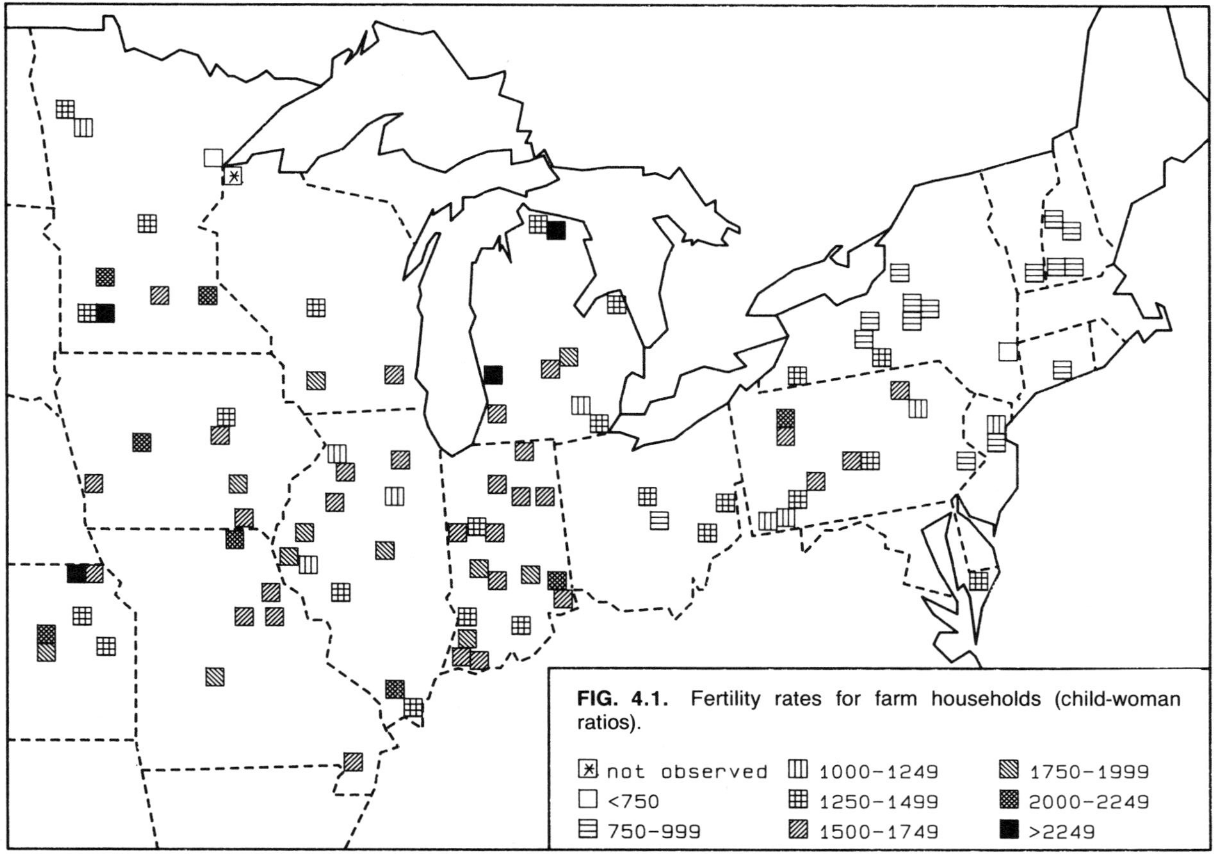

FIG. 4.1. Fertility rates for farm households (child-woman ratios).

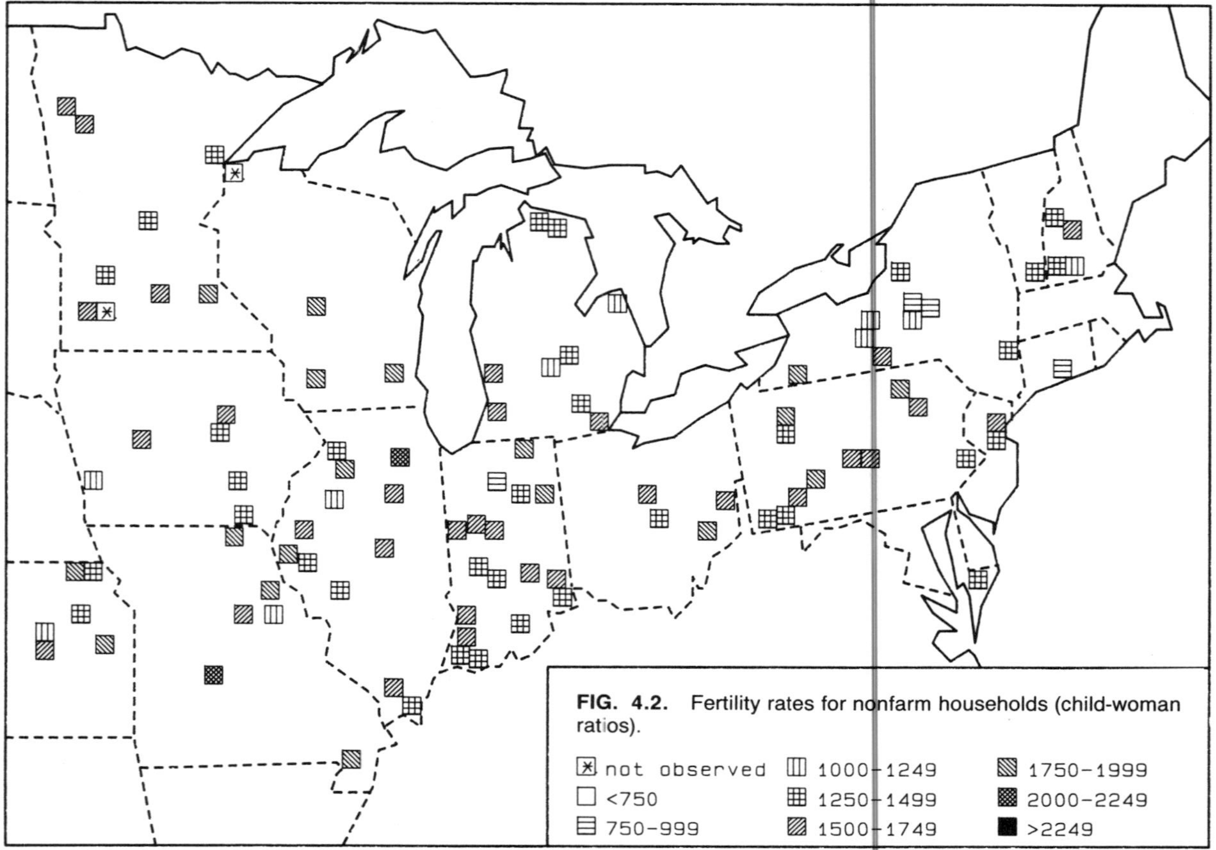

FIG. 4.2. Fertility rates for nonfarm households (child-woman ratios).

TABLE 4.1. Child-Woman Ratios by State in Sample, 1860

	Child-Woman Ratios[a]	
State	Farm Households	Nonfarm Households
Conn.	810	975
Md.	1490	1300
N.H.	957	1350
N.J.	928	1473
N.Y.	943	1172
Pa.	1343	1535
Vt.	833	1500
Ill.	1637	1529
Ind.	1648	1549
Iowa	1708	1431
Kans.	1572	1531
Mich.	1568	1438
Minn.	1732	1571
Mo.	1683	1766
Ohio	1202	1658
Wis.	1696	1833

[a]Children under 10/women, 16–44/1,000.

will have more children. This is borne out by the data. The age of marriage, estimated from the age of the oldest own child, varied significantly between the different populations.[5] For the cohorts of farm wives in the Midwest and Northeast aged 35–44, proportionately more midwesterners had been brides aged 16–24. The modal age for a midwestern bride was 23 (Fig. 4.4). In the Northeast, where the mode was 25, there existed a

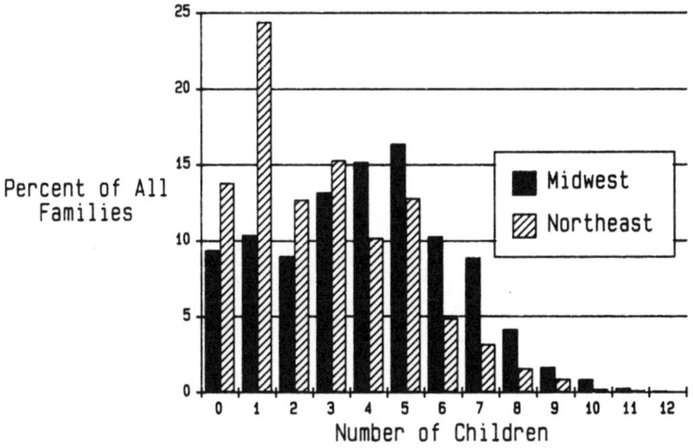

FIG. 4.3. Frequency distribution of the number of own children born to women aged 35–44, 1860.

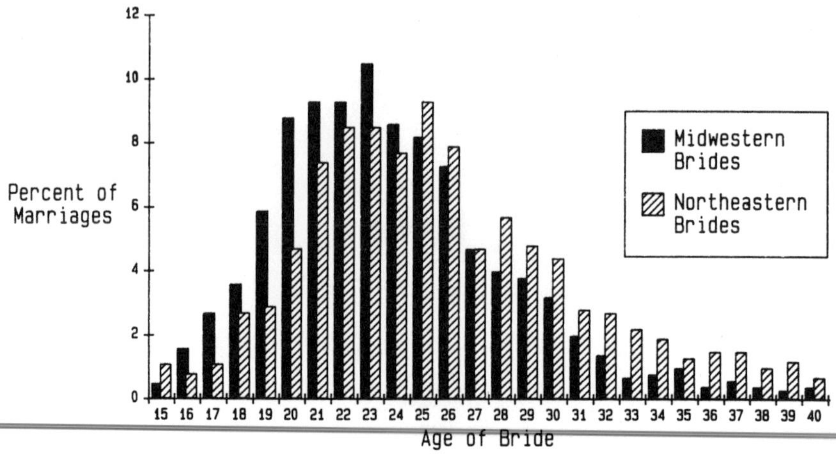

FIG. 4.4. Age at marriage of farmers' wives.

significantly higher proportion of older brides. This alone would depress northeastern fertility rates relative to the Midwest because of the shorter span of childbearing years and the loss of high-fertility years in the early twenties.[6]

However, this aside, there remained substantial East-West fertility differences. Nonfarm couples in the Northeast, for example, were comparable in age and length of marriage with farm couples in the Midwest, yet there were significantly fewer surviving own children in the northeastern households. Midwestern farm couples averaged one surviving child for every 3.9 years of marriage, whereas in the Northeast nonfarm couples managed only one child per 5.4 years. Eastern farm wives had the lowest fecundity, with only one own surviving child per 6.6 years of marriage; nonfarm midwestern couples, the highest, at 3.7. These differences seem too great to be accounted for totally by the greater average age of northeastern brides.

Regional and group differences aside, fertility in 1860 was not particularly high in the rural North. In the West, there were 36 infants under 1 per 1,000 population; in the East, 28.[7] These figures understate the true crude birth rate by the number of infant deaths, but they cast serious doubt upon the national estimate of the white birth rate adjusted for mortality, 41.4, or the Massachusetts infant mortality data. If we correct by the estimated infant mortality rate among Massachusetts babies between 1855 and 1859 of 122.9 per 1,000 births, then our best estimate of the 1860 birth rate in the rural West is 40; in the East, 32.[8] The rural birth rate in both regions is thus below the national average, despite evidence of higher fertility in the rural, as compared with urban, areas and in the North vis-à-vis the South.[9] To make our estimates of the birth rate consistent with the national average, the infant mortality rate would have to be about 250–275 per 1,000 births. This does not seem remotely plausible.

Although the birth rate, or its approximation by the ratio of children under 1 to total population, may be used to measure fertility, we have chosen to use the child-woman ratio as our measure at the township level because sample sizes are larger.[10] This is the ratio of the number of children under 10 to women aged 16–44.[11] It is highly correlated with the birth rate and is affected by the same forces such as infant mortality. We have limited our analysis to the white population.[12]

Our child-woman ratios were generally higher than those reported by others.[13] The difference is almost certainly attributable to the rural bias of our sample and the costs and incentives of child rearing relative to the city, but it may also reflect errors in the published census. Like Yasuba's series, however, ours shows a lower child-woman ratio in the Northeast than the Midwest. Only one eastern township had a ratio exceeding 1,750 children per 1,000 women of childbearing age; in most the ratio was under 1,250. On the other hand, only a few western townships had ratios that low and many were in excess of 1,750.

Farm-women fertility largely accounts for the high rate of population growth in the Midwest as well as the low rate of growth in the Northeast. Midwestern farm-women fertility rates were often double those of northeastern farm families. These differences are even more significant when the age differentials between the populations are considered. There were proportionately more women in their younger childbearing years in the Midwest relative to the Northeast, and midwestern farm wives were, on average, more than five and a half years younger than northeastern farm wives. With an average age of only 37, midwestern farmers' wives were probably not at the end of their reproductive history, whereas northeastern farm families were more likely to be completed ones.

Following Yasuba's lead, subsequent researchers have emphasized two factors as explanations for the declining fertility over time and the higher fertility characteristically found the farther westward one looks at any time in the nineteenth century: the economic opportunity for establishing new households and the extent of urbanization and industrialization.[14] Other things equal, economic opportunity and fertility are positively correlated, while fertility and urbanization tend to be negatively so. Since farming was the major source of employment and real estate the principal form of wealth in most parts of the country in the nineteenth century, agriculture constituted the principal economic opportunity for most people. This opportunity was less easily realized in the South primarily because of the institution of slavery.[15] And it was less possible in the Northeast as well because of the relative scarcity of land.[16] In the Midwest, however, especially on the frontier, land was abundant and entry costs low. Land clearing, farm formation, crop cultivation, and livestock tending provided employment opportunities. This labor created capital through improvements to the land and increases in livestock populations. As a potential "nest egg," unoccupied land probably influenced the proportion of women who married. It almost certainly affected their age at marriage and the incentives for couples to regulate their fertility.

Consider the situation facing a newly married, childless couple on an eastern farm who viewed farming as the ideal way of life. Because custom decreed partible inheritance to male offspring, having more than one son created problems.[17] If most or all available land was already taken, the settlement of suitable inheritances forced undesirable choices upon the family: an existing farm could be purchased at great expense; the family farm could be fragmented; an obligation could be placed upon the eldest son to buy out the financial interest of the other heirs to the family farm; and the family could be fragmented through the westward migration of younger sons to where land was available, thus striking at the roots of the family.[18] Faced with these options, the couple may well have preferred instead to limit fertility.

In the midwestern region and particularly on the frontier, however, good land was readily and cheaply available in the neighborhood. Moreover, as a result of initial overbuying, the family farm itself was often larger than could be farmed effectively by family labor using the existing technology. Work could always be found for family labor, especially on the newest farms: there were fences to build, ditches to dig, and land to clear in addition to the daily routine of farm life. In these circumstances, there were few if any incentives to check fertility.

Although the relationship between land availability and economic opportunity seems clear, a universally acceptable measure of land availability has proved more elusive. Yasuba used 1949 cropland acreages to calculate population densities. However, the use of data so far removed from the period under consideration provided the principal source of criticism of his work by Forster and Tucker. Instead, they used data for 1850, 1860, and 1880 to construct alternate estimates before expressing a preference for 1880 as a basis. Easterlin adopted yet a different measure. He computed the ratio of improved acreage in 1860 to the maximum ever improved. This has the advantage that it relates more directly to agricultural development. Quintiles of the distribution of settlement classes were then used for the analysis.

A student of Easterlin's, Donald Leet, subsequently utilized a more sophisticated measure of economic opportunity. He attempted to measure the percentage excess supply of, or demand for, farm sites in Ohio. Supply was measured by the number of farm sites expected to become vacant between 1850 and 1860 through the death of the owner, plus the number of sites that could be developed if the potential cultivable land in the area were immediately brought under the plow and divided into lots equal in size to the average improved acreage per farm in 1850. The demand for these farms was then approximated by the number of white males, aged 15–24, in the county on the assumption that those males might be expected to form new households and seek farms during the 1850s. The difference between the demand and supply formed the excess demand for farms during the 1850s. If it was greater than supply, the excess demand was expressed as a percentage of the total demand for farm sites. If demand was less than supply, then the "excess" demand was expressed as a percentage of the total supply of farm sites. As a result the variable was bounded by +/−100 percent. It was set to −100 percent for those counties that were unorganized in 1850. We have extended this methodology to cover all townships in our sample.

One important virtue of this measure in explaining differences in child-woman ratios is its direct relevance to farming and its structure at the time in question. Specifically, it takes account of potential family formation by existing residents and provides testable hypotheses about the attractiveness of places for migrants and immigrants: places with the greatest excess supply should be most attractive to outsiders.

Other factors besides land availability might also be expected to influence fertility. Urbanization and industrialization in America were associated with decreased demand for child labor and increased employment opportunities for women. By increasing child-rearing costs, children could no longer be regarded as producer goods but became instead consumption. Because of the rural bias of the sample, however, no variable for urbanization or industrialization was included. On the other hand, a variable was included to capture the demand for child labor on farms. We used the percentage of households operating farms in the township and expected a positive correlation between this and the child-woman ratio.

We also tried to capture some of the cultural and social values that might influence fertility. We included the percentage of households headed by New Englanders, expecting that migrants from those areas would have lower fertility. New England passed through demographic transition long before 1860 and had witnessed the deleterious social and economic effects of population pressure on land. Similarly, we included the percentage of foreign-born heads of households excluding the Irish and southern Germans, as a proxy for the proportion of families from areas that for the most part had neither undergone demographic transition nor experienced great pressure upon land. We utilized a separate variable for the percentage of households headed by southern Germans and Irish. In their homelands both groups had high fertility rates. They were also predominantly Roman Catholic. These considerations should result in this variable correlating positively with the child-woman ratio. However, if the Potato Famine was viewed as a Malthusian population check, then the relationship could be negative.

We included a wealth variable, although its effects upon fertility and the child-woman ratio are ambiguous. Consequently, we expected the coefficient of this variable to be approximately zero. Wealth in rural areas was dominated by real estate, therefore the effect could be positive through the demand for child labor on farms. This would be reinforced if children are considered as consumption rather than as producer goods; more wealth should mean more children. On the other hand, lower fertility is often associated with increasing wealth; the emphasis shifts from family quantity to "quality." We did not include variables for urbanization or industrialization in the model because of the sample's deliberate rural bias.

The model was thus:

CW = f(Land Pressure, Percent Farm, Percent New England, Percent Irish and German, Percent Other Immigrants, Wealth)

Our expectations regarding signs were Land Pressure (−), Percent Farm (+), Percent New England (−), Percent Irish and German (?), Percent Foreign (+), and Wealth (?). The question mark signifies either no prior expectations or contradictory forces that would reduce the significance level of the variable. We estimated this equation for all households in the townships and for a variety of subgroups—farmers and nonfarmers and native-born and foreign-born (Table 4.2).

All but the immigrant regression explained a significant portion of the total variability in intertownship child-woman ratios. The best, that for all households, explains 55 percent of the variability in the child-woman ratio between townships in terms of variations in the six independent variables. Although the four independent variables in the immigrant child-woman ratio regression failed to explain a significant proportion of the variation in the dependent variable, we chose to report the results to emphasize that the forces driving immigrant fertility were not those that drove the fertility of other groups, although the forces were consistent in direction across all of them.

TABLE 4.2. Explaining Intertownship Variations in Child-Woman Ratio for All Households and Various Groups, 1860 (standard errors in parentheses)

Group	Constant	Land	Wealth	Percent Farm	Percent New England	Percent Irish or German	Percent Other Immigrants	R^2	Number of Observations
All Households	1328.61	–135.95[b]	–0.09[b]	592.92[b]	–477.96[b]	87.55	381.98[a]	0.55	101
		(45.23)	(0.02)	(132.84)	(115.47)	(251.29)	(156.00)		
Farm	1790.96	–137.82[a]	–0.09[b]	–	–661.78[b]	–126.74	286.27	0.50	101
		(65.77)	(0.02)		(156.05)	(313.64)	(204.28)		
Nonfarm	1501.64	– 93.80[a]	–0.06[a]	–	– 63.35	–64.11	347.89[a]	0.17	100
		(43.84)	(0.03)		(126.61)	(292.35)	(164.35)		
Natives	1312.63	–188.27[b]	–0.08[b]	583.21[b]	–498.91[b]	–	–	0.48	101
		(47.04)	(0.02)	(147.10)	(117.34)				
Immigrants	1566.81	– 42.96	–0.03	93.88	–	669.32[b]	–	0.09	92
		(96.55)	(0.05)	(224.71)		(240.98)			

[a] Significant at 5 percent level
[b] Significant at 1 percent level

Land pressure had the predicted sign in every equation and was a significant explanatory variable in all but that for immigrants. Immigrants were apparently unresponsive in their fertility patterns to population pressure on the land. In the other equations, it had the strongest correlation of any independent variable with the dependent variable. Since this variable ranged between 0.8 (in parts of New York and elsewhere in the Northeast) and −1.0 (on the frontier), it potentially explains a differential of 250–300 in the child-woman ratio between townships. The major variations were between states and the two regions.

Among the native-born and for all households generally, a large fraction of farm households in a township was positively correlated with higher fertility. This result is consistent with the farm demand for child labor and also with the lower opportunity cost to farm women of having children. However, since variations in the percentage of farm households from township to township were smaller than for many of the other explanatory variables, its effect upon the child-woman ratio was not especially great.

Greater wealth was associated with lower fertility for each group, and this variable was significantly less than zero for all households, farmers, and natives. There is significant overlap between these groups. The child-woman ratio was not especially responsive to changes in this variable. For all households, for example, the mean township wealth was about $2,250. Doubling this would reduce the child-woman ratio by about 200 children per 1,000 women, or by about one-seventh. We have interpreted this variable as implying that wealthier communities tended to emphasize "quality" rather than quantity. However, there is some question regarding the direction of causation. It may be that wealth was higher in some communities because fertility there had been lower in previous generations.[19]

Among farmers, natives, and all households, the fraction of the population drawn from New England significantly reduced fertility. This is consistent with our hypothesis that people from areas that had already experienced population pressure upon land and had already undergone demographic transition would carry those cultural norms with them wherever they settled. This variable differed substantially from state to state and between regions. There were also tremendous variations between townships within particular states. In the New York townships, for example, the percentage of heads of household from New England ranged from 0.75 percent in Dutchess County to 21.7 percent in Oswego County. As a result, other things equal, the child-woman ratio between these two counties would differ by 100, or by somewhat more than the observed difference between them. Variations were as wide, and in some instances wider, outside of the Northeast.

The percentage of foreign-born other than German or Irish increased fertility among the population as a whole and among the nonfarm households but had little effect upon the farm households. Its role in influencing the fertility of farm families, while positive, was minor. Similarly, while farm ownership tended to raise immigrant fertility, the effect was not significant. This is further emphasized by the lack of significance of the percentage of farmers in explaining fertility among the foreign-born. The proportion of Irish-German peoples had a marginal and ambiguous role in all equations except that for immigrants. In that equation, a high proportion of Irish and Germans was positively associated with higher fertility rates in the township.

The child-woman ratio is only a measure of fertility. It does not explain it. Richard Steckel has developed a measure that is highly correlated with the child-woman ratio that has as its determinants four important vital statistics: the mother's age at last birth, the mother's age at first birth, the average birth interval, and the proportion of women having children. Because none of these variables can be measured accurately from the census data, he calls this a "synthetic total fertility rate."[20] The same forces that determine the child-woman ratio are also explanatory variables for the synthetic total fertility rate. However, it also allows us to decompose changes in fertility into the proportion due to changes in the average age of mothers at their first or last birth, child spacing, or the percentage of women who marry and have children. These represent some of the most important behavioral variables underlying human fertility.

The synthetic total fertility rate, R, is defined by the equation:

$$R = \left(\frac{L - F}{S} + 1\right)\beta$$

where L is the average maternal age at last birth, F is average maternal age at first birth, S is the average interval between children, and β is the proportion of women who eventually have children. These variables represent decision and behavioral variables reflecting family formation and affecting human reproduction. Yet they are subject to contradictory and uncertain measurement errors when estimated from the census data, and the degree of bias varies from component to component. Despite this, Steckel argues that the resulting estimate of total fertility is biased downward relative to the true fertility rate.

The average age at last birth was calculated by subtracting the age of the youngest surviving own child from the age of the mother for the cohort of women aged 45–54 at the time of the census. The forces underlying this are not amenable to quantification with our data. They reflect such factors as contraceptive efforts, nutrition, the regularity of intercourse, and death rates both among infants and children and their mothers. The potential biases are easier to document. If the mother bore her last child while she was in her late twenties or early thirties, then that child would be in his or her late teens or early twenties when the mother was aged 45–54. There is consequently a chance that he or she would no longer be living at home or may have died. A potentially more serious problem is the sharp rise in neonatal and infant mortality among children born to older women. Such events will lead to the misidentification of the last child and the synthetic total fertility rate will be biased downward. Choosing a younger cohort of women would reduce the downward bias, but only by raising the probability that women had not yet had their last birth. Even among the women 45–49 years old, 12 percent had an infant in the family.

The average age of the mother at her first birth is derived by subtracting the age of the oldest surviving own child from hers. In a noncontraceptive society, this is a close approximation to the age of marriage. High rates of infant mortality among children born to teenage women will tend to bias the mother's age upwards as will the out-migration of older children, thus reducing the synthetic total fertility rate. For these reasons, we estimated the average age at first birth among women aged 35–39 on the grounds that few, if any, women were likely to begin their reproductive history later than this. Furthermore, the number of own children is at or close to a maximum for this cohort and so out-migration is likely to have been minimal.[21]

The mean birth interval is affected by a diversity of forces. Contraceptive efforts, poor nutrition, infrequent intercourse, breast-feeding practices and related amenorrhea, and neonatal, infant, and child mortality all serve to lengthen the measured birth interval. We have calculated the birth interval for the cohort of women aged 15–49. By definition, it can only be computed for those women with at least two surviving children. However, almost 40 percent of all married women either had no children or only one child. It is therefore skewed towards those families with higher fertility rates who were more likely to have shorter birth intervals. This may in part be offset because the spacing interval between surviving children is greater than the interval between births by an amount that varies directly with neonatal, infant, and child mortality. From his studies, Steckel suggests that the spacing interval is too high by about 30 percent, biasing the synthetic total fertility rate downward by an equivalent amount.

The proportion of women ever bearing children is estimated by the proportion of women aged 35–39 with children. It is unlikely that many women would begin their reproductive history after 39. At the same time, few women this age would have lost all of their children through death or out-migration since the average number of children is close to a maximum for this cohort. The higher the cutoff age, the lower the probability of a woman subsequently beginning her reproductive history, but the greater the probability that children will have left the household.

The proportion of women who remained childless, other things equal, is an estimate of the proportion of women who did not marry. Fewer women married in the East than the West. This variable is likely to depend upon economic opportunity as well as the size of the potential pool of eligible males. As we have argued, economic opportunity in a predominantly agrarian society was reflected in the relative availability of farmland, which was comparatively scarce in the East. Furthermore, if males in their twenties were the most likely migratory group, then western migration would adversely affect the marriage prospects for eastern women. However, to the extent that this effect existed, it exerted minimal effect upon the age-sex structure of the northeastern population.[22]

Values of the various components of the synthetic total fertility rate for northeastern and midwestern farm and nonfarm populations are shown in Table 4.3. Among farm families, the synthetic total fertility rate in the Midwest was almost 50 percent greater than in the Northeast, while among nonfarm families it was almost 25 percent higher. The former understates the relative difference shown by the child-woman ratio; the latter overstates it.

Midwestern farm wives were almost eleven months older, on average, than their northeastern counterparts when they had their last live birth. There are three likely explanations for this difference. First, northeasterners may have practiced more effective birth control. Second, higher nutritional levels for midwestern women may have delayed the

TABLE 4.3. Determinants of Synthetic Total Fertility Rate among Farm and Nonfarm Households by Region, 1860

	Determinant				Synthetic Total Fertility Rate
Group	*F*	*L*	*S*	β	
Northeast					
Farm	26.90	39.42	3.08	0.69	3.49
Nonfarm	25.01	40.36	2.90	0.71	4.45
Midwest					
Farm	25.31	40.32	2.83	0.81	5.12
Nonfarm	23.47	41.34	2.76	0.74	5.53

F = Average age of woman at birth of first surviving child.
L = Average age of woman at birth of last surviving child.
S = Average interval between children.
β = Proportion of women who marry.

onset of menopause. Evidence for either of these explanations is sketchy. Third, recent medical research has shown a link between an early age of first birth and fecundity in later years and midwestern farm women were typically nineteen months younger than farmers' wives in the Northeast when they had their first child. As a consequence, midwestern women were at risk some thirty months longer than the typical northeastern farm wife. Nonfarm midwestern wives, however, married even earlier. They averaged almost eighteen years at risk of pregnancy, or about five and a half years longer than northeastern farm wives.

More women in the Midwest got married. Among the midwestern farm population 81 percent of the women married and all but about 4 percent of those had children. In the Northeast, the comparable percentages were 69 and 8. Among the nonfarm populations, the proportions marrying were similar but again the proportion of childless northeastern women was much higher. The percentages of childless married women were uniformly higher among the nonfarm than among the farm populations. This is consistent with the relative demands for child labor and the relative opportunity costs of having children between the two populations.

Lastly, the child spacing among midwesterners was considerably shorter than among northeastern families. It seems unlikely that the wider birth interval in the East could be attributed to more prolonged breast-feeding since the value of women's labor was greater in the East than the West. Although Wrigley argues that there are many populations that practice neither abortion nor contraception yet have comparable birth intervals of thirty-five to fifty months, we think it likely that northeasterners postponed children by some form of birth control since differences in the genetic traits of the populations, Northeast and Midwest, whether farm or nonfarm, are unlikely to explain these differences.[23]

The components of the synthetic total fertility rate can be used to decompose the differences between rates into the fractions attributable to each component.[24] The average difference in synthetic fertility rates between farm households in the Northeast and Midwest was 37.9 percent (Table 4.4). Almost half of this is explained by the smaller fraction of northeastern farm women who married. Not being at risk was one of the best methods of avoiding the consequences. A quarter of the difference is explained by the earlier age of marriage of midwestern women, 18 percent by the closer child spacing, and the remaining 14 percent by the prolonged fertility of midwestern farm wives.

Among nonfarm families the most important influence, one explaining 37 percent of the fertility differential in favor of midwesterners, was the earlier age of marriage of women in that region. The extended period

TABLE 4.4. Explaining Fertility Differences between Different Groups

Group	Percentage Difference in Synthetic Total Fertility Rate Attributable to[a]				Percentage Difference in Synthetic Total Fertility Rate
	F	L	S	β	
Farm:					
East v. West	25	14	18	42	37.9
Nonfarm:					
East v. West	37	24	20	19	21.1
East:					
Farm v. Nonfarm	46	23	20	12	24.2
West:					
Farm v. Nonfarm	123	67	26	–115	7.9

Source: Computed from Table 4.3.
[a]See Table 4.3 for key to symbols.

of fertility that midwestern women experienced accounted for another 24 percent. Thus, more than half of the differential between the two groups was accounted for by the period of time for which women were at risk. The shorter birth interval and the higher fraction of midwestern women who married accounted for only 20 and 19 percent respectively of the fertility differential.

Northeastern farm fertility was considerably lower than nonfarm fertility within that region. Almost half of the difference resulted from the earlier age of marriage among the nonfarm population. They married, on average, almost twenty-three months earlier than their farm compatriots and, if economic opportunity were a sine qua non for marriage, then this is a measure of the greater relative opportunities in the nonfarm sector of the Northeast. Farmers' sons may have been reluctant to marry without an independent source of income. In addition nonfarm women continued to bear children almost a year longer than farmers' wives, but the effects of this and the other two determinants (child spacing and the fraction of women who married) were relatively minor compared with the role played by their earlier marriage.

The differential between farm and nonfarm synthetic total fertility rates in the Midwest was not only small, but the factors that determined it were contradictory. The earlier marriage, longer lasting fertility, and closer child spacing favored the fertility of the nonfarm group, but the higher proportion of farm women marrying tended to offset some of these influences. Earlier age of marriage, by itself, is capable of explaining the entire fertility differential between the two midwestern groups but its effect is almost totally negated by the smaller fraction of nonfarm midwestern women who married. As a consequence one could argue that the tendency for nonfarm women to bear children later plus the marginally closer spacing of their children can account for the small fertility difference between the farm and nonfarm groups in the Midwest.

So far we have not distinguished between the fertility rates of two other important population subgroups: immigrants and the native-born. In 1860, except in Ohio, child-woman ratios were substantially higher among immigrants than among natives in each of the sample states.[25] In Connecticut, the differential approached 3 to 1; elsewhere it was typically 20 percent or more. The margin of immigrant fertility over native was generally greater in the Northeast than in the Midwest, but the general pattern mirrored that for the nation as a whole with fertility rising from East to West. Although we will argue in Chapter 5 that immigrant and migrant groups from similar backgrounds tended to cluster together, the fertility pattern is independent of this. Within the same communities, immigrants still had more children per 1,000 women of childbearing age than natives (Figs. 4.5 and 4.6). In general, the difference was at least 250. It was rarely lower.

Why was immigrant fertility so high relative to that of the native population? The regressions reported in Table 4.2 indicate that the forces explaining so much of native fertility rates and those of groups such as farmers do a poor job of explaining them for immigrants. The synthetic total fertility rate helps cast some light on the sources of the fertility differential between immigrants and natives and between the two regions (Table 4.5). Some sharp differences are apparent. Children were spaced much more closely together by immigrants than any other group, which suggests that they were less interested in checking their fertility. It also implies that extended breast-feeding, which has a prophylactic effect on pregnancy, was probably not the only means of birth control being practiced. Had this been the principal means of birth control, then we would have expected closer child spacing among natives because their opportunity cost of extended breast-feeding was greater. In each region, more immigrants than natives married, but the difference was slight in the East and large between East and West. We have argued that it and the age of marriage are heavily influenced by economic opportunity. If so, then natives in the West may have found it easier than immigrants to accumulate a nest egg since they married on average almost two and a half years earlier; immigrants may have viewed the long-term opportunities more optimistically since 90 percent eventually married. For the immigrant, these opportunities were not in farming or related to plentiful available land. In the East, immigrants married younger than any other group. Their childbearing also ceased sooner. This contradicts medical wisdom of unchecked human fertility and suggests either very high infant mortality among this group, which we view as unlikely, or the use of very effective contraceptive methods.

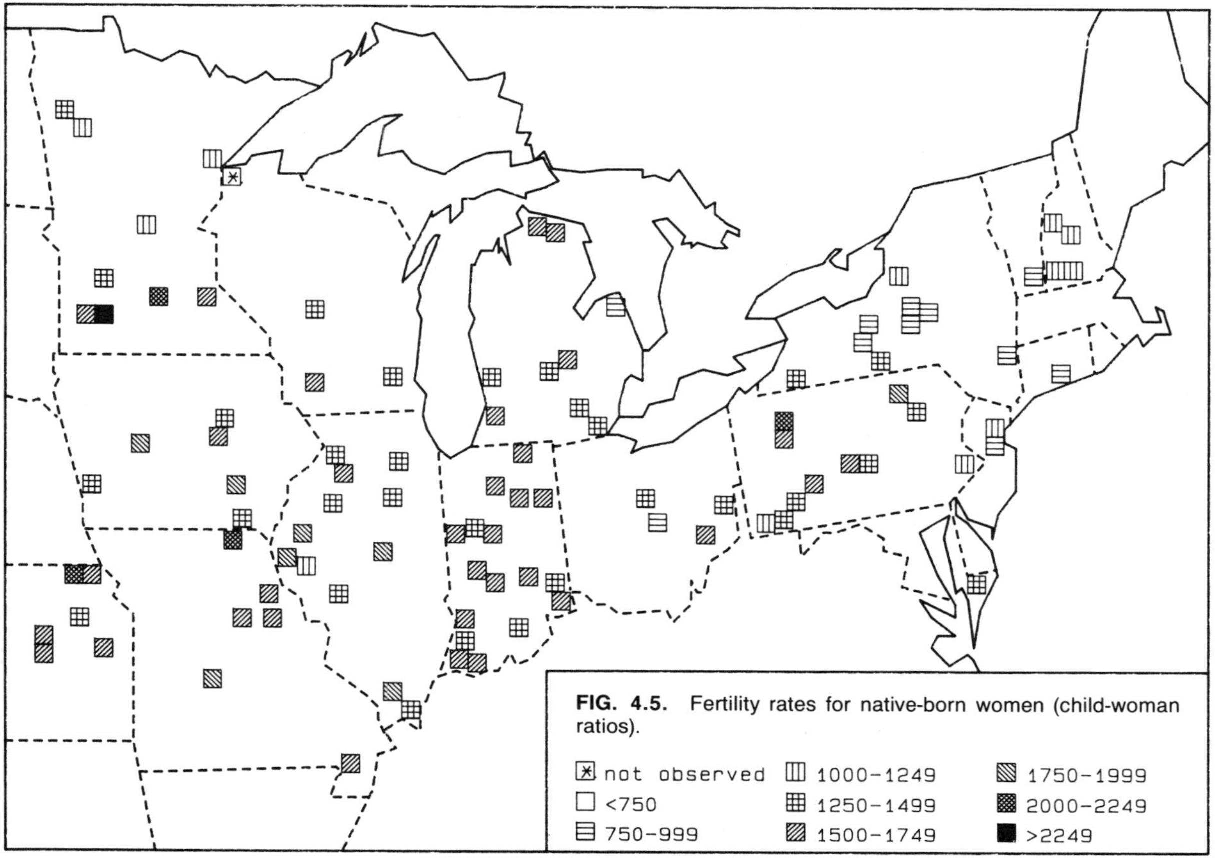

FIG. 4.5. Fertility rates for native-born women (child-woman ratios).

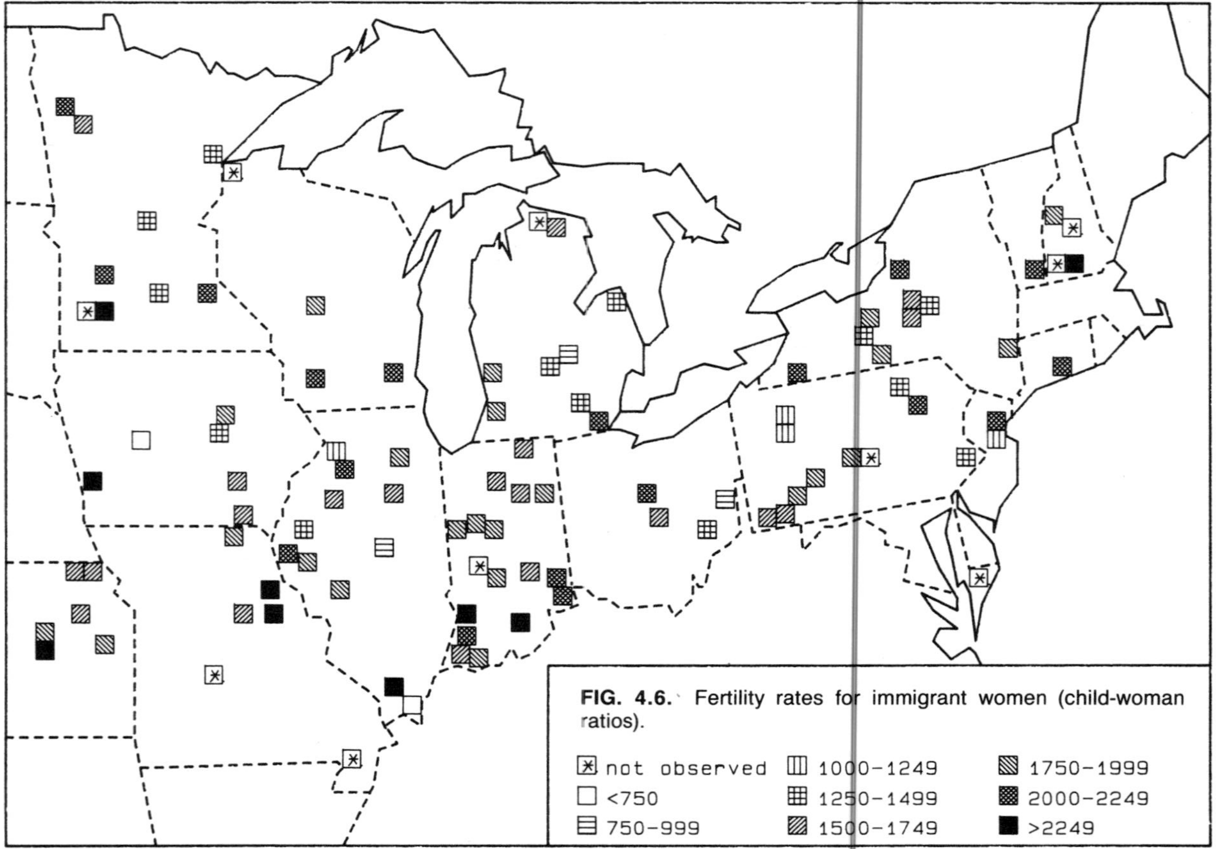

FIG. 4.6. Fertility rates for immigrant women (child-woman ratios).

TABLE 4.5. Determinants of Synthetic Total Fertility Rate of Natives and Immigrants in the East and West

Group	Determinant of Synthetic Total Fertility Rate[a]				Synthetic Total Fertility Rate
	F	*L*	*S*	β	
Native					
East	25.95	39.60	3.06	0.69	3.77
West	24.29	40.21	2.84	0.78	5.18
Immigrant					
East	24.02	37.59	2.55	0.70	4.41
West	26.71	41.94	2.51	0.90	6.33

[a]See Table 4.3 for key to symbols.

Some of the determinants of the total synthetic fertility rate are therefore contradictory between the various groups. For example, while the greater proportion of women having children, closer child spacing, and later last births should boost immigrant fertility above that of natives in the West, this was partly offset by the older age at first birth among immigrants. Indeed, this almost balanced the effect of the higher nuptiality rate (Table 4.6). Similarly in the East, the fertility effect of the younger age of immigrant brides was completely offset by their early cessation of childbearing vis-à-vis natives. As a result almost the entire 15.6 percent fertility differential is attributable to closer child spacing by immigrants. Among natives, higher midwestern fertility was promoted by each of the determinants. No single factor dominates. These people, principally migrants from the East, must have found accumulation easier, economic opportunity better, nutrition superior, and demand for child labor higher

TABLE 4.6. Explaining the Fertility Difference between Natives and Immigrants and between East and West

Group	Percentage Difference in Synthetic Total Fertility Rate Attributable to[a]				Percentage Difference in Synthetic Total Fertility Rate
	F	*L*	*S*	β	
East:					
Native v. Immigrant	73	–76	94	9	15.6
West:					
Native v. Immigrant	–63	45	50	68	20.0
Native:					
East v. West	30	11	20	39	31.5
Immigrant:					
East v. West	–44	71	4	69	35.8

Source: Computed from Table 4.5.
[a]See Table 4.3 for key to symbols.

than their contemporaries who stayed in the East. Midwestern immigrants, however, married later but in greater numbers than those who remained on the East Coast and maintained their fertility later.

Fertility differences between natives and immigrants were to become an issue of national policy after 1880 when Francis A. Walker in his official position as superintendent of the 1880 Census suggested that the children of the foreign-born were substitutes for those of the native-born, leading to a "dilution" of the native stock.[26] This fertility pattern was apparent before 1880. The child-woman ratios for immigrants were negatively correlated ($R = -0.21$) with the child-woman ratio among native-born at the township level and this relationship is statistically significant. It is also consistent with the "Walker thesis."

Despite the negative correlation between immigrant and native fertility, the pattern of fertility for the foreign-born mirrored that of the population as a whole. Fertility rates were higher in the West than the East and highest of all among midwestern farmers. The population in that region was growing rapidly through natural increase which, for all groups except immigrants, was strongly influenced by the economic opportunities presented by available land for farm creation. The midwestern population was also growing rapidly because of migration, both foreign and native, as we discuss next.

CHAPTER FIVE

Migration and Immigration in the Rural North

REALIZATION OF THE AGRARIAN DREAM often demanded geographic mobility. The reward for those who took the risk was a chance for improved economic and social mobility gained from the acquisition of physical capital rather than through family lineage. Land in nineteenth-century America promised an opportunity for wealth accumulation necessary for upward mobility, but since land grew relatively more abundant westward, movement through the economic classes was often inseparable from physical relocation. Adjustment towards equilibrium required mobility of resources, both human and financial. As a result, people were on the move during the nineteenth century as rarely, if ever, before. It was this capacity and propensity of Americans to migrate in response to opportunity that became the dominant theme in Frederick Jackson Turner's "Safety Valve" thesis of the American frontier.[1]

In 1860 almost a quarter of all native-born Americans were living in a state or territory other than that of their birth. In addition, the country had more than four million foreign-born.[2] Comparatively little is known about migration until the Census began to collect information on place of birth in 1850.[3] Prior to that, information is incomplete and indirect. The best data are for immigrants and provide information on age, sex, occupation, and country of origin. Coverage, however, was limited to seaborne passengers delivered to Atlantic and Gulf ports until 1850 when Pacific ports were added. No records of overland migration, especially that through Canada, were kept until the twentieth century.[4] Evidence on internal migration before 1850 is much more sketchy; however, despite the lack of hard evidence, the westward press of the population is indisputable. In 1790 the population center was 23 miles east of Baltimore. By 1820 it had moved to 16 miles north of Woodstock, Virginia, a westward movement of 127 miles in thirty years. After 1820, rising rates of immigration and liberalized public land sales in the West caused an even more rapid recession of the frontier and westward shift of the center of population so that by 1860 it was located 20 miles south of Chillicothe, Ohio, approximately 275 miles further west.[5]

Beginning in 1850, the Census classified population by state of birth and state of residence. These data have formed the core of most studies of migration in America.[6] In 1860 the Census showed that more than two-thirds of the population on the Eastern Seaboard had been born in their current state of residence, whereas in the Midwest slightly less than half the population had been born in the state where they lived. Not surprisingly, the fractions of persons then living in the state of their birth were lowest among the newest states and territories, where the only people born there were the children of very recent settlers.

Despite the relative homogeneity of the native East Coast populations, immigrants formed a larger fraction of the population there than in the West. New York City, for example, had over 380,000 foreign-born in 1860 and about a million immigrants lived in the state.[7] These immigrants, mostly Irish, stayed where they had landed.[8] The balance of the East Coast population was generally drawn from the contiguous states. Migrants in the West, on the other hand, came from more distant states rather than from more easterly contiguous ones. One-half of Iowa's population, for example, had been born in states east of Illinois or south of Missouri, while two-thirds of Kansas's population was from east and south of Missouri. Immigrants aside, midwestern migrants completed longer distance moves than did northeasterners.

All northeastern and midwestern cities had large immigrant populations.[9] A majority of the residents of St. Louis and Milwaukee were foreign-born in 1860, and almost half of the population of New York City and Chicago had been born overseas.[10] As a result, the rural bias of our sample may lead us to misrepresent some of the migratory flows. However, most of the 4.1 million foreign-born enumerated at the Eighth Census lived in small towns or rural areas where they could aspire to be a part of the agrarian Jeffersonian America. In much of the analysis that follows, immigrants are simply treated as a special group of migrants who traveled further and brought less human capital with them than did natives.

Studies of migration that have focused upon the Census place-of-residence by place-of-birth matrices are fundamentally flawed by the implicit assumption that the current place of residence is a discretionary variable for each individual.[11] Such an analysis treats everybody residing in a place other than that of their birth as migrants and all living in the state of their birth as "stayers." However, place of birth is an historic accident determined by one's mother. Current place of residence is a family, or more likely head-of-family, decision.[12] Consequently the macro-view of migration patterns is provided by a comparison between place of birth and current place of residence for heads of family.

Consider, for example, the Bowman family from Persifer township in Knox County, Illinois. In 1860 this nuclear family consisted of George Bowman (age 38, born in Pennsylvania), his 37-year-old wife (also native to Pennsylvania), three children (two daughters, age 14 and 13; one son, 8) who were born in New York, and two children (a son, 6, and a daughter, 4) who were born in Illinois. The usual place-of-birth by place-of-residence matrix would show five migrants to Illinois (two from Pennsylvania and three from New York) and two stayers. In reality, this was one family that migrated to Illinois from Pennsylvania by way of New York. The two stayers simply had no say in the choice of their current state of residence, nor for that matter did the three children who were born in New York. Moreover, by preserving the data as a family unit we gain some additional implicit information. The Bowman family must have migrated from Pennsylvania to New York sometime between 1822 and 1846, moving from New York to Illinois between 1842 and 1844. Whether or not they stayed in one place during their time in New York and in Illinois is unknown.[13]

The differences between a place-of-birth-by-residence matrix for heads of household in the East and for everybody in the region are minor. Furthermore, except for a lower percentage of immigrants, presumably because farm entry costs in the region were high (Chap. 8) while cities offered superior nonfarm employment opportunities for people with their skills, such a matrix from the sample data mirrors what can be produced from the published census. In the western states, particularly the newer ones, our matrix of place of birth by residence for heads of household is substantially different from the census one because of our exclusion of children born during and after the migration. As a result, in 1860 at least one-third of the inhabitants of rural townships in the northern United States were living in a state other than that of their birth (Table 5.1).

The arrangement of Table 5.1 is such that in reading down or across one moves from East to West via contiguous sample states. Read in this manner, not only do the data show the geographic heritage of the population in each sample state but also an immediate visual impression of the direction of migration and the distance traveled. The upper diagonal represents a movement to the West; the lower, to the East. Along the diagonal, people are still in the states of their birth. These are the stayers. The

TABLE 5.1. Nativity and State of Residence of Heads of Family, 1860[a] (percent of all families, reading down)

State/Country of Birth of Heads of Family	Current State of Residence (percent of heads of family)															
	N.H.	Vt.	Conn.	N.Y.	N.J.	Md.	Pa.	Ohio	Ind.	Mich.	Ill.	Mo.	Iowa	Wis.	Kans.	Minn.
New Hampshire	90	2	–	1	–	–	0	0	0	1	1	–	1	1	2	2
Vermont	3	66	1	4	0	–	0	5	1	3	4	0	2	3	3	4
Connecticut	0	2	85	4	2	–	1	1	0	2	2	0	2	1	2	1
New York	0	3	2	75	8	–	5	4	3	36	11	1	16	21	11	13
New Jersey	0	–	–	1	66	–	2	2	1	1	1	0	1	0	1	1
Maryland	–	1	–	0	0	97	1	9	2	0	1	2	2	0	1	–
Pennsylvania	0	–	0	1	1	–	76	25	8	2	8	2	16	3	10	4
Ohio	–	–	–	0	0	–	0	39	13	3	15	4	23	2	17	5
Indiana	–	–	–	0	–	–	–	0	26	0	4	1	6	1	7	1
Michigan	–	–	–	0	–	–	0	–	0	11	0	–	0	–	1	3
Illinois	–	–	–	–	–	–	–	–	1	–	7	2	1	0	5	1
Missouri	–	–	–	–	–	–	–	–	0	–	0	16	1	0	4	0
Iowa	–	–	–	–	–	–	–	–	0	–	–	–	1	–	0	–
Wisconsin	–	–	–	–	–	–	–	–	–	0	0	–	–	1	–	4
Kansas	–	–	–	–	–	–	–	–	–	–	–	–	–	–	1	0
Minnesota	–	–	–	–	–	–	–	–	–	0	–	–	–	–	–	6
Other Northern States	4	16	1	5	1	–	3	2	1	3	2	0	4	5	4	7
Southern States	0	0	0	0	0	3	1	7	25	1	30	69	12	2	19	3
Total U.S.	98	91	90	91	79	100	89	94	81	63	84	98	85	41	89	55
English-speaking Foreign	2	8	6	7	14	–	6	5	5	8	11	1	11	36	5	15
Non-English-speaking Foreign	0	1	4	2	7	–	5	1	14	29	5	1	4	23	6	30
All Foreign	2	9	10	9	21	–	11	6	19	37	16	2	15	59	11	45

Totals (downward) may not equal 100 due to rounding error.
Zero indicates a move involving less than 0.5 percent of the families.
– indicates no observation of such a move for sample family heads.
[a]Includes female- and other-male-headed households as well as husband-wife families.

farther one moves above or below the diagonal, the greater the distance a family has migrated from the place of birth of the head. Below the table is a reconciliation for the remaining heads of family from other northern states (primarily Massachusetts, though some were from Delaware, Maine, or Rhode Island), southern states (Kentucky, Tennessee, and Virginia by far the most important sources), or overseas.

The most obvious implication from the pattern in these data, of course, is that people moved from East to West. The lower diagonal is nearly devoid of entries. Virtually all of these "reverse" migrations took place within New England or the Middle Atlantic states. Thus 22 of the 791 New Hampshire families in the sample had moved there from Vermont and 26 had migrated northward from Massachusetts. A few families had moved back from the Old Northwest to the Middle Atlantic area, but the numbers were small—4 from Ohio, 1 from Michigan, and 1 from Indiana went east to New York State, while 26 families had moved there from Pennsylvania. One family also migrated to New York from Maryland. Perhaps more significantly, no families in the sample made a long-distance move from a state west of Indiana to one east of that state. People who migrated to the frontier stayed in the West, although in a few cases they seemingly decided that they had located too far westward originally. For example, 2 Wisconsin families moved to Michigan, as did 2 from Minnesota. They, however, were exceptions.

On the Eastern Seaboard, at least two-thirds of heads of family were classified as stayers and, except for a very small foreign-born but predominantly English-speaking population, the rest of the families were headed by people from neighboring states. Eighty-eight percent of Vermont households, for example, were headed by persons from that or the adjacent state (New Hampshire, New York, and Massachusetts). In the West, population tended to be more culturally heterogeneous. There, not only did the proportion of stayers fall drastically, but the bulk of the population was drawn from nonadjacent eastern states or from overseas. The decline in the proportion of stayers was to be expected in frontier locations, but it is surprising to discover that in Illinois, which had achieved statehood in 1818, more heads of families came from Kentucky, New York, Ohio, Pennsylvania, or Tennessee than had been born in the state. If a crude measure is made of cultural heterogeneity by the minimum number of states and countries of birth necessary to account for a majority of the heads of family in each state, then the Eastern Seaboard states were clearly the most homogeneous, while Illinois, Kansas, and Minnesota were the most heterogeneous.[14]

The two border slave states, Maryland and Missouri, differ substantially from other sample states nearby. All heads of family in Maryland were born either there or in Virginia. There were also no foreign-born in the Maryland sample, although the 1860 Census shows about 13 percent to have been so in the state. Two-thirds of Maryland's immigrant population lived in Baltimore and over 80 percent lived within Baltimore County.[15] Opportunities for yeoman farming may have been few, and most European immigrants seem to have had a strong aversion to slavery. Further, the cultural homogeneity of rural Maryland probably closed this society to them. Similarly, few immigrants found their way to rural Missouri, although in the towns and cities along the Mississippi River there were substantial immigrant populations.[16] Like Maryland, very few northern families chose to settle in rural Missouri, whereas almost 40 percent of the sample families were headed by Kentuckians and 14 percent by Virginians.

Scholars have long speculated on the motivations for the internal and international migrations.[17] Explanations may be broadly classified into two groups. One emphasizes factors in the migrants' homeland that drove them to leave, such as unemployment, starvation, and political or religious repression; the other stresses the attractions of the migrants' new home. These are termed "Push" and "Pull" theories respectively. Thus, for example, analyses of the massive Irish emigration that occurred in the wake of the Potato Famine of the early 1840s or the German migration that followed suppression of the 1848 revolutions tend to emphasize those forces pushing people from their homelands. On the other hand, higher wages, cheap land, greater social and economic mobility, and the favorable home reports of earlier waves of migrants were often powerful lures to migrants. The role of such pull factors may be seen, for example, in the decline in immigration that transpired during American domestic recessions. Migration also responded to the domestic economic situation in America and the longer lines of communication. Which force dominated in any particular case is disputed in the literature and seems to reflect the techniques of analysis as much as anything else.[18] Turner's thesis, however, incorporates both forces. The push was provided by discontent with social and economic conditions in the East.[19] The pull came from the availability of "free," or at least cheap, land on the frontier that proved an almost irresistible attraction to many.[20] Our data bear only on the latter hypothesis but the causality is clear. Because of the high proportions of migrant midwestern household heads, we expected and found a high correlation between that proportion and our measure of land availability, discussed in Chapter 4. We also found a strong positive correlation of 0.31 between the proportion of immigrants and land availability.[21] We regard this as evidence that immigrants responded to the economic opportunities that abundant land provided, regardless of whether they became farmers.

The availability of land does not explain migration directly unless one believes that people migrated for the simple pleasure of owning land. Rather, the demand for land is derived from the desire to become a farmer. This, in turn, depended in part upon the profits to be made. If we crudely approximate the returns to farming by the price of the principal northern farm cash crop, wheat, then, between 1834 and 1860, a rise in the price of wheat was followed by an increase in land sales two to three years later and the evidence suggests that many of the purchasers were migrants and immigrants.[22]

Not only did people move from East to West, but they also migrated within narrow bands of latitude. This may be explained by the desire of farmers to maximize the return on human and physical capital investments. Western lands, at least initially, were generally more productive than the heavily utilized, often abused lands of the East. Frequently, this alone was enough to encourage westward migration.[23] Returns, however, could be further increased by farming lands with soil and terrain that approximated those with which the migrant was already familiar and where the amount of daylight was the same as that to which seeds and livestock were already adapted.[24] Terrain and soils, for example, owe much to the effects of glaciation, while crops are photoperiodic and affected more by north-south movements than by east-west. Based on agricultural experiment results from Champaign, Illinois, where corn seeds from around the country were grown side-by-side, Steckel found that corn yields from seeds adapted 250 miles east of Champaign were slightly higher than those adapted to Champaign, while yields from seeds adapted 250 miles west were 93 percent of those from Champaign.[25] On the other hand, seeds from 250 miles north had yields only 72 percent of those from Champaign and seeds from 250 miles south produced only 62 percent as much as the Champaign seeds. Within 100 miles north or south, yields changed relatively little, but declined at an increasing pace beyond these tolerance limits. Consequently, "[F]armers who went too far north or south had poor yields, and sent relatively unfavorable reports back to the community from which they left. Thus the reputations of agricultural areas became established and influenced the migration patterns of subsequent settlers."[26]

The incentives to maximize the economic return from migration were further reinforced by ties of kinship, friendship, or common cultural heritage. Families gravitated towards those areas about which they had some information. This often came through personal, albeit sometimes remote, relationships. Letters sent home from migrants and immigrants were generally upbeat and optimistic. People clustered around others with similar cultural or ethnic backgrounds on the frontier. David Davenport, in his tracing of out-migrants from Schoharie County in upstate New York, found them clustered in individual communities that he located by searching Schoharie newspapers for letters sent home. Seven families, for example, had migrated to Logan County, Illinois; five had moved to the town of Milford in Otsego County, New York; and other groups had similarly clustered in other communities.[27] Immigrants similarly clustered together. Thus, for example, almost half of the Norwegians who were recorded at the Eighth Census were living in Wisconsin and a third of the Swedes had settled in Illinois.[28] Virtually all of the Dutch immigrants in our sample were located in one Michigan township.[29]

The ages of children in combination with information about their birthplace enables us to date the migration or immigration, within birth-interval limits. The average error is thus equal to half the mean birth interval, which was under three years. Various groups settled areas at different times. The age of the youngest child born overseas provides an estimate of the earliest date at which the immigration could have occurred. The age of the oldest child born in the United States of a foreign-born father gives an approximation of the latest date at which the immigration could have taken place. Similarly, the age of the youngest child born somewhere other than the current state of residence provides an estimate of the earliest date at which a family could have moved to its current state of residence. The age of the oldest child born in the current state of residence is a measure of the latest date at which the family could have moved.

Although 61 percent of the husband-wife families had two or more surviving children, there were relatively few families, particularly among immigrants, for which we have both the age of the youngest born out of state or overseas and the oldest born in-state or in the United States. Our estimates of the range of dates for various groups are therefore based on observations from different families. Most immigrants in the sample probably arrived during the early and middle 1850s, although the largest numbers of Bavarians, Dutch, Scots, and Swiss arrived in the late 1840s. The Swedes were the most recent immigrant group. Native-born migrants, on the other hand, had pushed westwards earlier, and they were already established when the immigrants started to arrive.

Although migrants or immigrants with similar ethnic or cultural backgrounds tended to settle in close proximity to one another, not all locations were equally attractive throughout the 1840s and 1850s. In part, this reflects the wider range of choices facing later migrants. New Yorkers migrating in the 1830s and 1840s, for example, probably did not regard Minnesota or Kansas as suitable places for settlement while those who delayed migration until the 1850s did. Consequently, patterns tended to change. Similiarly, whereas migrants from Connecticut who moved westward in the early 1840s typically chose to settle in Indiana (Table 5.2), somewhat later they preferred Pennsylvania and some never went beyond New York state. By 1852, however, Michigan was favored by Connecticut migrants, and subsequently Iowa attracted them. This pattern is consistent with the hypothesis that they sought to maximize agricultural returns by minimizing north-south movement. Similarly, migrant Tennesseans moved to southern Indiana during the late 1840s, then moved further west to southern Illinois by the early 1850s. Tennesseans later pushed even further westward into Missouri and Kansas.

The older midwestern states, Ohio and Indiana, were the preferred destinations for migrants in the 1840s. However, Illinois and Wisconsin were major recipients in the early 1850s, Iowa and Michigan before mid-decade, and Kansas and Minnesota in the latter part of the decade. Immigrants seem to have been less decisive in their push westward. During the mid- to late 1840s, the new English immigrants tended to settle in Indiana, Ohio, and Wisconsin, but in the next decade they seem to have preferred the Middle Atlantic and New England states at the same time that some of their compatriots were settling in Iowa and Michigan. The earliest German immigrants established themselves in Indiana and Pennsylvania; the next wave seemed to favor New Jersey and New York, and the last, Illinois and Michigan.[30] Immigrants were thus divided in their preference for the newer areas of settlement over the old.

At the same time that we located the oldest child born in the United States of an immigrant father, we also noted the state of birth (Table 5.3). Except for those who were settled in Iowa and Kansas in 1860, the majority managed to delay fertility until they reached their destinations. Thus, 76 percent of the 151 immigrants in the sample who settled in Illinois and had American-born children produced their first-born American child in Illinois, whereas only 34 percent of the immigrants in Kansas had theirs in that state. When children were born to immigrants in states other than their state of residence in 1860, it tended to occur in states that were directly on migration routes from major ports of entry: New York, Massachusetts, Pennsylvania, and Ohio. The generally low incidence of births to immigrants en route may be interpreted in two quite different ways. On the positive side, it could be argued that they must have reached their destinations quite speedily, particularly given the mean birth intervals discussed above. However, it is likely that ocean passage and the rigors of overland transport, particularly beyond the limits of the rail network, must have been especially arduous for pregnant women and newborn infants, making miscarriages and infant death common.

The figures in Table 5.3 also reveal some noteworthy migration patterns. These are marked by superscript [a]. Some represent back-migrations by immigrants, who for whatever reason, relocated eastward away

TABLE 5.2. Mean Period of Residence by Migrant and Immigrant Groups

	Average Number of Years since Migration to[a]															
Place of Birth	Conn.	Md.	N.H.	N.J.	N.Y.	Pa.	Vt.	Ill.	Ind.	Iowa	Kans.	Mich.	Minn.	Mo.	Ohio	Wis.
Migrants																
Connecticut	–	–	–	–	13	15	–	12	16	7	–	8	–	–	–	–
Kentucky	–	–	–	–	–	–	–	10	12	10	5	–	–	9	–	–
Massachusetts	–	–	–	–	16	–	9	9	–	8	9	11	–	–	–	14
New York	–	–	–	11	–	10	–	9	12	6	4	8	4	–	16	9
Pennyslvania	–	–	–	–	10	–	–	8	11	7	5	6	4	6	12	9
Tennessee	–	–	–	–	–	–	–	9	13	–	–	7	–	6	–	–
Vermont	–	–	6	–	13	–	–	10	15	9	8	10	–	–	17	12
Virginia	–	7	–	–	–	–	–	12	13	7	5	–	–	9	13	–
Immigrants																
Bavaria	–	–	–	–	–	–	–	–	10	–	–	–	–	–	–	–
England	–	–	–	–	8	8	–	8	13	8	–	8	–	–	14	10
France	–	–	–	–	–	–	–	–	11	–	–	–	–	–	–	–
Germany	–	–	–	7	7	9	–	4	9	–	–	4	–	–	–	–
Holland	–	–	–	–	–	–	–	–	–	–	–	6	–	–	–	–
Ireland	–	–	–	9	7	8	–	10	12	7	–	6	6	–	–	10
Norway	–	–	–	–	–	–	–	–	–	–	–	–	–	–	–	6
Scotland	–	–	–	–	–	–	–	–	11	–	–	–	–	–	–	–
Sweden	–	–	–	–	–	–	–	–	–	–	–	–	3	–	–	–
Switzerland	–	–	–	–	–	12	–	–	9	–	–	–	–	–	–	–
All Migrants and Immigrants	8	7	9	9	11	10	10	9	11	7	5	7	5	8	13	9

A minimum of 10 families was selected on which to base averages.
[a]Date = 1860 – average number of years.

TABLE 5.3. State of Residence and Place of Birth of First Surviving American-born Child of an Immigrant Father (percentages, reading down)

	State of Residence in 1860								
State of Birth	Ill.	Ind.	Iowa	Kans.	Mich.	Minn.	Mo.	Ohio	Wis.
Arkansas	–	0.2[a]	–	–	–	–	–	–	–
Connecticut	–	–	1.2	–	–	–	–	–	–
Illinois	76.2	0.3[a]	18.3	13.2	0.9[a]	5.3	10.0	–	1.5
Indiana	1.3	79.1	2.4	2.6	–	4.2	5.0	–	–
Iowa	2.0[a]	–	35.4	5.3	–	2.1	–	–	–
Kansas	–	–	–	34.2	–	–	–	–	–
Kentucky	0.7	1.3	–	5.3	–	–	5.0	–	–
Louisiana	–	0.3[a]	–	–	–	–	–	–	–
Maine	–	0.2[a]	–	–	–	1.1[a]	–	–	–
Maryland	–	0.3	3.7	–	0.3	–	–	–	–
Massachusetts	–	–	3.7	–	0.3	3.2	–	–	1.5
Michigan	–	0.2[a]	2.4[a]	5.3	86.7	1.1[a]	–	–	0.5
Minnesota	–	–	–	–	–	56.8	–	–	–
Missouri	–	0.2[a]	1.2[a]	21.1	–	–	60.0	–	–
New Hampshire	–	–	–	–	0.3[a]	–	–	–	–
New Jersey	0.7	–	–	–	–	–	–	2.6	1.5
New York	8.6	3.1	13.4	2.6	6.9	7.4	5.0	5.1	10.8
North Carolina	–	–	–	–	–	–	–	–	0.5
Ohio	2.6	12.4	8.5	5.3	2.0	2.1	–	89.7	0.5
Pennsylvania	6.0	2.1	8.5	5.3	0.3	5.3	10.0	–	2.5
Tennessee	–	–	–	–	–	–	5.0	–	–
Texas	–	–	–	–	–	–	–	–	0.5[a]
Vermont	–	–	1.2[a]	–	0.9[a]	2.1[a]	–	–	1.0[a]
Virginia	0.7	0.2	–	–	0.3	–	–	2.6	0.5
Wisconsin	0.7[a]	–	–	–	1.2[a]	9.5	–	–	77.9
Nebraska Territory	–	–	–	–	–	–	–	–	0.5[a]
Utah Territory	–	–	–	–	–	–	–	–	0.5[a]
Washington Territory	–	–	–	–	–	–	–	–	0.5[a]
Number of Cases	151	607	82	38	347	95	20	39	204

[a]Unusual migration path.

from the frontier.[31] Three immigrant families, for example, that eventually made Illinois their home had moved at first to Iowa. In other cases, there were families who moved initially to other states of recent settlement (Wisconsin or Michigan) that would not be on a direct migratory path but whose subsequent moves did not involve backtracking to reach their final destinations.

There were also a number of atypical intermediate destinations. Some immigrant families apparently at least passed through Vermont, New Hampshire, or Maine and were there long enough to deliver a surviving child before moving on to settle further west. A few immigrant families who settled in Indiana and Wisconsin had particularly unusual migratory patterns compared with those of their contemporaries. At least two entered the country via New Orleans, one came through Arkansas, another via Texas, and three came from western territories. One even came from the West Coast.

Migrants and immigrants did not always move speedily and directly to the states in which they resided in 1860. Although most only made one move that we can document through the census data, a few did so at least six times before settling where the census located them. One well-known multiple migrant was Thomas Lincoln, father of Abraham. He was born in Virginia in 1778, moved to Kentucky in 1782, on to Indiana in 1816, before making his final move to Illinois in 1830. Our indicator of the frequency of family moves is the number of own children with birthplaces different from one another, from the head of the family, and from the current state of residence. By this criteria, Thomas Lincoln would be counted as a two-time mover. Our measure therefore understates the frequency of moves. There are three sources of downward bias. First, we can only identify interstate and international moves. Second, our tracing of the migratory pattern depends upon a surviving child being born at each intermediate destination.[32] Third, the birth of a child was a relatively infrequent, albeit significant, event in the history of a family. At the same time, our assumption that a birth was indicative of something more than a fleeting, temporary residence somewhere may impart a small upward bias in the fraction of families making two or more moves.[33] It is almost certainly dominated by the downward biases of sample truncation and our inability to identify intrastate moves.

The percentage of families making at least one move is the same as the fraction of husband-wife families born out of state (Table 5.4).[34] In the Northeast, fewer than 10 percent of the families moved two or more times, except in Vermont. Only in New Jersey and Pennsylvania did families make as many as four interstate or international moves. Indeed, in the region as a whole, fewer than 4 percent of the families initiated two or more migrations. For the Midwest, on the other hand, an average of 20

TABLE 5.4. Minimum Frequency of Interstate and International Moves, 1860

	Percentage of Families Making at Least					Mean Number of Moves by	Mean Number of Moves by
State/Region	1 Move	2 Moves	3 Moves	4 Moves	5 or More moves	Migrants	Immigrants
Connecticut	22.7	4.9	1.5	0	0	1.29	1.28
Maryland	3.9	0	0	0	0	1.00	n.a.
New Hampshire	15.7	5.0	0.2	0	0	1.23	1.59
New Jersey	37.9	7.4	1.4	0.4	0	1.11	1.33
New York	27.7	2.9	0.1	0	0	1.10	1.13
Pennsylvania	25.5	4.2	0.4	0.0	0.0	1.16	1.22
Vermont	38.7	13.4	1.7	0	0	1.42	1.30
Northeast	26.3	3.9	0.3	0.0	0.0	1.14	1.20
Illinois	93.2	20.7	2.3	0.3	0	1.25	1.23
Indiana	73.7	10.9	1.0	0.1	0.0	1.15	1.21
Iowa	99.4	46.2	13.3	2.8	0.9	1.59	1.87
Kansas	99.6	52.9	12.0	3.2	0.2	1.69	1.65
Michigan	91.4	22.2	3.2	0.2	0.2	1.34	1.21
Minnesota	96.3	38.4	7.7	1.5	0.7	1.49	1.53
Missouri	85.0	22.6	4.9	0.3	0.1	1.32	1.60
Ohio	62.4	5.5	0.2	0	0	1.09	1.10
Wisconsin	99.3	26.9	4.3	1.3	0.4	1.38	1.30
Midwest	83.5	20.1	3.4	0.6	0.2	1.29	1.29
Northern States	59.6	13.4	2.2	0.3	0.1	1.27	1.27

0.0 indicates less than 0.5 percent.
0 indicates no observations.

percent of the families made two or more moves. About 3 percent of the households experienced interstate moves three or more times. The most persistent movers were in Iowa, Kansas, Michigan, Minnesota, Missouri, and Wisconsin.

No consistent, clear pattern emerged between immigrants and native migrants in the relative frequency of moves. The average number of moves for the two groups were similar, although in a few cases there were quite sharp divergencies. For example, the twenty-nine immigrant families who had moved to the sample New Hampshire townships by 1860 made substantially more moves, an average of 1.59 per family, than the seventy-one native migrants there, who averaged only 1.23; yet native migrants to Michigan changed locations more than immigrants who came to that state. They averaged 1.34 moves against 1.21 for immigrants. There were also often pronounced differences in the number of moves that groups made to different destinations. Migrants from Kentucky moved more frequently before settling in Iowa than did Kentucky migrants who settled in Illinois; Massachusetts migrants en route to Wisconsin moved more than those settling in Iowa. Similarly, English-born immigrants seem to have been more sure about settling in Illinois and Wisconsin than they were about moving to Iowa or Michigan. Similarly, the Irish who settled in Iowa made more moves than their compatriots going to Illinois, Michigan, or Wisconsin. What pattern there is to these data is consistent with a stepwise migration to points progressively further westward.

Different migrant and immigrant groups within the same state displayed significant variations in the number of moves. This pattern is also consistent with a stepwise migratory pattern. Kentuckians residing in Illinois, for example, made fewer moves than Virginians who settled in the state, but no more than New Yorkers who located there. In Iowa migrants from New York State made significantly fewer transfers than families from Pennsylvania. The Dutch immigrants to Illinois and Michigan moved less frequently than any other immigrant group. Distance may partly explain some of these variations. Furthermore, the later that a state opened for settlement, the higher the number of moves were likely to have been because some settlers who had earlier migrated to more easterly states of then-recent settlement decided to move on.

Whatever their migration or immigration pattern, come they did to the United States or to its western states. To an economy hungering for people, they were a valuable asset. Their choice of settlement, family size, and other family characteristics ultimately would influence the course of American history. Those who chose to leave their native surroundings or even only their current place of residence were people unlike those who for generations rarely left the environs of their birthplace. Indeed the "nation of immigrants" never became a nation of peasants hesitant to change. They were an atypical group, willing to break ancient family ties, to traverse oceans or undeveloped continents, and to gamble on success in a new world. Obvious optimists, they clearly expected improvement in their lives or that of their offspring. While political freedom or social equality no doubt intrigued some, material advance and economic improvement appears to have driven most.

CHAPTER SIX

Wealth and Egalitarianism among the Yeomanry

IF MOBILITY WAS A MEANS, wealth accumulation was an end for Americans in the rural North. Beyond the hope of independence, one of the presumably most attractive prospects in nineteenth-century agrarian America was that of equality of opportunity. This promised not only a comfortable level of material welfare, but also a relatively equal dispersion of wealth and income among the citizenry. Idealistic as it was, economic egalitarianism in the eyes of many represented the material corollary of political equality. According to the American legend, each individual, starting afresh and unencumbered by existing concentrations of wealth and power, could eventually attain economic parity with his neighbor. Northerners especially expounded this ideal. Nowhere were conditions riper for realizing this goal than in the antebellum Midwest with its small farms, rural communities, and abundant land. If it were ever to be achieved, conditions could hardly have been more propitious than in that rural, agrarian world of the North before the rise of big business and industrial capitalism. The sample of northern households provides an opportunity to examine how closely American society came to realizing this egalitarian ideal.

Access to land was a critical factor in promoting equality by creating economic opportunity, and Jeffersonian land policy played a central role in creating an independent self-sufficient yeomanry with a strong vested interest in the existing system. The degree of success of this policy is reflected by Alexis de Tocqueville's statement that "nothing struck me more forcibly than the general equality of condition among the people" on his travels in the United States.[1] Scholars could hardly ignore such an intriguing academic proposition and this comment with which de Tocqueville begins his book, *Democracy in America*, has sparked an enduring debate that continues to the present.[2] Much of the continuing controversy only serves to cloud the issues and we would argue that the notion of economic egalitarianism, particularly for the era before the Civil War, remains a part of national folklore.

Equality may be judged against an absolute standard–Was wealth divided equally? Or it may be judged relatively against some yardstick. Few would seriously argue the absolute case, although Edward Pessen, despite denials to the contrary, steps across the boundary.[3] On the other hand, if the distribution of wealth is to be judged on a relative basis, then we also need to establish a standard of comparison. Surprisingly too, we have to measure the wealth dispersion in the rural North since the few empirical studies covering this region have focused on narrower geographic areas that may not be representative.[4] Our argument is twofold. First, that the distribution of wealth in the rural North was more egalitarian than that in other places and at other times. Second, that regardless of the degree of inequality our estimates reveal, this distribution is more equal than might reasonably have been expected.

In 1860, the wealthiest 1 percent of the rural northern population owned about 12 percent of the total wealth; the wealthiest 5 percent held 31 percent (Table 6.1). In the Northeast, the distribution was marginally less egalitarian than in the Midwest since the richest 1 percent held just over 1 percent more of the total wealth, but the difference was surprisingly small. Thus land availability in the West per se seems to have had a marginal effect, at best, upon the distribution of wealth.

By comparison, the wealthiest 5 percent nationally in 1860 held 54–57 percent of the wealth, while the richest 1 percent of the population had about a quarter of the total.[5] These levels are essentially the same as those for the period since 1945.[6] For the Cotton South, Gavin Wright has concluded that "there is little reason to reject the traditional view that the social implication of the slave-cotton regime was a highly unequal distribution of wealth," with the richest 5 percent holding 39.5 percent of the wealth in 1850 and 36.2 percent in 1860.[7] These estimates are biased downward because the distributions are based on samples of farm operators rather than heads of household, and farmers were, by definition, wealthy. They thus ignore all those in the community who had little or no wealth.[8] On the South's frontier, Texas, wealth was even less equally distributed. Based on a sample of households from Texas, Randolph B. Campbell and Richard G. Lowe estimate that the richest 5 percent held

TABLE 6.1. Distribution of Wealth in Rural North in 1860 Compared with That Elsewhere and at Other Times

State/Region	Percentage Total Wealth Held by Richest 1%	Richest 5%
I *Rural North in 1860*		
Midwest	11.21	30.1
Northeast	12.40	31.7
Entire North	12.00	31.2
II *Comparative Data*		
Contemporary Estimates for Other Parts of the U.S.		
Maryland (excluding Baltimore)[a]	16.21	45.41
Cotton Counties[a]	16.61	42.01
Wisconsin[b]	–	–
North[c]	27.00	53.00
South[c]	27.00	59.00
U.S. Distribution of Wealth in the Twentieth Century		
1922[d]	31.60	–
1939[d]	30.60	–
1949[d]	20.80	–
1956[d]	26.00	–
1962[e]	26.20	–
1972[e]	24.10	–

[a] Robert E. Gallman, "Trends in the Size Distribution of Wealth in the Nineteenth Century: Some Speculations," in *Six Papers on the Size Distribution of Wealth and Income,* ed. Lee Soltow, NBER, Studies in Income and Wealth 33 (New York: 1969), 1–25.

[b] Lee Soltow, *Patterns of Wealthholding in Wisconsin Since 1850* (Madison, 1971).

[c] Lee Soltow, *Men and Wealth in the United States, 1850–1870* (New Haven, 1975).

[d] Robert S. Lampman, *The Share of Top Wealth-Holders in National Wealth, 1922–1956* (New York, 1962).

[e] U.S. Congress, "Data on the Distribution of Wealth in the United States," *Hearings Before the Task Force on the Distributive Impact of Budget and Economic Policies,* 95th Cong. 1st sess., 1977.

about 50 percent of the total wealth.[9] Wealth was much less equally distributed among the urban population. In Texas, the richest 5 percent of city residents owned about 58 percent of the total wealth in 1860.[10] This was low by urban standards at the time. In Milwaukee, it was somewhat higher, perhaps 65 percent.[11] Elsewhere in the older urban areas, wealth was less equally distributed. Pessen estimates that the richest 4 percent of New York City residents in 1845 owned 66 percent of the noncorporate wealth, while in Boston in 1848 they held 64 percent of the wealth.[12] In Baltimore, New Orleans, and St. Louis their shares were even higher.[13]

Compared with more recent periods and with other regions at the same time, wealth was much more evenly distributed among the population of the rural northern townships of 1860. The richest 1 percent of the population owned only about half as much as that group has held in the United States since the end of World War II. Only in the slave-holding township of Costin District in Worcester County, Maryland, did inequality approach the levels in other geographic locations in the nineteenth century or of today's economy.

The wealth distribution for the North is shown in Figure 6.1. Those for the two regions separately are indistinguishable from it. The horizontal axis measures the cumulative percent of households ordered poorest to richest, and the vertical measures the cumulative percentage of wealth held by those households. The diagonal line indicates perfect equality, for if the observations lay along this line, then households would own wealth only in exact proportion to their weight in the population. These curves are known as Lorenz curves and have given rise to a summary statistic for distributions known as the Gini index. This varies from zero (perfect equality) to 1 (perfect inequality) as the Lorenz curve deviates from the line of perfect equality.

The distributions in each of the states west of the eastern continental divide were quite similar. Excepting Minnesota, the Gini index lay in a narrow range from 0.58 (in Michigan) to 0.62 (in Missouri) and the richest 5 percent of the populations held from 26 to 32 percent of the total

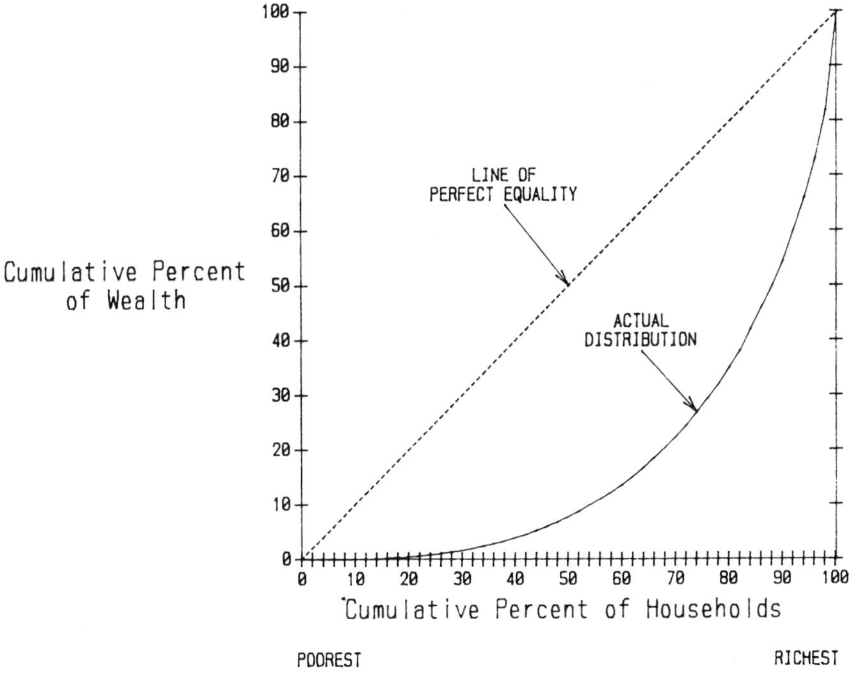

FIG. 6.1. Distribution of wealth in the rural North in 1860.

wealth. Among the eastern seaboard states, distributions varied more widely than in the West. Even excluding Maryland because of its slave status, where the Gini index of inequality was 0.85, the distributions for the eastern states ranged from New Hampshire's 0.54 coefficient, which was more egalitarian than that for any of the sample western states, to New Jersey's 0.68, which was at least as concentrated as the most concentrated of the western states.[14]

The dispersion was most unequal in Maryland where the wealthiest 1 percent of the population held more than one-third of the total. Wealth in Worcester County, Maryland, less evenly distributed than in the rest of Maryland, approached the level of concentration estimated for Baltimore by Gallman and was the same as that estimated by Lee Soltow for the South as a whole.[15] It indicates an extreme inequality in the distribution of wealth by mid-nineteenth-century American standards, but one that differs little from that for the United States in the 1920s or for Australia in 1915.[16] In Costin District of Maryland's Worcester County, the richest 10 percent of households owned more than three-quarters of the total wealth, while the poorest 40 percent held no wealth whatsoever.

The dominant characteristic distinguishing wealth holders from the nonwealth holders in Maryland was race. Three-quarters of those households with no wealth in Worcester County were black. Of the 197 free black families in the District, only 13 possessed any wealth. Only 1 black family possessed a sufficient accumulation to place it as high as the second decile. The Gale family owned a 110-acre farm, valued at $1,500, which supported the family of eight. The farm, together with their estimated $400 in personal property, made them the richest black family in the District. Compared with most blacks in the District, Edward Gale's attainment was impressive; relative to the richer whites, the Gales were still poor. Contrast them, for example, with the Dennis family, whites who owned two farms comprising 2,950 acres valued at $65,000 together with personal property worth an additional $52,000. Much of this personal property was probably accounted for by slaves because the Dennis family was listed in the slave schedules as owning eighty, some of whom were in trust for their children.

The distribution of wealth was more equal in the other sample slave state, Missouri. There the richest 10 percent of the households owned less than 45 percent of wealth, and only 5 percent of the population in the five sample counties possessed no wealth at all. Here too, race was a major factor influencing position in the wealth distribution. Of the 58 families with no wealth, 18 were black. More importantly, no blacks held any wealth in these counties. What relative degree of equality existed in these Missouri townships reflects greater equality among the white population, particularly their ownership of real estate, and the complete equality in poverty among blacks, rather than greater equality for the entire population. One could argue, depending upon the choice of reference group, whether or not the more than half of the population in Maryland who possessed no wealth (including slaves) felt more deprived and disadvantaged than the 20 percent of Missouri's population who lacked any wealth.[17]

Except in New Hampshire, the average wealth of the top 1 percent of households in the Northeast exceeded that of midwesterners, often by 50 percent or more. However, the median wealth levels were remarkably consistent across the sample states, ranging between \$500 and \$1,500, except in Maryland, and they were over \$1,000 in most.[18] This was sufficient to start a midwestern farm.[19] The low median in Maryland, \$100, reflects the high percentage of landless and propertyless free black families in Worcester County.

Everywhere the wealthy shared certain definable, but not unexpected, social and demographic characteristics. So did the poor. These characteristics (Table 6.2) are present regardless of which upper percentage of the total population is considered. The richest 1 percent of households had white heads of household and were with few exceptions headed by males who were literate, native-born, and middle-aged, and included larger households than did poorer families. Given these age characteristics, however, it is doubtful whether the smaller family sizes of the poorer group, who generally were younger, represents completed family size, while that of the richest 1 percent almost certainly did. An overwhelming proportion of the free black population found themselves among the poorest households in the community. Free blacks constituted less than 2 percent of the free population in the sample states but were overrepre-

TABLE 6.2. Demographic and Social Characteristics of Heads of Household of Richest and Poorest Percent of Households, 1860

	Richest 1 Percent	
	Midwest	Northeast
Percent White	100.0	100.0
Percent Male	97.0	94.0
Percent Literate	99.0	100.0
Percent Native-born	94.0	99.0
Mean Age	50.0	50.3
Mean Family Size	7.5	6.9
	Poorest 1 Percent	
Percent White	60.0	62.0
Percent Male	56.0	73.0
Percent Literate	55.0	67.0
Percent Native-born	86.0	88.0
Mean Age	22.8	36.5
Mean Family Size	2.7	3.7

sented among the poorest households in every state, as were female-headed households. Among the poor families, the heads of household exhibited high illiteracy rates, frequently were immigrants, and typically were young.

Differences among the richest 1 percent in each subregion are slight. Those among the poorest 1 percent are more pronounced. Relative to eastern families, the poor households in the West were more likely to be headed by women, immigrants, younger adults, or some combination of these. Because of their comparative youth, midwestern families were somewhat smaller. The higher percentage of female-headed households generally indicates widows left with small children. Work in an eastern factory, which offered little chance of passing along an inheritance, would make child rearing more difficult; trying to operate a midwestern farm on the other hand could place the children under direct supervision, provide employment for them, and perhaps make possible an inheritance. The higher percentage of immigrants is explainable by the attraction of midwestern agricultural land.

Although age proved to be the single most important factor accounting for differences in wealth, it was not the only one. Race, nativity, literacy, sex, and occupational status all helped determine rank in the wealth distribution. To establish the importance of each of these in determining the level of family wealth and to measure their relative importance, regression estimates of the form:

$$\text{Family Wealth} = g(\text{Age}, \text{Age}^2, \text{Race}, \text{Sex}, \text{Literacy}, \text{Farm}, \text{Birth})$$

were made for the two regions. The variables, Race, Sex, Literacy, Farm, and Birth were dummy variables where:

Race = 1 if white, 0 otherwise
Sex = 1 if male, 0 if female
Literacy = 1 if literate, 0 otherwise
Farm = 1 if farm operator, 0 otherwise
Birth = 1 if native-born, 0 otherwise.

The squared term for Age was included to capture life-cycle effects. The variables are represented by the abbreviations: AGE, AGESQ, RACE, SEX, LIT, FARM, and BIRTH.

The raw regression coefficients from these estimates have an immediate and obvious interpretation. They represent the dollar increments (or decrements) to family wealth for each of the social and demographic attributes (Table 6.3). Wealth was generally increasing with age because the positive age coefficient was an order of magnitude larger than the negative coefficient on AGESQ. At any age, however, the level of wealth

TABLE 6.3. Change in Family Wealth in Response to Social and Demographic Attributes[a]

Region	Constant	Age	Agesq	Race	Sex	Lit	Occ	Birth
Midwest	−7951.82	213.87[b]	−1.69[b]	1578.84[b]	474.00[b]	1046.24[b]	985.58[b]	1228.46[b]
Northeast	−8000.78[b]	220.54[b]	−1.81[b]	1623.11[b]	318.18	1025.04[b]	2144.69[b]	1222.16[b]
North	−8350.68[b]	220.59[b]	−1.75[b]	1585.61[b]	448.42[b]	1134.18[b]	1388.97[b]	1355.06[b]

[a] See text for a description of the variables.
[b] Significantly different from zero at better than 5 percent level.

depended upon the value of the other social and demographic variables. Thus, for example, being a male-headed household (SEX = 1) raised family wealth an average of $474; being able to read and write (LIT = 1) would raise it by $1,046. In the East, however, there was no significant difference in wealth levels depending upon the sex of the head of household. The equation also indicates that farmers were significantly wealthier than any other occupational group. In the Midwest a farm raised family wealth $986 over an otherwise identical but nonfarming one. In the Northeast a farm contributed more than twice as much to family wealth. The foreign-born (BIRTH = 0), however, were $1,228 poorer, other things equal, than an equivalent native-born family. Free blacks, however, paid the greatest penalties. In the Midwest the color of their skin alone was sufficient to reduce accumulated household wealth by almost $1,600. The penalty in the East was slightly higher, but the difference was not statistically significant. This is strong evidence of discrimination in the distribution of wealth based on race, but it does not tell the full story since the probability that the head of a nonwhite family was either literate or a farmer or both was also much smaller than for white families. The only discrimination that blacks escaped was that against the foreign-born.

The inclusion of other variables in the model such as family size, the number of dependents (persons under 15 and over 65), and the number of adult family members with no occupation weakens the strength of the life-cycle relationship between wealth and age. This is to be expected since each of these new variables is also a family life-cycle phenomenon. The coefficients of the other variables, however, keep the same relationship to one another, though their values change. Wealth increases with family size, but is decreased by people not in the work force. More particularly there was almost a one-to-one relationship between the increase in family wealth from addition of a family member and the decrease that resulted if that person was a child or retired adult.

The wealth model can also be respecified in semilogarithmic form, that is with the natural logarithm of the dependent variable substituted in its stead. Expressed in this way, the coefficients are of the form $e^{(1+g)x}$

and hence can be interpreted as the percentage change in total household wealth for a unit change in each social and demographic attribute (Table 6.4).[20]

The regression coefficients imply that households headed by a white had, on average, thirteen and one-half times as much wealth as an otherwise identical one headed by a black. Similarly, farmer-headed households had seven times more wealth than nonfarm; the literate, more than twice as much as the illiterate; male-headed households, 182 percent more wealth than female-headed households; and natives almost 180 percent more than immigrants. Among the various groups, the proportionate

TABLE 6.4. Change in Wealth Holding with Social and Demographic Attributes[a] (*t*-statistics in parentheses)

Group	Age	Age sq	Race	Sex	Literacy	Occupation	Nativity	Mean Wealth of Group
All	.103 (18.41)	−.001 (−14.44)	2.600 (26.77)	.599 (11.04)	.763 (15.67)	1.963 (73.89)	.587 (16.93)	$ 717
Natives	.108 (18.24)	−.001 (−14.46)	2.579 (26.29)	.635 (11.10)	.786 (14.59)	1.950 (67.33)	–	800
Immigrants	.068 (4.03)	−.001 (−2.79)	2.993 (4.91)	.338 (1.99)	.647 (5.64)	2.028 (30.22)	–	410
Farm	.095 (15.11)	−.001 (−11.27)	1.969 (12.25)	.245 (3.55)	.610 (10.88)	–	.555 (14.48)	1991
Nonfarm	.111 (11.75)	−.001 (−9.57)	2.713 (20.20)	.781 (9.31)	.897 (11.18)	–	.625 (10.54)	209
Black	.078 (1.55)	−.001 (−1.06)	–	.906 (2.72)	1.355 (5.27)	2.830 (8.92)	.682 (0.85)	21
White	.103 (18.46)	−.001 (−14.50)	–	.575 (10.43)	.720 (14.40)	1.954 (73.63)	.587 (17.04)	766
Men	.089 (16.88)	−.001 (−12.91)	2.495 (23.78)	– –	.800 (15.78)	1.931 (71.54)	.597 (17.13)	760
Women	.160 (6.40)	−.001 (−5.79)	3.039 (10.43)	– –	.459 (2.54)	2.464 (18.57)	.401 (1.95)	293
Literate	.106 (17.98)	−.001 (−14.33)	2.300 (17.39)	.634 (10.77)	–	1.935 (69.94)	.600 (16.54)	798
Illiterate	.065 (3.82)	−.000 (−2.16)	2.875 (19.97)	.340 (2.46)	–	2.323 (24.44)	.406 (3.47)	203

[a]Percentage change is calculated by taking e^x of these regression coefficients.
Age (and age²) = Age of head of household (in years).
Race = 0 if black, 1 otherwise.
Sex = 0 if female, 1 otherwise.
Literacy = 0 if illiterate, 1 otherwise.
Occupation = 0 if nonfarm, 1 otherwise.
Nativity = 0 of foreign-born, 1 otherwise.
Regression: wealth = f(age, age², race, sex, literacy, occupation, nativity).

wealth loss from being born black was lowest for farmers. The burden of illiteracy bore least heavily upon women, and the wealth loss to female-headed households was lowest for those with farms. The percentage reduction in wealth due to being an immigrant was the smallest for women.

Collectively these results imply that the possession of a particular attribute – being middle-aged, white, male, literate, a farmer, or native-born – did not necessarily endow that family with more wealth, but they certainly did not detract from it. On the other hand, not possessing one or more of these attributes generally penalized the family in its wealth holdings.

The age coefficient may be interpreted as the annual rate of wealth accumulation. For the North, this rate was almost 11 percent, which seems plausible and consistent with the data on interest rates as well as the estimates of profit rates in agriculture and manufacturing. Indeed, the wealth accumulation rate for farmers, the wealthiest group, was estimated to be almost 10 percent. This figure is close to our estimate of the rate of return on capital invested in farms in Chapter 14.[21] Women accumulated wealth faster (17 percent per year) than any other group, but since they were poor this rapid accumulation rate did not result in large fortunes. Accumulation rates were lowest for illiterates, immigrants, and blacks, ranging from 6.7 percent per year for illiterates to 8.1 percent for blacks. Blacks, however, were the poorest of all, averaging only $21 of wealth. Consequently, accumulation to put them on a par with the next poorest group, the illiterates, whose wealth was also growing, would take a considerable period of time.

The strength of the age variable and other related variables suggests that a person's position in the wealth distribution was strongly influenced by the stage in his life cycle. According to the Life Cycle hypothesis individuals save during the economically productive part of their lives to ensure some minimum level of consumption upon retirement.[22] This is consistent with our regression results in Table 6.3. The positive coefficient on AGE and a negative coefficient on AGESQ means that wealth increases with age, reaching a maximum at age:

$$\partial \text{WEALTH} / \partial \text{AGE} = 0$$

and declines thereafter. In the Midwest, wealth increased up to age 63.[23] In the East, it peaked somewhat earlier, at age 61.

The Life Cycle hypothesis makes a number of simplifying assumptions that population is uniformly distributed by age and everyone faces the same life expectancy, consumption pressures, and tastes, has the same lifetime earnings, and saves just enough to provide for consumption during retirement, passing along no wealth to heirs. Despite perfect equality in each of these attributes, however, wealth would still be unequally distributed. It can be shown that in this stylized world, the top X percent of the population owns:

$$X(200 - X)/100$$

of all wealth. Thus the richest 1 percent would possess about 2 percent (actually 1.99 percent) of the wealth and the richest 5 percent, 9.75 or a little less than one-third of what this group actually held. The resulting distribution of wealth by age is shown in Figure 6.2.

This model can be extended to provide greater realism, such as to allow for differential mortality rates based on age and for death as a random element. If there is no longer certainty about the moment of death, individuals can no longer plan to just exhaust their wealth balance. Some provision would therefore have to be made for those who lived longer than they had anticipated and so exhausted their resources before death, and for the disposal of excess balances held by those who died earlier than anticipated. A desire to provide a bequest to heirs would result in positive wealth balances at death and the resulting intergenerational transfer would produce a discontinuity in the recipient's wealth balances. Each such extension of the model has the effect of increasing inequality.

The correspondence between the actual wealth-age distributions by quinquennia age groups and the stylized life-cycle distribution is remarkable (Fig. 6.3). Without making allowance for other influences, mean total

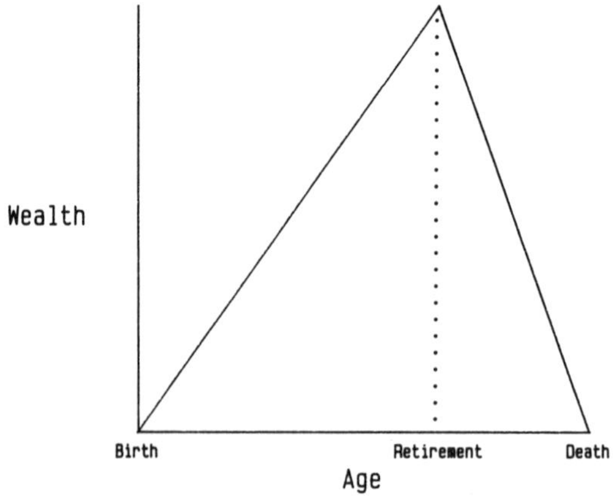

FIG. 6.2. Wealth accumulation by age: The Life Cycle hypothesis.

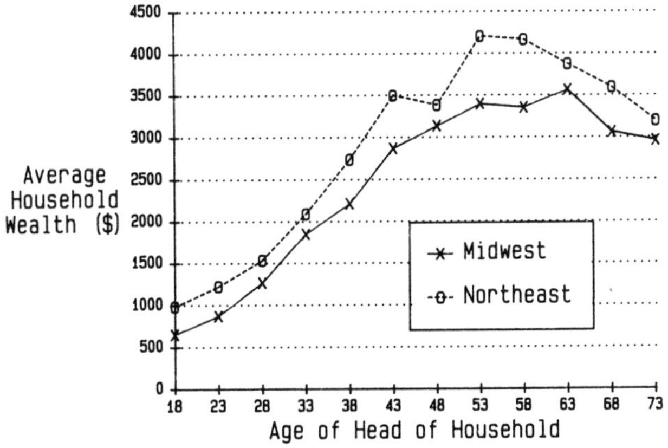

FIG. 6.3. Wealth accumulation by age: The Life Cycle hypothesis in 1860.

family wealth increased with the age of the head of household, peaking at about $4,200 in the East for household heads aged 51–55 and peaking at about $3,550 in the Midwest for heads of household aged 61–65. The difference between wealth levels and the age of the head of household when the maximum wealth levels are attained may be explained by a variety of influences not least of which is the apparently higher rate of accumulation in the Northeast relative to the Midwest, which for identical consumption patterns between the regions would permit earlier retirement in the former area.

The nonzero mean wealth estimate for those heads of household aged 16–20 who are just beginning their life cycle may reflect intergenerational wealth transfers, which are also implied by the relatively high-wealth levels of octogenarians—persons who, at least according to life-expectancy tables, had no reasonable expectations for many more years of life in 1860. Octogenarian-headed households held mean family wealth between $2,300 and $2,900, which, given an average family size of 5.3–4.9 persons, would be consistent with inheritances of $600–$1,000 as observed assuming a partitive inheritance system.[24]

Lee Soltow has recently shown that a partitive inheritance system to sons, starting from a perfectly equal distribution of wealth and given the distribution of sons between families, would lead to growing inequality in the distribution of wealth from generation to generation.[25] Assuming that sons were distributed with a Gini of 0.3, which is consistent with what we observe in the sample, then after one generation the index of inequality would be 0.42, 0.5 after two, 0.56 in three, and 0.61 after four generations. After ten generations, the index of inequality would be 0.8.[26] Within from two to four generations inequality through a partitive inheritance system alone would be as great as that which we observe in 1860.

The life cycles in Figure 6.3 also seem plausible with what we know about work habits and life expectancy in the mid-nineteenth century. By age 20 about three-quarters of all males were in the labor force (Fig. 3.4) and their life expectancy was about 40 years, that is they could expect to live to age 60.[27] At age 40 their life expectancy was 27, and at age 60 they could expect to live to be 74. Persons thus wishing to enjoy some years of leisure before death would presumably begin to reduce their labor output sometime after their half-century, at which point they would begin to draw down their wealth balances. Participation rates also begin to decline for those in their late 50s. This is exactly what the distributions reveal, though whether it was what was rationally intended is another matter. In the Midwest, even though wealth did not peak until 61–65, accumulation beyond age 51–55 was minimal.

The cross-sectional life-cycle patterns for some of the groups in Table 6.4 are presented in Figure 6.4.[28] These show the widely divergent rates of accumulation by age that each experienced. If we interpret the peak in the age-wealth distribution as signaling the onset of retirement, then farmers, the wealthiest group, were the first to retire. Blacks also retired early, but we posit a different explanation; namely a shorter life expectancy for this group. For other groups, wealth peaks for heads of household in their late 60s. Despite these differences, however, the general

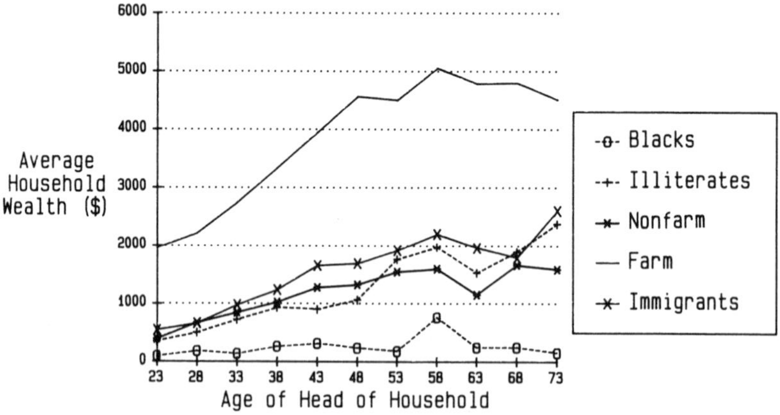

FIG. 6.4. Wealth by age of head of household for various groups in 1860.

pattern is the same across the various groups and emphasizes the importance of the absolute level of wealth that a head in any group on average attains at a given age. Unfortunately, our reliance upon dichotomous independent variables precludes an explanation of the distribution of wealth after the effect of age is removed.

Wealth became more equally distributed with increasing age. The Gini coefficients by age cohort for the various groups (Table 6.5) bear directly upon Robert Gallman's assertion that "the more numerous the young were, relative to the old, the more unequal would be the cross section of wealth distribution."[29] Although wealth among the young was very unequally distributed, its dispersion generally became more egalitarian for older age groups except among nonfarmers for whom inequality increased with age. Cohort inequality changed relatively little for some of the poorer groups because the distortions produced by inheritances, received principally by the young, were minimal.

Although the life-cycle patterns of wealth distribution may be similar between groups and the degree of inequality by age cohorts similar across the groups, the measured degree of inequality will still be influenced by the age structure of the population of heads of households. For example, although wealth holding by age for both farm and nonfarm households peaks at age 55–65, 31.9 percent of the nonfarm households were headed by individuals under 30 years of age, while only 17 percent of farm household heads fell in that age category. So the much greater equality among farmers may merely reflect the clustering of the population about a specific, older age range and their greater wealth nothing more than their longer period of accumulation. The mean age of the heads of household in each group was about 42, but because the age structures varied widely

TABLE 6.5. Gini Coefficients by Age Cohorts, 1860

	Age Cohort					
Group	Under 20	20–29	30–39	40–49	50–59	60 and over
All	.79	.68	.62	.61	.60	.59
Natives	.79	.67	.61	.60	.59	.58
Immigrants	–	.63	.59	.62	.60	.59
Farm	.57	.54	.50	.50	.51	.46
Nonfarm	.62	.70	.69	.73	.74	.73
Black and Mulatto	–	.72	.69	.71	.81	.69
White	.78	.67	.61	.61	.59	.58
Men	.77	.67	.61	.61	.59	.57
Women	.87	.76	.76	.72	.68	.66
Literate	.69	.67	.61	.60	.59	.58
Illiterate	.80	.71	.68	.68	.66	.65

the hypothesis that they were identical to one another could be rejected in almost every case.[30] Standardizing the distributions to compensate for these variations in age dispersions resulted in greater equality both within and between groups.[31]

Was the notion of economic equality then only a myth? Wealth was clearly not perfectly equal, but when compared with the wealth inequality in urban areas, the South, or the entire United States in 1860 or at other times, one is struck by the much more equal distribution prevailing in the rural North during the late antebellum era. About a third of the inequality could have stemmed from a life-cycle pattern of accumulation. Differential rates of population growth then aggravated this. Inheritance would also lead to a concentration of wealth similar to, indeed possibly greater than, that observed and determined by forces no more sinister and conspiratorial than decisions regarding family size. Only the high degree of inequality among blacks in the sample approached the levels found in the slave South or the urban centers. Even in this case, our age correction suggests that this could be due to the peculiar age structure of black heads of household. Regarding the effect of similar adjustments upon the urban and southern population, one would speculate that the correction for the urban areas might be quite large, whereas for the South it would be much less influential.

Although wealth was more evenly distributed in the rural North in 1860 than it is in that region today, and more egalitarian than the slave South or urban areas of its time, one cannot conclude without additional evidence that the rural North was nondiscriminatory in its distribution of wealth or egalitarian in a political sense. Money provided power, influence, and comfort—whether in urban areas, on the plantation, or on a northern farm in the antebellum years—just as it has throughout history. Indeed one could argue that in terms of relative deprivation, the poorest 5 or 10 percent of the northern rural households who had no wealth probably felt even worse off there than the 40 percent of poor-white and free-black households in the slave South or urban centers who had no wealth, or the approximately 30 percent in 1962–1966 with none. Certainly the immediate reference point for the former was more likely to have been a wealth-holding group than for the latter. Although wealth was greater in the older, more settled areas of the country, the median wealth holding, particularly in the nonslave states, was remarkably uniform across states, suggesting that migration took place among households lying towards the middle of the eastern states' range of wealth distributions. This, together with the flow of immigrants, would explain both the similarities between East and West as well as the differences in wealth patterns and in the social and demographic characteristics of the wealth holders. Most importantly the patterns of age and wealth accumulation are consistent with the Life Cycle hypothesis, while the social characteristics of the wealth holders are consistent with a hypothesis of racial and sexual discrimination. Wealth indeed was more equally dispersed among rural northerners than among other groups, but one fact remains: to be wealthy in the antebellum rural North, as elsewhere in America, meant being middle-aged, white, male, educated, and native-born.

PART TWO

The Rural Community: The Farm as an Economic Unit

As the industrial development of the nation proceeded, the importance of the purely economic dimension in agriculture intensified. While the more traditional psychic values of the independent farming life lingered on throughout the century, farmers operating and surviving within the increasingly industrialized environment were forced to pay greater attention to the business and financial aspects of their operations. At midcentury the two dimensions, the "love of the land" and the desire for cash income, remained precariously balanced. Some northern agriculturalists, especially those in the western states, could still indulge their psychic goals at the expense of the economic, but others located nearer to industrializing centers probably found the trade-off increasingly, if not prohibitively, costly.

Certain decisions had always been dominated by economic considerations, most notably whether one could afford the initial costs of establishing a viable farm enterprise. As time and the frontier moved on, the expense of buying land and equipment grew. So did the cost and difficulty of reaching available land parcels. Tenancy rates, even as early as 1860, proved quite high and were higher on the frontier than elsewhere in the nonslave states. It was at this point that the dream of farm ownership and the independent agrarian life began to confront the reality of economics. This issue that concerned the nineteenth-century northern farmer so seriously has interested generations of scholars ever since.

Once the initial investment was made, the farmer knew that ultimately he would face yet another choice between familial independence and financial interdependence with the marketplace, between psychic and monetary income. The latitude for choice could be wide–depending upon constraints imposed by climate, soil conditions, market proximity, and similar conditions–among varying degrees of self-sufficiency or market participation. How far a family farm could expand output beyond its own consumption needs, assuming adequate demand conditions, depended upon how high it could raise its land or livestock yields through the application of improved practices and technological advances.

Whether as a totally self-contained family operation, a purely economic endeavor, or some combination of the two, from an economic perspective the utilization of national resources by the agricultural sector can be evaluated by the rate of return being earned on the farm investment relative to other economic pursuits. Farmers in the settled regions who had committed themselves to commercialized farming became increasingly concerned with the profit being earned by their farms. Those in the less developed areas during the late antebellum years whose commitment lay closer toward the goal of independence and personal satisfaction could still be more cavalier about their earned rate of return, accepting–oftentimes unwittingly–one that was well below that prevailing in alternative economic pursuits.

In the chapters ahead we follow this sequence of economic choices by northern farmers, examining the costs of farm investment, the degrees of self-sufficiency, and market involvement as they varied across geographic areas and farm-size classifications, the levels of land and animal yields and the sources of their improvement, and finally, the rates of profit being earned in northern agriculture. In the process, the economic forces and individual decisions that influenced American agriculture at this time can be examined in the detail permitted by the sample of individual farming enterprises.

CHAPTER SEVEN

A Sample of Northern Farms from the Census Manuscripts

IN ADDITION TO COLLECTING DATA from the population schedules for the sample townships that were the primary focus of Part I, the information on the agricultural schedules was also recorded. These provided data for almost 12,000 farms that were then linked to the population schedules. The name of the farm operator was used as the key. Most farms were matched successfully, but no match was made for about 4 percent of the farms overall.[1] The proportion of failed matches varied from zero in Connecticut and Vermont to almost 8½ percent in Kansas. Unmatched farms were presumably operated by people who lived in other townships and not on the farm. Those with farms elsewhere but residing in the sample township were included among the group of "farmers without farms."[2] The overall picture was further complicated because in 1,022 of the households linked to farms no one reported their occupation as farmer. Inspection of the data shows that in about half of the cases nobody gave an occupation. These may thus reflect reporting errors. In most of the others at least one person listed himself as "laborer," but who provided the managerial direction is unclear. There were thus "farms without people" and "farms without farmers," as well as farmers without farms. However, there were only 1,476 farms lacking a farmer compared with 4,927 farmers without farms. This disparity corroborates the view that most farmers without farms were not agriculturalists.. The same holds true even if those farmers without farms who lived on farms (see Chap. 3) are excluded.

Farm operators were asked to respond to forty-eight questions regarding their agricultural enterprise in the year ending 1 June 1860 (see App. this chap.). The crop data reflected results for the 1859 crop year. The enumerators recorded output levels for twenty-three major and minor crops, as well as such products as butter, cheese, and wine. They also reported the dollar value of orchard products, market garden produce, total holdings of livestock, livestock slaughtered, and home manufacturing. The number of horses, mules, sheep, swine, milk cows, working oxen, and "other cattle" also were indicated. Completing the survey, the enumerators inquired into and reported the total improved and unimproved acreage, the cash value of the farm, and the value of implements and machinery used on that unit.

These data therefore provide a fairly comprehensive picture of the farm and its operations during the preceding year and, in conjunction with other sources, facilitates a reasonably wide range of economic analyses of agricultural operations and decisions at the level of the individual farm. To illustrate the basic source from which the sample was drawn, we have reproduced in Figure 7.1 one of the completed Schedule 4 (the Agricultural Schedule) pages for Honey Creek in Adams County, Illinois. This is the same township that we used as an illustration for the population schedules.

The first line is for a 200-acre farm operated by Apollo Shriver (see also Fig. 2.1). This farm had 125 acres of improved land (i.e., cleared) on which were grown 200 bushels of wheat, 1500 bushels of corn, 75 bushels of oats, and 30 tons of hay in 1859. In addition, the farm supported 4 horses, 4 milk cows (from which 100 pounds of butter were produced), 16 beef cattle, and 56 hogs. The livestock was valued at $720, and $400 worth of livestock had been slaughtered during the year ending 1 June 1860. This farm had a cash value of $4,000, and $100 of farm implements were used upon it.

Similarly, the second farm, operated by William Stout (see also Fig. 2.1) was valued at $2,000 and had 45 improved acres and 115 unimproved (uncleared) acres. The farm used $100 in implements and had 4 horses, 4 cows (again producing 100 pounds of butter), 5 beef cattle, 6 sheep, and 27 hogs. This livestock was valued at $500. Farmer Stout during the 1859 crop year produced 100 bushels of wheat, 800 bushels of corn, and 10 bushels of irish potatoes, and slaughtered livestock worth $70.

None of the farms on these pages cultivated a great diversity of crops. No rye, rice, tobacco, cotton, sweet potatoes, barley, wine, market garden crops, clover seed, grass seed, hops, hemp, flax, flaxseed, silk, maple sugar, cane sugar, beeswax, or honey were produced. A few produced wool, two grew buckwheat, and six had orchards. One farm, operated by Roland Gray (line 11) made 100 pounds of cheese and $20 worth of home-manufactured products. Two farms (line 8 and line 29) produced some molasses from sorghum, which was introduced to American farmers by the U.S. Patent Office in the 1850s. It quickly became a "fad" crop, grown by most "improving" farmers.

A number of the other farms on this page are noteworthy for one reason or another. The farm of Joel Darrah (line 10), for example, had an extraordinary number of horses (34), suggesting that one aspect of its operation was horse breeding. This same farm also had a substantial stockyard with 75 head of cattle and 100 hogs. Darrah slaughtered $4,250 of livestock during the year. He produced 150 tons of hay and 600 bushels of corn, but no oats for the horses. This farm probably purchased additional feed if the livestock were fed according to typical standards. Although not shown, the population schedules for Honey Creek Township indicate that Joel Darrah was a 52-year-old doctor and that his farm was probably operated by hired help who lived in the Darrah household.[3] This farm was one of those for which no farmer was recorded but two nonnuclear males in the household, one 19, the other, 22, reported occupations as laborer. Similarly, L. A. Weed whose farm is listed on line 35 reported his occupation as broom maker. So too did his son and father, but there was a 17-year-old in the household who listed his occupation as laborer. The farm operated by Joseph Hunter (line 26) was one of those not matched with the population schedules.

The census questionnaire seems relatively straightforward and unambiguous, except for the questions relating to the value of the farm, its implements, and livestock. Yet, even a casual examination of the records reveals pervasive rounding errors in the measurement of almost every item. While it is conceivable that farm acreages were frequently multiples of five and ten, it is less plausible that crop outputs were. Only livestock inventories appear to have been immune from this kind of bias. However, to the extent that the numbers were subject to true round-off error, the errors should cancel in the aggregate.

The 1860 Census did neglect one important aspect of farming: Tenancy. Indeed, no statistics were collected on tenancy until 1880. Occasionally, however, an enumerator made a notation on the manuscripts that his respondent, the farm operator, was a tenant. Allan Bogue, for example, discovered that an assistant marshal of Jones County, Iowa, in 1860 had noted the tenure status of those persons who did not own real estate and we also discovered similar marginal notation on the census manuscripts from time to time.[4] The infrequency of such notation has, however, led to other efforts to identify tenants. Bogue argued that those persons named in the agricultural schedules as operating a farm and who listed their occupation as farmer on the population schedules but reported

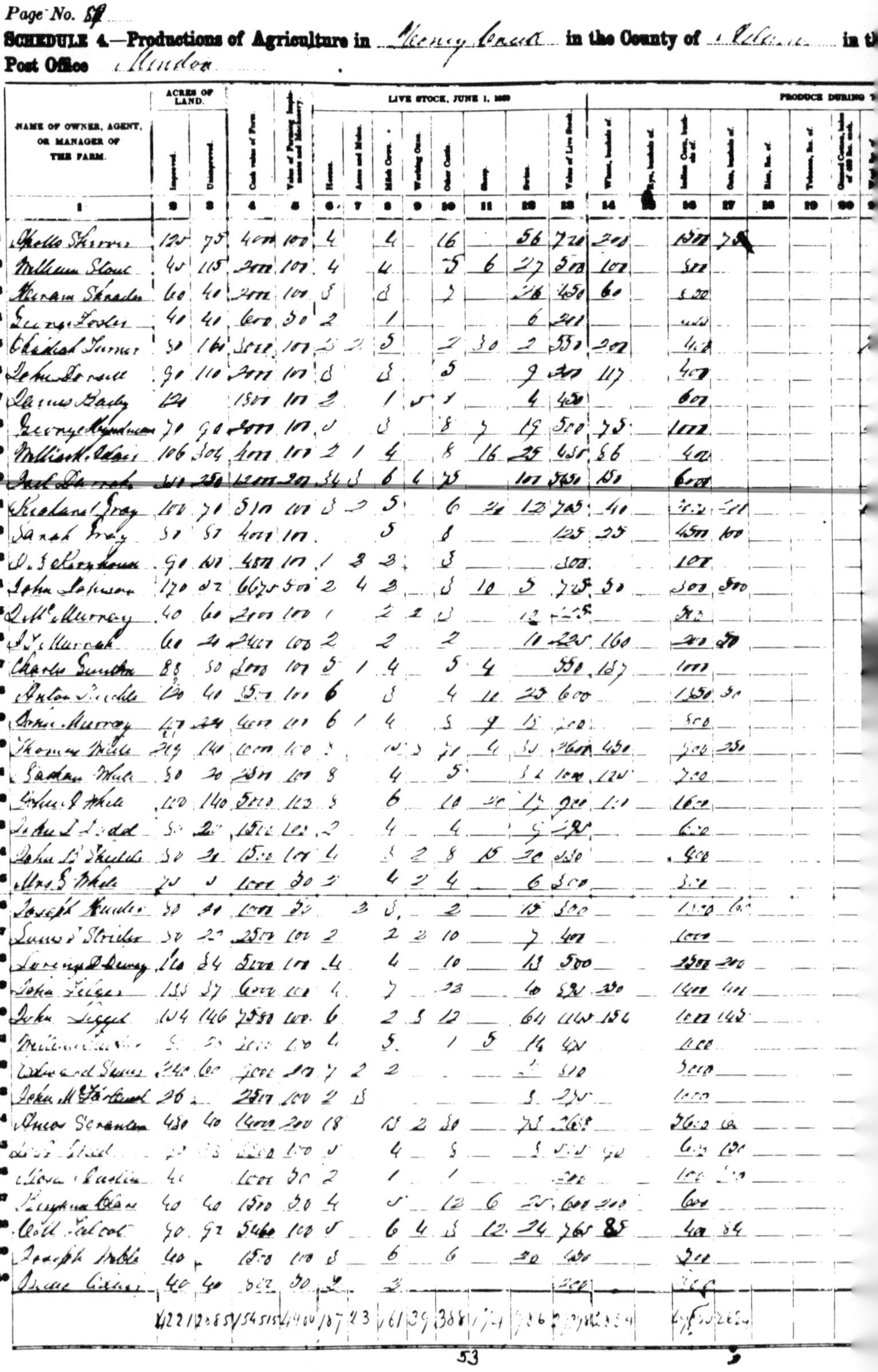

Page No. 59

SCHEDULE 4.—Productions of Agriculture in Honey Creek **in the County of** Adams? **in th**[e]

Post Office Mendon

NAME OF OWNER, AGENT, OR MANAGER OF THE FARM.	ACRES OF LAND. Improved.	ACRES OF LAND. Unimproved.	Cash value of Farm.	Value of Farming Implements and Machinery.	LIVE STOCK, JUNE 1, 1860. Horses.	Asses and Mules.	Milch Cows.	Working Oxen.	Other Cattle.	Sheep.	Swine.	Value of Live Stock.	PRODUCE DURING [THE YEAR] Wheat, bushels of.	Rye, bushels of.	Indian Corn, bushels of.	Oats, bushels of.	Rice, lbs. of.	Tobacco, lbs. of.	Ginned Cotton, bales of 400 lbs. each.
1	2	3	4	5	6	7	8	9	10	11	12	13	14	15	16	17	18	19	20
1 Skello Shrover?	125	75	4000	100	4		4		16		56	720	200		1500	75			
2 William Stone	45	115	2000	100	4		4		5	6	27	300	100		300				
3 Hiram Shrader	60	40	2000	100	5		8		2		26	450	60		500				
4 George Fowler	40	40	600	50	2		1				6	200			400?				
5 Obadiah Turner	30	160	3000	100	2	2	5		2	30	2	550	200		400				
6 John Dorsell	90	110	3000	100	8		3		5		9	300	117		400				
7 James Baily	120		1800	100	2		1	5	1		4	450			600				
8 George Hyndman	70	90	2000	100	3		3		8	7	19	500	75		1000				
9 William Adair	106	304	4000	100	2	1	4		8	16	25	635	56		400				
10 Joel Darrah?	350	250	12000	200	34	3	6	4	75		107	3450	150		6000				
11 Richard Gray	100	70	5100	100	3	2	5		6	4?	12	705	40		300?	50?			
12 Sarah Gray	50	50	4000	100			5		8			125	25		450	100			
13 D. J. Stephens?	90	100	4800	100	1	2	2		3			300			100				
14 John Johnson	170	32	6675	500	2	4	2		3	10	5	725	30		300	500			
15 D. McMurray	40	60	2000	100	1		2	2	3		12	225			500?				
16 J. McMurrah?	60	20	2400	100	2		2		2		10	225	160		200	50			
17 Charles Smith	88	50	5000	100	5	1	4		5	4		550	187		1000				
18 Anton [illegible]	120	40	3500	100	6		3		4	11	23	600			1350	50			
19 John Murray	47	24	4000	100	6	1	4		5	4	15	200			500				
20 Thomas White	219	140	6000	100	3?		10	3	70?	4	33	2600	450		900	250			
21 Gideon White	50	30	2500	100	8		4		5		32	1000	120		700				
22 John S. White	100	140	5000	100	8		6		10	20	17	900	100		1600				
23 John S. Dodd	50	20	1500	100	2		4		4		9	325?			600				
24 John W. Shields	30	21	1500	100	4		3	2	8	15	30	350			400				
25 Mrs. S. White	75	5	1000	50	2		4	2	4		6	300			300				
26 Joseph Kunkle?	30	30	1000	30		3	3		2		15	300			1500	100			
27 Samuel Strider?	30	20	2500	100	2		2	2	10		7	400			1000				
28 Lorenzo D. Dewey	160	84	5000	100	4		4		10		13	500			2500	200			
29 John Tilden?	133	37	6000	100	4		7		23		40	590	350		1400	400			
30 John Siggel?	154	146	7580	100	6		2	3	12		64	1100	154		1000	145			
31 [illegible]	5?	55?	2000	100	4		5		1	5	14	425			400				
32 Edward Stone	240	60	9000	100	7	2	2				2	510			3000				
33 John McFarland	26		2500	100	2	3					3	225			1000				
34 Amos Scranton	430	40	14000	200	18		13	2	30		73	2650			3600	100?			
35 [illegible]	20?	50?	2200	100	5		4		5		3	500	90		600	130			
36 [illegible]	40		1000	30	2		1		1			200			100	50?			
37 Benjamin Blair?	40	40	1500	30	4		5		12	6	25	600	200		600				
38 Colt? Talcott	40	92	5460	100	5		6	4	3	12	24	765	85		400	84			
39 Joseph Noble	40		1500	100	3		6		6		30	430			300				
40 Oscar Chiss?	40	40	800	30	2		3					200			300				
	4221	2085	154515	4400	187	23	161	39	388	174	786	27982	2354		41950	2684?			

53

FIG. 7.1. Copy of the Agricultural Manuscript Form Used and Data Collected by the Census Enumerator for the Eighth Census, 1860.

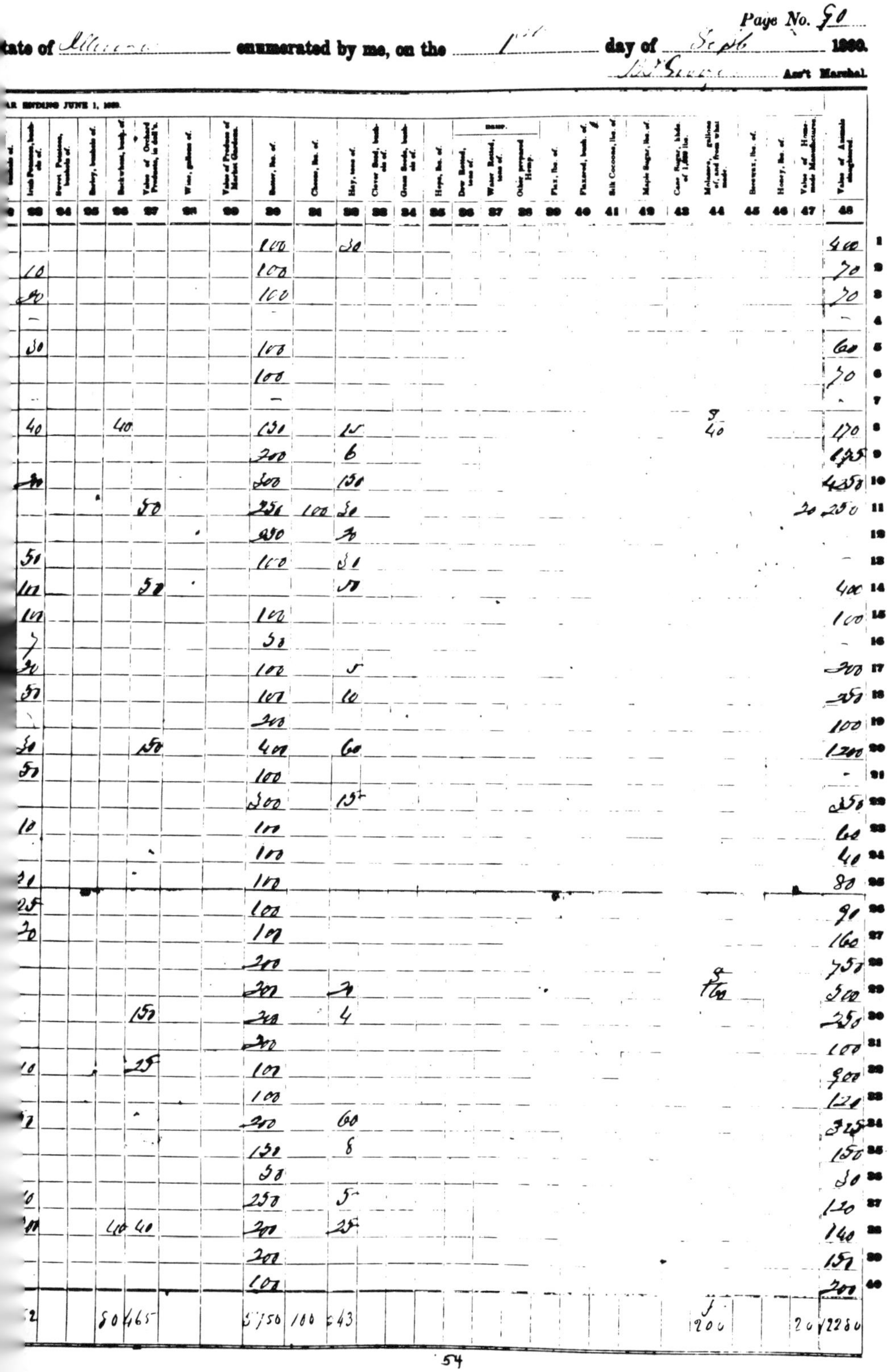

Page No. 90

[S]tate of Illinois enumerated by me, on the 1st day of Sept 1860.

[illegible] Ass't Marshal.

[YE]AR ENDING JUNE 1, 1860.

Row	22	23 Irish Potatoes, bushels of	24 Sweet Potatoes, bushels of	25 Barley, bushels of	26 Buckwheat, bush. of	27 Value of Orchard Products, in dollars	28 Wine, gallons of	29 Value of Produce of Market Gardens	30 Butter, lbs. of	31 Cheese, lbs. of	32 Hay, tons of	33 Clover Seed, bushels of	34 Grass Seeds, bushels of	35 Hops, lbs. of	36 Hemp: Dew Rotted, tons of	37 Hemp: Water Rotted, tons of	38 Other prepared Hemp	39 Flax, lbs. of	40 Flaxseed, bush. of	41 Silk Cocoons, lbs. of	42 Maple Sugar, lbs. of	43 Cane Sugar, hhds. of 1,000 lbs.	44 Molasses, gallons of, and from what made	45 Beeswax, lbs. of	46 Honey, lbs. of	47 Value of Home-made Manufactures	48 Value of Animals slaughtered
1									100		30																400
2		10							100																		70
3		20							100																		70
4		—							—																		—
5		30							100																		60
6									100																		70
7		..							—																		.
8		40			40				130		15												8 40				170
9									200		6																175
10		20							300		150																425
11						50			250	100	30															20	250
12									200		20																
13		50							100		30																—
14		100				50					50																400
15		100							100																		100
16		7							50																		—
17		20							100		5																200
18		50							100		10																250
19									200																		100
20		30				150			400		60																1200
21		50							100																		-
22									300		15																250
23		10							100																		60
24									100																		40
25		20							100																		80
26		25							100																		90
27		20							100																		160
28									200																		750
29									200		20												8 160				500
30						150			200		4																250
31									200																		100
32		10				25			100																		900
33									100																		120
34		7							200		60																325
35									130		8																150
36									30																		30
37		10							250		5																120
38		20			40	40			200		25																140
39									200																		150
40									100																		200
Total		2			80	465			5750	100	243												8 200			20	2280

54

FIG. 7.1. *(continued)*

no real estate were tenants.[5] He also identifies a separate class of "farmers without farms" who gave occupations as farmer but for whom no farm was located and no real estate value was reported. In his study of tenancy in Iowa, D. Winters has a similar definition except that in computing tenancy rates he uses a different denominator to that employed by Bogue.[6] Whereas Bogue used all persons who listed themselves as farmers on the population schedules for the denominator, Winters used only those listed in the agricultural schedules.

According to Donald Ginter, enumerators in the South deliberately listed persons who called themselves farmers but who were really tenants as having no real estate. But he further argues that they would also list no farm value or acreage on the agricultural schedules. Production data would, however, be recorded. This convention seems not to have been followed in the North, otherwise tenancy rates were extremely low. Ginter also mentions variants of this convention such as recording acreage and farm value in whole or in part, but not listing any real estate value on the population manuscripts.[7] To the extent that tenants by implication were poorer than owner-occupiers, we would expect—other things equal—they would have smaller farms with fewer improvements and there is thus no way of distinguishing this hypothesis from Ginter's alternative of partial recording of these values.

We argue that there existed two kinds of tenants. There were those who had no land of their own. They are identified as those who listed their occupation as farmer and for whom a farm was located in the agricultural schedules but who reported no real estate. Bogue, Winters, and Ginter would also classify them as tenants. There was, however, a second group of tenants who listed their occupation as farmer and for whom a farm was located in the agricultural schedules but who owned only a fraction of the land that they farmed. This group is identified by a value of real estate on the population schedules that was less than the value of the farm that they operated. Such farmers are common today and they also proved numerous in the nineteenth century. About a third of all tenants, they have been ignored by other researchers.

In Table 7.1 we show the breakdown by state and tenancy of the farms in the sample. The tenancy rate was highest in Maryland, where more than half of the farms were operated by tenants. It was lowest in Michigan. Tenancy proved to be surprisingly high on the Kansas and Minnesota frontiers where the rate exceeded one-third, despite the abundance of cheap land in the immediate vicinity, and the rate was generally higher in the Midwest than the Northeast.

As we show in Chapter 8, tenant farms as a class differed in a number of ways from those of the yeomanry, but individually they were indistinguishable from one another. Three of the farms on the sample page for

TABLE 7.1. Distribution of Sample Farms by State and Tenancy Including Those without Farmers and Those without Population

State/ Region	Total Number of Farms	Farms without People	Farms without Farmers	Farms Matched with Population	Yeomen Farms[a]	Tenants in Part[b]	Tenants in Whole[c]	Tenancy Rate per Thousand[d]
Illinois	937	31	56	850	698	36	116	179
Indiana	3,314	193	211	2,910	2,298	170	442	210
Iowa	366	12	28	326	264	19	43	190
Kansas	318	27	52	239	159	22	58	335
Michigan	623	7	40	576	535	29	12	71
Minnesota	210	3	16	191	121	10	60	366
Missouri	899	18	87	794	631	44	119	205
Ohio	518	40	56	422	364	41	17	137
Wisconsin	363	5	15	343	304	22	17	114
Midwest	7,548	336	561	6,651	5,374	393	884	192
Connecticut	102	0	17	85	78	3	4	82
Maryland	290	19	14	257	113	25	119	560
New Hampshire	462	16	49	397	359	28	10	96
New Jersey	151	9	37	105	89	9	7	152
New York	2,062	33	132	1,897	1,748	71	78	79
Pennsylvania	1,241	41	207	993	788	64	141	206
Vermont	83	0	5	78	66	8	4	154
Northeast	4,391	118	461	3,812	3,241	208	363	150

[a]Farms matched with population for which the value of the farm was less than or equal to the reported value of real estate owned by the household.

[b]Farms matched with population for which the value of the farm was greater than the value of real estate owned by the household, but the household reported ownership of some real estate.

[c]Farms matched with population, but the household reported no real estate.

[d]Tenants in whole or part per one thousand farms matched with population.

Honey Creek Township, for example, were operated by people whom we identify as tenants—J. L. Murnah (line 16), Nathan White (line 21), and Mrs. G. White (line 25). Other than the zero value of real estate on the population schedules, they appear little different from other farms in the area.

Data for the average farm with 3 or more improved acres are shown in Table 7.2. Farms in New Jersey were by far the most expensive in the sample, averaging $5,274 for a 69-acre farm or $76.40 per acre. Their high value per acre may be due in part to their high ratio of improved to unimproved land which, judging from the crop output and livestock data, must have been farmed quite intensively. Furthermore, these New Jersey farms used, on average, more farm implements than others despite their smaller average size. Farms in Minnesota, on the other hand, show the lowest average value per acre, $6.78, partly because fewer than 20 percent of the acres on the average farm were under cultivation. Neverthe-

TABLE 7.2. Average Sample Farm Characteristics for Farms with 3 or More Improved Acres, 1859–1860

	A. Farm Statistics					B. Livestock Inventories							
State/Region	Number of Farms	Farm Value ($)	Value of Implements ($)	Improved Acreage	Unimproved Acreage	Horses	Oxen	Milk Cows	Cattle	Sheep	Hogs	Value of Livestock ($)	Value of Livestock Slaughtered ($)
Connecticut	101	3.445	72	78	42	1.1	2.6	3.4	4.5	2.8	2.4	436	146
Maryland	290	2,097	35	70	84	1.5	2.3	1.9	3.8	5.2	11.6	245	73
New Hampshire	462	1,860	87	90	44	1.2	1.8	2.4	3.5	15.6	1.2	358	59
New Jersey	151	5,274	195	51	18	2.5	0.4	3.5	1.7	1.9	4.0	370	65
New York	2,059	3,905	142	88	28	2.7	0.6	6.3	4.1	22.6	3.6	590	82
Pennsylvania	1,196	3,861	127	67	46	2.8	0.4	4.3	4.8	10.3	6.4	458	104
Vermont	83	3,327	123	78	32	1.8	1.5	2.7	6.0	4.0	4.5	493	62
Eastern Region	4,342	3,581	125	79	39	2.4	0.8	4.9	4.2	15.8	4.7	493	86
Illinois	930	2,676	135	95	53	3.6	0.7	3.5	5.5	3.7	14.1	502	110
Indiana	3,213	2,611	88	2	61	3.3	0.4	2.7	4.4	7.5	19.8	409	80
Iowa	366	2,066	84	55	95	2.6	0.9	2.7	4.9	4.2	13.4	361	68
Kansas	315	1,716	97	45	136	2.7	2.1	3.1	5.4	2.3	14.3	438	72
Michigan	612	1,568	64	33	54	1.5	0.9	2.7	3.8	7.6	5.5	272	51
Minnesota	208	990	58	29	117	0.8	1.6	1.7	2.3	0.0	5.6	180	42
Missouri	792	1,977	87	80	117	4.5	1.4	3.5	7.4	12.8	22.9	622	88
Ohio	508	3,443	69	82	40	3.4	0.3	3.8	4.5	41.5	8.2	450	60
Wisconsin	362	1,756	84	52	88	2.1	1.5	3.4	4.9	4.2	4.9	252	46
Western Region	7,306	2,367	90	65	72	3.1	0.8	3.0	4.9	9.2	15.7	420	77
North	11,648	2,819	103	70	59	2.9	0.8	3.7	4.6	11.6	11.6	447	80

TABLE 7.2. *(Continued)*

C. Output of Principal Crops and Products (rounded to whole numbers)

State/Region	Wheat (bu)	Rye (bu)	Corn (bu)	Oats (bu)	Wool (lb)	Tobacco (lb)	Irish Potatoes (bu)	Barley (bu)	Buck-wheat (bu)	Butter (lb)	Cheese (lb)	Hay (ton)	Maple Sugar (lb)	Home Manufac-tures ($)
Connecticut	2	41	73	55	7	12	40	0	25	241	8	26	1	0
Maryland	28	0	450	153	9	0	35	0	0	45	0	0	0	5
New Hampshire	12	4	36	25	57	0	107	3	1	203	82	20	79	0
New Jersey	58	17	306	211	0	0	55	0	26	329	0	14	0	0
New York	46	32	106	203	89	1	95	27	27	567	423	18	67	4
Pennsylvania	40	29	144	176	28	0	69	1	41	389	40	12	27	3
Vermont	5	19	141	137	14	122	84	0	1	189	19	22	7	42
Eastern Region	38	26	139	169	57	3	82	13	26	421	221	16	48	4
Illinois	147	4	818	87	10	185	30	2	2	223	15	15	0	17
Indiana	127	2	539	42	18	102	27	2	3	136	3	5	5	9
Iowa	103	5	679	85	11	7	53	3	4	178	8	11	8	6
Kansas	54	0	748	21	4	5	50	0	10	205	6	11	0	2
Michigan	57	7	128	31	24	2	77	1	9	236	37	10	121	2
Minnesota	69	10	158	94	0	1	113	4	2	116	13	17	42	0
Missouri	18	3	656	21	30	49	10	0	2	105	2	4	3	20
Ohio	34	4	315	110	139	1114	38	4	22	253	194	10	17	5
Wisconsin	240	2	96	158	15	0	55	3	1	160	7	14	37	2
Western Region	105	3	520	58	26	151	37	2	5	166	22	8	17	9
North	80	12	378	99	37	96	54	6	13	261	96	11	29	7

less, these Minnesota farms achieved creditably high outputs of field crops. The implement value on Maryland farms was lowest among all sampled states, possibly because slaves were substitutes for mechanization. The average western farm used fewer implements than its eastern counterpart; it was also somewhat larger but with a higher ratio of unimproved to improved land, and was less valuable.

The livestock inventories show that western farms generally used more draft animals than eastern farms, which would be consistent with the rigors of breaking new land and the more extensive cultivation of field crops on western acreages. They also kept more hogs and beef cattle, a well-known means of marketing surplus grains in areas with poor transportation. On the other hand, the eastern farms had more milk cows because of their proximity to market for perishable dairy products. Indeed, the average eastern farmer produced ten times as much cheese as the western and about two and a half times as much butter. As these ratios greatly exceed those of cows on eastern farms to those on western farms, we can conclude either that the eastern animals were much more productive than their western counterparts, or that western farmers found alternate uses for milk such as for livestock feed.

The crop data emphasize the preeminence of grain crops in the Midwest, particularly corn and wheat. Midwestern farms produced on average almost three times as much wheat and four times as much corn as those in the East. Oats, rye, and buckwheat on the other hand were much more extensively grown there than in the West. Hay was another major eastern crop, possibly because of the demand for winter horse fodder from the cities.

These data have been tested against the published census totals for significant differences in means. The results are not reported because we consider the exercise to be of dubious scientific value and more likely to lead the reader to erroneous conclusions. Hypothesis testing involves the implicit assumption that the population values are known with certainty. Unfortunately, there is considerable evidence of error in the compilation of those data.

We are able to gauge, to a degree, the extent of error in the published census by using the original manuscripts to retabulate summary data for four counties in Minnesota–Cottonwood, Mahnomen, Murray, and Polk–which were so sparsely populated that complete recompilation was both feasible and simple. There were numerous errors and omissions, particularly in the reports for Mahnomen and Murray. None were made with Polk. The variations between manuscript and published data are shown in Table 7.3. None of these errors arose from totaling long strings of figures. There were only two farms in Cottonwood, sixteen in Mahnomen, and three in Murray. In Polk County, where the clerks preparing for

TABLE 7.3. Differences between the Manuscript Census Data for Three Minnesota Counties and the Published County Totals

Item	Cottonwood		Mahnomen		Murray	
	Manu-script Census	Pub-lished Census	Manu-script Census	Pub-lished Census	Manu-script Census	Pub-lished Census
Improved Acres					44	40
Horses			28	33		
Cows			35	38		
Swine			65	69		
Livestock Value			4,610	5,210		
Rye			346	65		
Oats			7,775	8,175		
Peas and Beans					9	12
Potatoes			6,985	7,065	145	285
Buckwheat	7	70				
Butter			1,640	1,810	580	1,080
Cheese					0	50
Hay	10	40	750	850	54	94
Value of Livestock Slaughtered ($)			1,050	1,250	57	113

Source: U.S. Census Office, Eighth Census, 1860. *Agriculture of the United States in 1860* (Washington, D.C., 1864), 80–83.

the published census made no mistakes, there were six farms. Furthermore, the errors, rather than offsetting one another, tended to be mutually reinforcing. One cannot, therefore, rely upon appeal to the Central Limit theorem as a basis for using the published census. Mistakes such as these discovered in relatively small populations must give rise to concern about the extent of error in more complex populations such as might be found in Illinois, Ohio, New York, or Pennsylvania. More limited, specific examination suggest that they were common.

Among users of census data, the heavy hand of the "Washington gnome" is well known. Crossing out information reported by the original enumerators and substituting what they considered appropriate numbers, the Washington compilers often greatly altered the published summary of figures. Most experienced users are skeptical of the validity of these alterations, believing the original data to be, on balance, more accurate. Certainly our comparisons of the original data with the published summaries would provide sufficient evidence to impeach any work based upon those published figures.

Our census data were supplemented by a sizable amount of additional source materials, all of which are discussed in the text. One merits specific elaboration here. There is evidence of systematic variations resulting from soil type, thus we have deliberately introduced soil differences into our analyses at various points. Although we took our soil types from

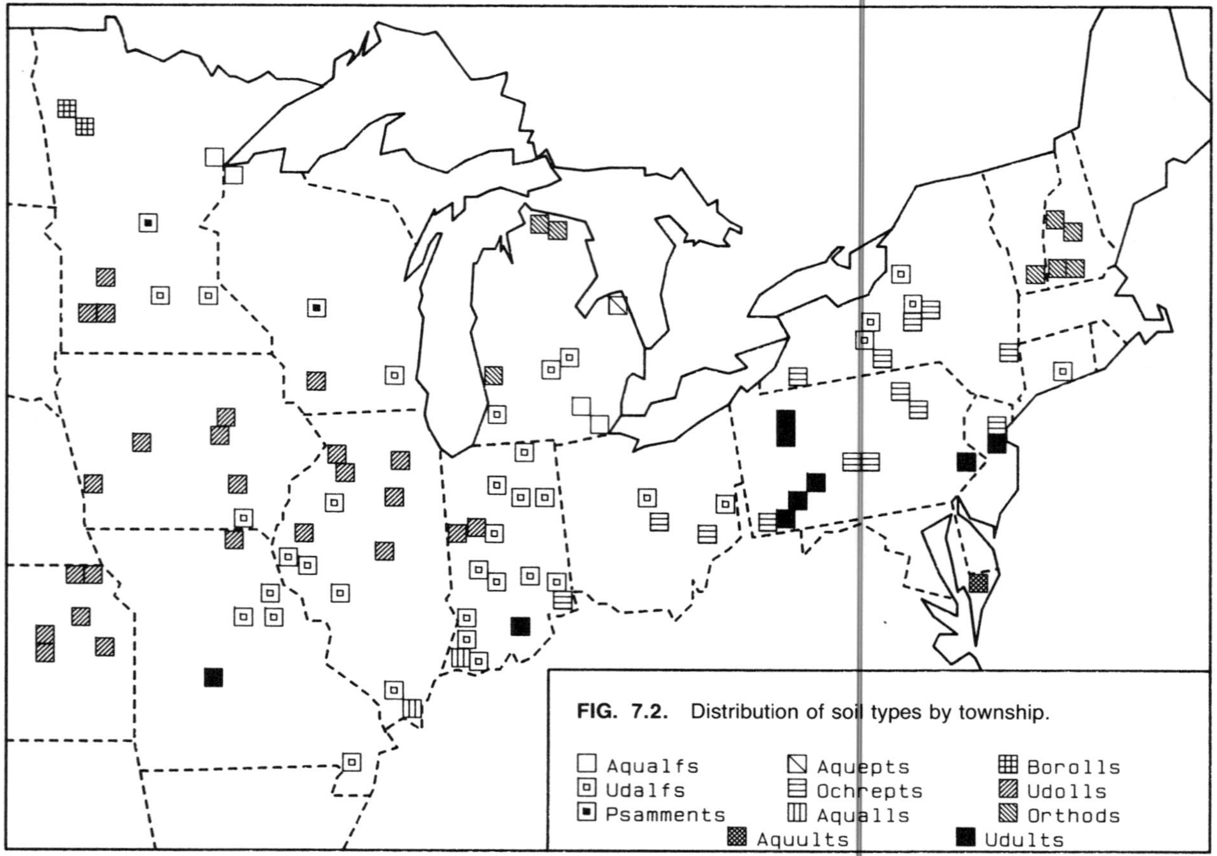

FIG. 7.2. Distribution of soil types by township.

a map with a scale of approximately 1 inch to 120 miles (1:7,500,000), thirty-nine subgroups of soils were distinguishable. We therefore reduced these to eleven groups for which the U.S. Geological Survey provided an appraisal of their agricultural suitability.[8] These belonged to six major soil types. The geographic distribution of the eleven soil groups is shown in Figure 7.2. Their suitability for crops is shown in Table 7.4. This soil classification is far from comprehensive. Modern soil surveys classify

TABLE 7.4. Soil Types and Farming Suitability

Soil Type	Use
Aqualfs	Used for general crops where drained and for pasture and woodland where undrained.
Udalfs	Row crops, small grains, and pasture
Psamments	Used for range and wild hay
Aquepts	Pasture, hay, and woodland pasture
Ochrepts	Pasture, silage corn, small grains, and hay
Aqualls	Pasture and, where drained, small grains, corn, and potatoes
Borolls	Small grains, hay, and pasture
Udolls	Corn and small grains
Orthods	Woodland, hay pasture, fruit, and, on gently sloping areas, potatoes and truck crops
Aquults	Used for limited pasture and woodland. Where drained, some hay, corn, and truck crops
Udults	General farming, woodland, and pastures. Cotton and tobacco in some parts

soils covering areas as small as 5 acres if markedly different from neighboring soils and all of our townships contained more than one separately identifiable soil. Our classification is only a broad generalization of that diversity, characterizing the dominant soil type.

Finally, to allow the reader to know the exact specification of questions asked of farmers, we reproduce in the following Appendix the instructions given to the census enumerators. The responses gained are the foundation for what follows in ensuing chapters.

APPENDIX TO CHAPTER SEVEN

SPECIAL INSTRUCTIONS

SCHEDULE NO. 4—AGRICULTURE

This schedule is to be filled up in the following manner: Insert in the heading the name of the district, town, or township, and the county or parish, and the State in which the farms enumerated are located, and insert the date when the enumeration was made. This is to be attested on each page of every set by signing the schedule.

In many agricultural returns, the amount stated must sometimes be *estimated*, as the number of bushels of wheat or of oats; but under other headings, as to the number of live stock, the precise number or amount can usually be stated. The Assistant must use his discretion in assisting a farmer to estimate fairly and accurately the amount of his crops, when he keeps no exact account; and in all instances it is desired to make the nearest approximate returns which the case will admit of.

The returns of all farms or plantations, the produce of which amounts to one hundred dollars in value, is to be included in this schedule, but it is not intended to include the returns of small lots, owned or worked by persons following mechanical or other pursuits, or where the productions are not one hundred dollars in value.

1. *Name of Owner.*—Under heading 1, entitled *Name of individual managing his farm or plantation*, insert the name of the person residing upon or having charge of the farm, whether as owner, agent, or tenant. When owned or managed by more than one person, the name of one only may be entered.

2. *Quantity of Land Improved.*—Under general heading, *Acres of land*, and under particular heading, *Improved land*, insert the number of acres of improved land, by which is meant, cleared land used for grazing, grass, or tillage, or which is now fallow, connected with or belonging to the farm which the Assistant Marshal is reporting. It is not necessary that it should be contiguous, but it must be owned or managed by the person whose name is inserted in the column. By improved land is meant all pasture, meadow, and arable land which has been reclaimed from a state of nature, and which continues to be reclaimed and used for the purposes of production.

3. *Unimproved Land.*—Under heading *Unimproved*, insert the number of acres of unimproved land connected with the farm. It is not necessary that it should be *contiguous* to the improved land, but may be a wood lot, or other land at some

distance, but owned in connection with the farm, the timber or range of which is used for farm purposes. By unimproved land is meant all the land belonging to each proprietor which does not come within the term improved. The quantity embraced under the two heads "improved and unimproved" includes the whole number of acres owned by the proprietor.

Should there be irreclaimable marshes of great extent, rendering the land unimprovable, you will not include them, and you will not omit all bodies of water of greater extent than 10 acres. That is to say, if a body of land comprises ten thousand acres, and nine thousand thereof be covered by a lake, you will return the land at 1,000 acres.

4. *Value of Farms.* – Under heading No. 4, *Cash value of farm,* include the actual cash value of the whole number of acres returned by you as improved and unimproved. In this, as in all cases where an amount of money is stated, make your figures represent dollars; thus, if the cash value of the farm by five thousand dollars, insert simply the figures 5,000. This rule must be particularly and carefully observed in all cases amounts of money are to be entered in the columns.

5. *Value of Farming Implements.* – Under heading No. 5 place the aggregate value of all the farming or planting implements and machinery, including wagons, threshing-machines, cotton-gins, sugar-mills; in fact, all implements and machinery used to cultivate and produce crops and fit the same for market or consumption.

6 to 10. *Live Stock.* – Under general heading, *Live stock, 1st June, 1860,* of the whole number of animals which belong to the farm on the 1st day of June, the number of each description thereof are to be inserted under the proper headings, taking care that under heading *Other cattle,* you insert the number of all cattle not before enumerated, which are one year old and older.

11. *Sheep.* – The number of all sheep which, on the 1st day of June, were of one or more years old, is to be inserted in column 11.

12. *Swine.* – under heading 12, insert the number of swine on the farm on the 1st day of June.

13. *Value of Live Stock.* – Inasmuch as the foregoing entries will not embrace all the live stock, it is intended that the aggregate *value* of every description of live stock owned on the 1st day of June shall be inserted in column 13.

14 to 45. *Produce of the Year.* – Insert in the appropriate columns the whole number of tons, bales, bushels, pounds, or value, according to the several headings, of the various crops produced within the year ending June 1, 1860. The quantity of grain gathered during the year is to be recorded, and all productions of the year, although they may not have been sold or consumed, are to be enumerated in their proper places; but nothing produced after the first day of June is to be inserted. Enumerate such hemp as may have been prepared for market, or give the quantity of prepared hemp which would be produced were it in marketable condition – the growth of the year ending the 1st day of June.

Market Gardens.—By market gardens (29) are meant such as are devoted to the production of vegetables and other articles for sale, and may include nurseries. *Clover and Grass Seeds.*—In enumerating clover and grass seeds, (33, 34, *sic*) you are to include only that which has been cleaned for use or prepared for the market.

46. *Molasses.*—In column (46) for molasses, wherever this article is not produced from the cane, you will designate the kind of molasses, by inserting in the space over the figures in each case the letter M maple, and the letter S for sorghum; or you may write out these words in full over the figures describing the quantity; the latter would be the most satisfactory mode. Where the molasses is made from cane, the space may be left blank, in other respects than by entering the quantity produced.

47. *Value of Home-made Manufactures.*—Under this heading is to be included the value of all articles manufactured within the year preceding the 1st day of June, in or by the family, whether for home use or for sale. If the raw material has been purchased for such manufacture, the value of such raw material should not be included; the object being to ascertain the value of manufactures by the family from their productions, or the value of the labor expended on the productions of others. This discrimination is important.

48. *Animals Slaughtered.*—Under heading 48, insert in dollars the value of all animals slaughtered during the year.

CHAPTER EIGHT

Farm and Frontier: The Relative Costs of Farm Making

ACQUISITION OF LAND WAS FUNDAMENTAL to creating a yeoman farm. Nineteenth-century legislation progressively liberalized the terms by which lands from the public domain were transferred to private uses.[1] For those with limited means, public sales offered a chance for land ownership and farm formation at minimum cost, while for the eastern farmer, selling out and moving westward, they offered the opportunity for a more extensive farm which could provide economically viable inheritances for family members. Many, however, could not afford the entry costs to farming, even in the Midwest. Tenancy rates were higher and economic opportunities outside farming, more restricted; despite this, people moved west, taking up these lands from the public domain.

Government-owned land sold at public auctions was subject to a reservation price determined by legislative edict. After 1820 this was set at $1.25 per acre, but under the terms of the 1854 Graduation Act prices were progressively reduced for unsold parcels. These legislative entry terms probably had some effect upon sales but a far stronger influence seems to have been the price of wheat (Fig. 8.1). The sharp year-to-year fluctuations in public land sales show a strong positive correlation with wheat prices.[2] Since wheat was a major cash crop, it can be argued that the demand for land was affected by the potential profits from commercial farming, but because the discounted present value of expected profits also determines the market price of land, the proof is not conclusive.

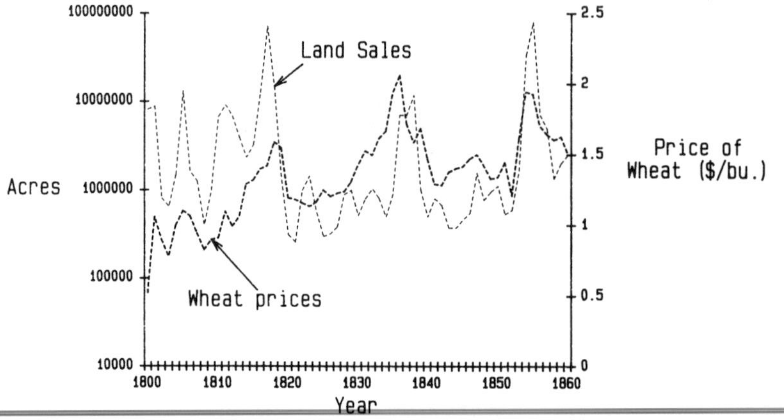

FIG. 8.1. Public land sales and the price of wheat, 1800–1860.

Pure land speculators purchased land in the sole expectation of a profitable rise in its market price. They are distinguished by the size of their land and their lack of active involvement in farming. The former is simply a distributional question of who captured the capital gains from land value appreciation: the government, the farmer, or the speculator. The speculator's lack of interest in farming, however, has a social cost to the extent that it involved foregone production.

Consider first the case of a land speculator with perfect knowledge, who would know the true time path of the price of any piece of land.[3] Suppose further that he alone possesses this knowledge. Let the time path be given by P_0P_t in Figure 8.2. The vertical axis is a ratio scale for the price of land, and time is measured along the horizontal axis.

When the government first releases land for sale at time t_0, it is worth less than the reservation price of $1.25 per acre and so is not sold at auction. Persons lacking information about the future trend in the price of this land would therefore be unwilling to buy it until time t_m when its market value has risen to the reservation price.

The speculator will, however, buy the land sooner, say $t_m - d$, where d depends in part upon the probability that others will discover the superior information. If this probability is very low then, other things equal, d will be small. This will increase the speculator's return and reduce the time he holds the land before reselling it. Having bought thc land at time $t_m - d$ for the government reservation price of $1.25 per acre, the profit-maximizing speculator could hold the land until time t_r, when it is resold for price P_r. The rate of return is given by the slope of the line RR', which is at a maximum when tangent to P_0P_t.

This solution is not the best the speculator can achieve. Once he acquires the land, his self-interest dictates revealing his specialist knowledge to the general population and convincing them, say at time t_z, that the land will be worth price P_z. If he is successful, then the price of the land will rise to its discounted present value (in this case, price P_x), which lies along line PV depending upon the time at which the speculator successfully convinces the populace of the validity of his knowledge. If the public becomes convinced any time before time t_d, the speculator will earn a rate of return higher than that offered by the "sit-tight-and-wait" policy. For example, if the market accepts his information at time t_x, the speculator's rate of return will be shown by the slope of the line RM, which is greater than the slope of RR'. The tendency for local taxing authorities to levy higher than average taxes on the land of absentee landlords provided yet another strong inducement for a quick resale.[4]

As drawn in Figure 8.2, time $t_x <$ time t_m, that is, the time at which the land is brought into production is earlier than it would have been in the absence of this speculator with superior information. Yet it could have been later, the timing being dependent upon how quickly he can impart

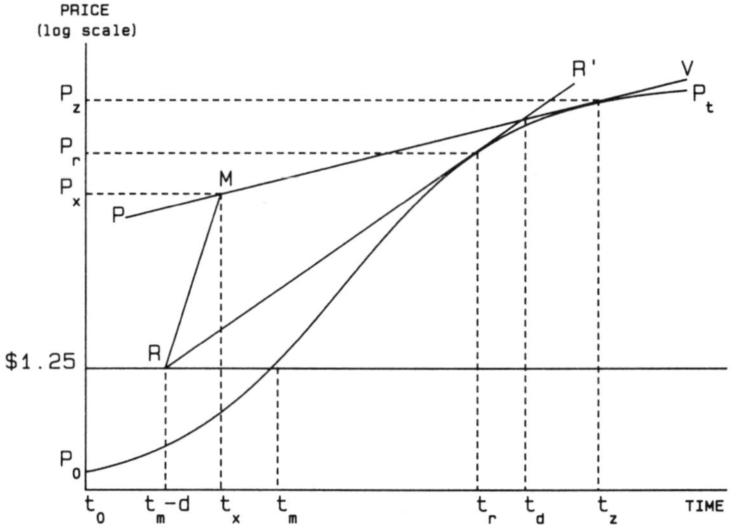

FIG. 8.2. Land speculator with superior information.

his knowledge and convince the buyers in the market of its veracity. The speculator adopting this strategy may be faced by a decision at time t_r: If the market is not as yet convinced of the value of his information, he must choose between the lower but certain return, RR', offered by the "sit-tight-and-wait" policy, or gamble that the information will be accepted sometime between time t_r and time t_d. If it is, he will still earn a higher return than offered by the naive "wait-and-see" policy. If the information still is not accepted, the return will fall below RR'. Part of the speculator's reward is for bearing such risks.

The contemporary literature is replete with examples of behavior as just described. Nathan Parker, author of travelogues such as *Iowa as It Is*, *The Iowa Handbook*, and *The Minnesota Handbook* were aimed at potential migrants and immigrants and described in glowing terms the fertility of the Iowa soil:

> . . . Robert Rawlins, of Washington county, exhibited 8 stalks of corn, 11 feet high, 11 ears, 10 rows in each ear, and 47 kernels to a row, making 88 feet of stalk, 5170 kernels of plump white corn, the produce of a single kernel! Messrs. Harrow of Wappello county exhibited specimens from a field of corn which produced the extraordinary yield of ONE HUNDRED AND SIXTY-EIGHT BUSHELS TO AN ACRE! Jerome Parsons, of Jefferson county, exhibited specimens of RED-CHAFF BEARDED WHEAT from the almost unprecedented yield of FORTY-SEVEN BUSHELS TO THE ACRE. In Jefferson county, 105 bushels of potatoes were raised to an acre; some specimens exhibited at the fair measured 9 to 16 inches in circumference. Of beets, some were 27 inches in length; other specimens, 31 inches in circumference, weighed 17 pounds. Squashes in western Iowa weighed 100 pounds; and, in northern Iowa, a vine, 275 feet long, bore, among others, five squashes, which averaged 80 pounds each. I have had apples weighing 24 ounces each and pears of 28 ounces. . . .[5]

Parker's self-interest in promoting land sales was only revealed in a postscript. He was a principal of the Iowa and Minnesota Land Agency and as a postscript to his travelogues advised those whose appetites had been whetted where they could write regarding land purchases. He also rigorously defended the activities of speculators, reproducing the following quote regarding their activities:

> So far from speculators being a drawback to the settlement of a new country, they are the very men who contribute most to the rapidity of its settlement. Lands would be idle and unimproved for years, were it not for this class of men. They come out here and purchase wild lands in vast bodies, and then make a business of inducing farmers and others in the East to emigrate hither and cultivate them.[6]

Every farmer was a speculator in the sense that a relatively large fraction of total farm profits resulted from capital gains on land.[7] Many, if not all, farmers when given the opportunity bought and hoarded more land than they could cultivate intensively, hoping eventually to sell at a profit. According to Paul Gates:

. . . American farmers regarded their land as a means of quickly making a fortune through the rising land values which the progress of the community and their own individual improvements would give it. Meanwhile they mined the land by cropping it continuously to its most promising staple. They did not look upon it as a lifetime investment, a precious possession whose resources were to be carefully husbanded. . . . To them land was not an enduring investment but a speculation.[8]

Not everyone, however, bought land with the intention of making a quick fortune before moving on. But even where it was not a motivation, most new farm operations embodied an element of land speculation or hoarding as farmers tended to purchase more land than they could profitably manage. As a result, average farm size in the more recently settled parts of the country tended to decline and the number of individual farms increased in succeeding decades. This "speculation" was probably attributable to overenthusiasm or a desire to provide for children, as much as to a pure profit motive. It was certainly incidental to their activities as farmers, regardless of the ultimate profits they realized from the decision, and they did eventually adjust the size of their holdings to one more suited to their farm operation.

These farmer-speculators did not have any specialist, or superior, knowledge. They were pure gamblers in the sense that they had no knowledge not already reflected in the current market price. Their case is illustrated in Figure 8.3. The line P_0e^{it} is the expected path of the price of land, which is known to all. However, because the actual price at any

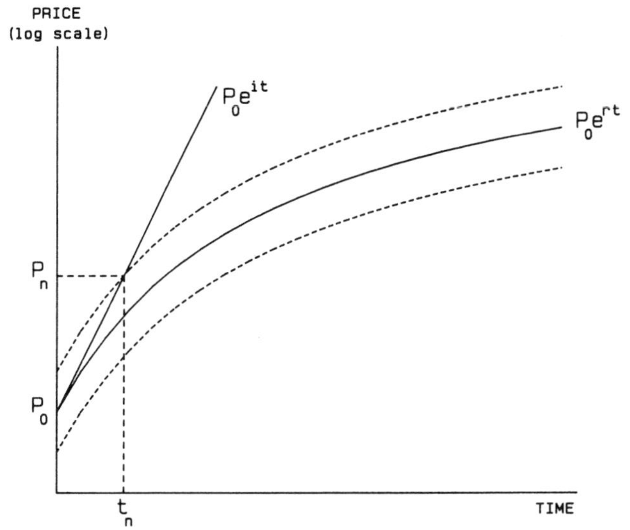

FIG. 8.3. Land speculation as a pure gamble.

moment is subject to random fluctuations about this path, the speculator hopes to make money by selling when the actual market price rises above that expected by some satisfactory margin. Suppose that a gambler has bought the land at time t_0 for the federal minimum price of $1.25 per acre (= P_0) and has adopted the strategy of selling when the price deviates from the expected path by, say, +1.65 standard deviations. Such an event will occur about 5 percent of the time. The slope of the line P_0e^{it} gives the mortgage rate of interest, which is the opportunity cost of buying too much land. The longer the speculator waits before selling, the less probable it is that he will earn a rate of return greater than the mortgage rate. After time t_n, even a price deviation of 1.65 standard deviations in excess of the expected price would be insufficient to make the speculation profitable.

Regardless of the actions of speculators who presumably were willing to sell land in whatever quantity the purchaser desired, federal land policy seems to have left its imprint upon midwestern farms. The published census has only limited information on the size distribution of farms and this is based upon improved rather than total acreage. Those data therefore serve to disguise rather than illuminate the effect of public land disposal on the size distribution of farms. Using the manuscript data, we show in Figure 8.4 the frequency distribution of farms by size for the sample in the eastern and western regions.[9]

There may have been some "heaping" in the data because of the increased relative frequencies of farm sizes that were multiples of 5 and

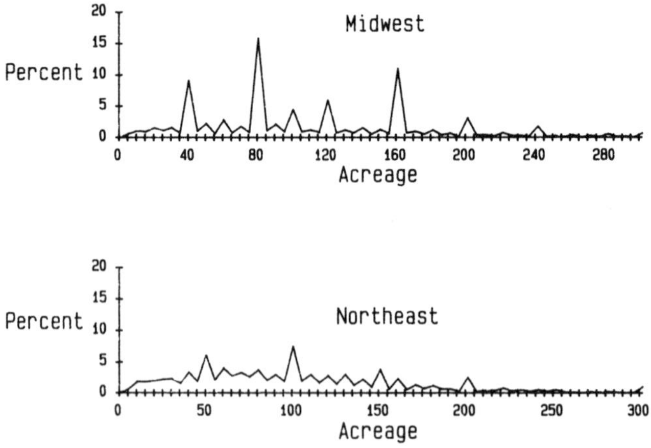

FIG. 8.4. Size distribution of farms 300 acres or smaller by region, 1860.

10 acres, but despite this, there were significantly higher incidences of particular farm sizes. In the Northeast, peaks at 50, 100, 150, and 200 acres were the most prominent. In the Midwest, farm sizes were clustered on multiples of 40–40, 80, 120, 160, and 200 acres–with the peaks at 40, 80, and 160 acres being the most prominent. These acreages are fractions, 1/16, 1/8, and 1/4, of the land survey section of 1 square mile or 640 acres and, we would argue, reflect one effect of public land sales on western agriculture.

Perhaps the clearest influence in the farm-size distributions is that of the Revision Act of 1820, which established 80 acres as the minimum purchase at public auction. The legislation became effective during the early settlement of Indiana, Michigan, Illinois, Wisconsin, and Iowa; in each of them 80-acre farms are the modal size, making up between 11 and 22 percent of the entire farm population.

However, by the time settlers were entering Minnesota and Kansas, preemption was limited to 160 acres and the minimum purchase set at 40. In these two states, 160-acre farms were the mode (Fig. 8.5); indeed, such farms were almost in a majority in each of these states. Furthermore, it is clear that the size distributions in Kansas and Minnesota differ markedly from that in the other western states.

Although land was not free until after the passage of the Homestead Act in 1862, few would contend that the cost of purchasing land from the federal government represented a major stumbling block for the aspiring farmer. Frederick Jackson Turner, to whom this relative ease of access to

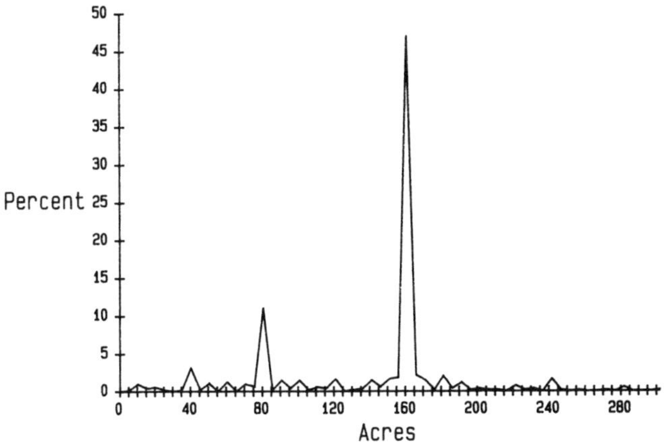

FIG. 8.5. Distribution of farm sizes on the frontier: Kansas and Minnesota in 1860.

agricultural lands functioned as a safety valve for social and economic unrest during the nineteenth century, argued:

> [W]henever social conditions tended to crystallize in the East, whenever capital tended to press upon labor or political restraints to impede the freedom of the mass, there was this gate of escape to the free conditions of the frontier. These free lands promoted individualism, economic equality, freedom to rise, democracy.[10]

The implication then is that eastern labor could cultivate the fertile western lands with little or no capital.

The extent to which eastern labor may have availed itself of these opportunities was addressed in our discussion of migration and immigration. People did indeed move into unsettled areas in a manner consistent with economic motivation. The cheap American lands were, for the most part, quickly taken up. The westward recession of the frontier kept the market continually supplied, thereby limiting both landlord and economic rents. Location, however, still carried a premium that continued development only served to enhance, but the further west one went the smaller the fraction of the total costs of establishing a farm represented by land acquisition. Here we propose to examine the actual costs of frontier farm making in the 1850s compared with the alternatives of purchasing already established, functioning farms further east or becoming a tenant. The role of tenancy in this debate has been largely ignored, yet our tenancy rates indicate that it was quite prevalent.

Consider first though, the costs of owner occupancy. Some commentators contented themselves with such generalizations as that a man "of small means" or with "the requisite funds (which indeed are but small)" could start a midwestern farm.[11] Many observers were much more specific. John Regan, for example, estimated costs for a 40-acre Illinois farm of "wild land, with nothing on it but grass and brushes" at $550, while "in Fulton, Knox, Macdonough (*sic*), Adams, Mercer, Henry, Stark and Peoria counties (in Illinois) . . . (the would-be farmer) can purchase improvements at from six to fifteen dollars an acre. . . . Say in all 1000 dollars."[12] Similarly for three different 80-acre Illinois farms, Gerhard quoted first year farm-making costs of $785, $1,411, and $2,127.[13] Further west in Iowa, the cost for an 80-acre farm was somewhat lower at $522, but the estimate made no allowance for breaking or fencing.[14] Horace Greeley, famous for his exhortations to "Go West, Young Man," was much more pessimistic about entry costs. He thought $5,000 an appropriate sum to start a farm in Kansas but noted that "[H]e who comes in with but $2,000, $1,000 or $500, must of course be much longer in working his way to a position of comfort and independence," but it was still possible.[15]

On the more northerly margins of settlement, individuals gave equally diverse estimates of farm-making costs. In Michigan the cost of buying and preparing 40 acres for crops was set down in one source at \$277.50, but no provision was made for implements, livestock, or living accommodations.[16] These could easily raise the cost to at least \$500.00. The state of Minnesota offered financial planning advice to would-be immigrant-farmers that was consistent with the conventional wisdom, albeit for a larger farm:

> . . . Counting at government price, one hundred and sixty acres is two hundred dollars. The cheapest and best fence, where lumber is cheap . . . is made of boards one inch by six and fourteen feet long, and two posts for every length of boards . . . the cost of fence complete, forty cents per rod. One mile of fence, inclosing forty acres, would cost 320 × 40 = \$128; though most have neighbors who help build line fences. . . . A man may build a comfortable house of logs by paying, say fifty dollars for lumber, nails, shingles, windows, &c., and he may make comfortable quarters for stock with poles and straw only, and men seldom put grain in barns when they have them. Horses are worth at present \$50 to \$100 each; oxen \$40 to \$50 per yoke; cows \$20 each. . . . it is highly desirable that all emigrants should have

The price of their land,	\$200.00
team and wagon,	150.00
two cows,	40.00
For building house,	100.00
Breaking twenty acres,	60.00
One steel plow, for crossing,	14.00
One harrow,	6.00
Axes, shovels, spade, forks, scythe, &c.,	25.00
House furniture and provisions for family, which must be bought till they can raise them,	200.00
	\$795.00

> Some men have started with nothing, and by working out or hiring farms have soon secured homes of comfort, and others will do the same; but to do this requires peculiar material in the man and his wife, and usually families with \$500 to \$1,000 on their arrival find they have need of the strictest economy.[17]

Costs were apparently much higher for prospective farmers in Wisconsin, who received the following advice about buying a 100-acre farm that was already partially improved:

. . . with 50 acres plowed and fenced, with a comfortable, cheap house and stable and not near enough to a large town for a fancy value could be bought for \$16 per acre, cash . . .	\$1,600
A good substantial low-priced horse team, including harness and wagon at	360
Plow, drag, cultivator, and small tools to start with	150
5 cows at \$30 per head	150

Other animals, including pigs, poultry, &c., &c.	50
Household furniture, stove, &c., usually necessary to be purchased by those who come from a distance	100
Incidentals, accidentals, and expesnes that cannot be foreseen or enumerated.	100
Making an aggregate amount of	$2,500

If one's means are moderate, one half of that sum can be made to answer every purpose, by going to the newer portion of the State, and purchasing as good but cheaper land—by substituting a yoke of oxen for the horses and harness, and starting with 3 cows instead of 5, &c., &c.[18]

Farm-making costs were primarily a midwestern concern, but there are some contemporary estimates of the costs incurred when buying into an eastern farm. For a 100-acre unit in New York State, the *Country Gentlemen* estimated that livestock would cost $1,010; implements $474.50; and seed, food, and hired labor, $525; or a total of about $2,000 the first year, not including the expenditure of buying (or renting) the farm. For those unable to afford this amount, the editor advised "expend less in land, and more in means to till it well."[19] These costs were about three times as expensive as those quoted for similar items in Wisconsin.

From examining evidence such as summarized in Table 8.1, Clarence Danhof concluded that "the farm-maker's wealth could not fall much short of $1000" for a 40-acre farm. This statement has been widely accepted and quoted.[20] Our purpose in reexamining the data is not to substantiate or refute earlier work but rather to examine the costs of buying and setting up farms of specific sizes on the frontier versus the alternatives of purchasing one in a more settled midwestern state, acquiring an eastern holding, or becoming a tenant, as reflected by the census. Rather than discuss hypothetical issues such as how much it was felt that farmers should have had to start a farm, we can examine actual farm data for areas undergoing early settlement as well as more mature areas and are able to offer insight into how much money farmers actually brought with them.

A number of items entered into Danhof's estimate of farm-making costs: $50–400 for land, $60–800 for clearing the land, $320 for fencing, $100 for implements, $150–200 for livestock, and $25–450 for housing. To these should be added allowances for incidentals, food and supplies until the first harvest, and the costs of travel, to produce his $1,000 cost estimate. However, he tempered this figure by noting that "no doubt farm-making was frequently undertaken by individuals possessing capital of less than $1,000" without ever specifying how much less.[21] Tenants were able to avoid those capital expenditures for the farmland, buildings, and improvements. They were, however, expected to supply their own implements, livestock, seed, and provide for the other incidental expenditures. As we will show, they made different decisions with regard to these expenses.

Reassessing Danhof's estimate, Robert Ankli proposed some new numbers for farm-making costs using the same manuscript census data that are the basis for this study. However, he changed the nature of the question addressed by Danhof by concluding that "it was probably correct to argue that an eastern working man (with a family?) needed closer to $1,000 than $500 to start farming immediately upon arrival in the West. But we should no longer be asking that question, for if a man were already out West, and wanted to own his farm, $500 would have been sufficient to begin the process."[22]

That conclusion was sharply criticized by Judith Klein because the manuscript census data do not provide all the cost elements in Danhof's estimate, because these data were thought to be deficient in some respects, and because Ankli changed the question originally asked by Danhof.[23] Danhof's purpose was to determine the economic validity of what he saw as three fundamental assumptions of the safety valve doctrine.[24] First, eastern labor found it desirable to take advantage of the opportunities afforded by the cheap western lands. Second, when faced with unemployment, onerous working conditions, or unsatisfactory wages, wage labor could take advantage of the opportunity with minimal difficulty. Third, labor did indeed avail itself of this opportunity in large numbers.

Tenancy offered substantially lower initial costs than owner occupancy. In the Midwest the average tenant of a 40-acre farm had $38 worth of implements and $219 of livestock, so that his basic capital outlay was $257 (Table 8.2). By contrast, the average owner-occupier of a similar unit had an outlay of $981, more than three times as much. For larger holdings, the relative capital costs of tenancy were even lower, so that the tenant of an average midwestern 160-acre farm had a capital outlay only one-seventh that of someone farming his own land. The differential between tenant and owner was even more pronounced in the Northeast, where the tenant of an average 40-acre farm had only one-sixth the investment of an owner-occupier, while someone renting a 160-acre spread had outlays almost one-eighth those of the owner. Although tenancy was thus relatively cheaper than owner occupancy in the Northeast, it involved capital outlays that were at least 20 percent greater than in the Midwest. Consequently, the agricultural ladder had on its bottom rung the farm laborer. Above him was a tenant in the Midwest, who was below a tenant in the Northeast. There was then a considerable gap between the resources of a northeastern tenant and those of a midwestern farmer, and

TABLE 8.1. Estimated Costs of Midwestern Farm Making: 1850–1860 by Contemporary Observers

Location	Total Cost ($)	Size (acres) ($)	Land Cost ($)	Breaking ($)	Fencing ($)	Seeding ($)	Harvesting ($)	Livestock ($)	Provisions ($)	Buildings ($)	Other ($)
Illinois[a]	550	40	50	†	100	20	†	140	50	20	170
Illinois[b]	785	80	100	130	320	40	195	†	†	†	†
Illinois[c]	895	34	170	87	100	468	71	†	†	†	†
Illinois[d]	920	200	320	†	173	†	†	†	†	100	27
Illinois[e]	930	45	500	†	†	20	†	140	50	†	220
Illinois[f]	1,411	80	360	150	400	145	456	†	†	†	†
Illinois[g]	2,100	160	1,000	400	400	†	†	†	†	300	†
Illinois[h]	2,127	80	1,200	175	320	326	196	†	†	†	†
Illinois[i]	2,290	320	240	1,500	†	*	*	†	†	*	550
Illinois[j]	2,750	160	1,600	225	400	†	†	†	†	500	25
Illinois[k]	2,800	100	1,000	1,250	*	*	*	†	†	†	550
Iowa[l]	440	40	50	80	160	†	†	†	†	†	150
Iowa[m]	522	80	100	†	†	5	†	156	75	70	116
Iowa[n]	850	160	200	320	320	†	†	†	†	†	†
Iowa[o]	1,034	80	†	†	†	†	†	310	†	450	374
Iowa[p]	1,175	80	240	75	75	†	†	200	100	100	385
Iowa[q]	1,500	80	250	75	75	75	†	200	100	100	550
Iowa[r]	2,650	160	200	600	600	150	200	†	†	650	250
Michigan[s]	277	40	†	220	40	17	†	†	†	†	†
Michigan[t]	2,475	160	225	1,015	*	*	338	†	†	900	†
Minnesota[u]	705	160	200	†	†	†	†	315	73	†	117
Minnesota[v]	795	160	200	60	†	†	†	190	†	100	245
Wisconsin[w]	1,690	200	250	480	400	160	400	†	†	†	†
Wisconsin[x]	2,500	100	1,600	*	*	†	†	560	100	*	250

Source: Adapted from Clarence Danhof, "Farm-Making Costs and the 'Safety Valve' 1850–1860," *Journal of Political Economy* 49(June 1941):327 with additions and deletions.

Note: An asterisk (*) indicates that the item is included in the first preceding figures; a dagger (†) indicates that the item is not included in the estimate.

[a] John Regan, *The Emigrant's Guide to the Western States of America* (1852), 353. "Other" includes $50 for furniture and $120 for implements.

[b] Fred Gerhard, *Illinois as It Is* (Chicago, 1857), 294.

[c] *Prairie Farmer* 15(1855):344.

[d] Josiah T. Marshall, *The Farmer's and Emigrant's Hand-Book* (Boston: H. Wentworth, 1852), 402–403. The estimate includes 160 acres of land at $1.25 per acre and 40 acres of timberland at $5.00 per acre. "Other" includes $15.00 for a well. The estimate applies to prairie lands in general and not to Illinois specifically. A very similar estimate by an English writer appears in *Working Farmer* 2(1850):270.

[e] Regan, *Emigrant's Guide,* 356–57. The estimate includes the purchase of 40 acres of improved land – fenced, broken, and including buildings; also 5 acres of timbered land at $20 per acre. "Other" includes $100 for furniture and $120 for implements.

[f] Gerhard, *Illinois as It Is,* 294.

[g] *Country Gentleman* 5(1855):141. Provisions for a year are specified in addition.

[h] Gerhard, *Illinois as It Is,* 295.

[i] James Caird, *Praire Farming in America* (London: Longman, Brown, Green, Longmans, and Roberts, 1859), 91. Includes 100 acres broken, fenced, sown, and harvested; also buildings. "Other" includes horses, implements, and harness.

[j] Gerhard, *Illinois as It Is,* 299.

[k] Caird, *Prairie Farming,* 89. The item of $1,250 is for breaking, fencing, and harvesting the first crop, as well as for buildings. The "Other" item is for hired labor.

[l] *Connecticut Valley Farmer and Mechanic* 1(1854):153.

[m] John B. Newhall, *A Glimpse of Iowa in 1846* (Burlington, Iowa, 1846), 59.

[n] *Northern Farmer* 1(1854):290–91.

[o] Nathan Parker, *Iowa Handbook for 1856* (Boston, 1856), 159–60.

[p] A. Cunynghame, *A Glimpse of the Great Western Republic* (London: Richard Bentley, 1851), 103.

[q] Ibid., 103–6, 108. "Other" includes $350 for passage from Great Britain to Iowa and $200 for miscellaneous and surplus. Implements included with seed. Original figures in sterling.

[r] *Iowa Farmer and Horticulturist* 5(1857):102.

[s] *Michigan Farmer* 8(1850):265. This is an estimate of capital required for undertaking farm making on a share basis, the land being owned by a second party with whom the produce is equally divided. Half the required seed is included.

[t] Sidney Smith, *The Settler's New Home* (London: J. Hendrick, 1849), 91 (citing William Ferguson).

[u] *New Hamspshire Journal of Agriculture* 14 April 1859. Includes $50 for transportation.

[v] Minnesota Commissioner of Statistics, *Minnesota: Its Place Among the States* (Hartford, 1860), 87–88.

[w] *Working Farmer* 2(1850):270.

[x] *Wisconsin Farmer* 8(1856):440–41. Specifies 50 acres broken. Includes $150 for implements. "If one's means are moderate, one-half of that sum can be made to answer every purpose, by going to the newer portions of the State, and purchasing as good but cheaper land – by substituting two yoke of oxen for the horses and harness, and starting with three cows instead of five. . . ."

TABLE 8.2. Capital Costs of Tenant and Owner-occupied Farms by Region and Farm Size in 1860

	40-Acre Farms		80-Acre Farms		160-Acre Farms	
	Owner-Occupied	Tenant	Owner-Occupied	Tenant	Owner-Occupied	Tenant
Midwest						
Farm Value	738	969	1,363	1,460	2,490	2,151
Implement Value	46	38	67	57	96	87
Livestock Value	197	219	285	268	426	335
Total Cost to Owner-Occupier	981		1715		3,002	
Total Cost to Tenant		257		325		422
(Number)	(494)	(130)	(885)	(232)	(565)	(213)
Northeast						
Farm Value	1,599	2,967	2,621	2,772	3,966	3,636
Implement Value	65	58	116	80	162	124
Livestock Value	256	256	401	277	615	501
Total Cost to Owner-Occupier	1,920		3,138		4,743	
Total Cost to Tenant		314		357		625
(Number)	(85)	(9)	(94)	(23)	(63)	(14)

another sizable gap between his financial resources and those of the yeoman farmer in the East.

Outlays for tenants were lower because they avoided the initial expense of land, buildings, and improvements. Tenancy, however, involved more than the substitution of annual rental payments for the one-time outlay on land or the resultant forfeiture of capital gains through land appreciation and the long-term benefits of land improvement (see Chaps. 13 and 14). The tenant generally had fewer, or at least less valuable, implements than the yeoman for any size farm. He also usually had fewer head of livestock. For example, yeoman farmers in the Midwest on a 160-acre holding averaged 3.1 cows, 5 beef cattle, 7.7 sheep, and 15.8 hogs, but a similarly situated tenant averaged only 2.7 cows, 4 beef cattle, 4.7 sheep, and 10 hogs. The relationship between tenant and yeoman livestock holdings in the East were similar, except that eastern farmers, regardless of tenancy status, had more cows, beef cattle, and sheep, while midwestern farmers had more draft animals and hogs.

Tenants often had more draft animals than yeoman, though cheaper oxen and mules were sometimes substituted for horses, which served to keep the livestock valuation lower. These draft animals reflected a greater commitment among tenants to cash-grain and root-crop production, rather than to general mixed farming. Given their greater need for cash, this was a rational decision even though it increased the risk exposure of the tenant family.

Tenant farms, acre for acre, were usually more valuable than those of the yeomanry because they had a higher proportion of improved to total acreage. Tenants, since presumably they did not capture the benefits of labor invested in capital improvements to the land, apparently wanted most of their land in current production. They, more than any other group, had the incentive to maximize short-term gains through repeated cropping in whatever currently had the highest yield measured in dollars per acre.

These distinctions between tenant and owner-occupied farms break down on the frontier. In Kansas and Minnesota tenant farms, while still more valuable than those of the yeomanry, had a smaller proportion of improved to total acreage, more livestock, and a greater implement value (Table 8.3).[25] The higher relative land value on the frontier suggests that

TABLE 8.3. Average Farm and Farm-making Costs for Owner-occupied Farms of Different Sizes in the Midwest in 1860

State	Number of Observations	Farm ($)	Implements ($)	Livestock ($)	Total Cost ($)
			40-Acre Farms		
Illinois	54	788	78	237	1,103
Indiana	215	769	43	206	1,018
Iowa	17	590	26	164	780
Kansas	3	267	37	153	457
Michigan	109	754	47	171	972
Minnesota	6	317	15	125	457
Missouri	44	329	34	219	582
Ohio	20	1,238	47	245	1,530
Wisconsin	26	858	44	113	1,015
			80-Acre Farms		
Illinois	128	1,345	105	297	1,747
Indiana	399	1,541	66	304	1,911
Iowa	33	1,060	45	221	1,326
Kansas	21	856	72	333	1,261
Michigan	124	1,282	52	222	1,556
Minnesota	19	630	34	141	805
Missouri	75	730	49	341	1,120
Ohio	40	2,323	73	388	2,784
Wisconsin	46	1,049	63	166	1,278
			160-Acre Farms		
Illinois	80	2,648	129	476	3,253
Indiana	195	3,457	113	509	4,073
Iowa	16	1,975	81	290	2,346
Kansas	74	1,744	92	354	2,190
Michigan	30	2,772	90	423	3,285
Minnesota	57	702	36	140	878
Missouri	61	1,434	73	522	2,029
Ohio	22	4,600	96	518	5,214
Wisconsin	30	1,633	84	294	2,011

these tenant farms may have been more favorably situated than those of owner-occupiers and reflects the comparative bidding strengths of large landowners. Their tenants must have received more advantageous rental terms to compensate them for the undeveloped state of their units. The number of draft animals they had suggests that they broke the farms for the landlord.

Prevalent as tenancy was, it was never the principal source of land tenure in any township in the sample. Most farms were bought by owner-occupiers. The average cost of 40, 80, and 160 acres of land in farms together with any improvements and capitalized rents in the sample midwestern states is shown in Table 8.4. We also show the cost of the average number of head of livestock for such a farm and the average value of farm implements. Since there were more 80-acre farms than any other size, except on the frontier, we focus upon them as the typical unit. However, for comparison with contemporary farm-making accounts and the existing farm-making literature, figures for 40-acre farms are more relevant.

For 80-acre farms, outlays on land, livestock, and implements range from as little as $805 in Minnesota to $2,784 in Ohio. The principal distinction between these bounds is the value of farm and land with its improvements and buildings. The costs of an 80-acre farm in Ohio were thus comparable with a similar unit in the Northeast. A northeastern farmer who sold and moved west to Ohio could purchase a farm perhaps

TABLE 8.4. Tenant and Yeoman 160-Acre Farms on the Kansas and Minnesota Frontier in 1860

	Tenant Farms	Owner-occupied Farms
Farm Value	$1,353	$1,291
Implement Value	$ 77	$ 68
Livestock Value	$ 296	$ 260
Capital Cost to Tenants	$ 373	
Capital Cost to Owner-Occupiers		$1,619
Percentage of Land Improved	20	23
Livestock Inventory		
Horses	1.4	1.2
Mules	0.1	0.2
Oxen	2.1	1.7
Total Draft Animals	3.6	3.1
Cows	2.5	2.3
Beef Cattle	3.5	3.7
Sheep	2.6	0.3
Hogs	7.0	10.0
Number of Farms	113	131

one-eighth larger than that which he vacated, but if he moved instead west or north of Indiana, he could purchase a farm at least twice as large.

The value of farms in each state, exclusive of implements and livestock, was considerably in excess of the minimum price for the public domain of $1.25 per acre. This reflected two factors. First, improvements such as breaking, fencing, and farm buildings had already been made to the land–even on the frontier–and these raised its physical productivity. Second, land had locational advantages that resulted in differential earnings even where physical productivity was the same.

According to Robert Gallman, improvements were valued at their reproduction cost.[26] Many of the contemporary farm-making cost accounts separate them from the purchase price of the raw land, but we are unable to do so. We have tried to estimate the value of an acre of land, both improved and unimproved, and the value of those items included in the price of the farm that were independent of acreage. Consider the ordinary least squares regression equation:

$$\text{FARM VALUE} = \text{constant} + b_1\text{IMPROVED} + b_2\text{UNIMPROVED}$$

To the extent that land within a locale was homogeneous with respect to such factors as fertility, proximity to markets, and transportation, and on which all farmers had made similar improvements, the coefficients b_1 and b_2 represent the price per acre for improved and unimproved land where the price for improved land includes the capitalized value of clearing, breaking, drainage, and fencing. The unimproved land may also have been fenced, but in the less densely settled areas it was probably not. The constant term in the equation reflects farm structures and other factors affecting land value to the extent that they were not related to acreage.

The value of structures on tenant farms in the East and West were comparable and accounted for between $545 and $600 of the value of the farm (Table 8.5). This should have been more than sufficient for a substantial farmhouse and outbuildings in the West. Those in the East would have been more modest. Compared with the structures on yeoman farms in the same region, those of tenants in the East were worth about half as much, but in the West they were almost double the value reported for owner-occupiers.[27] In the East some of the difference almost certainly reflects, in part, the relative importance of livestock on tenant versus yeoman farms. In the West it may reflect the yeoman farmers' determination to improve the productivity of his land before attending to his creature comforts.

Eastern land values generally exceeded those in the West. This was especially the case for eastern tenant farms where improved land was valued very highly but unimproved land had no value to the tenant. In-

TABLE 8.5. Value of Farm Buildings and Improved and Unimproved Land by Region and Tenancy in 1859 (standard errors in parentheses)

	Tenant Farms			Yeoman Farms		
	Constant (Farm Buildings) ($)	b_1 (Improved Land) ($ per Acre)	b_2 (Unimproved Land) ($ per Acre)	Constant (Farm Buildings) ($)	b_1 (Improved Land) ($ per Acre)	b_2 (Unimproved Land) ($ per Acre)
Midwest	599.89	25.26	1.94	321.02	27.92	3.39
	(67.53)	(0.77)	(0.38)	(32.03)	(0.35)	(0.21)
Northeast	545.18	41.91	–2.36	1,069.78	29.31	4.39
	(162.20)	(1.87)	(1.44)	(62.76)	(0.60)	(0.50)

deed, unimproved land actually reduced the value of the farm, but the coefficient was not statistically different from zero. To the extent that eastern unimproved land may have been unimprovable, this may capture land quality, but it also reflects the tenants' lack of use for such land. They gained no benefit from efforts to bring it under the plow, indeed, success would probably raise their rent. The value of an improved acre elsewhere was remarkably consistent between tenant and yeoman farms in the West, and on yeoman farms between West and East. Unimproved land in midwestern tenant farms was somewhat more valuable than raw land in the public domain. It probably could be improved. There is evidence that hay was harvested from such lands so it may also have been used for rangeland. On the other hand, unimproved land on owner-occupied farms, regardless of region, was substantially more valuable. Moreover, it was most valuable in the East, which is consistent with its relative scarcity, the potential gains from bringing it into cultivation, and the economic opportunity that it represented.

Farm values, however, also include economic rents from location. These were capitalized in its value, as contemporaries were well aware:

A bushel of grain is worth upon the farm as much less as the cost of carrying it to market. And the cost of transporting wheat or corn by railroad is about eight cents per bushel per hundred miles, and for meats about fifteen cents per hundred pounds, per hundred miles. The average cost per bushel for transporting wheat or corn from Chicago to Buffalo, by way of the lake, will not exceed seven cents, during the season of navigation; while from Cleveland to Buffalo, it is about four cents per bushel. . . .

The value of the crop upon a farm of 160 acres, at Columbus, Ohio, and upon one of the same size 80 miles from Chicago, are equal; whilst there is a difference in favor of the latter over the one at Iowa City, of 360 dollars; and over the one at

Fort Des Moines, in Iowa, of 660 dollars. Three hundred and sixty dollars will pay an interest of six percent upon a valuation of $6000; and $600 is the interest at the same rate upon $10,000. This shows that a farm of 160 acres within 80 miles of Chicago, is worth $6000 more than one of the same size in the vicinity of Iowa City; which is equal to $37.50 per acre, and $1100 more than one at Fort Des Moines; which is equal to $68.75 per acre, when appropriated to raising grain.[28]

We have attempted to measure these location rents by including dummy variables in our model of land values. The appropriate dummy variable was assigned a value of one if the farm was located within its borders, otherwise its value was zero. The coefficient of each dummy variable therefore represents the premium, or discount, on farms in that specific state relative to farms in Ohio for those in the Midwest, and New York for those in the East. The results are shown in Table 8.6.

The general relationship indicated above between the values of improved and unimproved land in tenant and yeoman farms remains unchanged, except that unimproved land in eastern tenant farms now has a positive value. It remains statistically indistinguishable from zero. In the Midwest the locational premium declines from East to West. Furthermore, the locational disadvantage in Missouri was higher than expected, being as much as double that in Iowa to the north and 50 percent higher than that in Kansas to the west. It is tempting to attribute this to slavery, especially since the same pattern is found with respect to Maryland. In the Northeast locational premiums declined to the north. Land in New Jersey was most valuable, with a premium of over $2,400 more than that in New York. Surprisingly, farmland in Pennsylvania also sold for premium prices vis-à-vis that in New York. This may be an artifact of the closer proximity of sample townships in Pennsylvania to urban markets.

The sample livestock values compare favorably with those given by contemporaries as desirable levels for the aspiring farmer. In Table 8.7 we give the breakdown of the number of head on the average 40-, 80-, and 160-acre farm by region and tenancy. Livestock inventories increased less rapidly than farm size, with 160-acre farms averaging about twice as much livestock as a unit of 40 acres. This reflects the relative land intensity of animal husbandry. The typical midwestern 80-acre yeoman farm had three draft animals, usually horses. Tenants worked somewhat fewer draft animals, but the average farm had sufficient horsepower for most jobs. Some farms in Iowa, Michigan, and Minnesota, however, had significantly fewer draft animals, but presumably any shortage for heavy jobs such as breaking or ploughing could be made up by cooperative arrangements. In Kansas, Minnesota, and Wisconsin most of the power was supplied by oxen. Contemporaries generally deemed them preferable to horses for the new farmer because they were better suited for the heavy job of breaking, subsisted better than horses without supplementary feed, and were much cheaper to purchase.[29]

In addition, each 80-acre farm usually included at least two milk cows, some beef cattle, and a breeding stock of pigs. Farms 80 acres and larger in the Northeast, regardless of tenure, had substantially more milk

TABLE 8.6. Land Values, Locational Rents, and Tenancy, 1860 (standard errors in parentheses)

Variable	Midwest: Owner-occupied Farms	Midwest: Tenant Farms	Northeast: Owner-occupied Farms	Northeast: Tenant Farms
Constant	919.63	1,478.80[a]	1,085.72[a]	450.87[a]
	(80.16)	(205.35)	(72.08)	(233.92)
Improved Acres	28.16[a]	25.01[a]	30.50[a]	40.62[a]
	(0.35)	(0.80)	(0.56)	(1.77)
Unimproved Acres	4.28[a]	2.27[a]	4.78[a]	0.87
	(0.21)	(0.39)	(0.47)	(1.38)
Locational Dummies				
Illinois	−1,137.65[a]	−1,244.65[a]		
	(94.58)	(253.88)		
Indiana	− 291.23[a]	− 706.95[a]		
	(82.20)	(210.95)		
Iowa	− 814.07[a]	−1,101.66[a]		
	(46.23)	(299.19)		
Kansas	−1,129.75[a]	− 916.14[a]		
	(137.64)	(281.84)		
Michigan	− 529.36[a]	− 623.36		
	(100.95)	(339.14)		
Minnesota	−1,160.58[a]	−1,660.80[a]		
	(155.40)	(310.76)		
Missouri	−1,689.36[a]	−1,663.59[a]		
	(97.10)	(273.21)		
Wisconsin	− 995.12[a]	−1,325.87[a]		
	(115.73)	(362.00)		
Connecticut			− 165.23	− 249.4
			(252.15)	(768.3
Maryland			−1,411.35[a]	−1,312.3
			(223.45)	(264.9
New Hampshire			−2,261.09[a]	−1,750.2
			(129.08)	(342.3
New Jersey			2,429.14[a]	3,229.2
			(219.22)	(471.8
Pennsylvania			385.92[a]	1,005.6
			(95.13)	(225.6
Vermont			− 336.14	48.5
			(282.40)	(702.3
Regression Statistics				
R^2	0.62	0.52	0.52	0.5
N	5,775	1,522	3,591	75

Excluded locational dummies: Ohio and New York.
[a]Significantly different from zero at more than the 5 percent level.

TABLE 8.7. Livestock Inventories by Farm Size, Region, and Tenancy in 1860

Region/Tenancy	Horses	Mules	Oxen	Cows	Beef Cattle	Sheep	Hogs
				40-Acre Farms			
Midwest							
Owner-Occupier	1.5	0.0	0.5	1.9	2.0	3.4	8.2
Tenant	1.6	0.0	0.5	1.6	1.9	2.2	9.0
Northeast							
Owner-Occupier	1.5	0.0	0.4	2.8	1.7	3.0	1.8
Tenant	1.9	0.0	0	2.1	1.0	0.1	2.7
				80-Acre Farms			
Midwest							
Owner-Occupier	2.3	0.1	0.6	2.4	3.0	5.4	11.8
Tenant	2.2	0.1	0.4	2.1	2.2	4.3	11.4
Northeast							
Owner-Occupier	2.2	0.0	0.7	4.2	2.9	8.7	3.5
Tenant	1.5	0.0	1.3	4.0	1.6	3.7	4.5
				160-Acre Farms			
Midwest							
Owner-Occupier	3.1	0.3	1.0	3.1	5.0	7.7	15.8
Tenant	2.2	0.1	1.3	2.7	4.0	4.7	10.0
Northeast							
Owner-Occupier	2.7	0.0	1.1	8.6	5.3	16.6	5.3
Tenant	2.8	0.1	1.9	5.2	4.4	9.4	9.4

cows and superior marketing opportunities for fresh dairy produce. Midwestern farms of all sizes had more hogs, which offered an alternative way of marketing farm surplus crops in areas with poor transportations.[30]

The census estimate for implements, $21–68 for 40-acre farms, is considerably out of line with the figures suggested by contemporaries. Indeed, even our estimates for larger farms usually lie below those cited by contemporaries for much smaller farms. There are two possible explanations: the farms may have had a mix of implements quite different from that suggested by contemporaries, or the census responses might have questionable validity. Instructions given enumerators were quite precise regarding what should be counted but were ambiguous about how these implements should be valued. Enumerators were directed to record "the aggregate value of all the farming or planting implements and machinery, including wagons, threshing-machines, cotton-gins, sugar-mills; in fact, all implements and machinery used to cultivate and produce crops and fit the same for market or consumption."[31] We believe that these implements were valued at current market value rather than original or full replacement cost and that their remaining useful life must have been in general quite limited.

At the very least, every farmer needed a plow, harness or yoke, and wagon, together with hand tools such as an axe, grain cradle, hoe, and rake. Based on prices of agricultural implements taken from a USDA report and independent observations drawn from the manuscript censuses of manufacturing for 1850 and 1860, we estimate that expenditures upon these items at the national level would range from $69 to as much as $280 and average about $110 at the state level (Tables 8.8 and 8.9).[32] The average is somewhat greater than provided for by Danhof, but purchasing a cheaper wagon would easily bring the total cost down to about $100. However, very few farms, even as large as 160 acres, reported an implements value this large. Even the lower limit exceeds the average implement value on 40-acre farms.

The census data do not include all the costs in Danhof's $1,000 figure. One missing element is the cost of provisions for the period before the first crops could be raised, which Danhof estimated at $100.[33] Seed, estimated at as much as $1–2 per acre or about $25–50 for the average 40-acre midwestern farm, would also be needed.[34] In some instances, an allowance for hired harvest labor would be appropriate.[35] Neglecting the latter unspecified cost, the average 40-acre farm in the Midwest cost about $1,200, but some substantial economies of about a third could be

TABLE 8.8. Cash Prices of Agricultural Implements and Machines Delivered FOB, Including Commissions and Allowances to Agents, but Not Including Discount for Cash within 30 Days, on About 1 July 1860

Implement or Machine		Price Range ($)	Implement or Machine		Price Range ($)
Carriages and Buggies		90–450	Planter:	Corn	20–32
Carts		28	Plow:	Walking	7–23
Corn Knife		0.75		Subsoil	6–12
Cultivators:	Shovel	4		Gang	18–60
	Horse Hoe	9		Breaking	8.50–15
	2-Horse			Shovel	4.50–5
	Riding	45	Rake:	Sulky	20–35
Cutters		12–65	Reaper		125–200
Drills		65–90	Roller		35
Fanning Mills		20–35	Scythe		1
Fertilizer Spreaders		10	Seeders and Sowers		30–53
Forks		5–25	Shellers		8–22
Grain Cradle		4	Spades		1
Harrow		10–45	Stackers		125
Harvester		150	Steam Engines		
Hay Carrier		10	(portable/hp)		90–135
Hay Press		250	Stump Pullers		125
Hoe		0.50	Thrashers		80–500
Mower		100–160	Wagons		50–150
Planter:	Hand	1.25	Weeders		7

Source: George K. Holmes, "The Course of Prices of Farm Implements and Machinery for a Series of Years," *USDA Division of Statistics, Miscellaneous Bulletins* 18 (Washington, DC: GPO, 1901).

TABLE 8.9. Range of Mean Factory Prices of Agricultural Implements and Equipment for the Northern States, 1850–1860

Implement	Price Range ($)	Mean FOB Price ($)
Axes	0.65– 1.00	0.66
Carriages	75.00–450.00	134.56
Carts	16.00– 40.00	24.38
Grain Cradles	4.00– 5.00	4.23
Harnesses	12.00– 50.00	23.18
Hatchets	0.38– 0.38	0.38
Hoes	0.30– 0.45	0.41
Horse Collars	1.50– 2.00	1.57
Plows	3.60– 33.33	7.94
Rakes	5.00– 6.80	5.60
Reapers	157.50–157.50	157.50
Saddles	10.00– 48.00	13.61
Threshers	148.00–375.00	266.23
Wagons	42.09–111.53	64.91
Wheat Fans	22.00– 22.00	22.00

Source: Bateman-Weiss samples from the manuscript censuses of manufacturing for 1850 and 1860.

effected, for example, by moving to the frontier, replacing oxen with horses, substituting a cart for a wagon, or improving fewer acres in the early years. For an 80-acre unit the cost was likely to have exceeded $2000, while expenditures for a 160-acre holding probably averaged $3000.

Farm costs and their composition proved to be similar between underdeveloped and developed rural communities. Costs in some of the sparsely populated areas exceeded those in other more densely settled townships, a difference that might reflect the tendency to take up the best lands first, leaving the poorer, lower-valued ones for later settlers. The potential farmer with Danhof's $1,000 could on average buy a farm of 40 acres or less in communities with fewer than 30 persons per square mile (Table 8.10). The cost of land in 1860 would have been somewhat greater than budgeted for by Danhof, but the aggregate value of implements much less. The farm-making costs in those communities with this population density were significantly lower than in the more densely settled areas. Land costs in the heavily populated communities were double or triple those in the less-settled areas. Livestock cash values and the value of implements were also noticeably higher. Our data suggest that an 80- to 160-acre farm on the frontier could be bought for about the same expenditure as would be made on a 40-acre or smaller farm in a more urbanized area, especially in the Northeast or Old Northwest. A 41- to 80-acre farm in a settled community could be exchanged for an 80- to 160-

TABLE 8.10. Average Farm and Farm-making Costs in the 1850s by Population Density

Population Density/ Farm Size Class	Cash Value of Farm	Aggregate Value of Imple-ments	Cash Value of Livestock	Farm and Farm-making Costs
I. 0–15 Persons/Sq. Mile				
0–40 Acres	$ 683.39	$ 37.20	$192.84	$ 913.43
41–80	988.75	51.53	254.46	1,294.74
81–160	1,930.04	82.58	341.55	2,354.17
II. 15–30 Persons/Sq. Mile				
0–40 Acres	536.19	35.53	162.10	733.82
41–80	1,091.72	62.60	254.24	1,408.56
81–160	1,803.14	90.16	401.25	2,294.57
III. 30–60 Persons/Sq. Mile				
0–40 Acres	1,041.97	48.97	201.27	1,292.21
41–80	1,736.03	75.76	298.06	2,109.85
81–160	2,981.95	104.78	454.49	3,541.22
IV. More than 60 Persons/Sq. Mile				
0–41 Acres	1,787.70	70.28	230.27	2,088.25
41–80	2,758.97	105.09	359.03	3,223.09
81–160	4,396.95	156.32	582.32	5,135.59

acre farm on the frontier, a condition entirely consistent with Fred Shannon's claim that "[F]armers might sell their eastern acres and move west and so they did in order to provide farms for each of their sons."[36]

Although the cash value of livestock rose with population density, farms in the more densely settled areas had fewer draft animals, cattle, sheep, and swine, but more milk cows. Farmers near urban areas produced less grain but more potatoes, orchard products, market garden produce, butter, cheese, and hops. Frontier farms cultivated hardy, nonperishable crops that could either be shipped to market if transport was available or walked there where it was not.

These costs compare favorably with those quoted by Danhof (Table 8.1), but are higher than estimated by Ankli. Recall that Danhof's estimates expressed the desirable level for settlers to have, while ours reveal the average amount they actually possessed. Some economies could be made, but typically it took a person of greater than average wealth to afford a farm. Someone with the median level of wealth could manage it, but most people that wealthy were middle-aged, native-born, white, literate males, who were also less likely to be in the pool of aspirant farmers.

Tenancy offered one alternative. Entry costs at this level may have been as little as $300, an amount affordable for perhaps three-quarters of rural households. However, this still exceeded the resources that most free blacks could command. Movement to the frontier offered some escape for tenant and yeomanry alike, but the savings were much greater for those who could afford to buy. Those who rented faced a constant challenge to produce cash surpluses despite distance from urban markets.

Establishing a farm was but the beginning. It did not measure the farmer's success as an agriculturalist, let alone guarantee his economic survival. He had to decide what to produce and how. Were livestock worth the care and attention that they demanded? Should he make extraordinary efforts to increase land yields by intensive, careful farming and how did these change over time? In the process, he had to make decisions regarding the allocation of his own time and that of family members among the wide variety of day-to-day and seasonal tasks. It is to these questions that we now move.

CHAPTER NINE

Livestock in the Farm Economy: Dairying as a Farm Enterprise

BY MIDCENTURY DAIRYING HAD BECOME a major agricultural endeavor, one contributing substantially to the aggregate agricultural output in the North. For their home consumption as well as for commercial sale, farmers produced fluid milk, butter, and cheese. Commercial creameries and cheese factories emerged as important industries in some locations where suitable supply conditions interacted with availability of markets and reasonably inexpensive transport facilities, but generally this remained a farm enterprise. Dairy cattle formed an important link in the ecological cycle on a farm, converting feeds and grasses into milk for consumption as well as providing fertilizer for crops and feed for other livestock. Dairy operations contributed importantly to cash flows and profits as well (see Chaps. 13 and 14). Most northern farmers kept at least one or two milk cows to serve these functions, but many maintained larger herds that allowed them to engage in market sales, and some had evolved into large commercial dairy producers. Production of milk and its products represented a rational adjunct to the farm economy, one that fit sensibly into the scheme of agricultural production across the continuum from remote self-sufficiency to full-scale commercialism that prevailed at this time. For our purpose, dairying provides an illustration of the role of livestock enterprises in the pattern of farming characteristic of this era, one for which we can gain a substantial amount of information from the federal census.

Despite its economic importance, dairying in the 1860s remained a woefully neglected branch of agrarian enterprise, particularly in the western states.[1] There were few agricultural endeavors where eastern and western attitudes, practices, and outcomes differed more markedly. The general neglect of this activity was both common and widely recognized. Said a contemporary observer early in the century: "Either the cows are the most worthless breed, or they are, as is most generally the case, utterly unprovided with nourishing winter food–and even in the summer, when milk is not wanted, their dairies are badly located, injudiciously constructed, and without one solitary vessel of convenience well adapted to that purpose."[2] Some fifty years later a writer in the *Journal of New York Agricultural Society* complained that, "Many dairymen habitually violate natural laws. . . . They dry [their cows] off thin and weak in the fall, winter very carelessly on poor feed, and then milk hard again next summer."[3] Even towards the end of the century an agricultural investigator gathering material on a questionnaire survey reported that he found, "on inquiry that there is not one man in a hundred of the average farmers who knows anything about what his cows eat, or how much it costs to keep them. In fact, they don't know anything about their cows except that they feed them something and get some milk and butter."[4]

Even in the "dairy region" of the Northeast effective and profitable dairying remained the exception rather than the rule. In 1864 a writer complained that "the dairy stock of New England has not been improved in its intrinsic good qualities during the last thirty or forty years."[5] In 1888 another observed: "One notable source of ill-success in dairying is inferior cows. It is said that even in the oldest and best dairy districts of New York, one third of the dairy stock will not more than pay the cost of its keep."[6] Similar comments abound for all the states of the northern dairy region. In the South, conditions were far worse, bordering on total disregard in some areas. Observers of that region's dairy husbandry, if it may be called that, were often appalled at its poor condition. In the South and on the western frontier areas cows truly were "kept for milk," in the passive sense that characterization implies.

In 1861 a correspondent to the Patent Office argued that no cow producing under 1,800 quarts a year was worth keeping, yet noted that for many the average yield did not exceed a thousand quarts.[7] Nevertheless, he accepted 1,800 quarts as the basis for his estimates of the total milk production in thirteen states. Using census data on the number of cows and this yield, he deducted the amount of milk used in the production of butter and cheese, to leave as a residual the amount of milk consumed as food. The error in this approach, assuming no regional yield variation, is apparent in his conclusion that almost 70 percent of Virginia's milk production was consumed fresh whereas only 27 percent of New York or Vermont milk was drunk by residents. This creates a paradox that a state with a great need to preserve dairy products because of inclement weather in fact did not do so while farmers in states with weather more favorable to keeping milk fresh, instead preserved it despite a potential price differential in favor of the fresh product.[8]

Nowhere in the United States, with the exception of the limited dairy regions of the Northeast and Ohio or those areas within the immediate proximity of large urban areas, was dairying a highly developed farm activity. For various reasons including the comparative profitability of other crops, the lack of suitable transportation for long-distance shipping of perishables, and the extensive, land-using nature of American agriculture at this time, most farmers tended to neglect their dairy activity or at best treat it as secondary. Even on its largest farms, America was a land of small dairy herds where most farmers held fewer than ten cows, a size that later in the century would be viewed as the minimum essential for a serious, profitable dairy enterprise. Although not a primary activity on most antebellum farms, dairying was nonetheless usually a subsidiary one on most. Even on the smallest acreages, farmers kept a cow to produce milk or butter for family consumption. The majority of farms owned three or four milk animals. Even so, dairying provided production of goods for home consumption or barter to the country store and of such by-products as fertilizer or animal feed.

Once family wants were met, if an excess could be produced the sale of milk and its products provided a means for entering commercial trade. Fluid milk was being supplied to nearby rural nonfarm or urban buyers long before the successful development of refrigerated transport. And butter or cheese, transportable over longer distances with lower risks of spoilage, became to some milk-producing farmers what liquor was to many who grew corn: a means of converting a product into a less immediately perishable and relatively higher-valued form. "Farmers in the vicinity of crossroads hamlets, county seats, and commercial and industrial centers," says Paul Gates, "found a market for milk. . . . Fresh butter, a standard item in the diet of most families, was always marketable."[9]

In the Northeast residents of urban centers demanded, but did not consistently receive, good quality butter or cheese and reasonably palatable fluid milk. The products they were supplied – lardlike butter, thin or dirty milk produced by poorly fed animals – were often inferior, as revealed both in the contemporary literature and in the long struggle for passage of city ordinances regulating quality, butterfat content, and sanitary practices. By 1860 milk and dairy products, particularly butter, had become integral to the human diet in the northeastern states. The New York, Boston, Baltimore, Philadelphia, and Washington milksheds already provided comparatively well-developed markets, even in an age before refrigerated rail transportation.

Market opportunities encouraged the formation of large commercial dairies in New York. There, cheese from Herkimer County and butter from Orange and Goshen counties gained reputations sufficient to command premium prices throughout the United States and abroad.[10] Specialized dairy farms with similar economic and physical characteristics existed in New England, and farmers within the milksheds of all large eastern cities frequently concentrated exclusively on fluid milk production.[11] Farther west specialized dairies were rarer, being found in substantial numbers only in the Western Reserve region of Ohio. Quality generally was poorer than that of eastern products, at least for those shipped over long distances, as reflected in the lower prices accorded western products sold in eastern markets. Interstate shipments of butter and cheese as well as of fluid milk, particularly in states serving nearby urban markets, would nevertheless have been insufficient to equalize per capita milk availability among the states.

After 1860, dairying was drawn increasingly into the commercial farm economy. Many farmers in the Northeast sought a cash product suitable for intensive mixed farming on relatively poor but high-priced land sheltered in some way from competition with better, cheaper land farther west. Production of fluid milk for city markets suited this requirement. Farmers distant from the city markets, in western New York for example, tended to specialize in milk for butter and cheese production, either on the farm or in the factories that had begun to develop during the 1850s. In a typical pattern farmers near cities specialized in fluid milk, often using barn-feeding methods; those more remote, especially where transportation was poor, produced butter and cheese. Improved transport began to influence New York City and Boston milksheds in a limited matter as early as the 1840s. The effect of rail transportation on size of urban milksheds remained limited, however, until refrigerated cars developed during the 1870s. Dairies from 10 to 30 miles distant from Boston were shipping some fluid milk to that city by rail in the early 1840s.[12] Yet, the Boston milkshed never extended beyond 65 miles before 1870; the New York milkshed no farther than 100 miles.

Dairy farming evolved similarly farther westward, although later than it had in the Northeast. Wheat farmers in Wisconsin, for example, when confronted with declining soil fertility and competition from the newly opened western farm lands where wheat could be produced at lower cost, often shifted to commercialized dairy production. Despite their distance from the eastern urban markets, these commercial dairy farmers tended to specialize in milk for butter and cheese production. Manufactured milk products, which could be shipped farther than fluid milk, could often be produced more cheaply in the Midwest than on the Eastern Seaboard, making western products competitive in eastern markets early in the postbellum period. Reinforcing these developments was the emergence throughout the nation of commercial fluid-milk suppliers wherever there were expanding urban markets. Consequently, as the century progressed, farmers became dependent on their dairy enterprise for a part of their cash income. This induced them to seek ways—imitating the techniques of farmers who were utilizing best available practices, innovating new techniques, or simply milking more days each year—to make dairying more profitable. Consequently, state and national average yields rose steadily after midcentury.

The figures in Table 9.1 show estimates of fluid-milk production in 1860 derived from the published census totals for butter and cheese production, after adjustment for butterfat variations and alternate uses of milk as indicated in contemporary sources. With a market value for fluid milk of about $0.075 a pound, America's dairy production in 1860 gener-

TABLE 9.1. Total Fluid-milk Production by State, 1859–1860

State	Total Milk Production (millions of pounds)
	Northeast
Connecticut	445.0
Maryland	268.2
New Hampshire	316.9
New Jersey	503.0
New York	5,188.0
Pennsylvania	2,565.2
Vermont	799.8
	Midwest
Illinois	1,349.0
Indiana	846.3
Iowa	552.9
Kansas	75.7
Michigan	717.1
Minnesota	141.5
Missouri	597.7
Ohio	2,540.7
Wisconsin	665.5

Sources: Derived from butter and cheese output data reported in the published census for 1860 adjusted to account for state variations in butterfat content and consumption of fluid milk. The total U.S. production was estimated to be 22,636.7 million pounds.

ated gross farm income of approximately $188 million, an amount almost equal to the value-added produced by the nation's textile (cottons and woolens) industry in that year.[13] Farmer neglect of the dairy clearly did not result from commercial unimportance but from inferior knowledge of breeding and feeding techniques, their preferred concentration on land-extensive food-crop production, and poorly developed markets. Over the remainder of the century as these conditions improved, so did dairy yields.

There were substantial state and regional differences in both milk yields and per capita output during the late antebellum era (Fig. 9.1). These variations, which reflect herd quality as well as care and feeding practices, indicate eastern dairy development to be comparatively advanced by standards of the time. The average yield in three northeastern states, Connecticut, New York, and Vermont, exceeded 4,000 pounds per cow and the mean annual milk yield in the Northeast was 50 percent greater than that in the Midwest.[14] Between 1850 and 1860, however, the gap had narrowed considerably. Whereas yields in the Northeast grew less than 10 percent (except on the southern borders of the region in Pennsylvania and Maryland), yields in a number of midwestern states increased by more than one-third and by more than 10 percent in all except Indiana. Most of this change resulted from the diffusion of improved dairy methods, especially feeding practices, into the developing

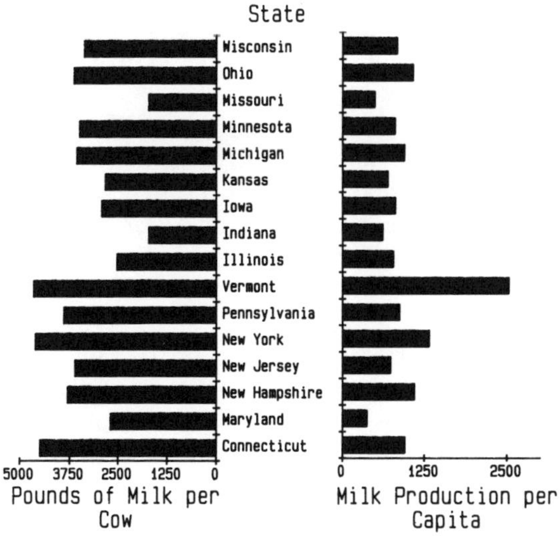

FIG. 9.1. Milk production per cow and per person by state, 1859–1860.

western states.[15] Among the sample states, all of those in the Northeast had yields exceeding the national average. Those in the Midwest were also above average, except in Indiana and Missouri, which fell below the national average and in Illinois where they were about average. Milk production per capita was especially low in Maryland. It was also lower in the other slave state, Missouri, than elsewhere in the North. At the opposite extreme, milk production per capita in Vermont was more than three times the national average and almost double that in New York.

The wide range in yields among regions cannot be accounted for by generic differences between breeds. Instead, it resulted from economic and geographic conditions as well as differences in care and feeding. Yields were highest in the northeastern states and in parts of Michigan and Ohio where proximity to urban markets and good transportation provided an incentive for farmers to try to increase yields through the adoption of superior care and feeding practices. Except on a comparatively small number of large, specialized commercial dairies, milk cows were almost exclusively dual-purpose (beef and dairy) mixed breeds or even triple-purpose (beef-dairy-draft) "native" animals. Their potential yields—those forthcoming even when the best available practices were used—were lower than those of specialized European dairy cattle, only a few of which had been imported into the United States before the middle of the century. Even the "improving" farmers who wished to raise the standards of their herds had a difficult time finding bulls or a breeding stock from which to start. In addition, both the quantity and quality of feed were considerably poorer outside the northeastern region.

Another influence on the yearly animal yield was the length of the milking season, the number of days the animals were milked each year. Before the Civil War the typical milking period in the Northeast extended from mid-March until the end of November. In the Midwest milking typically began in early April and continued through November. During the remaining months each year, the cow would be fed minimally and allowed to "go dry"—a practice usually thought desirable and necessary.[16]

The somewhat casual attitude toward milk production, particularly outside the northeastern states, reflected in the minimal care, feeding, breeding, and consequently in yields, carried over to labor usage. Rarely taken as seriously as field crops, dairying was typically assigned as a task to be done by the young, the old, and women. It was perceived as women and children's work, especially during peak planting or harvesting periods, and as a good means for utilizing otherwise idle family labor. Milking, cleaning of stables, feeding, and other chores associated with fluid-milk production as well as butter churning or cheese making thus employed labor with a low opportunity cost that was present as a fixed component of the family labor supply. Even so, the annual time devoted to obtaining milk varied across regions, the total on eastern farms being about 15 percent greater than on midwestern.

The low opportunity cost of the workers plus the generally minor position accorded the dairy by most farmers partially accounts for the slow pace of mechanization in this branch of agriculture over the second half of the century, but impediments to technological change existed as well. Milking was the most time-consuming daily chore, but successful machine-milking was not introduced until the twentieth century. Difficulties associated with adjusting machines to individual animals, avoiding irritation or injury to the cow, and preventing fire hazards deterred their implementation by farmers. Similar problems were encountered in other countries where inventors were also attempting to develop a practical machine.[17] Nor were there mechanical devices designed to reduce labor input time significantly in the other dairy work operations, including care and feeding. At this time, and indeed throughout the nineteenth century, dairying remained a manual task requiring large amounts of labor time.[18] In the more commercialized areas, several developments had tended to increase the time spent. Those eager to sell or barter milk or its products, for example, tried to ensure a long productive period in which their herd yielded milk, yet as a consequence they had to incur the labor expense of the more careful and time-consuming methods for housing, feeding, and maintaining animals throughout the year. Commercial milk sales also brought producers under stricter governmental regulation regarding sanitation and quality, which necessitated greater labor input usage. The vast majority of farmers in the antebellum period, however, did not yet face these conditions.

Typically, the number of milk cows held varied across farm size categories (see Fig. 9.2). Farmers with small landholdings (less than 80 acres) owned proportionately few, while those on larger farms (over 160 acres) had a disproportionately large percentage relative to their representation in number of farms. These larger units, constituting only 22.3 percent of the farms in the Midwest and 19.1 percent of those in the Northeast, owned 34.5 percent of the cows in the former region and 31.9 percent of those in the latter. As a result, herd size on the larger farms was typically double the national average.

Nevertheless, small herds characterized farms of all sizes, even the largest. The average holding on midwestern farms was fewer than three head, while in the Northeast it averaged fewer than five cows per farm (Fig. 9.3). Almost all farmers (about 99.9 percent) owned six or fewer cows, and most had fewer than four. Herd size alone reflects the general lack of a solid commercial orientation of dairying at this time. More than 40 percent of these farms kept two or three animals largely to provide for

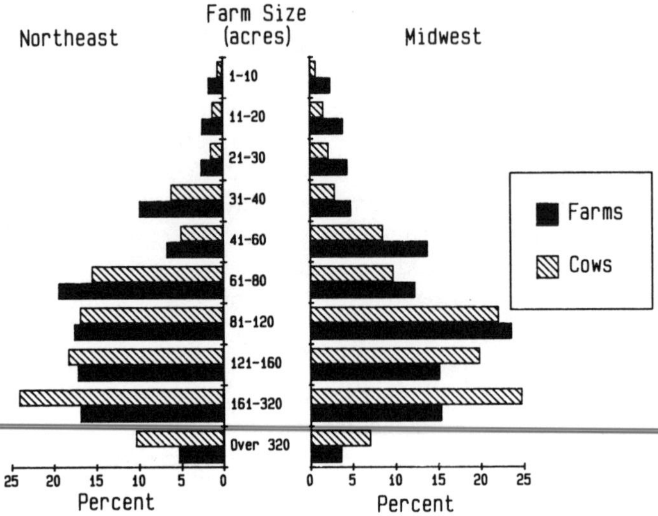

FIG. 9.2. Distribution of farms and cows by size of farm in each region, 1860.

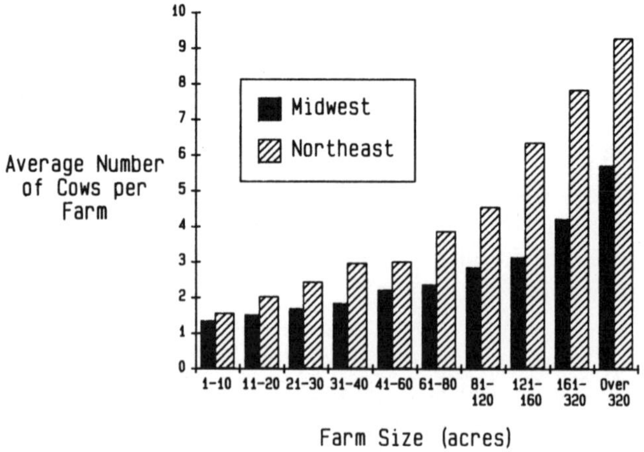

FIG. 9.3. Herd size by size of farm and region, 1860.

family use, while another one-third owned no more than an average of four. Only on units above 80 acres or so does herd size increase notably, reflecting the potential for sales (or barter) off the farm.

Clarence Danhof claims that commercial agriculture already was established in many northern states before the Civil War.[19] He was referring most specifically to such products commercially marketable under mid-nineteenth century technology as wheat, pork, or corn rather than to more immediately perishable foodstuffs such as milk. But even milk and dairy products, while not entering long-distance commerce to any major extent, were traded in local or even regional markets. Butter and cheese provided a means of converting fluid milk to a less quickly perishable and relatively higher valued form suitable to available transport facilities. According to aggregate quantitative evidence, northern farmers produced more milk and dairy products than were consumed on the farm (see Chap. 12 and Fig. 9.1). Such marketable surpluses were more pronounced in Vermont, New York, or Ohio than elsewhere, but total production in many northern states appears to have far exceeded the farm population's desire to consume these goods.

The large eastern farms, those above 120 acres, produced substantial amounts of butter and cheese per farm (Fig. 9.4). There is a noticeable break in the production level for eastern farms of this size and larger, with both butter and cheese production per farm rising dramatically at this point. No such sharp discontinuity is apparent in the western region.

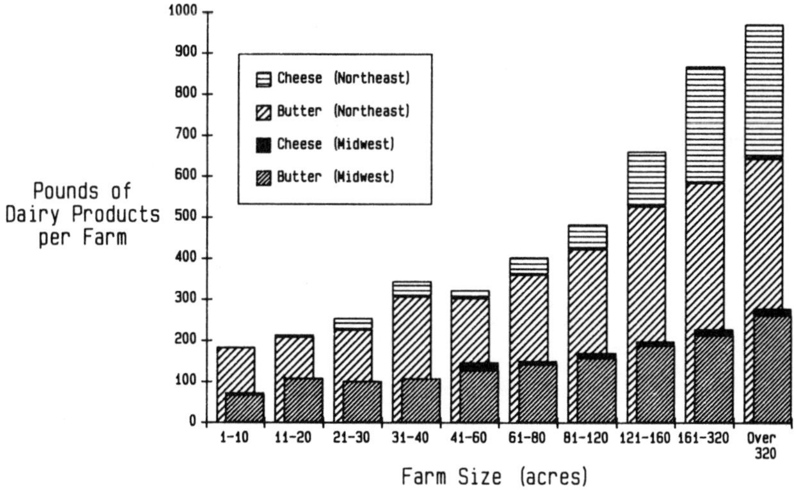

FIG. 9.4. Butter and cheese production by size of farm and region, 1859–1860 (in butter equivalents).

These indications are consistent with contemporary observations as well as with the size of herd on these farms. At this level eastern dairy farms assumed a commercial character, with most commercially oriented dairy operations in the urban Northeast occurring on relatively large units.

The yield of butter per cow in the East shows a marked downtrend with farm size, but without estimates of fluid-milk production this can be misleading. Consider the data for the Northeast in Figure 9.5. Butter output per cow falls by about 25 to 30 percent between farms of 60 acres or less and farms of 160 acres or more. Cheese production per cow, on the other hand, almost triples between those farms with fewer than 60 acres and those over 160, revealing the increasing tendency of the larger eastern farms to dispose of their dairy output as fluid milk rather than as butter. Smaller farms tended to convert their milk product into butter, both for family consumption and for local sale to nearby patrons or country stores.

Low butter production per cow on the larger farms, while implying an orientation toward greater fluid-milk production, does not necessarily reflect lower average output per person on such holdings. In fact, as Figure 9.6 indicates, the highest average output of butter and cheese per member of the farm's population occurred on farms exceeding 160 acres. Because of the larger average holdings of milk animals on the bigger farms, they were able to produce a greater amount of butter and cheese per farm

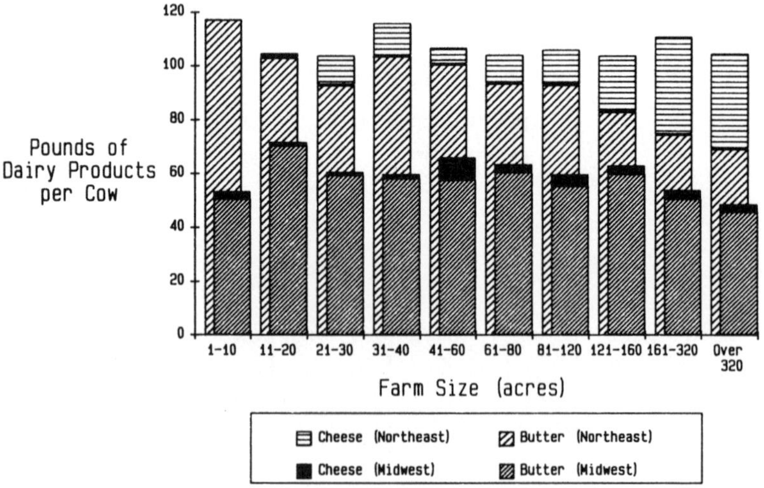

FIG. 9.5. Butter and cheese production per cow by size of farm and region, 1859–1860 (in butter equivalents).

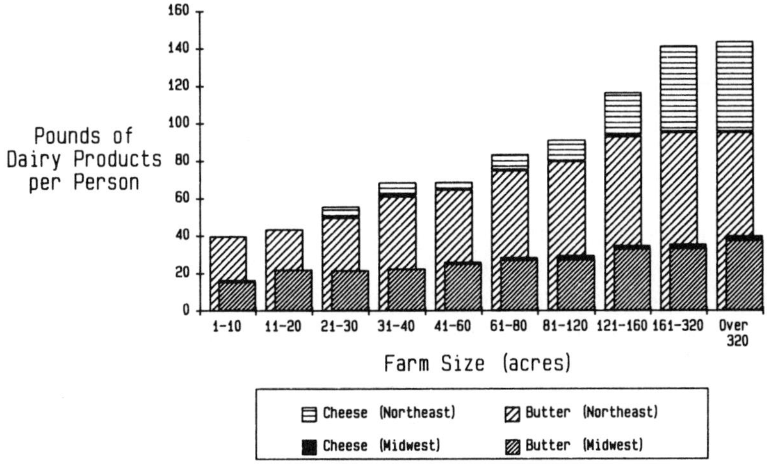

FIG. 9.6. Butter and cheese per person by size of farm and region, 1859–1860 (in butter equivalents).

member while using less of their total output of milk per cow for making butter or cheese.

We know that a market for dairy products existed at this time, but at what scale of operation for farmers did it begin to exert its influence? This issue is addressed for all commodities in our discussion of self-sufficiency in Chapter 12. The question here is at what size of farm, if any, did farms begin to produce surplus dairy products for market sale? The answer depends upon consumption levels, but unfortunately most of the "consumption" estimates at this time are really average production data, calculated by dividing butter output reported in the published census by population.[20] Edgar W. Martin's estimate of annual butter consumption in 1860, for example, of 14.6 pounds per capita was derived that way.[21] It also appears that Richard Cummings's estimate of an average annual butter consumption per capita of 15.1 pounds for 1850–1859, as well as that in USDA *Statistical Bulletin 25*, was similarly calculated from output data.[22] Other nineteenth-century sources attempt actual estimates of consumption. Silas Loomis, writing in the *1861 Report of the Commissioner of Patents*, speculated that daily average fluid-milk consumption per person in thirteen (mostly eastern) states was about 1 pint.[23] Henry Alvord, in the *1899 Yearbook of Agriculture,* estimated annual per capita consumption of butter to be 20 pounds.[24] F. N. Woll, in his *Dairy Calendar* for 1895, claimed that annual per capita consumption of butter was 33 pounds; of cheese, 17 pounds; and of fluid milk, 273 pounds.[25]

Twentieth-century estimates of nineteenth-century consumption also suffer from drawbacks. T. R. Pirtle's figures prepared for the Department of Agriculture are identical to those by Cummings.[26] Perhaps the best are those of Bennett and Pierce, who indicate an annual per capita consumption of 260 pounds of whole milk, 10.7 pounds of cream, one-third a pound of condensed and evaporated milk, and 15.2 pounds of butter for 1879.[27]

All these calculations, varying greatly in reliability, provide little insight into the distribution of consumption or variations among consuming groups. Our sample data give estimates of production per member of the farm population. Farm families reputedly consumed larger quantities of milk and dairy products than did nonfarmers, and rural families more than urban.[28] We therefore need estimates of their consumption to draw conclusions about available market output. The average national figures reported in most sources can only be suggestive since the sample data represent average output per farm member, a group whose consumption was probably the highest of any in the United States.

John Cassels, recognizing this problem in his *A Study of Fluid Milk Prices*, developed estimates based on four groups in the population for 1929. Employing production, net import, and net storage movement data, he derived estimates for per capita consumption for the entire population and for four groups of consumers.[29] As expected, a substantial difference existed between per capita consumption levels on farms, in rural areas, and in cities. Fluid-milk consumption, for example, on producing farms exceeded the average for the entire population by 37 percent, and butter consumption by 70 percent.

The 1860 Census reports only butter and cheese figures, thus Cassels's estimates for butter are the most useful guide for estimating consumption of dairy products by the farm population in 1860.[30] Assume that the same relationship between per capita consumption by the total population and that by the farm population held in 1860 as in 1929, with the latter exceeding the former by 70 percent. This is not an inappropriate assumption since other evidence suggests that it was consumption of fluid milk off the farm that was most affected by transport and marketing improvements after 1860, not butter or cheese. The relationship between farm and market butter consumption probably remained relatively stable over this period. Applying a factor of 70 percent to the total population average indicates that average annual per capita consumption of butter on farms in 1860 would have been 24.8 pounds.

Assuming this average consumption per farm member to be invariant across all farm sizes, a reasonable assumption given other evidence on nineteenth-century consumption patterns, we calculate the quantities of butter that would have been available for sale on commercial markets or for barter with a local country store. These figures (Table 9.2) indicate that even farms in the smallest size category would have averaged about 11 pounds of surplus butter production, almost enough to supply one nonfarm consumer for a year. Farms over 80 acres averaged 165 pounds of output beyond farm consumption.

What would such sales have meant in terms of cash income? The retail butter price in 1860 for the northern states averaged about $0.20 per pound. Assume that the price paid a producing farmer would have been $0.15, a low estimate if the fragmentary evidence on prices received by them is correct. Overall, producers in the North with more than 80 acres (see the last column in Table 9.2) could have gained a supplement to their incomes from $20.91 to $30.23 if markets were accessible. Earnings of this magnitude would have contributed substantially to a farm family's annual income, representing an amount equal to northern manufacturing wages for one to two months. Even smaller farms could expect reasonable cash earnings, or cash equivalent where barter or sale with a country

TABLE 9.2. Estimated Surplus Butter and Cheese Production by Size of Farm, 1859–1860

	Butter		Cheese	
Farm Size (acres)	Residual per Farm (pounds)	Residual Value per Farm (dollars)	Residual per Farm (pounds)	Residual Value per Farm (dollars)
		Northeast		
1–10	69.9	10.49	—	—
11–20	90.7	13.61	—	—
21–30	114.3	17.15	32.4	3.24
31–40	184.0	27.60	51.5	5.15
41–60	189.4	28.41	14.1	1.41
61–80	242.4	36.36	61.9	6.19
81–120	293.6	44.04	100.2	10.02
121–160	390.5	58.57	258.8	25.88
161–320	438.3	65.75	592.7	59.27
Above 320	480.8	72.11	684.1	68.41
		Midwest		
1–10	—	—	—	—
11–20	—	—	—	—
21–30	—	—	—	—
31–40	—	—	—	—
41–60	2.6	0.38	12.2	1.22
61–80	13.3	1.99	—	—
81–120	15.7	2.35	—	—
121–160	48.5	7.27	—	—
161–320	55.7	8.35	—	—
Above 320	90.3	13.55	—	—

Source: See text.

store occurred, from the sale of butter. In the Midwest small farms could not have met this higher level of farm consumption of butter, but the larger midwestern farms (those over 40 acres) could have collected a few additional dollars from the sale of surplus butter. In the Northeast even the smallest farms could have earned over $10.00 from the sale of surplus butter, while the larger farms could have gained quite substantial income from this source.

Farmers in most size categories could also sell fluid milk for additional income when they were located near cities or towns. Whether or not specific individual farmers actually were able to take advantage of and had sufficient information to be aware of this full earning potential remains uncertain. But even granting generous allowances for farm-family consumption, most farms produced sufficient output to generate a fairly substantial cash or barter income from sale of dairy foods in 1860. There is little doubt that they possessed this potential well before this time. Indeed sales of products such as butter, milk, and eggs often appear to have been a farmer's earliest venture into the commercial market and away from self-sufficiency.

If we assume a similar relationship between total and farm consumption for cheese, the average consumption of that product by each farm member would have been 5.6 pounds. The average northern farm over 40 acres produced sufficient cheese to allow for market disposal, but only those farms over 80 acres could have done so to any appreciable extent. For them, assuming a $0.10 per pound cheese price, these sales could have brought in from $4.00 to $20.00 annually. The great bulk of northern farms would thus have been producing this product almost completely for their own modest family consumption. In the Midwest it seems doubtful whether there was any cheese surplus to market from any size of farm, while in the Northeast earnings from cheese for large farms rivaled their earnings from butter sales and all but the smallest two size categories of farms had a marketable surplus.

We can extract some broad generalizations from our data regarding commercially oriented dairying in the antebellum North during this period. The bulk of northern farms, those with more than 40 acres, produced some surplus dairy products, particularly butter, which they sold directly to neighbors or to nearby local markets through country stores for cash or barter. Some farms of this size that were near small towns, whether in the Northeast or Midwest, sold excess fluid milk commercially. This, however, was more common among eastern farmers. Truly "commercial" dairying involving the selling of large quantities of butter and cheese and supplying substantial quantities of fluid milk to urban milksheds most generally occurred on the larger size farms, particularly those of 120 acres and more. Farmers in the Northeast, especially in the Hudson and Mohawk valleys of New York State and on larger farms everywhere tended to engage more seriously in a commercially oriented dairy operation. Compared with those in the Midwest or on smaller acreages, they had bigger herds, produced larger quantities of dairy products, and traded more actively in fluid-milk markets.

Nevertheless, few truly commercial specialized dairy farms existed before the Civil War. Dairying was a secondary economic activity for most farmers, but a primary one for only a few. Our figures offer convincing evidence that by 1860 dairying played a reasonably prominent role in eastern agricultural activities, providing a more substantive potential even on comparatively small farms for generating income through market trade than traditionally has been recognized. In the Midwest, where on the eve of the Civil War only the largest farmers had begun the transition to market participation, the potential for true commercial dairying lay well into the future.

CHAPTER TEN

The Pursuit of Surpluses: Crop Yields and Agricultural Practice

INCREASED PRODUCTION AND MARKETABLE SURPLUSES became goals of northern farmers as they entered commercial markets. In the aggregate they succeeded, raising productivity and output throughout the nineteenth century by adopting innovations in farm implements and practices as well as by exploiting the fertile lands available in the trans-Appalachian West. Crop yields grew in the process.

Contemporary yield estimates are available from a variety of sources for the mid-nineteenth century. These cover a wide range of values and there is often reason to suspect the impartiality of many of the estimates. Most researchers have favored figures that are close to the yields realized at the turn of the century, but it is not clear how typical they were for the mid-nineteenth century. Were they realizable only when utilizing the best available practices or were they attainable by the average farmer? Were there systematic geographic variations in yield? Did soil type make a difference? In this chapter we derive empirical yield estimates from the manuscript census data that represent the median yields realized by farmers in 1859. These also allow us to investigate any systematic variations in yields in that year.

Letters to the U.S. commissioner of patents furnished a major source of information on general farming practice and yields.[1] This correspondence has been used extensively by many writing on the history of agriculture during this period.[2] There are good reasons, however, to question the representativeness of yields and practices as reported in these letters. First, there is the obvious selection bias. People who write letters believe that what they have to say is interesting and important. Many of the letters consequently can be classified into two groups – those from "high"-practice farmers boasting, albeit sometimes discreetly, of their prowess and those complaining of low prices or the ravages of pests, disease, and poor weather. Letters of the former group dominate.

The following yield quotations, taken from some of the letters in the 1850 Report for northern and midwestern states in the sample, are fairly typical:

From Connecticut:

I think the average product per acre [of corn] to be about 40 bushels. Some extra fields go as high as 80 or 90 . . . the average yield of our oat crop is something less than corn. . . .[3]

From Illinois:

Average product per acre [of wheat] for 1850, about 19 bushels . . . [corn], fifty bushels; Oats – Average yield (5 farms, in fair season) 36 bushels. . . . Quantity of hay cut per acre? With reasonable farming 2 tons; I have known 2.5; average 1.5 tons. . . . Potatoes (Irish) – Average yield, 70 bushels. . . .[4]

From Indiana:

I raise from 1 and 1.5 to 2 tons per acre [of hay]. . . .[5]

From New Jersey:

[corn] yields an average of about fifty bushels per acre. . . . Average yield per acre [of potatoes], 100 bushels. . . . [wheat] average product per acre, 20 bushels . . . [rye] about 12 bushels harvested per acre. . . .[6]

From New York:

Since I have grown the flint-wheat, my average has been about 25 bushels per acre . . . Oats – Average crop per acre, about 50 bushels . . . Barley – Average yield per acre, about 35 bushels. . . . Clover and Grasses – Average quantity per acre, about 2 tons. . . .[7]

From Ohio:

the yield [of potatoes] is 400 bushels per acre. . . .[8]

From Pennsylvania:

Wheat – There are three kinds in use – the bald, which averages about 25 bushels per acre; Black Sea, average 25 to 30 bushels and red-chaff, average 20 bushels per acre. . . . Corn – Varieties, yellow and white: average crop, 50 bushels per acre. . . . Oats, average yield per acre, 40 bushels. . . . Rye, average yield per acre, 35 bushels. . . . Clover and Grasses–Average product per acre, 2 tons. . . .[9]

Thus corn yields, for example, were almost invariably estimated at around 50 bushels per acre in 1850. However, USDA figures show that no state had an average corn yield this high until 1939.[10]

The range of yields quoted in the *Patent Reports* for the three major grain crops–corn, oats, and wheat–is shown in Table 10.1. We believe that these estimates are subject to an upward bias. However, the claims in the commissioner of patents' reports are modest in comparison with many exaggerated ones in the popular press of the time. Frequently these overly sanguine estimates, advanced in connection with land sales promotions, were designed to stimulate interest in land purchases and to justify inflated prices. The Illinois Central Railroad, for example, made extravagant claims in its sales brochures in an effort to dispose of the millions of acres that it received in grants from the Federal Government. This sales literature was translated into various languages and distributed widely both at home and throughout Europe in an effort to attract settlers.[11] In one pamphlet, for example, satisfied farmers gave the following testimonials:

Our average crop of corn, say a field of eighty acres, did not vary much from fifty

TABLE 10.1. Commissioner of Patents Yield Estimates for Corn, Oats, and Wheat, 1843–1856 (bushels per acre)

	Corn		Oats		Wheat	
State/Region	Range	Median	Range	Median	Range	Median
New England	20–50	35	17–50	30	15–25	15
Maryland	—	30	9–50	20	6–20	15
New Jersey	35–50	45	30–50	40	12–30	20
New York	25–50	30	28–50	35	10–25	18
Pennsylvania	30–50	38	30–50	40	8–30	15
Illinois	40–50	43	—	—	10–20	16
Indiana	30–60	40	—	—	9–25	16
Iowa	22–40	35	—	—	10–20	15
Michigan	15–40	30	—	—	12–30	21
Missouri	30–60	40	—	—	10–20	15
Ohio	25–60	39	—	—	10–35	15
Wisconsin	25–50	45	—	—	12–40	20
Upper Midwest[a]	—	—	30–60	40	—	—
Lower Midwest[b]	—	—	20–55	40	—	—

Source: William N. Parker and Judith L. V. Klein, "Productivity Growth in Grain Production in the United States, 1840–1860 and 1900–1910," in *Output, Employment, and Productivity in the United States after 1800,* Studies in Income and Wealth, 30 (Princeton, 1966), Table B.1, p. 500.

[a]Michigan and Wisconsin.

[b]Ohio, Indiana, Illinois, and Iowa.

bushels per acre. Winter wheat . . . upon a field of thirty acres, varied in different years from nineteen to twenty-three bushels per acre . . . oats varied from forty to sixty bushels per acre. . . .[12]

and:

I raised over twenty-five bushels per acre of the best wheat last year, on corn ground, without ploughing, and sixty bushels of oats.[13]

Even the editor of the prestigious *Prairie Farmer* lent his name to the effort by quoting the following yields based upon eighteen years' experience:

With ordinary culture:	
Winter Wheat	15 to 25 bushels
Spring Wheat	10 to 20 bushels
Indiana Corn	40 to 70 bushels
Oats	40 to 80 bushels
Potatoes	100 to 200 bushels
Grass (timothy and clover)	1½ to 3 tons[14]

Land companies made similarly fanciful claims.[15]

Although such exaggerations can perhaps be dismissed out of hand as the poetic license of marketers, there were more disinterested parties who are less easily ignored. For example, Frederick Gerhard in his book *Illinois as It Is*, suggested the following yields (bu/acre):[16]

County	Wheat	Corn	Oats
Cass	18–25	50–70	40–45
Jo Daviess	15–40	30–100	45
McLean	20–30	45–70	40–50
St. Clair	15–30	30–100	30–60
Marshall	50–70		
Pike	20–40	50–70	40–50
Adams	20–40	60–70	
Peoria	15–25	30–60	
Will	40–60		

and concluded:

according to these observations which were made in nine different counties of the State, throughout her longitudinal extension . . . we receive the following average numbers, per acre:—Indian corn, 56 bushels; wheat, 24; oats, 44; . . .[17]

Government officials were similarly optimistic. The Minnesota commissioner of statistics, for example, quoted wheat yields in the range of 10–35 bushels per acre, corn yields of 23–70 bushels, and average oat yields of 35 bushels.[18]

More conservative estimates were given for 1849 by James D. B.

DeBow, superintendent of the Seventh Census. After the census had begun, a special resolution of the Senate had directed him to prepare a statement of the cultivated land devoted to various agricultural crops in that year. To satisfy this charge, DeBow obtained estimates of the average yield per acre for various crops by county, but was at pains to emphasize that the figures were for good crops and that "the table which follows [reproduced in part as Table 10.2 below] is very incomplete, but nothing better can be framed from the returns, which in general were very carelessly made or entirely neglected."[19]

If these yield estimates are compared with those in Table 10.1, which are from letters to the commissioner of patents, it is obvious that the letter writers were almost universally more optimistic in their claims. The 1849 figures lie toward the bottom end of the ranges reported in Table 10.1, despite DeBow's view that these were good yields.

The 1849 crop yields for corn, oats, and wheat compare quite favorably with the average ones realized over the period 1866–1875, but there was more variation between the 1849 yields and those for 1866–1875 among the other field crops.[20] Irish potato yields in 1849 were, for example, generally higher than in the post–Civil War decade while those of tobacco were lower. Because there was a gradual improvement over the decades, it is reasonable to suppose that average yields in the period 1866–1875 were probably quite similar to the best ones twenty years earlier.

TABLE 10.2. Actual Crops per Acre on the Average as Returned by the Marshals for 1849–1850

States	Wheat (bu)	Rye (bu)	Indian Corn (bu)	Oats (bu)	To-bacco (lb)	Peas & Beans (bu)	Irish Po-tatoes (bu)	Bar-ley (bu)	Buck-wheat (bu)	Hay (ton)	Hops (lb)	Dew-rotted Hemp (lb)
Connecticut	—	—	40	21	—	—	85	—	20	—	—	—
Illinois	11	14	33	29	—	—	115	40	15	1.5	—	—
Indiana	12	18	33	20	—	—	100	25	25	1	—	—
Iowa	14	—	32	36	—	—	100	—	—	—	—	—
Maryland	13	18	23	21	650	—	75	—	—	1	—	—
Michigan	10	—	32	26	—	—	140	—	14	—	—	—
Missouri	11	—	34	26	775	—	110	—	—	1.25	—	775
New Hampshire	11	14	30	30	—	—	220	22	—	1	—	—
New Jersey	11	8	33	26	—	—	75	18	16	—	—	—
New York	12	17	27	25	—	—	100	25	22	1.13	950	—
Ohio	12	25	36	21	730	—	75	30	20	1.63	—	—
Pennsylvania	15	14	20	22	—	—	75	—	—	1.75	—	—
Vermont	13	20	32	26	—	20	178	—	25	1	—	—
Wisconsin	14	—	30	35	—	—	125	18	—	—	—	—

Source: U.S. Census Office, *Statistical View of the United States . . . Being a Compendium of the Seventh Census,* (Washington, D.C., 1854), 178.

Despite the plethora of crop yield reports both for the pre–Civil War period and the decade following the war, there are surprisingly no general estimates for 1859. Nor is there any unanimity on what yields a farmer might reasonably have expected in an average year. Based upon our calculations, we argue that 1859 was a fairly unexceptional crop year and that our estimates are internally consistent with the acreage under cultivation in 1859.

It is impossible to estimate crop yields directly from the identity:

$$Y_i = Q_i/A_i$$

where Y is yield per acre, Q is output harvested, and A is acreage harvested for each crop; $i = 1, \ldots, n$, because no data on the acreage devoted specifically to each crop were collected at the Census. Enumerators were instructed to report physical production for the following field crops:

1. Wheat;
2. Rye;
3. Corn;
4. Oats;
5. Rice;
6. Tobacco;
7. Cotton;
8. Peas and Beans;
9. Irish Potatoes;
10. Sweet Potatoes;
11. Barley;
12. Buckwheat;
13. Hay;
14. Clover seed;
15. Grass seed;
16. Hops;
17. Hemp;
18. Flax; and
19. Flaxseed.

They also gathered information on total improved acreage, which included all acres under cultivation as well as land cleared and used for grazing or grass or which was fallow.

The census enumerators additionally collected information about a variety of other products produced on the farm: wool production, the value of orchard products and market garden produce, wine production, butter and cheese production, silk cocoons, cane and maple sugar and molasses, sorghum molasses, beeswax and honey. Although production of these outputs involved the use of land, the nature of the transformation from land into dollars of apples, pounds of butter, gallons of molasses, or other products is unclear. Consequently, we confine our attention to the field crops for which output is given in physical units.

The yield identity may be rewritten as:

$$A_i = Q_i/Y_i$$

This may then be summed across all crops: $\Sigma A_i = \Sigma(Q_i/Y_i)$.

This equation may be used to estimate yields from the data collected by the Census. Total acreage harvested, ΣA_i, is replaced by improved acres, IMPROVED. This introduces a constant term into the right-hand side of the equation that measures the acreage devoted to excluded crops such as those from orchards, market gardens, or viticulture as well as land devoted to grazing and pasture or fallow. Information on physical crop output, Q_i, is taken from the Census for the nineteen field crops that are separately identified. The error term represents yield variations due to differences in farm practice, farming ability, and "Acts of God":

$$\text{IMPROVED} = a + b_1Q_1 + b_2Q_2 + \ldots + b_{19}Q_{19} + u_i$$

This equation was estimated by ordinary least squares. The regression coefficients, b_i, are then the reciprocals of the crop yields per acre.[21]

Although this equation does not allow us to estimate yields directly, the formulation was forced upon us by the nature of the available data. Unfortunately, it causes a number of problems. We can make no tests of statistical significance for crop yields since yields are the reciprocal of the regression coefficient. Using the confidence interval about the regression coefficient as an estimate of the range of yields has no statistical validity; moreover, it generates an asymmetric interval which can be very wide despite a high t-value for the regression coefficient. Consequently we do not report any interval about our yield estimates. However, the yields we report are derived from regression coefficients that were significantly different from zero.[22]

Perhaps more serious than the lack of statistical tests of significance for our yield estimates is the implication to be derived from a regression coefficient that was not significantly different from zero: the yield (its reciprocal) is infinite. We offer a different and more plausible interpretation for such a result. Provided the regression coefficient is positive, such a finding can be intrepreted as implying that the acreage devoted to the particular crop was negligible (since as $A \rightarrow 0$, $Y \rightarrow \infty$).

Negative regression coefficients for crop outputs are clearly nonsensical. Crops whose coefficients were originally estimated to be negative were dropped from the model and the equation reestimated without them. These were usually the less frequently grown ones, such as barley, clover, flax and flaxseed, hemp, or tobacco. Dew-rotted hemp, flaxseed, and clover seed, for example, were excluded from the equation for the entire North. The average farm produced less than half a bushel of flaxseed or clover seed and only 17 pounds of hemp. Removal of those crops that have very small t-values from the equation had minimal effects. The biggest change in any coefficient was at the third decimal place, and much of the effect seemed to be dissipated by marginal changes in coefficients that were themselves not significantly different from zero.

Although our regression equation was suggested by an identity, and the particular form that it took forced upon us opportunistically by the available data, the causal relationship it implies is counterintuitive. The model asserts that farm size was determined by the vector of crop outputs, whereas the reverse is more likely true.[23] As a result, it violates the Gauss-Markov condition that errors be uncorrelated with the independent variable. In the single-crop case it can be shown that this "backwards" regression biases the yields upward. In the multicrop case, unfortunately the direction of bias cannot be specified a priori but depends upon the variance-covariance matrix of errors for the crops.[24]

Although our results are biased in an unknown direction, we believe that they are nevertheless worthy of consideration. We have subjected them to a variety of checks for internal consistency and plausibility, and compared them with a number of independent yield observations (see below). Each of the tests has served to reinforce our faith in the yield estimates we derive from this regression model.

The weighted equation for the entire sample of rural northern townships is shown in detail below:

$$\underset{(t\text{-statistic})}{\text{Improved Acres}} = \underset{(10.28)}{27.3078} + \underset{(6.24)}{0.0880}\text{ Wheat} + \underset{(2.17)}{0.0797}\text{ Rye}$$

$$+ \underset{(12.01)}{0.0336}\text{ Corn} + \underset{(4.79)}{0.0359}\text{ Oats} + \underset{(0.11)}{0.0214}\text{ Rice} + \underset{(0.95)}{0.0020}\text{ Tobacco}$$

$$+ \underset{(0.10)}{0.3999}\text{ Cotton} + \underset{(2.06)}{0.2862}\text{ Peas \& Beans} + \underset{(3.08)}{0.0799}\text{ Irish Potatoes}$$

$$+ \underset{(0.71)}{0.1265}\text{ Sweet Potatoes} + \underset{(3.60)}{0.1459}\text{ Barley} + \underset{(3.11)}{0.1337}\text{ Buckwheat}$$

$$+ \underset{(11.00)}{1.13425}\text{ Hay} + \underset{(1.86)}{0.2841}\text{ Grass Seed} + \underset{(1.18)}{0.0035}\text{ Hops}$$

$$+ \underset{(0.35)}{12.800}\text{ Dew-rotted Hemp} + \underset{(0.11)}{0.0946}\text{ Other Prepared Hemp}$$

$$+ \underset{(0.95)}{0.0712}\text{ Flax}$$

$$R^2 = 0.369, \quad n = 11{,}717, \quad F = 35.02$$

Clover seed, flaxseed, and dew-rotted hemp were dropped after their coefficients were estimated to be negative but not significantly different from zero.

The yield estimates implied by these regression coefficients are shown in Table 10.3. Nine of the coefficients were significant at better than the 5 percent level; one coefficient, that for grass seed, was significant only at the 10 percent level. We have also shown the range of yields implied by the 95 percent confidence interval about the significant crop coefficients. They are for illustrative purposes only.

We have used weighted regressions for the regional estimates because some states were oversampled. Since yields varied across states, those which were above or below the average in oversampled states will bias yields up or down, while the nonaverage yields in undersampled states would result in estimates that were biased downward or upward depending upon whether state yields are above or below average. Similarly, interstate variations in crop mixes, especially as these reflected differences in profitability or the feasibility of growing particular crops, would bias our regression coefficients if the sample observation weights were not corrected to reflect their relative importance in the population from which they were drawn.

TABLE 10.3. Yields per Acre on Northern Farms, 1859–1860 (Units as shown. All coefficients significant at the 5 percent level unless otherwise noted)

Crop	Regression Coefficient	Yields (bushels unless otherwise noted)	Range of Yields Implied by 95% Confidence Interval about the Regression Coefficients
Wheat	0.0880	11.4	8.6–16.6
Rye	0.0797	12.5	6.6–13.2
Corn	0.0336	29.8	25.6–35.5
Oats	0.0359	27.9	19.7–47.1
Rice	0.0214	46.7	n.s.
Tobacco	0.0020	500.0 (lb)	n.s.
Cotton	0.3999	2.5 (bale)	n.s.
Peas & Beans	0.2862	3.5	1.8–73.4
Irish Potatoes	0.0799	12.5	7.6–34.6
Sweet Potatoes	0.1265	7.9	n.s.
Barley	0.1459	6.9	4.4–15.1
Buckwheat	0.1337	7.5	4.6–20.3
Hay	1.1342	0.9 (ton)	0.7– 1.1
Grass Seed	0.2841[a]	3.5	1.9–31.7[b]
Hops	0.0035	286.0 (lb)	n.s.
Water-rolled Hemp	12.8000	0.1 (ton)	n.s.
Other Prepared Hemp	0.0946	10.6 (no units)	n.s.
Flax	0.0712	14.0 (lb)	n.s.

n.s. = not significant at the 10 percent level or better.
[a]Significant at the 10 percent level.
[b]Range implied by 90 percent confidence interval.

Some of the interstate variations in crop mix are shown in Table 10.4. Virtually all farmers grew corn in each state in 1859. Hay, potatoes, and oats were almost as widely cultivated. However, none of the 290 farms in Costin District, Worcester County, Maryland, reported growing any hay, and markedly fewer farms in Missouri grew potatoes (only 63 percent compared with 80 to 90 percent or more in other states).[25] In Kansas and Missouri less than a quarter cultivated oats. Producers in five of the sample states grew no tobacco at all, while 24 percent of those among the Ohio sample did so. Similarly, 69 percent of Pennsylvania farms cultivated buckwheat, a crop produced by only 1 percent of the sample farms in Maryland. Approximately two-thirds of all farms from New York to Iowa and Minnesota grew some wheat, which was for many the principal cash crop. Cultivation of the other crops in the table varied widely.

Fewer crop-yield estimates could be made at the regional or state levels than for the entire North because of the geographic dispersion and variations in the frequency particular crops were grown. Additionally, more crops had either insignificant but positive regression coefficients, or had negative coefficients in the first set of estimates. They were not included in subsequent reestimations.

Corn, oats, wheat, and hay yields could be estimated for most of the states (Table 10.5). For each there was a wide interstate variation in the yield. During 1859 in New Hampshire and Vermont, where the wheat crop apparently failed, output per acre was very low. Wheat yields, on the other hand, were high that year in Iowa, Kansas, and Minnesota. The

TABLE 10.4. Percentage of Farms Growing Various Crops by State, 1859–1860[a]

State	Barley	Buck-wheat	Clover	Corn	Hay	Irish Potatoes	Oats	Rye	Tobacco	Wheat
Connecticut	1	56	n.a.	97	100	100	75	84	1	13
Illinois	2	7	b	97	67	80	44	2	1	77
Indiana	3	9	2	96	67	77	42	8	7	85
Iowa	5	18	b	95	75	93	54	7	11	79
Kansas	1	23	b	91	84	82	19	2	1	38
Maryland	n.a.	1	n.a.	95	n.a.	84	58	n.a.	n.a.	31
Michigan	4	37	5	93	86	98	48	24	1	66
Minnesota	10	12	b	87	94	93	50	22	b	67
Missouri	1	10	b	93	49	63	24	5	9	35
New Hampshire	16	5	n.a.	81	98	98	63	21	n.a.	60
New Jersey	n.a.	51	15	94	90	80	83	33	n.a.	64
New York	22	52	4	76	94	97	87	28	b	69
Ohio	12	49	14	93	83	80	70	13	24	62
Pennsylvania	2	69	17	85	92	96	83	61	n.a.	63
Vermont	n.a.	10	n.a.	94	94	.96	80	43	10	33
Wisconsin	6	4	b	69	92	94	85	2	n.a.	96

n.a. = no observation.
[a] Calculated from sample.
[b] Less than 0.5%.

TABLE 10.5. Grain Crop Yield Estimates for the 1859 Crop Year by State and Region (bushels per acre)

State/Region	Barley	Buck-wheat	Corn	Oats	Rye	Wheat
Connecticut	—	—	3.4	—	—	—
Maryland	—	—	16.3	24.7	—	—
New Hampshire	0.7	—	4.6	4.0	1.8	1.8
New Jersey	—	—	—	—	—	—
New York	14.0	7.8	13.0	42.9	26.1	6.0
Pennsylvania	—	13.7	18.2	11.5	14.4	12.8
Vermont	—	—	—	8.7	4.1	0.7
Northeast[a]	8.8	10.0	15.8	33.9	—	7.3
Illinois	—	—	28.0	18.1	—	7.5
Indiana	—	—	34.4	12.1	2.9	10.4
Iowa	—	—	31.7	—	2.0	14.9
Kansas	—	8.7	43.1	8.5	—	29.4
Michigan	—	9.2	25.6	23.8	12.0	10.4
Minnesota	—	—	—	22.6	—	14.3
Missouri	1.7	—	16.7	20.1	—	9.8
Ohio	—	3.2	22.5	10.2	2.1	—
Wisconsin	3.7	—	—	22.1	—	9.6
Midwest[a]	—	3.1	29.9	20.9	—	12.2

[a]Weighted regression.

estimates for these latter states compare quite favorably with the ranges given in Tables 10.1 and 10.2. A portion of the high yields doubtless represented a bounty from the initial cultivation of land in these states or from their first sowing in wheat.

The corn crop in Connecticut and New Hampshire in 1859 also "failed" in terms of average output per acre, corn yields in the Northeast being about half those of the Western states. Kansas yields were very high and the standard error of the regression coefficient very small ($t = 9.93$); in Missouri, the figure was closer to that realized in the northeastern states, resembling the low corn yields for southern states reported by William Parker and Judith Klein.[26]

Oats were the principal feed grain for horses and were occasionally used as a supplement for other livestock. During 1859 this crop did poorly in New Hampshire and Vermont, as did all grain crops in that crop year, as well as in Indiana, Kansas, and Pennsylvania. Nevertheless, oat yields in the Northeast as a whole were 60 percent greater than in the West. The proximity in the eastern states of urban markets with large horse populations doubtless provided a profitable outlet for surplus oats that in general could not profitably be hauled any distance.[27]

Only a few estimates were obtained for nongrain crops (Table 10.6). Tobacco yields are too low to have much credibility. We would have expected a yield in the hundreds of pounds per acre. It was, however, infrequently grown and widely variable in its cultivation among farms growing it. Only one Connecticut farm reported any tobacco production, while it was grown on seventy-one Missouri farms that produced as little as 12 pounds to as much as 5,000 pounds. Yield estimates for peas and beans were also largely meaningless. Although beans were often produced for human consumption, farmers cultivated peas for feed (in which case livestock were simply turned out into the field) or ploughed them under for green manure.[28] Potato yields are also much lower than anticipated. Contemporaries suggested yields on the order of 60–100 bushels per acre (Table 10.2), compared with our estimates which range from 3.2 bushels per acre to 43.7 bushels.

Hay yields were estimated for most of the states in the sample. In the course of measuring acreages devoted to small grains, grass, and hay that might be harvested with a reaper-mower at the farm level, it became obvious that for some farms either hay yields were too low (that is, too much acreage would have to be assigned to hay production given the number of tons produced) or hay was also being harvested from unimproved acres even though the instructions to the census enumerators ought to have excluded such a possibility. For example, a Kansas farm of

TABLE 10.6. Miscellaneous Crop Yield Estimates for the 1859 Crop Year by State and Region (units per acre as shown)

State/Region	Grass Seed (bu)	Hay (ton)	Hops (lb)	Irish Potatoes (bu)	Peas & Beans (bu)	Sweet Potatoes (bu)	Tobacco (lb)
Connecticut	—	0.8	—	—	—	—	8.8
Maryland	—	—	—	—	—	—	—
New Hampshire	—	0.6	—	16.2	1.1	—	—
New Jersey	—	0.7	—	—	—	—	—
New York	—	1.0	413.7	6.3	4.5	1.0	—
Pennsylvania	—	1.9	—	—	—	—	—
Vermont	—	0.9	124.8	—	—	—	—
Northeast[a]	—	1.0	—	8.2	3.6	—	—
Illinois	0.7	—	—	3.2	—	—	—
Indiana	—	0.8	—	—	—	6.0	—
Iowa	—	—	—	—	—	0.5	—
Kansas	1.6	1.6	—	43.7	—	—	—
Michigan	—	—	—	—	—	—	—
Minnesota	—	—	—	—	1.5	—	2.2
Missouri	—	0.3	—	—	1.3	—	—
Ohio	—	0.8	—	—	—	—	—
Wisconsin	0.1	2.1	—	—	—	—	—
Midwest[a]	0.1	0.8	—	—	—	—	—

[a] Weighted regression.

160 acres with 30 improved acres produced 70 tons of hay in addition to other crops. Even if this farm produced no other field crop, the yield would have been 2.3 tons per acre, almost 50 percent higher than we estimate for Kansas overall. If, however, this crop had been garnered from the unimproved range land, the farm's production of hay could have been met with a yield of only 1,100 pounds per acre, which was probably well within the range for wild hay.

Despite the general plausibility of our results, the crop yields estimated from the manuscript census data may not be typical of the yields experienced over a longer period. Although the contemporary farm journals and the commissioner of patent reports frequently mention weather conditions and the ravages of disease and insects, it is almost impossible to assimilate the frequently contradictory reports, often for quite small geographic areas, into a general perception of their influence on yields at the state or regional level.

Consider the following crop reports for Illinois that illustrate some of the difficulties in making generalizations about the effects of weather.[29] The *Prairie Farmer* in February 1859 reported that "the uniform opinion is that at least half of the wheat saved last fall is totally winter killed," but by early March it was reporting "fields that looked dead a week ago are now getting green, and bid fair to make a good crop."[30] Weather was also often quite localized in its effects. For example, in April the *Prairie Farmer* published widely divergent reports from two correspondents. One, Charles Gilbert in Knox County, reported, "We are having a gloomy spring, wet and cold. Spring grain, wheat in particular, is rotting," while O. B. Nichols from Clinton County stated that "wheat looks as promising as I have seen it during the last twenty years."[31] The picture is further complicated because weather that was bad for one crop was not necessarily so for all. Quotations for wheat ofttimes contradicted those for corn. Thus Charles Gilbert, who reported to the *Prairie Farmer* that wheat was rotting, still expected a good corn crop from Knox County.[32] Weather and crop reporters did agree that the late frosts of 4 and 5 June badly damaged the wheat crop and hurt other small grains to a lesser extent.[33]

The ravages of insects and the weather do not seem to have been too serious. With the harvest in, the Chicago Board of Trade observed: "The new crop had realized our expectations, and although the yield had not been large for the area of ground sowed, the quality of our spring wheat was superior to any which has been raised for several years. The winter wheat, too, was of fair quality, although the yield was small."[34] For corn, however, "the yield of grain per acre in 1859 was large, the crop was generally good, and secured in good condition."[35] *Ex post*, then, the crop traded on the Chicago Board of Trade was probably about average for oats and wheat, and better than average for corn.

The Ohio commissioner of statistics' annual reports often contained a summary of observations of the crop and the influence of weather conditions "as made by competent persons." For the 1859 crop, those reporting frequently mention the serious effects of the early June frost on wheat and other crops.[36] Specific comments were made regarding three of the four sample counties in Ohio. For Licking County, in the central part of the state, wheat was reported to be of "good quality. 'Enough for seed' "; corn was described as "a fair supply"; oats a "good crop"; hay was described as very light; and potatoes were listed as the best for many years.[37] From Morrow County in the north-central part of the state, wheat was described as "one-fourth average"; corn as "more than average"; oats, "strong average crop"; and "hay 5/8 average. Buckwheat large crop." Rye was also described as being killed by the June frosts.[38] Wheat and corn were apparently much injured by the frost in Noble County in the southeastern part of the the state, but oats nevertheless realized eight-tenths of the average, hay and potatoes were average, and buckwheat did better than average.[39]

The diversity of views on yields suggests to us that 1859 was probably a fairly typical year. There were temporary setbacks and some areas did poorly while others did well, just as some crops did better than others. Many of the complaints about yields may perhaps be attributed to the overly sanguine expectations of farmers or to the minority who were adversely affected.

The data also show systematic yield variations related to soil type. Some soils are known to be more suited to one crop than another (see Chap. 7, especially Table 7.4). Oat yields on Udult soils (moist, warm soils described as suitable for general farming, woodlands, and pastures), for example, were significantly lower than those obtained from other soils while hay yields were much higher. We have tried to capture the effect of soil type upon farm operations and yields by incorporating dummy variables into our yield equations. Dummy variables usually provide for different constant terms depending upon soil type, but we also included interaction terms between the dummy variables and the various field crops. If the dummy-crop interaction term is positive, then yields on that particular soil for the crop in question are lower than those on the base soil since yield is calculated as the reciprocal of the sum of the base soil crop coefficient and the dummy interaction term. Conversely, if the dummy-crop interaction term is negative, then yields are higher than on the base soil type. The yield on the base soil type is simply the reciprocal of the crop coefficient.

This procedure has one serious drawback: it generates a large number of additional variables. If fully implemented for the sample, the model would involve 19 crop variables together with a constant term that represents yields and farming practice on the "base" soil type (any one of the eleven), plus 10 dummy variables and 190 interaction terms, or a total of 219 variables.[40] We have instead focused our attentions upon a subset of crops and attempt to identify those soil types that involved significant interactions with major crops (wheat, rye, corn, oats, potatoes, sweet potatoes, barley, buckwheat, hay, and grass). Once identified, the entire interaction sets for those soil types were introduced into the equation.[41] We report these results for the North as a whole as well as for the two subregions. Estimates for some of the more important crops are shown in Table 10.7.

In the Midwest wheat yields on Udalf and Ochrept soils were somewhat higher than the median of 10.6 bushels per acre on other soils. Corn yields were lower on them, and the difference was significant in the case

TABLE 10.7. Yields of Important Crops and Their Variation with Soil Type by Region

Region/Soil Interactions	Crop Yield per Acre							
	Wheat (bu)	Rye (bu)	Corn (bu)	Oats (bu)	Irish Potatoes (bu)	Sweet Potatoes (bu)	Hay (ton)	Grass (bu)
A. Midwest								
Base[a]	10.6	n.s.	33.6	n.s.	*	n.s.	0.8	0.8
Udalfs	+	n.s.	24.3	n.s.	*	n.s.	+	2.1
Ochrepts	+	n.s.	19.8	n.s.	*	n.s.	–	+
B. Northeast								
Base[a]	5.5	10.0	20.2	59.5	10.4	1.2	0.8	n.s.
Udalfs	+	++	–	11.0	–	–	1.2	n.s.
Udolls	–	–	+	–	–	*	–	n.s.
Aquults	+	+	+	9.0	+	+	+	n.s.
C. North								
Base[a]	12.3	n.s.	33.7	n.s.	n.s.	n.s.	0.6	3.9
Udalfs	–	n.s.	23.5	n.s.	n.s.	n.s.	+	*
Ochrepts	+	n.s.	15.8	n.s.	n.s.	n.s.	+	*
Aquults	–	n.s.	–	n.s.	n.s.	n.s.	3.0	*

Soil types are described in Table 7.4 and their distribution is mapped in Fig. 7.2

All reported values were significant at the 5 percent level or better (one-tail test).

n.s. = not significant.

*Negative coefficient, variable excluded.

The following symbols have been used in place of numbers when the result was considered implausible. They indicate the direction and general magnitude of the effect.

+ = yield higher than base (but interaction term not significant).

++ = yield much higher than base (interaction term signficant).

– = yield lower than base (but interaction term not significant).

[a]Following soil types were not included in the regression: Psamments, Aquepts, Borolls, Orthods, and Udults. They could not be distinguished from one another.

of Udalf soils. Northeastern wheat yields on the base soil were only about half those in the West, and yields were again higher on Udalf soils. Similarly, corn fared more poorly on these than on others. In general, soils that gave high yields for small grains gave poorer ones for corn.

We have also applied this methodology to estimate yields in Illinois (Table 10.8) because we have independent county estimates of crop yields

TABLE 10.8. Soil Type and Crop Yield Variations in Illinois, 1859–1860

	No Allowance for Soil Type		With Soil Type Dummies	
Variable	Regression Coefficient	Yield (bu)	Regression Coefficient	Yield (bu)
Constant	29.592[b]		43.216[b]	
Udalf Dummy (D2)			−16.470[b]	
Aquall Dummy (D6)			−24.537	
Wheat	0.1335[b]	7.5	0.0996[b]	10.0
Wheat[a] D2			0.0670[a]	6.0
Wheat[a] D6			− 0.0119	11.4
Corn	0.0357[b]	28.0	0.0368[b]	27.2
Corn[a] D2			− 0.0038	30.3
Corn[a] D6			− 0.0083	35.1
Oats	0.0554[b]	18.1	0.0512[b]	19.5
Oats[a] D2			− 0.0119	25.4
Oats[a] D6			none grown	—
Irish Potatoes	0.3103[b]	3.2	0.3286[b]	3.0
Irish Potatoes D2			− 0.2839[c]	22.4
Irish Potatoes D6			− 0.3144	70.4
Barley	0.0211	47.4	0.0251	39.8
Barley[a] D2			0.8224	1.2
Barley[a] D6			none grown	—
Buckwheat	0.0622	16.1	0.1706	5.9
Buckwheat[a] D2			− 0.4427	n.a.
Buckwheat[a] D6			− 0.0582	8.9
Grass Seed	1.5116[b]	0.7	1.3538[b]	0.7
Grass Seed[a] D2			0.4267	0.6
Grass Seed[a] D6			− 3.5359	n.a.
Dew-rotted Hemp	0.3459	2.9	0.0786	12.7
Dew-rotted Hemp[a] D2			none grown	—
Dew-rotted Hemp[a] D6			none grown	—
R^2	0.429		0.445	

The base soil was of type Udoll. See Table 7.3 for a description of soil types and Fig. 7.2 for a map of their distribution.

[a]Significant at better than the 10 percent level (two-tailed test).

[b]Significant at better than the 5 percent level (two-tailed test).

[c]Significant at the 10.7 percent level.

n.a. = nonsensical result (negative)

D2 = dummy variable for Udalf soil type counties in the Illinois sample (Adams, Brown, Knox, Macoupin, and Williamson) set to 1, if true; 0, if otherwise.

D6 = dummy variable for Aquall soil type county in the Illinois sample (Massac) set to 1, if true; 0, if otherwise.

in that state. Forty-four percent of the farms were in Udalf counties, 3 percent were on the Aquall soils in Massac County at the southern tip of Illinois, and the balance farmed on Udoll soils. The same variables that were significant in the original equation are significant in the expanded regression and there were some significant interaction terms. The results indicate significantly lower wheat but higher potato yields from Udalf soils than were realized from these crops grown on Udoll soils. Even where the interaction terms are not significant, the results are plausible.

Farmers specializing in wheat were concentrated in the prairie counties of Illinois, north of the Illinois River. Soils in these counties that were among the leading wheat producers in the nation were predominantly Udolls, which produced larger yields than the other major type, Udalfs, in the rest of the state. The Udolls extended westward and northward into Iowa and southwestern Wisconsin and Minnesota, with an eastern outcrop in western Indiana. In each case, wheat yields were higher from these than from others along the same latitude. Indeed, in Minnesota these soils produced superior yields of all crops.

In the East, Udult soils in Pennsylvania and New Jersey produced greater yields than Ochrepts in the same areas. This seems to be reflected in land values. In New York State, on the other hand, Ochrepts provided higher yields of corn but lower ones of small grains than the Udalfs in the northern part of the state.

There are a number of independent figures for 1859 that can be used as checks upon our estimates. We do not believe, however, that they can be used as a basis for rejecting our estimates because we can attach no confidence intervals to them. Nor should the reader necessarily be prepared to place more faith in these independent yield estimates, because they are sometimes internally inconsistent or conflict with other equally plausible and independent observations. Our purpose in presenting them is solely as a basis for comparison.

The auditor of public accounts for the state of Illinois presented a statement to the twenty-third general assembly of the "number of acres in cultivation of wheat, corn and other field products, in 1859" listed for the purpose of taxation.[42] Dividing the 1859 crop year outputs returned in the census by these estimates of acreage planted gives an estimate of the yield per acre (Table 10.9). The results derived from our regressions for the state are very similar to the weighted average yields calculated from the acres planted with corn and wheat as returned by the state auditor.

The state auditor estimated that the wheat yield on Udoll soils where farmers were relatively specialized in wheat production was 10.8 bushels per acre, while from Udalf soils it averaged only 7.2 bushels. By comparison, our regression model (see Table 10.9) put the wheat yield from Udoll townships in the sample at 10.0 bushels per acre and that in Udalf town-

TABLE 10.9. Illinois County Crop Yields, 1859–1860 (bushels)

Soil Type/County	State Auditor Yields		Regression Model Yields			
			Table 10.8		Table 10.5	
	Corn	Wheat	Corn	Wheat	Corn	Wheat
Aquall Soils:						
Massac	24.7	7.9				
Mean Yield	24.7	7.9	35.1	11.4		
Udalf Soils:						
Adams	576.1 (*sic*)	4.5				
Brown	33.4	6.8				
Knox	30.9	9.5				
Macoupin	32.8	7.7				
Williamson	27.9	7.6				
Weighted Mean Yield	30.1	7.2	30.3	6.0		
Udoll Soils:						
Bureau	18.1	11.5				
Dewitt	34.3	7.3				
Kendall	–	–				
Livingston	20.3	5.4				
McDonough	28.8	13.8				
Weighted Mean Yield	26.3	10.8	27.2	10.0		
Overall Weighted Mean Yield	27.0	8.7			28.0	7.5

Source: The state auditor yields are from Illinois State Auditor, *Biennial Report of the Auditor of Public Accounts . . . to the Twenty-Third General Assembly* (Springfield, 1863), 51–52, which provides estimates of acreages planted in 1859. Crop harvested is taken from the *Eighth Census, Agriculture in the United States in 1860* (Washington, D.C., 1864), 30–35. The corn yield estimate for Adams County is clearly an error. Acreage in corn in 1859 was reported as only 4,607 acres.

ships at 6.0 bushels. Corn yield estimates for these two soil groups were also similar. The yields from the Aquall soil county (Massac), however, differ substantially from those for the county overall. This may be because our sample township, which was adjacent to the river, contained very fertile bottom land.

We have also been able to derive county yield estimates for the 1859 crop year for a variety of crops in Ohio (Table 10.10).[43] In the sample counties from that state, the commissioner of statistics was of the opinion that wheat and rye failed, having been heavily damaged by the late frost of 4 June 1859. Our estimates of the corn and hay yields were of the same order of magnitude as the yields reported by the commissioner of statistics, but our yield estimates for wheat were more optimistic while that for barley was much more sanguine. No yields are reported for buckwheat, oats, or rye because the regression coefficients were not significantly greater than zero at the 10 percent level. We interpret this as indicating that little acreage was devoted to these crops in the sample townships.

Our estimates show great variations in yields from township to town-

TABLE 10.10. County Crop Yield Estimates by the Ohio Commissioner of Statistics for Sample Counties, 1859 Crop Year (bushels per acre)

	Crop						
County	Barley	Buck-wheat	Corn	Hay	Oats	Rye	Wheat
Harrison	7.8	16.6	29.3	1.0	26.0	2.0	1.8
Licking	11.3	16.8	30.7	0.8	22.7	4.9	3.2
Morrow	12.2	15.6	20.0	1.0	24.1	6.0	3.4
Noble	12.1	13.2	27.7	1.2	20.8	5.3	4.6
Weighted Mean	11.2	15.6	27.4	1.0	23.0	4.8	3.4
Regression Estimate:							
Licking and Morrow Cos.	2.3	n.s.	23.1	1.1	n.s.	n.s.	7.9
Harrison and Noble Cos.	"higher"	"higher"	16.7	0.6	"lower"	"higher"	"higher"

Source: Ohio Commissioner of Statistics, *Fourth Annual Report* . . . *1860* (Columbus: Richard Nevins, 1861).

n.s. = not significant at 10 percent level or better.

ship even within the same state. This is consistent with all the independent evidence that we have found. It would also be true today, though perhaps the relative range from high to low has narrowed. In the nineteenth century, however, county crop yields varied tremendously. A state census of Iowa in 1859, for example, shows average county corn yields varying between 8.4 bushels and 52.7 bushels per acre, oats from 0.3 bushels to 33.3 bushels, and wheat from 0.5 bushels per acre to 14 bushels per acre.[44] The range was probably even greater among townships and farms. The 1855 New York State Census, for example, shows a variation in corn yields between the sample townships from 9.7 bushels to 35.7 while between the sample counties the variation was only from 15.7 to 33.2 bushels. Similarly, winter wheat had a range of 1–14.7 bushels at the township level, but at the county level the range was 4.7–13.7 bushels. Although we cannot show it with our data, there were also major yield fluctuations from year to year. Corn in Ohio, for example, which had averaged 40 bushels per acre in 1853, produced only 26 the following year.[45]

The performance of our regression procedure in estimating yields in the sample townships may be gauged in part from the magnitude of the constant term in the equations. It should be remembered that the constant term originated in the substitution of improved acres as a proxy for acreage under cultivation. Since the former includes land not only under cultivation but also that cleared for grazing or grassland and fallow, the constant term should be positive, reflecting these other uses to which improved land might be put. In every case it was positive, though for Vermont farms it was quite small. Elsewhere, from 20 to 50 percent (averaging about a third) of improved acreage was not used for field crops (Table 10.11). This seems reasonable. J. B. D. DeBow, for example, estimated "improved land not in actual cultivation or in meadow and pasture" in 1849 at about the same fraction.[46] Furthermore, in 1880 when the census split improved acreage between "tilled, including fallow and grass in rotation (whether pasture or meadow)" and permanent meadow, permanent pasture, orchards, and vineyards, the ratio of the former to total improved acreage was 82 percent.[47] Since our measure excludes fallow, pasture, and meadow (unless hay was harvested from it) from the numerator, the ratio should be smaller, and it was.

The principal use for improved land not under field crops was livestock grazing, therefore Table 10.11 also shows the number of livestock on the average farm. The results seem quite consistent. The average Illinois farm, for example, had more livestock and more improved acres not under cultivation than did the average Indiana farm. Only the Vermont figures seem grossly out of line. With only 2.2 improved acres not

TABLE 10.11. Improved Acreage Not under Cultivation and Livestock Inventories on Mean-sized Farms in Sample Townships, 1860

State/ Region	Improved Acres Not Cultivated	Percent Improved Acres Not Cultivated	Livestock Inventory						
			Horses	Mules	Oxen	Cows	Cattle	Sheep	Hogs
Illinois	29.6	31	3.6	0.3	0.7	3.5	5.5	3.7	14.1
Indiana	22.9	37	3.3	0.2	0.4	2.7	4.4	7.5	19.8
Iowa	16.4	30	2.6	0.1	0.9	2.7	4.9	4.2	13.4
Kansas	20.5	46	2.7	0.2	2.1	3.1	5.4	2.3	14.3
Michigan	10.4	32	1.5	0.0	0.9	2.7	3.8	7.6	5.5
Minnesota	12.8	45	0.8	0.1	1.6	1.7	2.3	0.0	5.6
Missouri	21.6	28	4.5	1.1	1.4	3.5	7.4	12.8	22.9
Ohio	32.2	40	3.4	0.0	0.3	3.8	4.5	41.5	8.2
Wisconsin	10.3	20	2.1	0.0	1.5	3.4	4.9	4.2	4.9
Midwest	26.3	38	3.1	0.3	0.8	3.0	4.9	9.2	15.7
Connecticut	15.6	20	1.1	0.0	2.6	3.4	4.5	2.8	2.4
Maryland	29.6	42	1.5	0.3	2.3	1.9	3.8	5.2	11.6
New Hampshire	23.1	26	1.2	0.0	1.8	3.4	3.5	15.6	1.2
New Jersey	25.4	50	2.5	0.2	0.4	3.5	1.7	1.9	4.0
New York	25.3	29	2.7	0.0	0.6	6.3	4.1	22.6	3.6
Pennsylvania	28.5	43	2.8	0.0	0.4	4.3	4.8	10.3	6.4
Vermont	2.2	3	1.8	0.0	1.5	2.7	6.0	4.0	4.5
Northeast	26.9	33	2.4	0.0	0.8	4.9	4.2	15.8	4.7
Northern States	27.3	37	2.9	0.2	0.8	3.7	4.6	11.6	11.6

under crops in 1859, the average Vermont farm probably had too many head of livestock for the available grazing land if farmers there followed the same practices as elsewhere. Less grazing land per head meant that farmers had to substitute cultivated animal feed crops, particularly hay, oats, and silage in the diet. This was an important step toward improving livestock yields, and there is some indirect, independent evidence to support its early application in Vermont. Dairy cows there had the highest average milk yield per head in the country in 1860, producing 4,658 pounds per year, more than the national average at the start of the twentieth century.[48]

We can test the reasonableness of our yield estimates at the state and regional level using the published census gross production statistics for 1859 and our yield estimates to calculate the acreage devoted to each crop. The sum of the acreages can then be compared with the total land area under cultivation. J. B. D. DeBow used a similar procedure to rationalize the yield estimates he obtained at the Seventh Census.[49] This test is particularly stringent since a comparison of our yield estimates with those of most contemporaries (see Tables 10.1 and 10.2) suggests that ours may be too low. If that indeed should prove to be the case, then the larger will be our estimate of the acreage under cultivation for the given production levels reported in the census, and the greater will be the probability that our estimate of crop acreage will exceed the total acreage that was available.

In the aggregate, and in the two subregions, this was not the case (Table 10.12). Field crops accounted for only 68 percent of midwestern improved acreage. In the Northeast proportionately more land appears to have been devoted to field crops, which accounted for just over 80 percent of cultivable land. Given the relative importance in that region of livestock farming, particularly dairying, this result was unexpected. This may simply reflect the higher price of northeastern farmland, which dictated that it be kept in intensive and continuous cultivation. Unfortunately, comparable data on the percentage of improved acreage devoted to individual crops in 1849 are only available on a national basis.[50]

Corn, hay, and wheat were the most important crops to midwestern farmers in terms of acreage. They devoted double the proportion of land to corn that northeasterners did and more than a quarter of their available land to it in 1859. However, this is fractionally less than the nationwide percentage planted in corn in 1849.[51] The relative decline of corn was caused by a production shift between 1849 and 1859 away from corn toward wheat. The surge in wheat production was symbolic of its elevation to a major cash crop for export during the 1850s. The midwestern farmers responded by alloting almost 50 percent more of their land to wheat than did northeastern farmers. One consequence of this was that

TABLE 10.12. Regional Estimates of Acreage under Cultivation in Various Crops, 1859–1860

	Midwest[a]		Northeast[b]		North[c]	
Crop	Acreage[d]	Percent of Total	Acreage[d]	Percent of Total	Acreage[d]	Percent of Total
Corn	13,552,000	26.0	5,332,000	12.5	16,453,000	17.4
Hay	8,667,000	16.6	10,244,000	24.0	19,591,000	20.7
Wheat	7,752,000	14.9	4,355,000	10.2	11,124,000	11.7
Oats	3,006,000	5.8	2,447,000	5.7	5,244,000	5.5
Rye	459,000	0.9	532,000	1.2	1,314,000	1.4
Peas & Beans	n.a.	—	623,000	1.5	860,000	0.9
Irish Potatoes	n.a.	—	7,972,000	18.7	7,998,000	8.4
Sweet Potatoes	139,000	0.3	720,000	1.7	364,000	0.4
Buckwheat	1,312,000	2.5	1,273,000	3.0	2,247,000	2.4
Tobacco	125,000	0.2	944,000	2.2	248,000	0.3
Barley	n.a.	—	663,000	1.6	1,566,000	1.7
Hemp	1,000	0.0	1,000	0.0	23,000	0.0
Flax	73,000	0.1	132,000	0.3	220,000	0.2
Flaxseed	16,000	0.0	n.a.	—	0	0.0
Grass Seed	394,000	0.8	11,000	0.0	210,000	0.2
Hops	n.a.	—	36,000	0.1	42,000	0.0
Total Improved Acreage[e]	52,187,795	100	42,641,243	100	94,829,038	100
Improved Acreage Not in Crops Above	16,691,795	32.0	7,356,243	20.7	27,325,038	28.8

[a]Ill., Ind., Iowa, Kans., Mich., Minn., Mo., Ohio, Wis.

[b]Conn., Del., Maine, Md., Mass., N.H., N.J., N.Y., Pa., R.I., Vt.

[c]Conn., Del., Ill., Ind., Iowa, Kans., Maine, Md., Mass., Mich., Minn., Mo., N.H., N.J., N.Y., Ohio, Pa., R.I., Vt., Wis.

[d]Calculated as the product of the appropriate regression coefficient and the gross production as reported by the Census. See U.S. Bureau of the Census, *Agriculture . . . in 1860.*

[e]From U.S. Census Office, Eighth Census, *Agriculture in the United States in 1860* (Washington, D.C., 1864).

wheat acreage in the northern states in 1859 exceeded the nationwide acreage planted with this crop in 1849.

Hay was an important crop in both regions, but in the Northeast it was their most important. There, it found a ready market in urban areas and played a part in the generally superior feed given eastern livestock. Irish potatoes also seem to have been a particularly important product in the Northeast in 1859. If our yield estimate is correct, then acreage in this crop grew almost eightfold between 1849 and 1859. Farmers in both regions devoted similar fractions of their land to oats, almost 6 percent. Other crops accounted for small shares of improved acreage.

At the state level we can observe the acreage devoted to wheat, other small grains (barley, oats, and rye), and corn, together with an estimate of the total acreage under crops (Table 10.13). The leading wheat states

TABLE 10.13. Acreage Estimates for Various Crops by State, 1859–1860

	Wheat		Other Small Grains[c]		Corn		All Crops	
Region/State	Acreage[a]	%[b]	Acreage[a]	%[b]	Acreage[a]	%[b]	Acreage[a]	%[b]
Midwest								
Illinois	3,182,000	24.3	864,000	6.6	4,109,000	31.4	10,189,000	77.8
Indiana	1,618,000	19.6	600,000	7.3	2,082,000	25.3	5,149,000	62.5
Iowa	567,000	14.9	221,000	5.8	1,338,000	35.3	2,617,000	69.0
Kansas	7,000	1.6	10,000	2.6	143,000	35.2	171,000	42.0
Michigan	798,000	23.0	213,000	6.1	486,000	14.0	2,507,000	72.1
Minnesota	153,000	27.5	96,000	17.3	44,000	8.0	390,000	70.2
Missouri	433,000	6.9	329,000	5.3	4,366,000	69.9	6,717,000	107.5
Ohio	804,000	6.4	2,020,000	16.0	3,268,000	25.9	11,309,000	89.6
Wisconsin	1,683,000	44.9	718,000	19.2	n.a.	—	3,101,000	82.8
Northeast								
Connecticut	n.a.	—	95,000	5.2	606,000	33.1	2,094,000	114.4
Maryland	27,000	0.9	160,000	5.3	823,000	27.4	1,088,000	36.2
New Hampshire	131,000	5.5	569,000	24.1	308,000	13.0	2,362,000	99.8
New Jersey	n.a.	—	n.a.	—	n.a.	—	1,027,000	52.8
New York	1,456,000	10.1	1,303,000	9.1	1,548,000	10.8	13,253,000	92.3
Pennsylvania	1,017,000	9.7	2,769,000	26.5	1,546,000	14.8	7,080,000	67.7
Vermont	659,000	23.3	449,000	15.9	90,000	3.2	2,929,000	103.7

[a]Product of gross production reported to the Census and the relevant regression coefficient. See U.S. Census Office, Eighth Census, *Agriculture . . . in 1860.*

[b]Acreage as a percentage of total improved acreage reported at the Census. See U.S. Census Office, Eighth Census, *Agriculture . . . in 1860.*

[c]Barley, rye, and oats.

were Illinois, Minnesota, and Wisconsin, in each of which farmers planted more than a quarter of their acreage with this crop. Over a quarter of the acreage in Connecticut, Illinois, Indiana, Iowa, Kansas, Maryland, Missouri, and Ohio was planted in corn. In the more northerly states, relatively little acreage was devoted to corn.

There are also some obvious problem cases—Connecticut, Missouri, and Vermont, for example—where some of our yield estimates for important crops must be low since we overestimate acreage, but in general the results seem plausible.[52] In Illinois, for example, the state auditor estimated the 1859 acreage planted in wheat and corn at 2.3 and 4.0 million acres respectively, while we estimate wheat acreage at between 2.6 and 3.2 million acres and corn at 4.1 million acres.[53]

We believe that, overall, our yield estimates are reasonable. They are also lower than has generally been supposed. As a result, the rate of growth of output per acre and output per man-hour in the latter half of the nineteenth century may have been more rapid than hitherto supposed. Although the drive to improve family consumption levels no doubt provided an initial impulse to seek and implement methods that advanced output per acre or per animal, the more enduring impetus probably emanated from the farmers' heightening commercial involvement over the century. "By the 1850's," says Clarence Danhof, "market-oriented agriculture was firmly established as the dominant type, clearly distinguishable from the semisubsistence approach."[54] Expanded market production and yields were linked to other aspects of farm operations, two of which—productivity and mechanization—we consider in the next chapter.

CHAPTER ELEVEN

Mechanization and Productivity Change

INCREASING LAND AND LIVESTOCK YIELDS was one avenue toward the goal of creating marketable surpluses. While important for agricultural advance, it was not the most obvious solution to the farmers' problems at midcentury for two reasons. First, land was not the resource on which most farmers, especially those in the western states, needed most to economize. Second, once the initial gains in land yields from clearing and settlement were realized, additional advances became difficult given the technological possibilities of the day. The great improvement in acreage yields lay almost a century into the future when chemical fertilizers, hybrid seeds, irrigation, and various scientific developments became available to farm operators. Some technological devices designed to raise labor productivity were, however, becoming available during the nineteenth century. Mechanical rather than chemical or biological, these improvements operated primarily through their effect on the usage of labor.

Hired hands were scarce and high priced when available. Farmers depending upon casual wage labor lived in fear that workers, when needed, might not be available at any price that justified their hire. Wage labor was especially scarce in rural areas where population densities were low. There was widespread consensus that "manual labor . . . [of an] agricultural character, when followed as a necessary means of obtaining a livelihood, is considered by some as a degrading employment throughout our land."[1] A partial solution to the problem was the large farm family that created a pool of captive labor "bound to the entrepreneur by ties of custom, law, fear, and affection."[2] The implicit wage of this labor lay below that for hired workers because of the element of exploitation and the receipt of nonwage benefits, enhanced further by the farmers' ability to trade to their favor on the discounted present value of the potential inheritance to heirs.

As a consequence, the family farm tended to employ more labor and operate at a greater scale for the same costs than a farm that relied upon hired labor. This situation is graphed in Figure 11.1, where the horizontal axis measures the quantity of labor and the vertical capital and land. A farm using hired labor would operate at scale Q_1 employing L_h of labor while for the same cost the family farm would operate at Q_2 with L_f of labor. Since the level of output on the family farm is greater for the same costs, other things equal, the family farm would be more "profitable" than the wage-labor farm, but a part of that profit represents the expropriated value of the marginal product of family labor.

The reliance upon family labor on the farm constrained the farmer's ability to expand farm operations further. If L_f represented the total family labor supply, the family farm could only expand scale to, say, output level Q_3 by mechanizing and employing K_f of capital equipment and land with the L_f of available labor (the point F). This factor combination is not the cost minimizing input ratio for the level of output Q_3 and implies that

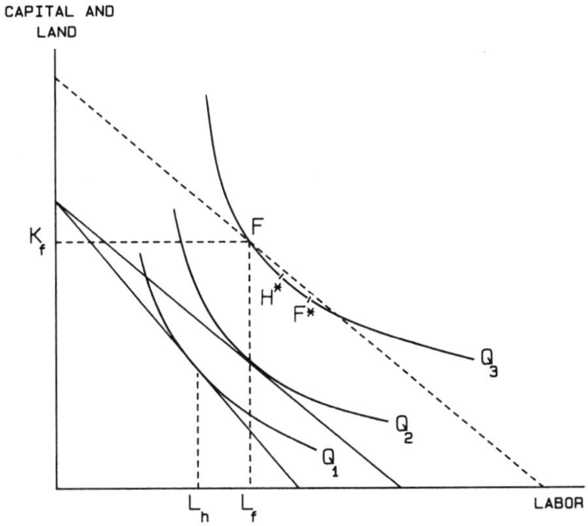

FIG. 11.1. Factor employment on family farms constrained by family labor.

the family farm has a greater propensity to mechanize and farm extensively than a purely commercial operation relying upon hired labor or a family farm not subject to the labor constraint (which would produce Q_3 at H^* and F^* respectively). The drive to increase output stemmed from the same forces that created the drive to produce a marketable surplus.

The element of exploitation in the use of family labor gave the farmer a strong incentive to improve labor productivity and capture those gains. Success promised greater profits, an easing of the labor constraint upon the family farm, and even the opportunity to expand. The response was quite dramatic. William Parker and Judith Klein have estimated that labor productivity growth between 1840–1860 and 1900–1910 averaged over 2 percent per year in wheat production and about 1.8 percent per year in corn and oat production, or a more than fourfold increase in wheat output per man-hour and a more than three and a halffold increase in corn or oats output per man-hour.[3] A very rapid pace of productivity growth by agricultural standards, this compares favorably with rates attained in other sectors of the economy.

The apparent success of American farmers in achieving such a rapid pace of labor productivity growth led some to question the underlying data. In particular, attention was focused on Parker and Klein's estimates of crop yields in 1840–1860 if only because they warned readers:

> The most dubious use of data lies in the combination of the estimates of land yield by state based on the USDA revised estimates, with an average of labor inputs per acre derived from a sample of contemporary evidence which . . . is drawn largely from the most productive farms.[4]

Although the use of labor input data from the most productive farms should bias their results against rapid productivity growth, their presentation of commissioner of patents' yield data that were higher than the USDA revised estimates for the post-1866 period and rejection of the former in favor of the latter potentially biased their results in favor of indicating rapid labor productivity growth. We have shown in Chapter 10 that the commissioner of patents' yield data are almost certainly too high because of the inherent biases in their collection. They are also higher than our yield estimates for 1859–1860. What has not been appreciated, however, is that the revised USDA estimates were above other contemporary ones.

Consider the evidence for Ohio. Except for the wheat yields, which drifted downwards between 1850 and 1875, there seems to be no secular trend in yields. Both the Ohio commissioner of statistics series and the USDA revised estimates also show a similar pattern of year-to-year yield fluctuations.[5] However, USDA revised yields for Ohio were higher than the state estimates, sometimes by as much as 50 percent. Overall between 1866 and 1875, the USDA corn yields averaged 1.5 percent more than the assessor yields, but oat yields were 12.5 percent higher and wheat 16.5 percent greater. This evidence does not offer conclusive proof of an upward bias in the USDA estimates because assessor yield estimates were used as the basis for land taxation, which created a strong motivation to bias yields downward in reports to assessors.[6] However, to the extent that the pattern was repeated elsewhere, we argue that Parker and Klein's use of the USDA yields imparts a downward bias to their estimates of labor productivity growth that is consistent with their other assumptions. Without these biases, labor productivity would have been seen to grow even more rapidly. Since we have shown that our yield estimates are plausible and consistent, we propose using them to study what they imply about labor productivity growth in the latter half of the nineteenth century within the framework laid down by Parker and Klein.

We do not intend to argue that the Parker-Klein index of labor productivity should be replaced. Rather, it is our intention to show that their index defines a reasonable lower bound for productivity growth over the period 1839–1910. We also demonstrate that modest changes in any of the parameters of that index will not merely modify the index, but may drastically alter the conclusions to be drawn from the partitioning exercise they performed.

The Parker-Klein labor productivity index is a regionally weighted index of average labor input per bushel of grain (corn, oats, or wheat) and is defined by

$$\sum_{R} \left(\frac{a + b}{y} + c \right) v$$

where R represents the regions (Northeast, South, and West), a and b are preharvest and harvest labor per acre respectively, c is postharvest labor per bushel, y is yield per acre, and v is the weight (regional crop production as a fraction of total production of each crop). Dividing a and b by yields per acre converts all the labor inputs to labor per bushel.

Because we are not proposing to replace the Parker-Klein results and have no new evidence on southern agricultural performance, we reworked Parker and Klein's figures to exclude the South and reestimate labor productivity growth with our regional yields substituted for those used by them (Table 11.1). The reworked figures excluding the South (Panel A of Table 11.1) show a slower pace of productivity change in corn and oats than when the South is included. The wheat figure is unchanged. The pattern for corn and oats thus accords with our expectations of lower productivity growth when the South is excluded from the calculations. According to Parker and Klein, yields in that region were especially low

TABLE 11.1. Labor Requirements and Labor Productivity in the Northeast and Midwest, 1840–1860 and 1900–1910

	Labor Requirements per Bushel of Output[a] Man-hours			Labor Productivity $(i_{1840/60}/i_n) \times 100$		
Period	Corn	Oats	Wheat	Corn	Oats	Wheat
A. Using 1859 Regional Yields[b]						
1840–1860	3.20	1.27	2.96	100	100	100
1900–1910	0.74	0.37	0.71	297	343	417
B. Using Revised USDA Average Yields[c]						
1840–1860	3.28	1.29	4.21	100	100	100
1900–1910	0.74	0.37	0.71	444	347	593

[a] $\sum_{R=1}^{2} \left(\frac{a+b}{y} + c\right)v$. Region 1 = Northeast; 2 = Midwest.

[b] Northeast: Corn = 33.5; Oats = 28.5; Wheat = 14.5.
Midwest: Corn = 32.7; Oats = 29.3; Wheat = 13.0.
Source: See Parker and Klein, "Productivity Growth," Table 1, 532.

[c] Northeast: Corn = 15.8; Oats = 33.9; Wheat = 7.3.
Midwest: Corn = 29.9; Oats = 20.9; Wheat = 12.2.
Source: See Table 10.5.

in the base period (1840–1860) and, while they did not equal those of other regions even in 1900–1910, they did increase proportionately faster. The index for wheat was unchanged albeit at lower labor inputs per unit of output because the change in weights from dropping the South just offset the slower productivity growth that would have resulted from excluding the region with the most rapid rise in yields (an almost 50 percent increase between 1840–1860 and 1900–1910).

Substituting our 1859 regional yields for the 1866–1875 USDA figures used by Parker and Klein increases the labor input per bushel of output in corn and wheat production in the base period; the labor input per bushel of oats was essentially unchanged (Panel B of Table 11.1). Using our yields, we estimate that labor productivity grew at an average annual rate of 2.15 percent for corn and 2.6 percent for wheat, compared with 1.5 percent and 2 percent respectively for the Parker-Klein regional estimates. Oat productivity did not differ between the two methods of computation because the weights largely compensated for the differences between our oat yield figures and the yields used by Parker and Klein. Our oat yields simply replaced one paradox of their results with another. Their data show a fall between 1840–1860 and 1900–1910 from 29.3 bushels per acre to 26.5 bushels. Our 1859 western oat yield, 20.9 bushels, is not only much lower than the one they used, but shows an expansion in yields between 1840–1860 and 1900–1910. Our 1859 northeastern oat yield of 33.9 bushels implies a decline in yields in that region over the course of the nineteenth century.

Our data suggest modest yield gains for corn and wheat between 1840–1860 and 1900–1910 in the West, but substantial ones in the northeastern states. Such advances could originate from the development of more tolerant strains adapted to lower humidity, to a shorter growing season, and more resistance to diseases that had become endemic in the Northeast. Nevertheless, a part of it must reflect that in 1859 the corn and wheat yields in the Northeast and oat yields in the West were depressed.

Partitioning the labor productivity increase in the manner of Parker and Klein produces eight indexes for all of the combinations of base and terminal period values of the parameters (Table 11.2). Changes in the weights, v, reflect shifting centers of production of the various crops (the "westward movement"). Changes in yields, y, represent advances in crop strains, farming practice, and so on ("scientific farming"). Lastly, changes

TABLE 11.2. Labor Requirements as Affected by Interregional Shifts, Regional Yields, and Regional Labor Inputs per Acre Comparing the USDA 1866–1875 Regional Yields with Those Obtained from the 1859 Manuscript Census Data

	Period Value of			Labor Requirements per Bushel[a]			Labor Productivity $(i_1/i_n) \times 100$[b]		
Index	v	y	a,b,c	Corn	Oats	Wheat	Corn	Oats	Wheat
				Parker-Klein Estimates for Northeast and Midwest[c]					
i_1	1	1	1	2.20	1.27	2.96	100	100	100
i_2	1	2	1	2.20	1.28	2.68	100	99	110
i_3	1	1	2	0.95	0.55	0.96	232	231	308
i_4	2	1	1	1.87	1.16	2.85	118	109	104
i_5	1	2	2	0.94	0.54	0.86	234	235	344
i_6	2	1	2	0.71	0.35	0.75	310	363	395
i_7	2	2	1	1.95	1.22	2.69	113	104	110
i_8	2	2	2	0.74	0.37	0.71	297	343	417
				Revised with 1859 Yields					
i_1	1	1	1	3.28	1.29	4.21	100	100	100
i_2	1	2	1	2.20	1.28	2.68	149	101	157
i_3	1	1	2	1.51	0.53	1.49	217	243	283
i_4	2	1	1	2.18	1.41	3.10	150	91	136
i_5	1	2	2	0.94	0.54	0.86	349	239	490
i_6	2	1	2	0.85	0.43	0.83	386	300	507
i_7	2	2	1	1.95	1.22	2.69	168	106	157
i_8	2	2	2	0.74	0.37	0.71	444	347	593

Source: From Parker and Klein, "Productivity Growth," Table 2.

[a] $\sum_{i=1}^{2} \left(\frac{a_i + b_i}{y_i} + c_i\right) v_i$. See text.

[b] i_1/i_n, $n = 1, \ldots, 8$.

in *a*, *b*, and *c*—the labor inputs per acre or bushel—reflect changes in mechanization and are considered collectively in our index here, although they could potentially be treated as separate factors.

Although our oat productivity indexes differ little from those of Parker and Klein, there are some subtle variations. The use of 1900–1910 weights (index i_4) reduces our index not only relative to the comparable Parker-Klein index but also to our base period labor inputs. This occurs because oat production shifted from the Northeast in 1840–1860 to the Midwest (and states farther west) by 1900–1910 because of the need to feed horses with a crop that could not bear heavy transport costs. In the context of our 1859 yields, this is a shift from a high-yield to a low-yield area. The use of 1900–1910 labor inputs also has a negative interaction with the 1859 yields such that although labor productivity increased when allowing for mechanization and the westward movement, it increased proportionally less by our index (i_6) than in the Parker-Klein measure.

Substitution of 1900–1910 labor inputs into the index (i_3) in the Parker-Klein measure accounts for two-thirds to three-quarters of the productivity gain in the two regions; in our productivity series this change accounts for 70 percent of the productivity gain in oats but less than half of that in wheat and corn. Regional shifts are also more important in our index than in their measure for the Northeast and West. The effect was positive in corn and wheat, with production moving from the low-yield region in favor of the high-yield region, but negative, as we have already noted, in oat production. Lastly, whereas mechanization and regional shifts (index i_6) accounted for more than 100 percent of the productivity gains in corn and oats and almost all those in wheat with the 1866–1875 USDA yields, these two changes account for only 85 percent of the productivity gains when the 1859 crop yields are substituted.

We do not think that our estimates of productivity are superior to those of Parker and Klein because our yields reflect performance only for one year. Moreover, there is evidence that the 1859 oat yields in the West and the corn and wheat yields in the Northeast were below average. Yet we believe that the Parker-Klein figures understate the improvement in yields during the course of the nineteenth century. These improvements stemmed from systematic selection of seeds from superior yielding varieties and from improvements in farming practice—crop rotation, use of nitrogen-fixing legumes, or employment of fertilizers whether natural or synthetic, for example. Although we have no direct evidence on this for field crops, we know that milk yields increased substantially during the nineteenth century as a result of improved breed selection and greater attention to care and feeding practices.

Regardless of which labor productivity growth estimates one accepts, they cannot be generalized to all farm activities without being at odds with Robert Gallman's estimates of total factor productivity growth.[7] Either the Parker-Klein estimated labor productivity growth is too rapid if generalized to all crops and livestock, or Gallman's estimate of total factor productivity growth is too low.

Suppose that agricultural production can be approximated by a Cobb-Douglas production function:

$$Q = AL^{\alpha}K^{\beta}T^{\gamma}$$

where Q is output, L is labor, K is capital, and T is land. The coefficients α, β, and γ are the output elasticities of labor, capital, and land respectively. If these output elasticities are equal to the factor shares in total output, then A is the geometric index of total factor productivity. This will be true if we assume perfect competition and constant returns to scale:

$$\alpha + \beta + \gamma = 1, \qquad \alpha, \beta, \gamma > 0$$

We may rewrite the production function:

$$A = Q/(L^{\alpha}K^{\beta}T^{\gamma}) = (Q/L)^{\alpha}(Q/K)^{\beta}(Q/T)^{\gamma}$$

Thus, total factor productivity is simply the weighted average of the three partial productivity indexes for labor, capital, and land, where the weights are the factor shares.

We can also rewrite it in terms of labor productivity (Q/L):[8]

$$(Q/L) = A(K/L)^{\beta}(T/L)^{\gamma}$$

and the rate of growth transformation of this expression:

$$(Q^* - L^*) = A^* + \beta(K^* - L^*) + \gamma(T^* - L^*)$$

where the asterisk indicates rate of change.

According to Parker and Klein's study the annual rate of growth of labor productivity $(Q^* - L^*)$ was of the order 1.8–2.0 percent. Over this same period, Gallman's estimate of the annual rate of growth of total factor productivity is 0.50 percent.[9] Suppose now, $\beta = 0.10$ and $\gamma = 0.30$, then:

$$2.0 = 0.5 + 0.1(K^* - L^*) + 0.3(T^* - L^*)$$

which implies that if there was no increase in the land/labor ratio, then the capital/labor ratio would have had to increase fifteenfold between 1840 and 1900. If we assume no increase in the capital/labor ratio, then the land/labor ratio would have had to increase fivefold. Neither alternative seems plausible.

Higher values for β and γ would reduce the increase in the capital/labor ratio or the land/labor ratio necessary to maintain the equality, but it is unlikely that $\beta + \gamma > 0.5$ (a labor share of less than half). It is also unlikely, of course, that either of the ratios experienced no change. Stanley Lebergott's data on the labor force allow us to make a crude estimate of the land/labor ratio assuming no changes in the age-sex composition of the labor force, the human capital that it embodied, or hours of work.[10] These data, considered in conjunction with census estimates of the acreage under cultivation, suggest that the land/labor ratio approximately doubled to 56 acres per person between 1840 and 1900, a growth rate of 1.16 percent a year. Nevertheless, the capital/labor ratio would have had to expand almost tenfold if our other figures are correct, and there is no reasonable set of values that will yield plausible results.

Although the substitution of 1859 yields into the Parker-Klein estimates of labor productivity reduces the contribution of mechanization, it remains the most important source of growth, accounting for more than half of the measured labor productivity gain between 1840 and 1910. Much of the large-scale mechanization postdates the Civil War, but there was one major innovation, the reaper-mower, between 1840 and 1860. Its history is well documented.[11] Moreover, its adoption by northern farmers has attracted widespread attention.[12] Here we use our yield estimates to approximate the number of acres each farm in the census sample planted in wheat, in other small grains (barley, oats, and rye), and in grasses and hay. We then compare the distribution of acreages with the threshold levels at which farms should have found it profitable to use the reaper or a reaper-mower. This produces a crude estimate of the probable number of farms that could have profitably owned a reaper for their own exclusive use in 1859–1860. We also examine the value of farm implements of farms above and below the threshold to detect any discontinuity that may indicate the presence of a reaper as a part of the machinery inventory of the farm.

Although the reaper was more satisfactory in harvesting grains than in cutting grasses and hay, there is evidence that it was used in both applications and that manufacturers often offered different cutting bars more suited to use on green grasses.[13] Farmers also had a revealed preference for combined reaper-mowers wherever possible.[14] The desirability of the combined implement was heightened by the simultaneous ripening of wheat and hay. The hay harvest could be delayed somewhat, but the wheat harvest could not without a sharp reduction in yields as ripened grain was lost through shattering within a day or two.

When the reaper was introduced, it did not immediately and everywhere displace older harvesting technologies. Instead, the two coexisted: the older technology, grain-cradling, was labor-intensive; the other, mechanical reaping, was laborsaving. The grain cradle was a modified scythe onto which a frame, composed of five tapering wooden fingers, had been attached alongside the blade. This "cradle" caught the grain as it was cut, facilitating binding and shocking. Its use required skill and endurance which, with the general scarcity of paid labor at harvesttime, ensured high wages.[15] The reaper-mower, patented in the 1830s but not perfected until the 1850s, replaced the skilled labor of the cradlers. While it simplified the task of raker-binders by depositing the cut grain in gavels rather than in swaths, it subjected them to the rhythm and pacing of the machine, thereby reducing the desirability of that work. However, the reaper-mower was not equally adept at all tasks to which it was put because:

> Some grasses are tall, large and easy to cut; but others are short, wiry and hard. Timothy grass stands well; clover is usually prostrated and tangled. The taller grains sway in the wind and incline away from the advancing machine, or laterally as often as they lean towards the cutting edge. Grain fields are weedy and sometimes difficult grasses are encountered in them. Rye is tall and wheat comparatively short. Both become tangled, lodged and straw-broken at times. Rusted wheat is difficult to handle. "Lodging" is the rule with heavy oats. Overripe grain becomes so "fluffy" that good work cannot be done in harvesting it. . . .[16]

Paul David estimated the labor saving per acre of the manual rake reaper over the grain cradle at 0.273 man-days; that of the self-rake reaper at 0.364 man-days.[17] These labor savings, which are almost certainly lower bound, are based on the assumption that the manual rake reaper needed eight men to harvest 11 acres and a self-rake reaper, seven men, compared with 11 men using the grain cradle.[18] A grain cradler, according to Leo Rogin, averaged 2–2.5 acres a day, while one raker-binder followed each cradler and one man was required to shock 10 acres of wheat.[19] The manual rake reaper required two men to operate it; one to drive the team and one to rake the grain from the bed behind the cutting bar. Only one person was required to operate a self-rake reaper. A reaper, which regardless of type could cut 10–15 acres a day, averaged probably 11 acres. Following behind each reaper were four to six binders. With a self-rake reaper the labor saving over the cradle was put at five men; David's figures suggest a labor saving of three to four men over the grain cradle.[20]

The monetary value of this saving in labor usage depended upon the wages paid to harvest labor, which varied from state to state, and whether labor was hired for the day, the month, or the season. David examined only Illinois data, based on which he suggested day-wages of $1.27 during 1849–1853 and $1.87 during 1854–1857.[21] Work by David Schob, however, suggests that David's figures for the periods in question may be low.[22] Our estimates of labor costs (Table 11.3) are for 1859 as shown in a survey of agricultural labor by Horace Greeley for the *New York Tribune*.[23] These are generally lower than David's figures for Illinois wages, reflecting an easing of demand for harvest labor with the passing of the wheat boom, the laborsaving effects of the reaper, and the unexceptional nature of the 1859 crop. They are much lower than Schob's estimate of wages. According to Greeley, harvest wages ranged from as little as $0.75 per day in Branchville, New Jersey, to $1.38 per day in Branch County, Michigan (on the Indiana-Ohio-Michigan border), though a correspondent from Lincoln, Illinois, quoted a rate of up to $2 per day.[24]

Grain cradles involved little or no fixed expense. In 1859 they cost on average $4.23 each with a range of $4.00–5.00.[25] It is therefore unlikely that established farmers would be any more reluctant than new ones to adopt the reaper because of sunk costs in the old technology. Purchase of a reaper on the other hand involved a considerable capital expenditure and the machine had a less than infinite life span. Citing evidence such as the Illinois State Agricultural Society's claim that reapers were "good for five years' wear," Alan Olmstead has argued that David was mistaken in his assumption that the reaper had a life expectancy of ten years.[26] Because the evidence seems convincing, we have assumed that reapers lasted five years, depreciated proportionately over the period, and had no scrap value. Estimates of the number of potential users are sensitive to this assumption. Increased longevity had the potential for increasing sharply the number of individual farmers who could economically use a reaper of their own. We further assume that all manufacturers offered their reapers for the same price as McCormick, namely $133 FOB at the Chicago factory for a hand-rake model.[27] On the basis of labor savings alone, the self-rake models could have sold for as much as one-third more (i.e., about $177).[28] To these prices must be added transport costs, which would add perhaps $20 at most to the reaper cost if farmers bought from the closest manufacturer.[29] The maximum cost of a reaper delivered to the sample townships then ranged from $134 (in Connecticut) to $153 (in Minnesota).

Probably few farmers could afford to pay cash, but most manufacturers seem to have offered credit terms. Paul David used a figure of 6 percent on the grounds that this was the rate charged by McCormick on credit sales. Alan Olmstead, however, has shown that this rate was for

TABLE 11.3. Wages for Farm Labor by State for Different Seasons and Different Contract Terms, 1859 ($)

State	By the Year	Per 8 Months (per month)	Planting Time		Hay and Harvest		Fall Work		Winter Work	
			per month	per day	per month	per day	per month	per day	per month	per day
Illinois	175	13–18	n.a.	1.00	20–25	1.25	13–18	0.75	12–15	n.a.
Iowa	n.a.	n.a.	15	0.50	n.a.	1.25	n.a.	0.50	n.a.	0.50
Maine	30–144	12–14+	15+	0.65–0.83	15–25+	1.25	11–15	0.50	8–11+	0.50
Massachusetts	150–200	16–18.50+	18–21+	0.83–1.00	30–45	1.00–1.25	15–18+	0.83–1.00	10.13+	0.67–0.83
Michigan	144	13.5+	13+	0.75	18+	1.38	12+	0.75	10+	0.50
New Hampshire	160	16–18	17+	0.92	28+	1.34	14+	0.87	12+	0.75
New Jersey	125–130	10–15	12–18	0.75	16–25	0.75–1.00	11–12+	0.62–0.75	8–13	0.50–0.62
New York	130–150	12–18	10–18	0.62–0.75	20–30	1.00–1.25	10–15	0.62–0.75	6–14	0.50–0.62
Ohio	118–150	12–15	13–15	0.56–0.75	18–22	1.00–1.25	11–14	0.50–0.75	10–12	0.50
Pennsylvania	108–120	10–15	10–14	0.50	16–25	0.75–1.25	8–10	0.50	6–8	0.50
Vermont	150–160	15–16+	16–18	0.75–0.83	24–30+	1.25–1.50	14+	0.75	12+	0.50–0.60

Source: *Hunt's Merchants Magazine* 41, 6 (Dec. 1859):759, quoting *New York Times.*

five months on three-quarters of the balance and there was a $5 additional service charge. The resulting true annual percentage rate of interest was over 19 percent.[30] Other manufacturers such as Atkin and Manny charged even more.[31] Such interest rates are about double the normal commercial paper rates.[32]

The depreciation rate, interest rate, cost of harvest labor, and the delivered cost of a reaper, assuming specific rates of labor saving, can be used to define the "threshold" acreage for profitable reaper use by a single user. This is the acreage of small grains and grasses for which the costs of using a grain cradle were the same as the costs of using a reaper. It is defined by:[33]

$$T = \left(\frac{d + 0.5i}{L_s}\right)\left(\frac{C}{w}\right)$$

assuming that costs are linear in the relevant range, where d is depreciation (0.2 by assumption), i is the rate of interest, L_s is the labor saving of the reaper over the cradle (assumed to be 0.273 for the hand-rake reaper), C is the cost of the reaper delivered, and w is the daily wage rate (see Table 11.3). With interest rates of between 12 and 30 percent, the first term varies from a little less than 1 to about 1.28. It is dominated by the second term, the cost of the reaper relative to daily harvest labor, which varied perhaps between 75 and 150 and was determined primarily by the wage rate given the small price variation for reapers.

What we think define the reasonable bounds for single-user thresholds are graphed in Figure 11.2 against the wage rate, which is read from the right-hand scale. Thresholds varied from perhaps as little as 63 acres for farmers able to borrow at 12 percent but paying harvest labor $2 per day to as much as 200 acres for farmers forced to pay 30 percent interest but able to hire harvest labor for $1 per day and located at a long distance from the nearest reaper factory. Even the minimum lower-bound threshold that we estimate is almost 80 percent greater than David's estimate because we assume double the interest rate that he used, twice as rapid a depreciation rate, and a lower wage rate for harvest labor. If Horace Greeley's harvest labor costs were accurate, then the actual threshold in 1859 was 100 acres or more.

Few farmers had this large a cultivable acreage and even fewer would devote a large proportion of it to just a limited number of crops, particularly ones with a high degree of positive covariation between their yields. Twenty-six percent of northern farmers had a total improved acreage exceeding 100 acres, but we estimate that no more than 4 or 5 percent had as large an acreage planted in small grains, grasses, and hay.[34]

Superimposed upon Figure 11.2 are graphs of the percentage of all northern farms harvesting more than specific acreages of small grains and of small grains and grasses combined. These are derived using our estimates of yields from Chapter 10. To the extent that our yield figures may be biased downward, our estimates of the harvested acreage will be biased upward; therefore we will tend to overstate the number of farms above the threshold. Farmers harvesting small grain acreages larger than the threshold should have found ownership of a reaper profitable. Only about 3 percent of northern farmers in 1859, however, are estimated to have harvested more than 63 acres of small grains. Less than 0.1 percent harvested 200 acres or more. More farmers would have found the reaper profitable if they could also harvest grass and hay, although the implement's poorer performance when cutting grass weakens the case. Factoring in its use as a mowing machine raises the percentage of farmers above the lower-bound threshold to 11 percent and those above the upper-bound to almost 1 percent. The potential for use as a mowing machine must have figured prominently in the machine's adoption.

Based upon these fractions, only 41,000 of the 1.3 million northern farmers should have been able to make profitable use of the reaper in small grain harvesting, and no more than 150,000 should have found it profitable as a combination reaper-mowing machine.[35] Estimates of the actual number of machines in use in 1859 fall within this range. Cyrus McCormick estimated that 73,200 reapers were in use west of the Alleghenies in 1858.[36] Another authority estimated that there were perhaps

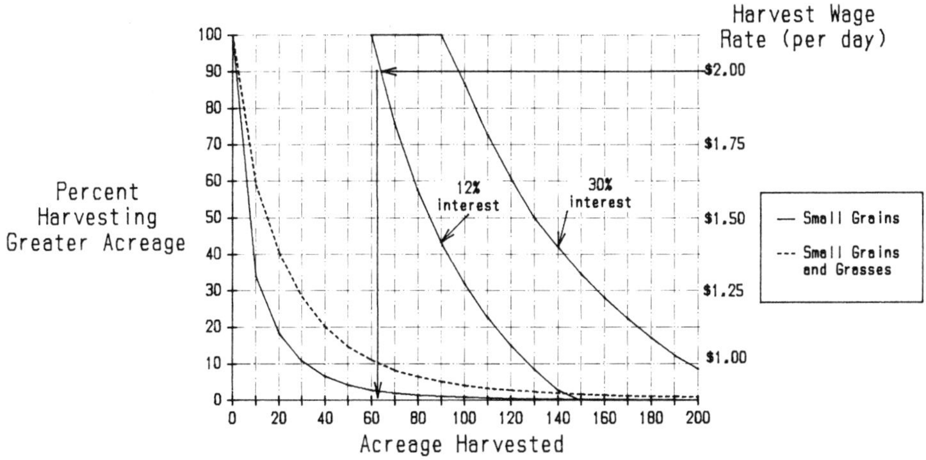

FIG. 11.2. Reaper thresholds and the percentage of farmers harvesting different acreages of small grains and grasses, 1859–1860.

200,000 machines in use in the 1861 harvest, of which perhaps 50,000–60,000 had been manufactured after 1859.[37] Consequently we cannot reject the argument that farmers bought reapers for their own use. However, there is a considerable body of evidence indicating a widespread prevalence of joint reaper purchases by groups of farmers. Olmstead, for example, found that one of every four McCormick reapers sold between 1854 and 1859 was purchased jointly by two or more individuals, most of whom did not have a last name in common.[38] Furthermore, machine harvesting was often performed on a contract basis.[39] Under these circumstances, the threshold is irrelevant.

The sample data provide some indirect evidence from which reaper ownership might be inferred. If we assume that a reaper cost $125–150 and farmers reported the replacement value of their machinery to the census, then farms larger than the threshold should have reported an implement value of at least $200–250 if their inventory included a reaper and all the other necessary farm implements (see Chap. 8). The average value of farm implements exceeded $200 only on those midwestern farms that were harvesting about 85–90 acres of small grains and grasses. In the East, however, farms harvesting 50–60 acres of grain and grasses had implement inventory values greater than this. This may reflect the lower rate of joint ownership of reapers in New York and Pennsylvania that Olmstead notes.[40]

Farm mechanization, then, as now, may not have been driven by purely economic considerations. Important as labor saving may have been in easing the constraints upon farm expansion imposed by the limited external labor market and family size, machine use was and is the symbol of progressive, modern farming. Furthermore, to the extent that the labor saved was the drudgery and toil of the decision maker, pure economic rationality may have been clouded by personal considerations.

The struggle to produce crops and care for livestock may have measured the farmer's success as an agriculturalist, but it was only half the battle. There remained the struggle not only for economic survival but ultimately a degree of economic independence. We now turn to the question of how much these farms produced for market. Were midwestern farms in general and frontier farms in particular self-sufficient, or did they specialize and produce a marketable surplus by the late antebellum period? What critical level marked the transition from self-sufficient, subsistence farming to commercial agriculture? Northern farmers, despite ambivalence regarding their surrender of some of their self-sufficient independence to commercial dependency, were edging into the industrializing economy.

CHAPTER TWELVE

Self-sufficiency and the Sources of the Marketable Surplus

GROWING URBANIZATION IN THE EAST coupled with an expanding transportation system both there and in the Midwest created new market opportunities for agriculture. Farmers responded by producing an excess, the so-called marketable surplus, beyond the needs of their farm and family to sell or barter in the exchange economy. Rising productivity and technological improvements facilitated achieving this objective. Market involvement began at the local level but expanded eventually to the international. As farmers became more enmeshed in this system, they found not only new opportunities to increase their incomes but also new problems such as market risks and heightened dependency on individuals or institutions outside their families or communities. Nevertheless, because the incentives for commercial production ultimately proved irresistible, the mid-nineteenth century marks the watershed in the transformation of agriculture across the northern United States from the family-oriented farm to commercial production.

There has been considerable debate about when and to what extent American farmers in the North became dependent upon markets. The issue has not been whether or not surplus commodities were marketed—for there had always been a demand for foodstuffs, particularly grain, originating from the nonfarm population—but rather whether such sales were incidental. Did farmers deliberately produce more than they could consume regardless of the probable states of the harvest, or were surpluses simply fortuitous outcomes seized upon by opportunistic farmers?[1] A related question is, how narrowly did farmers specialize at midcentury? Were farmers dependent upon trade to acquire a satisfactory basket of goods to meet their own consumption needs and those of their livestock?

James Lemon, in his study of southeastern colonial Pennsylvania, argues that "[R]omantic notions of the subsistent and self-sufficient farmer must be rejected."[2] He shows that by the middle of the eighteenth century perhaps 80 percent of the farmers had some surplus to sell and on average only 60 percent of output could be accounted for by on-farm consumption.[3] There is, however, some debate whether or not this constituted self-sufficiency or capitalist production. James Henretta argues the former, citing in support of his view Lemon's opinion that the average farmer "produced enough for his family and was able to sell a surplus in the market to buy what he deemed necessities," buttressing his argument with Clarence Danhof's assertion that farms devoting 60 percent or more of their net product to on-farm consumption should be classified as subsistence.[4] Lemon has, however, strongly disagreed with this view, contending that if anything, he understated the extent of capitalist involvement by colonial Pennsylvanian farmers who were quite firmly and deliberately enmeshed in the market.[5]

Whatever the resolution of this debate for the colonial period, there can be little doubt that the need for trade was increasing rapidly throughout the antebellum period. In 1820, 71 percent of the northern population lived on farms. Nevertheless, the commercial orientation of American farmers was so obvious that Alexis de Tocqueville remarked: "Almost all the farmers of the United States combine some trade with agriculture; most of them make agriculture itself a trade."[6] By 1860 the agricultural population in the North had fallen to about 40 percent of the total, so the level of marketing must have increased.[7] If we assume no difference in diet between farm and nonfarm populations and ignore such complications as the changing age structure of the population, these data imply that only 30 percent or so of foodstuffs in the North needed to enter into trade in 1820 but 60 percent or more must have been traded by 1860. Such figures perhaps overstate the geographic extensiveness of the trade because more than half of the northern nonfarm population in 1860 still lived in rural areas, presumably being provided food by farms in the immediate vicinity. But the data probably reflect the level of market trade in foodstuffs.[8] In addition, agriculture was an important source of nonfood raw material inputs to the developing manufacturing sector.

Evidence of growing commercialization and efforts to secure adequate markets and prices for surplus agricultural products abounds. Winifred Rothenberg has developed an impressive body of data from farm account books for Massachusetts farmers. These show long-distance trips of 150 miles or more by farmers to market their crops as early as the mid-eighteenth century, despite the high costs of overland wagon transportation. Not content simply to take advantage of casual marketing opportunities in the immediate vicinity, these farmers actively sought customers and widened the scope of their search until demand from nearby markets increased sufficiently to obviate that necessity.[9]

The growing commercialization of agriculture is also evident from the attention that it received in contemporary migrant and immigrant handbooks. Alexander Campbell, for example, in his 1856 pamphlet, *A Glance at Illinois*, followed his discussion of farm-making costs with this advice:

> Now if the following plan were adopted, it would probably be as profitable a division as could be made for farming purposes, and would suit the means and views of a majority of farmers, as well as any other which could be made: —Say with a farm of 160 acres, you appropriate 40 acres to buildings, orchards, and pasture grounds; upon which also may be raised the vegetables for the family, and a portion of the provender for the stock; 20 acres for mowing; 30 acres for wheat, and 70 acres for corn.
>
> We will assume that the wheat and corn crops are the only ones of which the farmer will have any surplus. This may of course be varied to suit the views and circumstances of the cultivator, but will not materially affect the general result. With fair farming, 20 bushels of wheat to the acre is not too large an estimate, nor are 50 bushels of corn by any means a large average yield upon our rich prairie lands. Therefore, assuming the above to be a fair estimate of the yield, we have 30 acres of wheat, at 20 bushels per acre = 600 bushels. 70 acres of corn, at 50 bushels per acre = 3500 bushels.
>
> Now if you retain 200 bushels of wheat, for seed and family use, and 900 bushels of corn, for working stock, and fattening animals for family use, both of which allowances are, undoubtedly, sufficiently large—you will have left for market, 400 bushels of wheat, and 2600 bushels of corn,—in all 3000 bushels of grain.
>
> Although there is a considerable consumption of meat and grain upon the sugar and cotton plantations of the south, and in the West Indies, the country south of the line we have named, is at all times fully adequate to the supply—except in case of a short crop.[10]

Despite this growing emphasis upon markets, however, the farmer who was able to provide virtually everything for his farm and family from the farm was regarded as a success as late as the 1840s, even in a relatively well-developed area such as New York State.[11] This soon passed as market orientation quickly increased with the expanding manufacturing sector and the spreading transportation network so that by the early 1850s, the president of the New York State Agricultural Society, Horatio Seymour, could say with conviction:

. . . now no farmer would find it profitable "to do everything within himself." He now sells for money, and it is his interest to buy for money, every article that he cannot produce cheaper than he can buy. He cannot afford to make at home his clothing,the furniture or his farming utensils; he buys many articles for consumption for his table. He produces that which he can raise and sell to the best advantage, and he is in a situation to buy all that he can purchase, cheaper than he can produce. Time and labor have become cash articles, and he neither lends nor barters them. His farm does not merely afford him a subsistence; it produces capital, and therefore demands the expenditure of capital for its improvement.[12]

At the aggregated level there have been a number of economic and historical studies examining self-sufficiency. These have generally focused upon the South or on a comparison between the South and Midwest rather than between the Midwest and the Northeast. In *The Economic Growth of the United States, 1770–1860*, Douglass C. North formally restated and lent added support to the notion of regional specialization by putting cotton exports from the South at the center of his model, with the Midwest supplying the necessary foodstuffs so that the South could devote even more of its resources to cotton cultivation.[13]

Subsequent research has weakened this argument. Albert Fishlow, using New Orleans cargo receipts from the Midwest, disputed the extent of the West-South trade assumed in North's formulation. Instead he showed a growing East-West interdependence with exchange of eastern manufactured goods for midwestern foodstuffs.[14] Studies by Diane Lindstrom on the interregional grain trade and by Lawrence Herbst on North-South commodity trade have corroborated Fishlow's critique.[15]

North's argument is further diminished by Robert Gallman's, and by Raymond Battalio and John Kagel's, findings of self-sufficiency in foodstuffs at the level of the individual farm.[16] William Hutchinson and Samuel Williamson's calculations reinforce this, indicating little need for southerners to have relied in the aggregate upon western foodstuffs.[17]

Northern farming has not been totally neglected. Colleen Callahan and William Hutchinson have made some preliminary regional estimates, analogous to those by Hutchinson and Williamson. For 1860 their data imply shortages of wheat, oats, and potatoes in either the Midwest or the Northeast that could be eliminated by interregional trade, and an aggregate deficit of meat and corn.[18] At the farm level, however, there have been no studies analogous to these for the South by Gallman or Battalio and Kagel. We have only James Lemon's estimate that in the late eighteenth century a family of five in Pennsylvania would have needed 73–78 acres to be self-sufficient.[19] The relevance of this estimate for the mid-nineteenth century is questionable.

One measure of self-sufficiency is the level of home manufacturing, which was quite low in northerners' homes at midcentury. According to the Census, in 1840, $14,347,000 of goods were manufactured in the home, but this had fallen to $8,039,000 twenty years later (Table 12.1). On a per capita basis, it had declined from $1.34 in 1840 to only $0.36 by 1860. Household manufacturing, "as a factor in the economic life and prosperity of the country as a whole," concluded Rolla Tryon in his study, "was practically nil at the end of the sixth decade of the nineteenth century."[20]

TABLE 12.1. Goods Manufactured in Households, 1840–1860

	1840		1850		1860	
Region	Total Value ($000)	Per Capita Value	Total Value ($000)	Per Capita Value	Total Value ($000)	Per Capita Value
North	14,347	1.34	10,688	0.72	8,039	0.36
South	14,667	2.31	16,805	2.04	16,608	1.60
United States	29,023	1.70	27,493	1.18	24,547	0.78

Source: Rolla M. Tryon, *Household Manufacturers in the United States, 1640–1860,* 308; U.S. Census of Manufacturing, 1870, Table 8-A.

Wholesale abandonment of home manufacturing was not possible or advisable in all parts of the country, thus in 1860 many northerners still engaged in it.[21] Domestic production never gained the foothold in the West that it had in the East despite greater distance from the manufacturing centers.[22]

Its decline in the North reflects the relative development both of the agricultural sector and of local commercial manufacturing. Local manufactories arose to supply nearby demand; farmers, in the belief that their time could be better spent on their agricultural activities, patronized these producers. The relatively rapid demise of home-produced clothing, furniture, and similar items in farm and other rural households indicates that a developing agricultural-industrial economy was emerging in the northern states during the antebellum era.

The small national output of household-manufactured goods that remained by 1860 was confined almost exclusively to the South where local manufacturing was less prevalent, agricultural ownership more concentrated, and farm production more specialized. If southern household production were counted as a separate industry, it would have ranked as the third largest in the region, exceeded only by combined flour and grist milling and by sawmilling. It would have been considerably greater than commercial cloth production. In addition, substantial amounts of cotton were ginned, sugar refined, and rice cleaned on southern plantations. Comparing the size of the cotton crop with the reported value of ginned cotton that appears in the published census suggests that perhaps $214 million worth of cotton was ginned by noncommercial gins. Further, plantations also often included flour mills, sawmills, tanneries, and similar manufacturing facilities. There, output generally was not considered commercial manufacturing by census takers or other governmental observers.[23] So prevalent were household industrial arts "that when hostilities broke out, in 1861, and the South was cut off from imported goods, these industries quickly expanded to take their place."[24]

While it is clear that Americans were producing fewer goods in their homes, regional variations did exist. Not surprisingly, western farmers, who were more remote from the established manufacturing centers, produced more domestically. Examining East-West differences as they varied across farm sizes is revealing (Table 12.2). Families on western farms of every size manufactured more goods at home than those on comparable eastern farms by a substantial margin, typically producing twice as much or more, and in the case of 11–20-acre farms, seventeen times as much. Significantly, however, the average value of home manufactures both per farm and per capita tended to increase on larger farms in both the Northeast and the Midwest. Even so, the absolute values of products manufactured in households both East and West were small and diminishing as time passed.

TABLE 12.2. Value of Goods Manufactured in Farm Households by Size of Farm, 1859–1860

Farm Size (Total Acres)	Value of Goods per Farm ($) East	West	North	Value of Goods per Farm Household Member ($) East	West	North
1–10	1.01	9.52	5.56	0.22	2.17	1.24
11–20	0.47	8.35	4.55	0.10	1.69	0.93
21–30	1.75	4.22	2.97	0.39	0.90	0.64
31–40	1.19	4.85	4.02	0.24	1.01	0.83
41–60	1.98	5.14	3.41	0.42	1.01	0.70
61–80	2.20	6.44	5.28	0.46	1.22	1.03
81–120	3.45	8.32	6.17	0.65	1.44	1.11
121–160	2.99	8.20	6.42	0.53	1.44	1.13
161–320	7.97	13.23	11.39	1.30	2.06	1.80
Above 320	3.19	21.52	16.21	0.47	3.08	2.34

Surprisingly little domestic manufacturing was reported by farmers on the frontier. The annual average value on holdings of 40, 80, and 160 acres in frontier townships was only $3.73 per farm. The mean for all sample farms in Kansas was $1.94; in Minnesota, $0.27. In contrast, farm production in Illinois and Indiana averaged $16.69 and $8.71 respectively.

Although northerners had generally relinquished the more traditional forms of household production, especially textiles, not every important item had passed into commercial production to become independent of the farm or rural family. The chief exceptions as discussed in Chapter 9 were butter and cheese. Butter especially was an important dietary component. Commercial creameries and cheese factories were late appearing, thus most butter and cheese was still not factory produced in 1860. Fortunately the output of these processed goods, which we would argue were as much manufacturing activities as flour milling or sawmilling, was reported separately in the agricultural enumerations.

Eastern farmers produced 224 million pounds of butter and 73 million pounds of cheese; midwesterners made 153 million and 28 million pounds respectively. Valuing these outputs at an estimated average national price of $0.15 per pound for butter and $0.10 for cheese, reasonable lower-bound price estimates for the northern states, indicates that the value of these products in the East would have been $40.9 million, in the West $25.8 million.[25] If these activities are counted as household manufacturing within the mid-nineteenth-century economy, they overwhelm the officially reported value of household manufactures and imply the persistence of substantial home production at this time.

The effect of valuing these dairy products as household manufactures for farms in the sample is shown in Figure 12.1. Eastern household manufacturing rather than being insignificant becomes an important element in farm income and is double or triple the value produced by the average midwestern farm exceeding 20 acres.

Consider the effect on the total value of household production when

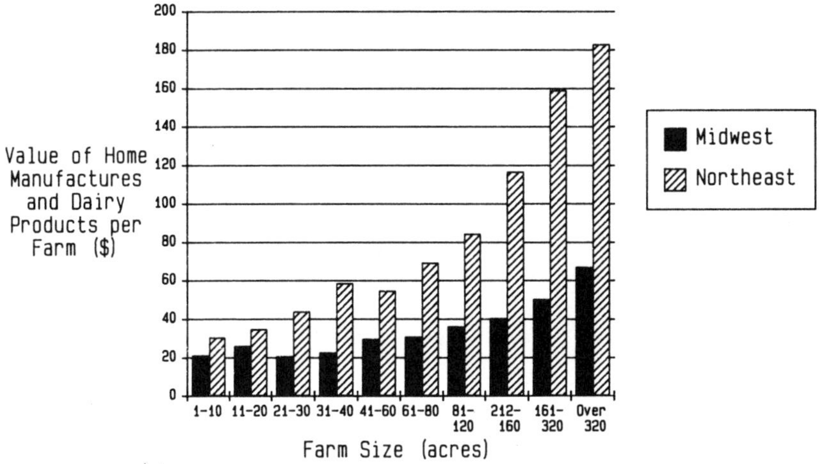

FIG. 12.1. Value of household manufactures including dairy products by size of farm and region, 1859–1860.

butter and cheese making are added to the reported totals for household manufacture (Table 12.3). Although the level in New England remains comparatively low, those in the other three settled regions–Middle Atlantic states, Midwest, and South–are virtually the same and quite substantial. Within this broadened definition of household production, the relative slowness with which the manufacture of dairy products was transferred from farm to factory, thereby sustaining home industry, becomes clearer. While most Americans had ceased to manufacture a wide array of products within their homes by the Civil War, the practice of churning butter and making cheese persisted as a vestige of the earlier era of farm self-sufficiency, not only in food, but in processed or manufactured goods as well.

TABLE 12.3. Value of Household Production by Region Including Butter and Cheese Output, 1859–1860

Region	Reported Household Manufactures ($ million)	Farm Production of Butter & Cheese ($ million)	Total Production Value ($ million)
New England	1.1	10.4	11.5
Middle Atlantic States	1.4	32.7	34.1
Midwest	5.0	26.7	31.7
United States[a]	24.4	83.1	107.5

Source: U.S. Census Office, Eighth Census, *Agriculture in the United States in 1860* (Washington D.C., 1864).

[a]Includes South and the Pacific West.

Cheese factories began appearing in substantial numbers in some eastern states during the 1850s, well before the emergence of commercial creameries. Butter production, in fact, remained predominantly a domestic process throughout the nineteenth century. Commenting on one important difference between factory butter and cheese making, the commissioner of agriculture's *Report* for 1865 said, "It takes more skill and science to make cheese than butter. Cheese-making is a chemical process; butter-making mechanical."[26] Thus butter churned on farms, and to a lesser extent farm cheese that could be marketed in nearby communities, provided an important cash income source for many northern farmers.[27]

The size of the potential marketable surplus for all crops and livestock products depends both upon production and consumption. Farms not only produced food and feedstuffs, they also consumed them. We must therefore account for the consumption needs of the farm population and livestock, as well as "set-asides" for next year's seed in measuring surplus production. Here, we focus solely upon the quantities of feed and food products. We have limited the analysis to grains, legumes, irish potatoes, and sweet potatoes. In Chapter 13 we extend this analysis to cover other products that might be sold and measure the cash income of farms. In the following sections we develop a basis for estimating consumption and seed requirements based, wherever possible, on contemporary data. Where such data are not available, we have sought estimates that will bias our results against surpluses.

Individuals at this time consumed comparatively large amounts of food, the mid-nineteenth-century American diet being rich in calories, if not in nutritional value. In a standard work on American eating habits, *The American and His Food*, Richard Cummings suggests a diet for the 1850s consisting in part of 183.9 pounds of meat, 13.2 pounds of lard, 15.1 pounds of butter, 205 pounds of wheat flour, and 29.7 pounds of sweeteners.[28] Much of the meat was consumed as fat salt pork; yet despite its unpalatability by modern standards, meat consumption in the 1850s was close to record high levels.[29] These figures exclude poultry, fish, and wildlife.[30] The diet was heavy on fats and salt but light on fluid milk, fresh fruit, and green vegetables. Indeed, vegetables were often referred to as "sauce," suggesting a role limited to providing flavor or as a garnish, rather than as foodstuffs in their own right.

Cummings's estimates appear to have been incorporated in the more comprehensive national diet estimates for 1879 made by Merrill Bennett and Rosamond Peirce. Their diet was composed of thirty-eight separately identified foodstuffs that provided 3,741 calories a day.[31] This caloric intake should have been sufficient to maintain body weight under moderate to heavy work conditions for ten hours a day.[32]

These estimates of the free diet are supported by contemporary evidence derived from the widow portions provided for in the wills of farmers. These instructed sons to supply their mothers with specified quantities of meat, grain, other foodstuffs, beverages, and money. The wills analyzed by Lemon for the end of the eighteenth century in Pennsylvania specified about 150 pounds of meat, a variety of grains (12 bushels of wheat being the most frequently mentioned), the dairy products of one or two cows, rights to garden produce, and 2.4 barrels of cider a year plus a variety of nonfood items, including cash.[33] Further work on widows' portions in Massachusetts from the seventeenth through the early nineteenth centuries by Sarah McMahon is consistent with Cummings's data. For the period 1809–1831, the portions examined by McMahon allowed about 200 pounds of meat (about two-thirds of it in pork), 12.1 bushels of corn, and 5.6 bushels of rye. Moreover, 98 percent of the portions contained dairy products, 93 percent specified vegetables and garden produce, and more than half made an allowance for orchard products.[34]

Slaves by all accounts had a potentially superior diet, in nutritional terms if not in taste, to that consumed by the free population because of the greater emphasis on fresh garden produce and greens. Their diet provided more calories, but more work was required of them.[35] Slaves in Maryland and Missouri, according to Battalio and Kagel, were fed 3 pounds of bacon or meat of equivalent value and 1 peck of cornmeal a week.[36]

The dietary allowances that we assume in our analysis are equal or superior to those cited above: a free diet composed of 771 pounds of milk (as fluid milk, butter, or cheese), 200 pounds of meat, and 13.5 bushels of grain (in corn equivalents) per year for each adult equivalent.[37] Slaves are assumed to have been fed according to the Battalio and Kagel diet modified to allow for the consumption of dairy products in the amounts given by Fogel and Engerman.[38] This diet provides for an annual consumption of 237 pounds of milk, 182 pounds of meat, and 16.25 bushels of corn per adult equivalent slave. These dietary allowances provide more than 5,000 calories a day for both slave and free adult males, assuming no spoilage or waste.

Livestock today customarily receive substantial feed supplements of grain and concentrates. With the widespread dissemination of scientific feeding methods, there is relatively little variation in standards from region to region and farmer to farmer. Such was not the case in the mid-nineteenth century. Contemporary accounts suggest that few supplements were fed to livestock in the 1850s. They were expected to subsist, if not prosper, on pasture and forage. According to Gates: "Whether sheep, cattle, or hogs, the livestock were required to get most of their forage from unenclosed fields and woods, were given little or no grain or root crops, and rarely had protection against wintery blasts. Such feeding practices did nothing to maintain quality."[39] Our feed allowances (Table 12.4) are more generous than those used for southern livestock by Battalio and Kagel or Gallman, but they are consistent with the contemporary

TABLE 12.4. Livestock Supplementary Feeding Standards for 1859–1860 Based upon Contemporary Accounts

Animal	Feed per Year in Corn (bu)
Cattle	3.0
Dairy Cows	2.0 per 1000 lb milk
Hogs	10.0
Horses	25.0
Mules and Oxen	17.0
Sheep	0.5

Source: U.S. Patent Office, *Reports, 1851-56.*

evidence from the *Commissioner of Patent Reports* and the claims that northern livestock was better fed than southern.[40]

The generally inadequate feeding standards for livestock were reflected in the low slaughter weights and poor yields. Until these practices changed, animal husbandry made little progress. For example, Bateman has shown that most of the rise in milk yields between 1850 and 1910 was attributable to improved care and feeding techniques rather than to the introduction of inherently more productive breeds.[41]

Dairy cows fared better than steers. Farmers, more cognizant of the close links between feed and milk production, fed them accordingly. In New York State, where milk yields were among the highest in the country, cows were at pasture during the summer. During the winter they were fed corn fodder, oat straw, and hay, supplemented occasionally by 2 quarts of wheat bran or cornmeal a day for the two months prior to spring calving.[42] The feeding standard that we assume is somewhat more generous than this and is based on the estimated milk yield per head.

Other cattle were fed only scanty supplements to pasturage, and even then only for a brief period immediately prior to slaughter. A correspondent for the commissioner of patents from New York state wrote: "[T]he first winter, they are fed with hay and a little meal or roots. The second and third winter they are kept mainly on straw, and the autumn following are sold directly from the pasture" while in Ohio "steers are raised to three years old, without much grain."[43] Further west in Illinois, three steers were fed more generously, receiving "one ton of hay per head, with the gleanings of the corn fields and corn shucks, and perhaps two bushels of corn each is sufficient for the winter," but in Iowa "Some corn is given to calves the first winter; afterwards they are kept on hay made from the native prairie grasses, or on corn fodder."[44] Bidwell and Falconer were more sanguine in their description of cattle feeding, which they characterized as wintering around the strawstack in which cattle often had to dig grass out of the snow.[45]

Farmers traded upon hogs' recognized capacities as scavengers. The practice of turning fields over to hogs for gleaning after harvest was apparently widespread. Hogs were not, however, fattened until immediately prior to marketing, at about 18–24 months. A Pennsylvanian described the following feeding regimen for his hogs: "During their first winter [they] are fed just sufficient to keep them alive. The second summer they have the run of a clover field, and in the fall they are allowed the range of the orchard and woods. Six weeks before killing time, they are penned up and provided with as much corn, in the ear, as they can destroy."[46] Seven to 10 bushels fed in this way would add 100 pounds or so to the animal.[47] We have assumed a supplementary feeding rate for pigs of 10 bushels per hog in the farm inventory, which is equivalent to 12.5–20 bushels per hog fattened for slaughter, depending upon the age at which they were butchered. It is consistent with animals weighing 200–300 pounds at market.[48]

Sheep apparently were expected to survive all varieties of weather with minimal attention. Feed supplements were small and often given only to breeding ewes. Various Patent Office correspondents described sheep care as: "Sheep get most of their fat on grass;" or "Sheep are kept in pasture from seven to eight months, and the remainder of the year on hay and straw," while another was somewhat more generous: "Sheep may be wintered on straw and chaff, with a small daily allowance of a gill of corn, or its equivalent."[49] We assume that they were fed as well as those kept by this latter correspondent.

Farmers appear to have been most conscientious in the care and feeding of their draft animals. Although there seem to be no direct contemporary estimates of the quantity of feed provided horses, mules, and oxen in the *Commissioner of Patent Reports* we examined, data on the cost of raising draft animals in conjunction with the price of oats and corn permit us to estimate the range of probable consumption levels at midcentury.[50] For horses the range is about 16–34 bushels a year, which is somewhat higher than that used by Battalio and Kagel for southern horses.[51] We assume horses were fed the equivalent of 25 bushels of corn, and mules and oxen two-thirds as much.[52]

We made two independent checks on these feed allowances. First, we compared our aggregate feed allowances against those provided to livestock in 1899. Data from the 1900 Census show that livestock consumed on average 24 percent of gross production by value.[53] Using the feed allowances we have described, the aggregate fraction of gross production consumed by livestock on sample farms ranged from 17 to 36 percent by state including the value of hay fed as a supplement to the corn rations.[54] Second, we also tried to estimate the appropriate diet by an alternative approach. We eventually elected not to employ the latter for technical reasons but we report some of the results here because they give further insight into the care that livestock received if farmers followed the regimen outlined above.

By the late nineteenth century, agriculturalists were beginning to appreciate the close links between livestock diet, yields, and profitable livestock management through the promotion and teaching of scientific feeding standards. The problem was to feed livestock the most economical diet that was consistent with their role and economic purpose on the farm. Today we can recognize this as a variation on the classic linear programming exercise–the diet problem, where the objective is to minimize the cost of feed subject to satisfying the dietary needs of the livestock, given the nutritional values of the various feedstuffs and their prices—but linear programming was not developed until the Second World War.[55] Although its promoters did not express it in quite this manner, the algorithm is consistent with the thrust of scientific feeding at the end of the nineteenth century.

Information on the nutritional content of livestock feeds was obtained from tables of the average composition of digestible nutrients in American feedstuffs published by W. A. Henry.[56] This source lists some 200 feedstuffs in common use in 1901, while a later edition, published in 1936, by F. B. Morrison lists over 1,000.[57] We focused attention upon just 6 of these—barley, corn, hay, oats, straw, and wheat—using simple averages of the analyses where necessary.

Henry furnishes estimates of the minimum daily requirements of total digestible nutrients, protein, dry matter, carbohydrates, and ether extract for each farm animal by weight and by workload. These standards, for example, suggest that hogs of 225–250 pounds live weight, which was approximately the average for hogs at Chicago being fattened for market, require approximately two-thirds of a pound of protein a day.[58] This requirement could be satisfied by feeding 8.5 pounds of corn, 7.3 pounds of oats, or 6.6 pounds of wheat. According to the price data for Illinois given above, the cost would have been $0.08 for corn, $0.07 for oats, or $0.10 for wheat.

Livestock feed requirements were converted to an annual basis by assuming different periods of pasturage when no supplemental feeds were provided. The objective function was to minimize the cost of livestock feed subject to satisfying the weighted dietary needs of the livestock, given feed costs and the nutritional value of each feedstuff. No price was assigned for pasture. Weights were provided by different farm animals.

It was impractical to solve this problem for every farm in the sample so we concentrated our attention on sensitivity tests, measuring the effects of varying the number of days at pasture for a subset of the data. We discovered that one set of possible implicit assumptions in the feed allowances we have described above is that cattle were fed 50 days a year; cows, 80 days; hogs, 190 days; draft animals, 140 days; and sheep, not at all.

We also made allowances in our estimates of the potential marketable surplus for crop replacement. Seed was deducted from production to provide for next year's planting. Aggregate estimates of these (and livestock feed allowances) are available in estimates of the percentage of crops marketed and entering into gross farm income.[59] They have not been used since they assume what we expect to show, namely, that farms on average produced surpluses, beyond their own consumption needs, that could be sold. Instead, we subtracted percentages of each farm's gross production of individual crops on the basis of contemporary yield and seed productivity data for the sample states (and sample counties to the extent possible) that are given in the replies to the commissioner of patents circulars.[60] It seems plausible that these reports lend an upward bias to yields and seed productivity, thereby biasing seed requirements downward. Moreover, to the extent that yields in 1859 were low-to-average, a fixed percentage of gross production for seed might be insufficient to seed a like acreage in 1860.[61] We have therefore tried to take account of this in arriving at our estimates by raising the contemporary estimates somewhat. We assumed the following amount of "set asides" from gross production to provide for next year's seed: wheat and barley, 9 percent; corn, 4 percent; oats, 6 percent; rye, 6 percent; other seeded crops (buckwheat, peas, and beans, etc.), 8 percent; and 10 percent for all root crops.[62]

We measured overall food surpluses and deficits as farm production, net of seed, human food, and livestock grain requirements, all expressed in corn equivalents using the appropriate conversion rates. Dairy allowances were met by multiplying the number of cows on the farms by statewide milk yield estimates.[63] Meat consumption was met by dividing the reported slaughter value of livestock by the average price of undressed meat and multiplying by 0.76 as the ratio of dressed to undressed carcass weights. These relationships we assume to be reversible so that any dietary shortfall in meat or dairy could be rectified by substituting corn equivalents in suitable amounts. Grain requirements were met out of the corn equivalents.

The map in Figure 12.2 gives an overview of the mean farm surplus by township expressed in bushels of corn equivalent. Surplus milk was converted into corn at the dairy cattle feed rate of 2 bushels of corn per 1,000 pounds of milk, and meat was converted into corn at the rate of 1 bushel per 7.6 pounds of meat. The largest surpluses were found on Illinois, Indiana, Iowa, and Kansas farms.

A preponderance of marginal farms existed in the Northeast, especially in New Hampshire and Vermont, but even along the Erie Canal. At our assumed free diet, which represents 41.4 bushels of corn equivalents per adult male equivalent a year, farms in the smallest surplus category could feed no more than 3.6 nonfarm adults. Yet the average surplus from a farm in Livingston or Dewitt counties, Illinois, could have supported at least 36 such individuals.

With the exception of Polk and Mahnomen counties in northwestern Minnesota, farms in townships of the upper northern states were comparatively marginal surplus producers. They produced enough to satisfy their own needs but had little left over to feed the nonfarm local population. Furthermore, farms in nineteen townships (Table 12.5)–Cheboygan,

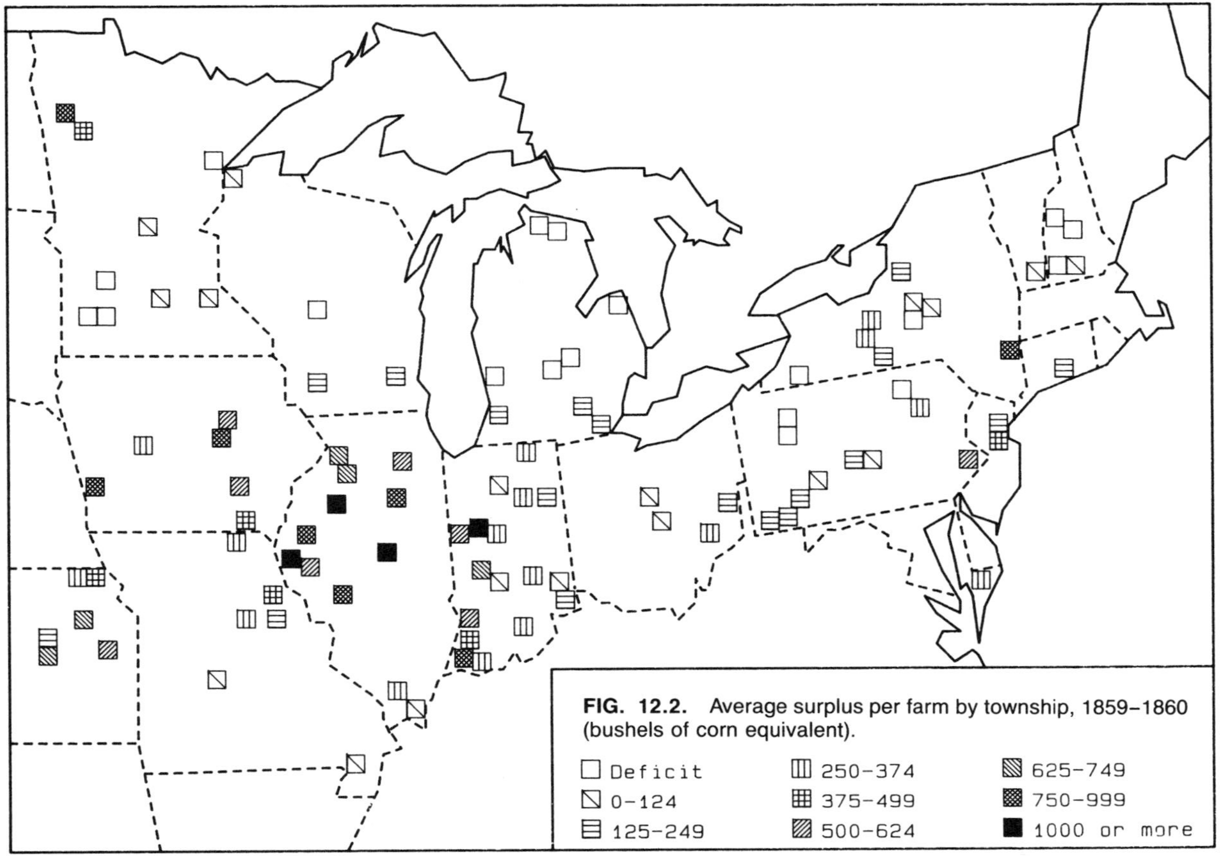

FIG. 12.2. Average surplus per farm by township, 1859–1860 (bushels of corn equivalent).

TABLE 12.5. Farm Food and Feed Deficits in Deficit Townships, 1859–1860

County and State	Average Deficit				Number of Adult Equivalent Consuming Units Short on:[a]			
	Dairy (lb milk)	Meat (lb meat)	Grain (bu corn)	All (bu corn)	Dairy	Meat	Grain	All
Cheboygan, Mich.	1,601[b]	185.9	78.7	99.9	—	0.9	5.8	2.4
Clinton, Mich.	4,987[b]	100.3	71.9	75.1	—	0.5	5.3	1.8
Emmet, Mich.	1,566	347.3	78.3	127.1	2.0	1.7	5.8	3.1
Huron, Mich.	1,986	675.5	81.8	174.6	2.6	3.4	6.1	4.2
Ottawa, Mich.	5,091[b]	61.3	37.3	35.1	—	0.3	2.8	0.8
Shiawassee, Mich.	5,457[b]	256.8	59.9	82.7	—	1.3	4.4	2.0
Cottonwood, Minn.	5,695[b]	263.0	99.2	122.4	—	1.3	7.3	3.0
Murray, Minn.	3,681[b]	199.0	90.2	109.0	—	1.0	6.7	2.6
Renville, Minn.	3,716	964.0	135.3	269.6	4.8	4.8	10.0	6.5
St. Louis, Minn.	4,059[b]	185.0[b]	39.6	7.2	—	—	2.9	0.2
Belknap, H.H.	7,702[b]	131.1[b]	79.8	47.1	—	—	5.9	1.1
Cheshire, N.H.	8,589[b]	321.5[b]	98.1	38.6	—	—	7.3	0.9
Grafton, N.H.	7,720[b]	246.0[b]	87.1	39.3	—	—	6.5	0.9
Cattaraugus, N.Y.	24,172[b]	5.2[b]	68.6	19.5	—	—	5.1	0.5
Chenango, N.Y.	29,690[b]	179.5[b]	99.5	16.5	—	—	7.4	0.4
Clarion, Pa.	7,534[b]	142.7	46.1	49.8	—	0.7	3.4	1.2
Forest, Pa.	6,569[b]	58.9	92.8	87.4	—	0.3	6.9	2.1
Sullvian, Pa.	6,090[b]	312.9	91.1	120.1	—	1.6	6.7	2.9
Juneau, Wis.	6,551[b]	517.7	51.2[b]	83.8	—	—	2.6	0.1

[a] Adult equivalent consumption = 771 lb milk, 200 lb meat, and 13.5 bu corn = 41.4 bu corn equivalent.

[b] Surplus.

Clinton, Emmet, Huron, Ottawa, and Shiawassee counties in Michigan; Cottonwood, Murray, Renville, and St. Louis counties in Minnesota; Belknap, Cheshire, and Grafton counties in New Hampshire; Cattaraugus and Chenango counties, New York; Clarion, Forest, and Sullivan counties in Pennsylvania; and Juneau County, Wisconsin–had on average a deficit in food and feedstuffs for the farm family and farm livestock. In general the deficits were not large. However, in six of the townships it exceeded 100 bushels per farm, and in Renville County, Minnesota, the shortfall was 270 bushels of corn equivalent per farm, an amount equal to the annual consumption of 6.5 adults. The deficit in Huron County, Michigan, was not quite so acute, 175 bushels of corn equivalent per farm, but was substantial nonetheless. Farms in these townships produced little food in 1859, partly because they had only recently been established.

Although farms in these nineteen communities in the aggregate could not feed themselves according to our assumed standards, let alone meet the needs of the local nonfarm population, they were not usually short of every food. Most had a dairy surplus and a deficit of grains and meat. The dairy deficit, which when present was comparatively small, would have been eliminated if there had been two more cows to every three farms. Some of the meat deficit probably could also have been made up by hunting; it certainly could have been met by a higher slaughter rate. Since this latter strategy was apparently not adopted, one could argue either that less meat was consumed and other foods substituted, or that hunting made up the deficit without recourse to market purchases.

The shortages of grain were much more serious. These could not be closed even by eliminating livestock feed supplements in Cheboygan, Cottonwood, Emmet, Huron, Murray, Renville, and Sullivan counties. In Clarion and Forest counties, reduced hog rations would have eliminated the grain shortage. How realistic the reduction in hog feed would be is debatable and is dependent upon alternate feed sources such as acorns or other "mast." Elsewhere in deficit townships, purchases must have been made to close the gap for it is doubtful if the prudent farmer allowed his draft animals to go without an adequate diet.

Surpluses varied systematically with farm size. The average surplus by region in each of the food categories for several size groups of farms is shown in Table 12.6. Grain surpluses were largest in the West, where the average was typically at least three times greater than in the Northeast. The four smallest size classes of producers faced a grain deficit in the East. Even eastern farms of about 40 acres were only marginally self-sufficient. Dairy surpluses were largest in the eastern states, where they were generally four or five times greater than in the West. Only western farms over 40 acres kept at least one surplus cow on average, but even the smallest northeastern farms had a surplus of one or two. Overall, for grains and all foods combined, except in the smallest size category, western farms had 50 to 100 percent more surplus to market than northeastern farms of the same size.

Surpluses increased linearly with farm size in the Northeast but at a decreasing rate for every food crop in the West. Given these conditions, a different size distribution of farms, one with more small units, would have produced a larger aggregate marketable surplus from the northern region. For example, western farms of 31–40 acres produced an average surplus (in grain equivalents) equal to 35 percent of that on 121–160-acre units. Overall, replacing one 121–160-acre farm with four 31–40-acre ones would have increased the marketable surplus by 42 percent in the West if all else remained the same.

Consequently, public land policy, discriminating in favor of larger farms by specifying minimum but not maximum purchases, resulted in a smaller agricultural surplus and less food available for export. It also resulted in fewer farmers in the total population and higher tenancy rates. Furthermore, because large farms were worked extensively rather than intensively, the farmer economized on both capital and labor, substituting land in their input mix and receiving smaller yields per acre but greater total production at a lower cost.

TABLE 12.6. Average Food and Feed Surpluses by Size of Farm and Food Group, by Region, 1859–1860

Foodstuff/	Farm Size (acres)										All
Region	1–10	11–20	21–30	31–40	41–60	61–80	81–120	121–160	161–320	320+	Farms
Dairy (lb)											
Midwest	208	822	1,289	1,755	2,735	2,679	3,651	4,443	5,859	8,446	3,721
Northeast	3,666	5,568	7,928	9,735	9,927	13,665	16,294	23,909	30,258	35,973	17,570
Meat (lb)											
Midwest	33	–4	142	61	303	387	446	571	1,184	2,149	589
Northeast	1,447	572	266	219	293	661	623	954	1,118	1,632	736
Grain (bu)											
Midwest	83	141	176	129	156	179	230	317	457	835	281
Northeast	–32	–25	–15	–3	35	38	56	63	104	226	53
All Foods (bu)											
Midwest	88	142	197	141	201	235	296	402	624	1,134	366
Northeast	166	62	37	46	94	152	170	237	311	513	185

Tenants in both regions generally produced larger surpluses than owner-occupiers (Table 12.7). In the Midwest, for example, tenant farms of every size produced more than comparable ones operated by the yeomanry. Indeed, those of 31–40 acres produced almost three times the surplus of owner-occupied farms of the same size, but overall they only averaged about 17 percent more. Nevertheless, it is the direction that is significant, for the same result appeared in the Northeast. The relative surplus was considerably larger, with tenants averaging almost 50 percent more. The smallest yeoman farms in the Midwest (those under 40 acres) and the very largest (those over 320 acres), however, managed to generate bigger surpluses than comparable northeastern tenant farms.

The product mix of tenant and yeoman farms in both regions accounts for this differential between them. The yeomanry emphasized mixed farming relatively more than tenants, who grew more cash grains and tended fewer head of livestock (see Chap. 8). In the Northeast, for example, yeoman farms produced a milk surplus that was 30 percent larger than generated on tenant farms, but they produced only one-third the grain surplus. In the Northeast, too, tenant farms had larger average meat surpluses, but this proved to be a consequence of larger surpluses on tenant farms of 80–160 acres and it is tempting to speculate that we see here the beginnings of feedlot operations since these farms produced substantial quantities of corn as well. In the Midwest, owner-occupied farms also produced a larger milk surplus, but the differential was much smaller, while there was virtually no difference in meat surpluses. Tenant farms of every size, however, produced more grain. By placing less emphasis on mixed farming, tenant farms needed less labor. Their family size was therefore smaller; fewer mouths to feed contributed to the amount of their surplus production. Consequently, if the surplus is measured in terms of bushels of corn equivalents per adult equivalent, tenant farms in the Midwest generated surpluses that averaged 62 percent more than those of the yeomanry and in the Northeast tenant farms produced an average of 79 percent more.

Estimates of the surplus per acre for all farms of various sizes by region for the different food categories are shown in Table 12.8. The surplus per acre under cultivation generally declines with increasing farm size, the land in large farms yielding less surplus per acre than that in small ones. Consider, for example, grain production in the West, where farms of 1–10 acres produced almost nine times the surplus per acre of those 320 acres or more, and farms of 11–20 acres yielded almost twice as much net surplus per acre as these large ones. These figures also point to substantial productivity differences between East and West. The dairy surplus per acre on eastern farms was at least three or four times that on western ones, but conversely grain surpluses in the latter region were

TABLE 12.7. Average Surplus per Farm by Farm Size, Region, and Tenancy, 1859–1860

Region	Farm Size (acres)										All
	1–10	11–20	21–30	31–40	41–60	61–80	81–120	121–160	161–320	320+	Farms
Midwest (bu)											
Owner-Occupier	–7.1	69.9	125.0	100.7	149.2	203.2	288.7	399.8	627.8	1,033.1	358.6
Tenant	81.6	215.1	276.9	278.5	383.0	345.4	326.4	405.6	589.3	1,480.7	417.9
Northeast (bu)											
Owner-Occupier	345.3	65.8	33.2	47.0	72.7	152.1	157.8	212.5	284.8	530.2	174.5
Tenant	20.8	14.4	48.8	36.6	216.9	152.6	227.4	325.1	433.6	450.3	256.2

TABLE 12.8. Average Food and Feed Surpluses per Improved Acre by Size of Farm and Food Group, by Region, 1859–1860

Foodstuff/ Region	Farm Size (acres)										All
	1–10	11–20	21–30	31–40	41–60	61–80	81–120	121–160	161–320	320+	Farms
Dairy Surplus (lb per acre)											
Midwest	86	52	57	72	83	66	65	66	55	41	59
Northeast	747	370	355	328	253	257	230	246	211	128	224
Meat Surplus (lb per acre)											
Midwest	14	0	6	3	9	10	8	9	11	10	9
Northeast	295	38	12	7	8	12	9	10	8	6	9
Grain Surplus (bu per acre)											
Midwest	34.2	9.0	7.8	5.3	4.7	4.4	4.1	4.7	4.3	4.0	4.5
Northeast	–6.5	–1.6	–0.7	–0.1	0.9	0.7	0.8	0.6	0.7	0.8	0.7
All Surplus Foods (bu per acre)											
Midwest	36.2	9.1	8.7	5.8	6.1	5.8	5.2	6.0	5.9	5.5	5.8
Northeast	33.7	4.1	1.6	1.5	2.4	2.9	2.4	2.4	2.2	1.8	2.4

four times or more those in the former. Overall, a western acre was at least twice, and frequently three times, as productive as a northeastern one (see Fig. 12.3). The most productive soils were those in Indiana, Illinois, Iowa, and Kansas; the least productive were found in the northernmost states.

More western than northeastern farms produced dairy deficits, while about the same fraction in each region had meat deficits (Table 12.9). Because they placed less emphasis upon the dairy, more tenant than owner-occupied farms had dairy deficits. In the Midwest 26 percent of tenants fell short on dairy products compared with 22 percent of owner-occupiers, while in the Northeast 12 percent were short compared with only 3 percent of yeoman farms. In the East far more farms, both tenant and yeoman, faced grain deficits. These data suggest that the most commercially oriented and market-dependent farms were in Illinois and Iowa in the West, and in Maryland and New Jersey in the East. Farmers in Indiana, Kansas, and Wisconsin would also have sought commercial markets for the sale of surplus produce. The fraction of farms with overall food deficits in these states was substantially lower than in most others. In Illinois the percentage of farms with deficits overall was smaller than the fraction with deficits of each of the three food groups; farms with a dairy deficit had, for example, a grain surplus offsetting that shortfall. A similar phenomenon is apparent in Indiana, Iowa, and Maryland. In eight states concentrated in the East, more than a third of the farms had deficits in grains, which generally could not have been eliminated even by reducing animal feed supplements to zero. These farms must therefore have made market purchases to meet at least some of their consumption needs.

The probability of being a deficit producer declined with increasing farm size in both regions. Whereas 48 percent of the farms in the West with 1–10 acres had deficits, only 16 percent with more than 320 acres were in that position (Fig. 12.4). In the Northeast, two-thirds of farms in the smallest size class were deficit producers, but this fraction dropped to only 22 percent among the largest-sized farms. The fraction of deficit western dairy farms was usually four times that in the Northeast for each size class of farm, whereas the fractions of deficit meat farms were approximately the same in each region. In grains, however, more than 48 percent or more of farms in each size class in the Northeast had deficits compared with about a third or less of western farms over 10 acres.

Reducing hog feed to 4 bushels per animal on the assumption that they gleaned more from the fields, or that fields of corn, oats, or rye were "hogged down" without being harvested and that they obtained more mast from general foraging, changes the figures in favor of western farms. The average surplus in grain equivalents is increased by about 25

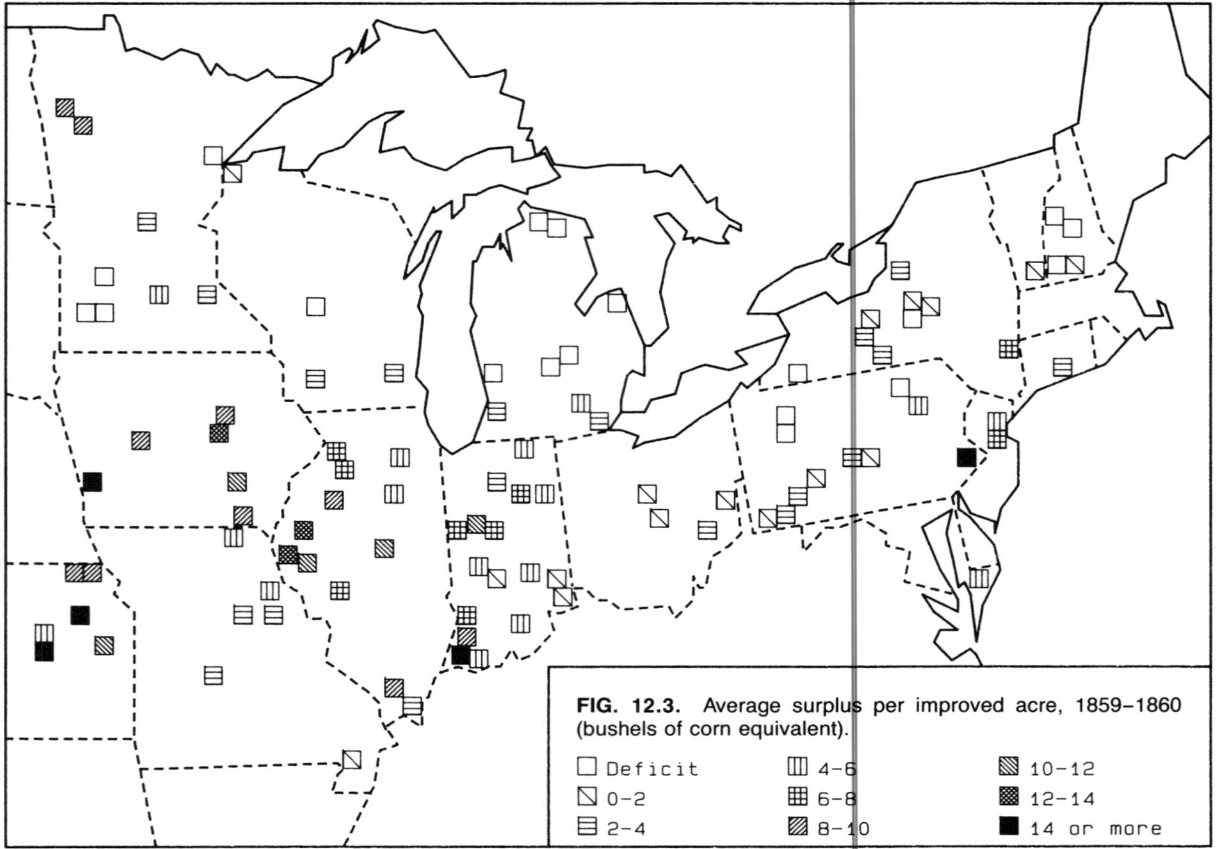

FIG. 12.3. Average surplus per improved acre, 1859–1860 (bushels of corn equivalent).

TABLE 12.9. Percentage of Deficit Farms by Food Category and State, 1859–1860

State	Percentage of Farms with Deficits of:			
	Dairy	Meat	Grain	All
Illinois	16	29	12	10
Indiana	34	34	24	22
Iowa	14	49	12	11
Kansas	15	41	17	18
Michigan	12	54	61	56
Minnesota	20	64	33	37
Missouri	26	28	38	31
Ohio	2	44	38	34
Wisconsin	6	61	23	27
Midwest	24	38	28	25
Connecticut	5	22	82	31
Maryland	36	35	16	17
New Hampshire	3	44	95	69
New Jersey	6	39	13	18
New York	2	35	52	34
Pennsylvania	4	36	51	38
Vermont	2	46	64	46
Northeast	5	37	54	37
North	17	38	37	29

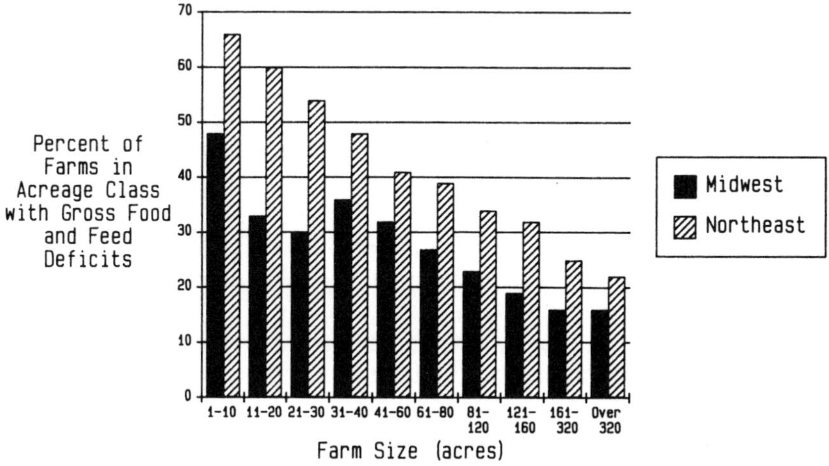

FIG. 12.4. Percentage of farms with gross deficits of food and feed by size of farm and region, 1859–1860.

percent and the fraction of overall deficit farms falls to 16 percent, whereas this change increased eastern surplus by only 14 percent and reduced the fraction of deficit farms by only 3 percentage points to 31 percent. Such a change is also more favorable to owner-occupiers than tenants.

Our conclusions do not depend critically upon our food and animal feedstuff assumptions. We have not performed a sensitivity analysis on the human diet on the grounds that an existing allowance of 5,200 or more calories a day per adult equivalent is an upper-bound one biased against our finding of substantial surpluses. We have, however, estimated the effect of increasing livestock feed allowances by 50 percent over those shown in Table 12.5. Such allowances, which far exceed any mentioned in the contemporary literature, are generally greater than those recommended in modern stock feed guides for best-practice farmers. The result of these calculations was to reduce the surpluses but not eliminate them totally in the West. Agriculture in the Northeast would, however, have had little or no surplus beyond local requirements and urban areas would have been forced to depend almost totally upon western agricultural imports. This change would increase the fraction of deficit grain farms in the western region from 26 to 43 percent, and increase the proportion in the northeast from 49 to 65 percent. In the event of a shortfall in production to meet farm needs, it is likely that livestock would suffer some diminution of their feed allowance before the farmer resorted to market purchases of feedstuffs. Hence, we feel that our principal estimates are better approximations to the circumstances of mid-nineteenth-century agriculture.

The average midwestern farm in 1859 produced sufficient surplus food to feed 8.8 adults or about two other families. In the Northeast, however, the surplus from a farm would only feed 4.5 adults, and in New England, farms did not produce sufficient extra to feed even 1 extra adult. Nevertheless, despite selecting parameters designed to bias our results against marketable surpluses, at midcentury most farms were not only able to meet their own consumption needs but also produced a surplus that could be marketed. The most serious deficit facing many eastern townships was in grains, both for human and animal consumption. But they often had an abundance of dairy products that found a market in the urban centers of the East Coast. Except on the furthest reaches of the frontier and in the exhausted soils of some eastern communities, northern agriculture in the United States had moved far beyond self-sufficiency to market dependency on the eve of the Civil War, and in the next chapter we examine the farmers' quest for markets and measure their income from these sales.

CHAPTER THIRTEEN

Producing for the Market: Gross Farm Revenues and Income

COLLECTIVELY, NORTHERN FARMS IN 1859–1860 WERE PRODUCING substantial surpluses of feed and foodstuffs beyond their own consumption needs. These, however, were of little value unless they could be sent to market at acceptable prices. Sales, not production alone, were the stepping stone to economic success. One market for these commodities lay at the farm gate since in every sample township resided a substantial nonfarm population, but in many communities farmers had to seek more distant markets if they were to sell all their surplus produce. Whether consumed locally or by distant consumers, we shall assume that all farm products beyond the needs of livestock and the farm family were sold. Farmers were thus passively dependent upon prices. Moreover, to the extent that markets lay far beyond the farm, they were also at the mercy of the transport system.

Markets at the farm gate varied greatly both in absolute size and relative to the number of farms serving them. At one extreme the nonfarm population in Madison County, New York, numbered more than two thousand and had to be fed to the extent possible largely by the 298 farms in the sample township. At the opposite extreme all twelve residents of Cottonwood County, Minnesota, lived on farms. Both townships failed to feed their entire populations from within, but the shortfall per person in Madison County was only half that in Cottonwood. As a proportion of the rural population, nonfarm residents made up anywhere from zero to more than 80 percent. Overall, however, 44 percent of the households and about 40 percent of the rural northern population was classified as nonfarm.

Presumably, as many as possible among the nonfarm residents would try to satisfy their needs from local sources to avoid the high costs of transportation and minimize spoilage. Farms in nineteen of the townships, however, did not produce sufficiently to meet their own needs, let alone those of the general population.[1] Fifteen other townships would have faced deficits if the nonfarm population had consumed rations equal to those allocated to the farm population and would have needed to import food from elsewhere (Fig. 13.1). Deficits were most acute in the Northeast, where more than half the townships in the region were unable to feed their populations from within. As a result, the net surplus for the Northeast over and above farm and local nonfarm needs averaged only 6 bushels of corn equivalents per adult equivalent. This was about one-seventh of the per capita consumption, so that one urban northeasterner could be fed for every seven who lived in rural areas. However, since more than one-third of the northeastern population lived in cities, it could not be fed from regional surpluses alone.[2] Furthermore, the diet of those who could be fed from regional surpluses in the Northeast would have left much to be desired if interregional trade had not been possible. They would have consumed almost three times as much dairy produce as contemporaries suggested, very little meat, and virtually no grain.

In the Midwest, on the other hand, the average surplus per person was much greater. Measured in corn equivalents, individuals had available from regional sources at least twice as much as they could eat. Again, however, the diet would have been far from nutritionally ideal. If trade were impossible, people in the West would have had a diet with an abundance of grain – enough grain in fact to feed three – but insufficient meat and dairy products.

In ten townships scattered throughout the North, the deficit could have been eliminated by less than a 25 percent cut in human food consumption. This may have involved nothing more than the elimination or minimization of waste and spoilage. Adults would still have had a potential dietary intake of about 4,000 calories a day. In fifteen townships the shortages were far more severe, exceeding 20 bushels of corn equivalents per person, or about half of the nutritional intake of the diet discussed above (see Chap. 12). It is inconceivable that these could have been eliminated by any plausible diminution of human and livestock consumption.

Although many of these townships with severe deficits were located in the Midwest, the overall situation there was more optimistic than that facing communities in the Northeast. Deficit and marginal townships were usually on the geographic periphery of midwestern settlement.

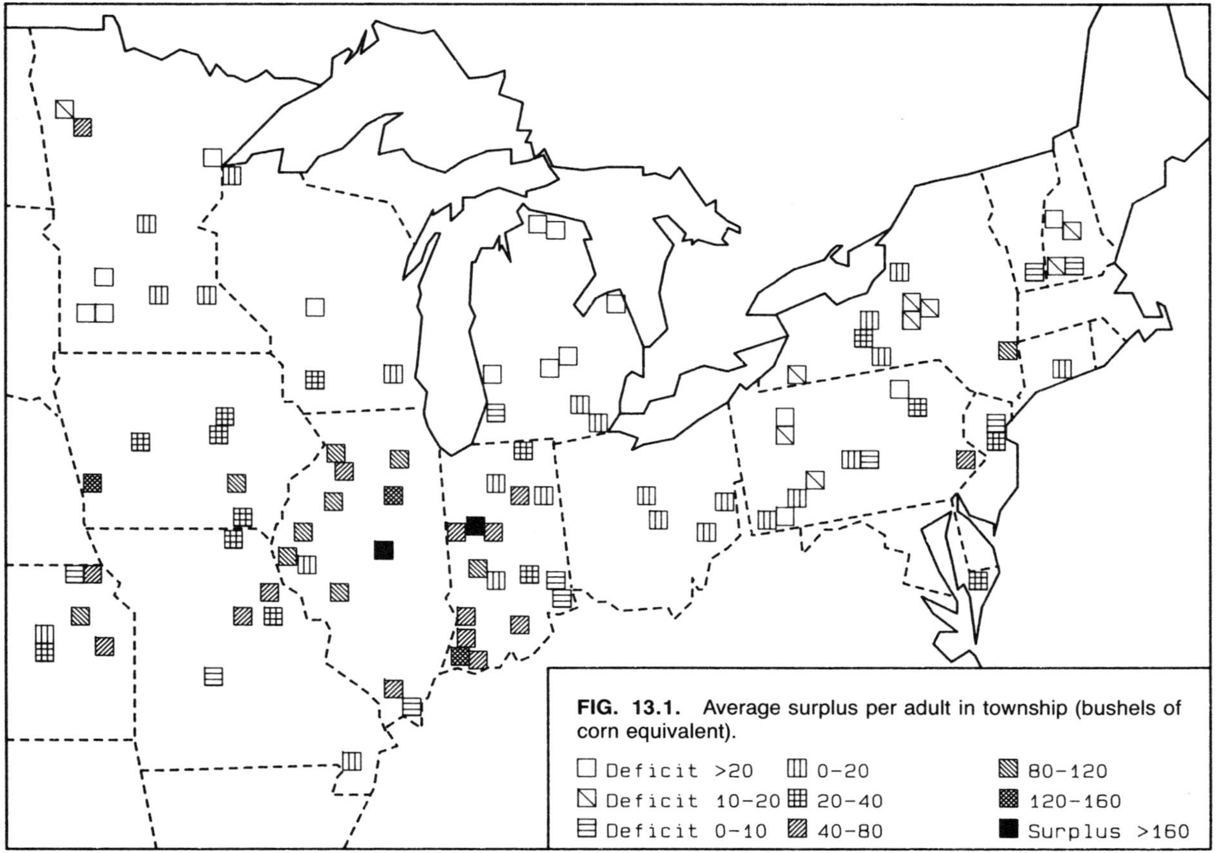

FIG. 13.1. Average surplus per adult in township (bushels of corn equivalent).

They were counterbalanced by large surpluses from the Indiana and Illinois heartland. Many of these produced surpluses of at least 80 bushels per person, or twice as much food as someone could eat.

Meat surpluses (and deficits) per capita were generally small, averaging only 18.4 pounds in the Midwest and 8.2 pounds in the Northeast, compared with a per capita consumption of about 200 pounds. However, these limited surpluses of meat do not necessarily imply that fresh meat was scarce. Indeed, we would argue that they are proof of an active trade between town and country, but the market was in meat on the hoof rather than the carcass. In the absence of refrigeration, animals commonly were slaughtered near where they were consumed, not where they were produced. Markets for fresh meat were geographically quite limited. Where good transportation was available, however, meat surpluses were larger. Among those townships located on or close to rail or water transport, they averaged 26.2 pounds per person; in those townships lacking good transport, there was a small meat deficit, 19.6 pounds per person.

There were also markets beyond the farm gate for those who had larger surpluses than needed by the local residentiary population. The major markets were in the urban centers of the East, but there were doubtless other deficit areas in closer proximity. The size of the average farm surplus shows a systematic variation with ease of access to transportation. Where it was available, farmers produced more. Most of the large surpluses were produced by farms in townships within 30 to 40 miles of navigable rivers such as the Illinois, Wabash, Mississippi, Missouri, and Hudson. Water transportation was the most economical for bulky, relatively low value-to-weight agricultural commodities, but railroads often paralleled these routes and competed for traffic. For farms close to transportation, surpluses averaged 346 bushels of corn equivalent, but those lacking access to distant markets produced only about half as much (172 bushels). Although it is tempting to infer causality from the provision of transport to the production of surpluses for market sale, it worked in both directions. While farmers with access to markets had an incentive to produce more, railroads and canals tended to be built through the more productive areas where demand for their services would be higher.[3]

Large farm surpluses, however, did not necessarily translate into a high demand for transportation; rather, they measure production for market whether those sales are made locally or elsewhere. Townships on transportation routes tended to be more populous, with a fractionally greater proportion of nonfarmers. Nevertheless, even after allowing for local consumption, those on transport routes produced an average surplus of 32.7 bushels of corn equivalent per person, or 3.2 bushels per improved acre, whereas those without easy access to transport averaged only 9.7 bushels per person and 1.1 bushels per acre.

Townships from Ohio eastward generally contained higher percentages of nonfarm households than those further west. Farms there also typically produced smaller surpluses. As a result, these communities had relatively little to export after meeting the needs of the local population. Only three townships in this area had surpluses exceeding 60,000 bushels of corn equivalent surplus, and two of these – Dutchess County in New York and Montgomery County, Pennsylvania – were within a day's wagon haul of major urban markets. For the rest, distant markets were less important.

In the western heartland, however, farms were so productive that large surpluses remained after feeding the local nonfarm population. Moreover, the bulk and weight of these surpluses was such that water or rail transportation was almost a sine qua non for the kind of agriculture that had evolved in the West, particularly the emphasis upon cereal grains. The drive for overland transport improvement characteristic of these years was obviously and rationally motivated, given these pressures to move bulky goods.

The tonnage to be moved from western townships was an order of magnitude greater than that in eastern ones (Fig. 13.2). About a quarter had at least 1,000 tons of surplus produce to be shipped during a year, almost half had 500 tons or more. It is difficult to imagine that this volume and weight of commodities could have been shipped by wagon. According to Paul Gates, a two-horse team could haul about a ton 25 miles a day.[4] If we assume a mean distance to market of 50 miles, then moving 1,000 tons would have employed at least ten teams full time for a year. The occupation data, however, show few teamsters in these communities and it seems unlikely that farmers could have done it themselves while still managing to be so productive in the field. Consequently, marketing such a surplus would probably have been impossible without the railroad.

The surplus of western grains was shipped East to meet the shortages there in both urban and rural areas. So far as the demand for transportation was concerned, however, deficits and surpluses were equivalent except to the extent that there might be a back-haulage problem in certain areas. Townships with surpluses had food to sell beyond the immediate environs; those with deficits needed to import from elsewhere. Thus the size of the township surplus or deficit provides a reasonable proxy measure for the demand for transportation services.

So far, this discussion of marketable surpluses has been confined to grains, legumes, and tuberous root crops because they could be substituted in both the livestock and human diet. Farmers, however, produced a

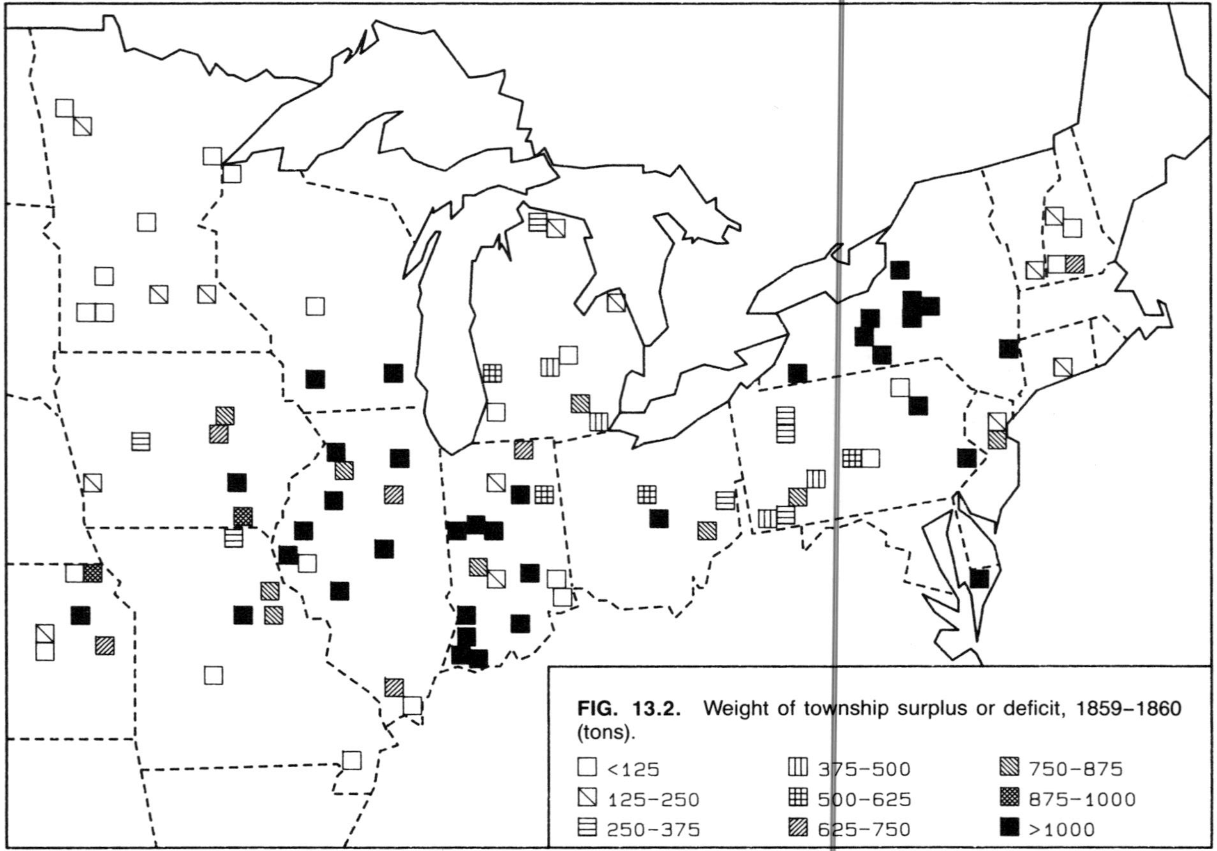

FIG. 13.2. Weight of township surplus or deficit, 1859–1860 (tons).

wide range of other crops. Some were industrial or commercial crops such as tobacco and flaxseed, others were primarily for human consumption, such as dairy, orchard, and market-garden products; and some, such as hay, were only for livestock. These crops, together with any surplus for food and feed grains, could be sold and we assume that they were. Not all farm products, however, were recorded by the census enumerators. There were four important omissions: poultry, eggs, fluid milk, and lumber. We have derived estimates for each using other sources.

Our estimates of gross poultry and egg production are based upon extrapolations from the Strauss and Bean figures for the post–Civil War period.[5] This procedure indicated a chicken and hen inventory of 73.5 million fowl for the 1859 crop year, with sales of poultry amounting to 106.9 million fowl in that year. We assumed that the average chicken weighed 4 pounds and was valued at \$0.053 to \$0.077 a pound.[6] These figures are consistent with the national diet in 1879, for which Bennett and Peirce estimated consumption of poultry at 15 pounds per head.[7] Our estimates imply a per capita consumption of poultry in 1860 of 15.9 pounds. The chicken and hen inventory, and sales of poultry were divided between farms on the basis of the 1900 census distribution of chickens by farm size and state using the ratio of the estimated 1860 chicken inventory to that reported for 1900.[8] Sales of poultry were entered into farm gross revenues and the value of the chicken inventory was added to the reported value of livestock. Egg production, also extrapolated from the Strauss and Bean data, was estimated to be 158.8 million dozen eggs, which is 2.16 dozen per year per chicken in the farm inventory.[9]

The Census did not separately report fluid milk production. Only that portion converted into butter and cheese was captured by the census data. Using the milk yield estimates shown in Chapter 9 and assuming conversion factors of 22:1 for milk to butter poundage and 10:1 for milk to cheese, we were able to derive the residual fluid milk production.[10] From this estimate we deducted the milk equivalent of the Bennett and Peirce adult annual consumption of dairy products by the farm family members.

No mention is made of forest products by the Census before 1880, at which time the value of wood sold or consumed (\$96 million) exceeded the value of orchard and market-garden products and contributed over 4 percent to gross farm revenues.[11] Estimates by Robert Gallman for 1859–1860 place a value of \$50.4 million on forest products representing between 3.5 and 6.5 percent of gross farm income in that year.[12] This is probably too low. Rather than rely upon aggregate estimates of cords of wood per capita, we have chosen instead to calculate the 1879 ratio of cords of wood cut to unimproved acreage for each sample county from the Census.[13] These ratios were then applied to the unimproved acreage at the farm level in the sample to estimate the number of cords cut in 1859–1860. Nationally this procedure would place cordwood production in 1859–1860 at some 50 million cords.

These commodities were then valued at farm gate prices. However, there are no comprehensive and consistent data series on prices paid to farmers in each state for 1860, but there are numerous scattered estimates. Whenever there was no consensus between sources, we used the lowest price so that farm revenues will be biased downward. The prices we used for the major crops are shown in Table 13.1. These were assembled from various, diverse sources of data. At least one price was found for each crop and commodity. Where we were unable to find an appropriate price for a particular commodity in a state, we took the price from the nearest state for which we had a quote. In addition, we assumed that milk sold for $0.0083 a pound, and eggs between $0.08 and $0.15 per dozen.[14]

A major source of data were studies published by agricultural experiment stations in Illinois, Indiana, Iowa, Maryland, New York, and Wisconsin giving prices received by farmers, often on a monthly basis, during the nineteenth century for many of the crops in the agricultural schedules.[15] These prices were generally taken from contemporary newspapers, typically on or about the fifteenth of each month.[16] The annual average price was the weighted sum of monthly prices, the weights being the fraction of total sales of the crop taking place in the month. These newspaper prices were often supplemented by data from mill, farm, and store accounts (summarized in Table 13.2).

Prices in Illinois, New York, and Wisconsin have also been supplemented with figures collected by local commercial interests (see Table 13.3). The Chicago Board of Trade, for example, reported weekly grain prices and monthly prices of less important (in the Chicago trade) agricultural commodities such as clover seed and potatoes.[17] These are generally higher than the estimated prices received by farmers in Illinois because they include the cost of transportation. A similar range of prices was obtained from the Milwaukee Chamber of Commerce.[18] A more extensive set was available for New York.[19] While there was less consistency between these figures and the estimates of prices received by farmers in New York than in the comparable cases of Illinois and Wisconsin, the size of the New York City market and the concentration of transportation routes upon the port of New York makes these differences entirely plausible.

We have also obtained prices received by Massachusetts farmers in 1855 for corn, rye, oats, and potatoes. These data, supplied by Winifred Rothenberg, are taken from farm account books. Corn realized between $1.12 and $1.50 per bushel; potatoes, $0.33–1.42 per bushel; rye, $1.125–

TABLE 13.1. Prices Received by Farmers by Crop and State, 1859–1860 ($)

	State															
Crop	Ill.	Ind.	Iowa	Kans.	Mich.	Minn.	Mo.	Ohio	Wis.	Conn.	Md.	N.H.	N.J.	N.Y.	Pa.	Vt.
Wheat (bu)	0.90	1.00	0.68	0.79	0.89	0.75	0.89	1.15	0.88	1.51	1.22	0.98	1.30	1.25	1.13	0.98
Rye (bu)	0.40	0.37	0.50	0.48	0.48	0.41	0.42	0.50	0.25	0.87	0.71	0.95	0.84	0.80	0.69	0.95
Corn (bu)	0.43	0.30	0.30	0.35	0.30	0.38	0.41	0.50	0.41	0.90	0.74	0.93	0.77	0.68	0.65	0.99
Oats (bu)	0.40	0.33	0.25	0.26	0.26	0.26	0.33	0.43	0.29	0.43	0.38	0.45	0.40	0.36	0.39	0.43
Tobacco (lb)	0.09	0.09	0.09	0.09	0.09	0.09	0.09	0.09	0.09	0.12	0.04	0.08	0.08	0.08	0.10	0.25
Wool (lb)	0.32	0.28	0.35	0.33	0.33	0.33	0.30	0.41	0.20	0.37	0.24	0.31	0.51	0.23	0.13	0.49
Peas & Beans (bu)	1.21	1.21	1.21	1.21	1.21	1.21	1.21	1.21	0.87	1.03	0.86	1.03	1.03	0.86	1.03	1.03
Irish Potatoes (bu)	0.50	0.48	0.48	0.48	0.48	0.48	0.48	0.48	0.46	0.48	0.73	0.48	0.48	0.39	0.48	0.48
Sweet Potatoes (bu)	0.51	0.51	0.51	0.51	0.51	0.51	0.51	0.51	0.51	0.51	0.51	0.51	0.51	0.51	0.51	0.51
Barley (bu)	0.57	0.77	0.44	0.66	0.66	0.50	0.60	0.55	0.69	0.66	0.66	0.66	0.90	0.65	0.66	0.66
Buckwheat (bu)	0.50	0.45	0.41	0.50	0.59	0.46	0.47	0.68	0.45	0.60	0.40	0.59	0.68	0.40	0.50	0.59
Butter (lb)	0.15	0.19	0.19	0.19	0.19	0.19	0.18	0.13	0.13	0.15	0.23	0.15	0.15	0.17	0.15	0.15
Cheese (lb)	0.15	0.11	0.11	0.11	0.11	0.11	0.11	0.11	0.09	0.11	0.11	0.11	0.11	0.11	0.11	0.11
Hay (ton)	5.68	10.30	10.30	10.30	10.30	10.30	10.30	10.30	5.86	10.30	14.55	10.30	10.30	13.93	10.30	10.30
Clover Seed (bu)	4.94	4.94	4.94	4.94	4.94	4.94	4.94	4.94	6.13	4.94	4.94	4.94	4.94	5.13	4.94	4.94
Grass Seed (bu)	2.83	2.83	2.83	2.83	2.83	2.83	2.83	2.83	1.95	2.83	2.83	2.83	2.83	3.06	2.83	2.83
Hops (lb)	0.20	0.15	0.20	0.33	0.20	0.19	0.20	0.16	0.19	0.15	0.18	0.18	0.13	0.25	0.18	0.20
Flax (lb)	0.20	0.20	0.20	0.20	0.20	0.20	0.20	0.20	0.20	0.20	0.26	0.20	0.20	0.20	0.26	0.16
Flaxseed (bu)	1.03	1.03	1.03	1.03	1.03	1.03	1.03	1.03	1.06	1.61	1.61	1.61	1.50	1.61	1.61	1.61

Source: See text.

TABLE 13.2. Average Prices Paid to Farmers in Illinois, Indiana, Maryland, New York, and Wisconsin during Census Year 1859–1860 ($)

	Average Price Received by Farmers in:					
Commodity	Illinois	Indiana	Iowa	Maryland	New York	Wisconsin
Barley (bu)	0.51	0.85	0.49	n.a.	0.62	0.49
Beans (bu)	n.a.	n.a.	n.a.	n.a.	0.68	0.87
Beeswax (lb)	0.25	n.a.	n.a.	n.a.	n.a.	n.a.
Buckwheat (bu)	n.a.	n.a.	n.a.	0.40	n.a.	1.13[a]
Butter (lb)	0.15	0.15	0.15	0.21	0.17	0.13
Cheese (lb)	0.15	n.a.	n.a.	n.a.	n.a.	0.09
Clover Seed (bu)	n.a.	6.01	6.83	5.50	5.13	6.13[b]
Corn (bu)	0.50	0.59	0.53	0.68	0.82	0.39
Flaxseed (bu)	n.a.	n.a.	n.a.	n.a.	n.a.	1.06[c]
Grass Seed (bu)	n.a.	1.79	1.50	2.25	3.06	1.95
Hay (ton)	5.84	9.30	4.38	13.03	13.93	5.86
Honey (lb)	n.a.	n.a.	n.a.	n.a.	n.a.	0.15[d]
Hops (lb)	n.a.	n.a.	n.a.	n.a.	n.a.	0.25[e]
Oats (bu)	0.30	0.50	0.37	0.36	0.42	0.29
Potatoes (bu)	0.55	0.77	0.55	0.65	0.39	0.46
Rye (bu)	0.56	0.60	0.54	0.74	0.87	0.58
Wheat (bu)	0.95	1.06	0.79	1.21	1.33	0.88
Wool (lb)	n.a.	0.32	n.a.	0.22	0.23	0.20

Source: See Chap. 13, n. 15.
[a] December 1859 only.
[b] Average price, January 1851–March 1858.
[c] Average price, January 1851–July 1857.
[d] Average price, January 1855–December 1855.
[e] Average price, 1861.

TABLE 13.3. Average Board of Trade Prices in Illinois, New York, and Wisconsin during Census Year 1859–1860 ($)

	Average Board of Trade Prices in:		
Commodity	Illinois	New York	Wisconsin
Barley (bu)	0.58	n.a.	0.57
Butter (lb)	n.a.	0.19	0.13
Cheese (lb)	n.a.	0.08	n.a.
Clover Seed (bu)	4.25	5.55	n.a.
Corn (bu)	0.56	0.82	0.66
Grass Seed (bu)	2.12	2.27	1.66
Hay (ton)	n.a.	12.25	n.a.
Hops (lb)	n.a.	0.12	n.a.
Oats (bu)	0.31	0.51	0.39
Potatoes (bu)	0.48	n.a.	n.a.
Rye (bu)	0.73	0.83	0.68
Wheat (bu)	0.95	1.30	0.93
Wool (lb)	0.25	0.36	0.34

Sources: Illinois: Chicago Board of Trade, *Second Annual Statement of the Trade and Commerce of Chicago for the Year Ending December 31, 1859* (Chicago: Hyatt, 1860); Chicago Board of Trade, *Third Annual Statement of the Trade and Commerce of Chicago for the Year Ending December 31, 1860* (Chicago: Tribune Steam Printing, 1861); New York: New York State Chamber of Commerce, *Annual Report of the Chamber of Commerce of the State of New York for the Year 1859–60* (New York, 1860); Wisconsin: Milwaukee Chamber of Commerce, *Second Annual Statement of the Trade, Commerce and General Business of the City of Milwaukee for the Year 1859* (Milwaukee, 1860).

1.50; and oats between $0.50 and $0.75. Judging from the Rothenberg index for Massachusetts, prices in 1855 were high, a judgment borne out by corroborative evidence cited below.[20] These prices supplement our other data for the New England sample states of Connecticut, New Hampshire, and Vermont.

We obtained additional price figures for two urban markets, Cincinnati and Philadelphia, from studies of wholesale prices (Table 13.4). Thomas Berry provides wholesale figures in the Cincinnati market for sixteen of the thirty-three agricultural commodities by month during 1861.[21] On the basis of the Warren-Pearson price index for farm products these should be slightly lower than those for the 1859–1860 period partly due to the Union and Confederate blockade of the Mississippi that interrupted regular lines of shipment.[22] The competitive position of Cincinnati as a terminus of steamboat traffic may also have reduced prices in that market below those received by farmers elsewhere in Ohio. Anne Bezanson's study of wholesale prices in the Philadelphia market provides reports on seventeen agricultural commodities.[23] The average prices over the year June 1859–May 1860 computed from the relative monthly series given in Bezanson using the base prices per unit are shown in Table 13.4.

The Bateman-Weiss samples from the 1860 census of manufactures

TABLE 13.4. Wholesale Prices of Agricultural Commodities in the Cincinnati and Philadelphia Markets ($)

Commodity	Cincinnati 1861	Philadelphia June 1859–May 1860
Barley (bu)	0.55	n.a.
Beans (bu)	1.22	1.03
Beeswax (lb)	0.26	0.36
Butter (lb)	0.13	0.15
Cheese (lb)	0.07	0.11
Corn (bu)	0.30	0.81
Clover Seed (bu)	n.a.	4.94
Flaxseed (bu)	1.03	1.61
Grass Seed (bu)	n.a.	2.83
Hemp (ton)	145.00	121.40
Molasses (gal)	0.35	0.48
Oats (bu)	0.26	0.43
Rice (bu)	3.98	2.49
Rye (bu)	0.48	0.87
Sugar (lb)	0.08	0.07
Tobacco (lb)	0.09	0.08
Wheat (bu)	0.89	1.50
Wool (lb)	0.33	0.40

Sources: Cincinnati: Thomas S. Berry, *Western Prices before 1861: A Study of the Cincinnati Market* (Cambridge, 1943); Philadelphia: Anne Bezanson, *Wholesale Prices in Philadelphia, 1852–1896* (Philadelphia, 1954).

manuscripts provided another important source of price data.[24] By state, these figures cover nineteen of the thirty-three agricultural commodities identified in the census of agriculture; they also provide price estimates for the value of lumber imputed to the farm. Since they represent the average prices paid by manufacturers for raw material inputs, they are assumed to reflect cash, insurance, and freight (CIF) prices for the census year. The series are incomplete. Only prices for wheat, corn, and lumber were obtained for every state, but fairly inclusive coverage was obtained for barley, buckwheat, hops, oats, rye, and wool (Table 13.5). There is a marked similarity between the prices in Table 13.5 and those in Tables 13.2, 13.3, and 13.4. This suggests that the CIF prices paid by manufacturers may be reasonable approximations for those received by farmers during this period. Relative to the Rothenberg price data from Massachusetts farm account books, the prices paid by manufacturers for agricultural products in neighboring states were generally much lower. Given a choice between contradictory data, we always chose figures that bias our results toward understating revenue and income. We therefore use these lower prices.

Remaining gaps in the data were filled by using the average U.S. prices received by farmers in 1896 derived from Strauss and Bean.[25] For many commodities, these 1896 prices represent historic lows. They are therefore below the prices that the farmer could reasonably have expected to receive in 1860, biasing our revenue estimates downwards.

The sale of crops and other produce were not the only sources of income, realized or potential, for farmers. Over the decade of the 1850s the value of farm livestock grew at an average rate of between 0.6 percent and 5.6 percent per annum, reflecting an increase in the absolute numbers of farm livestock, rising prices, and a shift to a younger, more vigorous stock.[26] For our calculations, we assumed that the farmer realized these capital gains through the sale or slaughter of that livestock. Similarly, average farm values increased between 1850 and 1860 despite declines in mean farm size in every sample state except New Hampshire. Consequently, value per acre was rising faster than the value of the farm, reflecting changed supply and demand conditions, increased investment in agricultural improvement, and the impact of the spreading railroad network that widened market opportunities. This rate of growth of land value per acre varied from a low of 1.5 percent per annum over the decade of the 1850s in New Hampshire to as much as 10.7 percent in Kansas, with a higher rate of growth in the West than the East.[27]

As Paul Gates has stated:

TABLE 13.5. Prices Paid by Manufacturers for Agricultural Commodities in Census Year 1860 ($)

	State														
Commodity	Conn.	Ill.	Ind.	Iowa	Kans.	Md.	Mich.	Minn.	Mo.	N.H.	N.J.	N.Y.	Ohio	Pa.	Vt.	Wis.
Barley (bu)	—	0.57	0.77	0.44	—	—	0.50	0.50	0.55	—	0.90	0.65	0.68	—	—	0.69
Buckwheat (bu)	0.60	0.50	0.45	0.41	0.50	0.50	0.30	0.46	—	—	0.68	0.40	0.68	0.50	—	0.45
Butter (lb)	—	—	—	—	—	—	—	—	—	—	0.20	—	—	—	—	—
Clover Seed (bu)	—	—	—	—	—	4.00	—	—	—	6.20	—	—	—	4.33	—	—
Corn (bu)	0.90	0.43	0.30	0.30	0.35	0.67	0.52	0.38	0.44	0.93	0.77	0.68	0.50	0.65	0.99	0.41
Cotton (bale)	44.00	—	—	—	—	—	—	—	—	—	56.00	56.00	—	—	—	—
Flax (lb)	—	—	—	—	—	—	—	—	—	—	—	—	—	0.26	0.16	—
Flaxseed (bu)	—	—	—	—	—	—	—	—	—	—	1.50	—	—	—	—	—
Hemp (ton)	—	—	—	—	—	—	—	—	100.00	—	—	—	—	141.30	150.00	—
Hops (lb)	0.15	0.20	0.15	0.20	0.33	—	0.15	0.19	—	—	0.13	0.25	0.16	—	—	0.19
Lumber (cord)	2.46	2.34	1.38	1.10	2.30	—	1.69	1.44	—	2.34	2.66	2.60	1.09	1.01	3.30	1.48
Molasses (gal)	—	0.50	—	0.50	—	—	—	—	—	—	—	0.90	0.63	—	—	—
Oats (bu)	0.43	0.40	0.33	0.25	—	0.65	—	—	—	0.45	0.40	0.36	—	0.39	—	—
Potatoes (bu)	—	—	—	—	—	—	—	—	—	—	—	—	—	—	0.17	—
Rye (bu)	0.87	0.40	0.37	0.50	—	0.63	0.72	0.41	—	0.95	0.84	0.80	0.50	0.69	0.95	0.25
Silk (lb)	—	—	—	—	—	—	—	—	—	—	11.94	—	—	—	—	—
Tobacco (lb)	0.12	—	—	—	—	0.38	0.15	—	0.22	—	—	—	—	0.10	0.25	—
Wheat (bu)	1.51	0.90	1.00	0.68	0.79	1.19	1.04	0.75	0.97	0.98	1.30	1.25	1.15	1.13	0.98	0.88
Wine (gal)	—	0.26	—	0.37	—	—	—	—	—	—	—	—	—	—	—	0.25
Wool (lb)	0.37	0.32	0.28	0.35	—	0.33	—	—	0.30	0.31	0.51	0.40	—	0.13	0.49	0.32

Source: Bateman-Weiss Manufacturing Census Samples, 1860.

Unlike the urban laborer working in a mine or mill his twelve or fourteen hours daily, creating profits and capital for others, the farmer on his own land was creating capital for himself as well as for the community. The community was also creating capital value for him. As population pressed into an area, the demand for land and its market value increased.[28]

These capital gains are assumed to accrue to the yeoman farmer. We assume that tenants received none of the benefits, except those reflected in increased productivity and higher prices for agricultural commodities. The average annual rates of growth of land and livestock values during the 1850s for the sample states are given in Table 13.6.

For both tenant or yeoman alike, however, the farm not only provided employment and sustenance, it also provided shelter, thereby giving services that otherwise would need to be bought. Towne and Rasmussen estimated this gross rental value in 1860 at $89 million or about 1.3 percent of the cash value of farms.[29] Not until the 1930 Census are data on the value of the farmhouse reported separately from those on farm value or farm buildings.[30] We have taken the ratio of the 1930 value of the farmer's dwelling to the value of the farm for each sample county and applied these ratios to the 1860 data to obtain an estimate of the value of the farmhouse in 1860. We assumed that the rental value was 10 percent per year of the value of the farmhouse, an approach yielding estimates that are approximately the same as those given in the Weeks' Report at

TABLE 13.6. Average Annual Growth Rates of Livestock Value per Farm and Land Value per Acre by State, 1850–1860

	Value of Livestock per Farm			Value of Land per Acre		
State	1850	1860	Rate of Growth (%)	1850	1860	Rate of Growth (%)
Connecticut	$333	$449	3.0	$30.57	$36.43	1.8
Illinois	318	506	4.7	7.98	19.55	9.4
Indiana	239	318	2.9	10.68	21.82	7.4
Iowa	249	367	3.9	6.08	11.88	6.9
Kansas	—	320	(4.3)	—	6.89	(10.7)
Maryland	366	575	4.7	18.81	30.19	4.8
Michigan	235	380	4.9	11.80	22.81	6.8
Minnesota	—	200	(5.6)	5.61	10.15	6.1
Missouri	366	579	4.7	6.50	11.54	6.0
New Hampshire	304	358	1.7	16.29	18.58	1.5
New Jersey	447	584	2.7	43.72	60.38	3.3
New York	431	527	2.0	28.76	38.47	3.0
Ohio	307	447	3.9	19.96	33.07	5.2
Pennsylvania	325	446	3.2	27.32	38.84	3.6
Vermont	425	515	1.9	15.32	22.13	3.7
Wisconsin	243	257	0.6	9.55	16.61	5.6

Source: Eighth Census, *Agriculture in the United States in 1860* (Washington, D.C.: Government Printing Office, 1864). Figures in parentheses are estimated.

the Tenth Census.[31] In New Jersey, for example, the Weeks' Report gave the rental on a six-room house as $96 a year, while our estimate of the average rental value in 1860 of a New Jersey farmhouse is $103. Similarly, in rural Indiana the report gave a figure of $60 for a six-room house in Aurora; we estimate an average rental value of $47.

The sum of crop values (including those commodities omitted by the Census but excluding seed and animal feed) plus capital gains on land (for yeomen only) and livestock and the value of shelter provides an estimate of gross farm income. No allowance is made for capital recovery, the value of labor, or home consumption (Fig. 13.3). Farmers in New York, whether tenant or yeoman, had the highest gross farm income, averaging about $1,250 per farm. Income was also high in New Jersey, Pennsylvania, and Vermont in the East, and Illinois and Ohio in the West. In general, however, western income was much smaller than that in the East, averaging $794 for yeomen and $547 for tenants compared with $1,062 and $830 respectively. The slave states, Maryland and Missouri had the lowest gross income.[32]

Whereas tenant gross income levels in the Northeast were often close to those earned by the yeomanry, in the Midwest they were generally much lower, averaging perhaps two-thirds those of owner-occupiers and reflecting the higher rate of capital gains in the region. The difference is particularly marked in Indiana and Illinois. In both regions, though, tenants earned only 90 percent of the yeoman gross farm income even excluding the effects of capital gains.

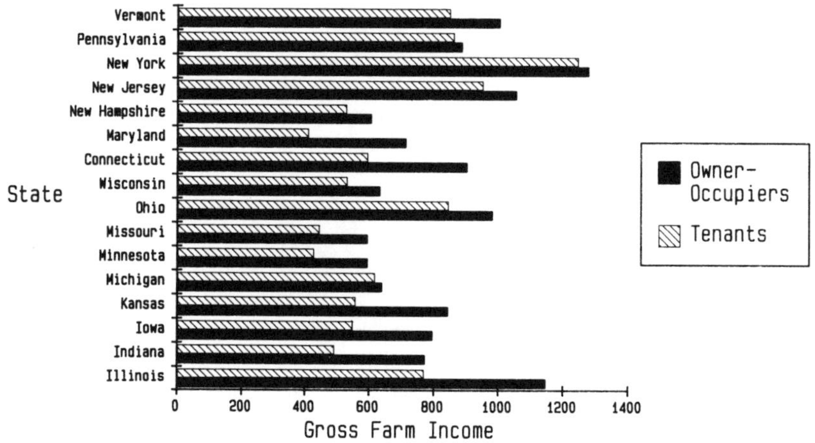

FIG. 13.3. Average gross farm income by state and tenancy, 1859–1860.

For the North as a whole we estimate gross farm income for yeomen at $897 per farm and for tenants, $646. The difference between them reflects not only the absence of capital gains for tenants, but also lower average earnings. Even without the disallowance of capital gains on farms for tenants, their gross income would still have been $93 per farm lower than earned by the yeomanry. If these figures hold across all twenty northern states, then our estimate for regional gross farm income is a little less than $1.2 billion and fractionally over if the $34 million accruing on tenant lands are included.[33]

Estimates by tenancy and size of farm reveal little difference between tenant and yeoman income in the West on small farms (60 acres or less), but income rises much more rapidly for the yeomanry as farm size increases up to about 320 acres after which tenant farms close some of the gap (Fig. 13.4). The same rapid acceleration in gross income with farm size for owner-occupied farms is apparent in the Northeast. The largest farms, whether tenant or owner, earned substantial gross incomes, averaging at least $1,500, while owner-occupied farms of over 320 acres in the Northeast had gross earnings of $2,700.

Gross farm income, however, grew much less rapidly than farm size. In the Midwest, a doubling of farm size from 41–60 acres to 81–120 acres generated only 43 percent more income.[34] In the East, the comparable figure gain is only slightly larger, 51 percent. Nowhere, however, was the gain in gross farm income proportionate to that in farm size. This illus-

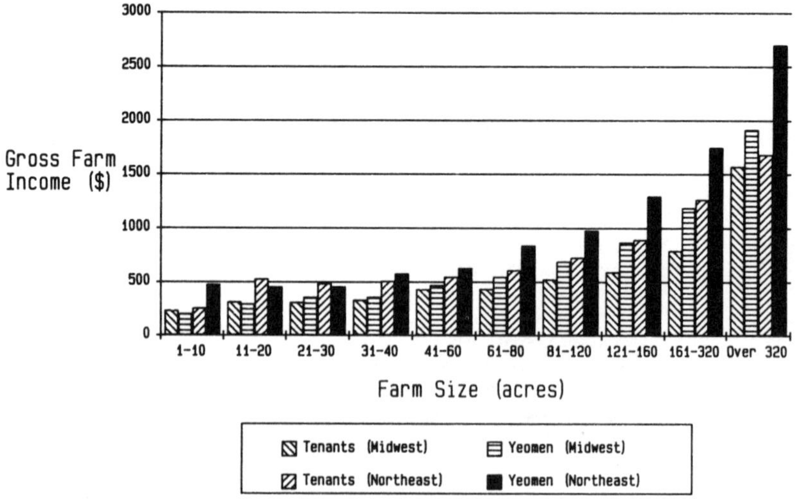

FIG. 13.4. Gross farm income by farm size, region, and tenancy, 1859–1860.

trates the revenue side of the substitution of land-extensive farming practices on larger farms that was noted in Chapter 12.

Gross farm income was not the income received ultimately by farmers. They had to pay wages to nonfamily farm laborers and cover annual depreciation on farm equipment, which we estimate at 14 percent.[35] In addition, tenants had to meet their rental payments. Information on rents is sketchy at best; our assumptions, though crude, are consistent with the available evidence. Paul Gates cites rents in Illinois in the 1850s of $1.50–3.00 in the countryside and $3.00–5.00 nearer to cities. Rents in Iowa are quoted at $1.25–2.00.[36] We have assumed that tenants in Iowa, Kansas, Michigan, Minnesota, and Wisconsin paid $1.25 per *improved* acre; those in Illinois, Indiana, New Hampshire, and Vermont, $2.00. Rents closer to eastern markets and urban areas were assumed to be higher. Tenants in Ohio and Maryland are assumed to have paid $3.00 per improved acre; those in New York and Pennsylvania, $4.00; while farmers in the New Jersey townships close to New York City were assessed $5.00 per acre. The range is well within that cited by contemporaries and reflects general proximity to markets. They are also plausible in comparison with our estimates of tenant gross earnings per improved acre that averaged about $14 in the East and $10 in the West. Rents were not varied between townships within states.

There are a variety of data on agricultural labor costs, some of which were cited in Chapter 11. They are consistent with those discussed here. The Massachusetts Bureau of Labor collected statistics on the wages paid to agricultural laborers beginning in 1792, but records for other states during the antebellum period are patchy.[37] Scattered local records for 1859–1860 exist for most of the sample states but because they are presented in the form of ranges rather than averages these data are not particularly useful.[38]

Of potentially greater value than these other data are the series on monthly wage rates paid to farmhands that were collected at the Eighth Census.[39] Agricultural labor was either "with board" or "without board" depending upon whether or not the farmer provided hired workers with food. Data reported by the Eighth Census are with-board rates, although the Census also estimated the "price of board to laboring men per week" which averaged $2.28 for the sample states.[40] The estimates for 1859–1860 wage rates from local records are also predominantly for the with-board rate.[41] Not until 1866 were series of wage data both with and without board rates published.[42] Table 13.7 summarizes the wage data that we have used.

The figures reported in the U.S. Department of Agriculture's *Farm*

TABLE 13.7. Monthly Wages Paid to Agricultural Labor by State 1859–1860, 1860, and 1866 ($)

State	1859–1860[a] With Board	1859–1860[a] Without Board	1860[b] With Board	1866[c] With Board	1866[c] Without Board
Connecticut	12.00–16.00	22.00–35.00	15.11	14.78	23.12
Illinois	16.00–17.00	n.a.	13.72	13.18	20.09
Indiana	n.a.	n.a.	13.71	13.18	19.51
Iowa	12.00	n.a.	13.18	13.28	19.95
Kansas	13.00–20.00	n.a.	16.12	13.95	23.96
Maryland	n.a.	n.a.	9.71	8.98	14.33
Michigan	14.00	n.a.	15.27	14.42	22.01
Minnestoa	"Similar to Wisconsin"	n.a.	14.10	14.85	22.28
Missouri	13.00–15.00	n.a.	13.63	12.73	18.83
New Hampshire	n.a.	n.a.	14.34	15.83	23.05
New Jersey	11.00–16.00	n.a.	11.91	13.36	22.72
New York	11.50–15.00	n.a.	13.19	13.60	20.82
Ohio	12.00–15.00	18.00	13.11	13.35	20.04
Pennsylvania	12.00	Board valued at $6 per month	12.24	13.26	21.06
Vermont	n.a.	n.a.	14.14	15.16	24.11
Wisconsin	Less than $15	n.a.	13.96	13.99	21.71

Sources: [a]U.S. Department of Agriculture, "Wages of Farm Labor in the United States," Division of Statistics, *Miscellaneous Series Report 4* (Washington, D.C., 1892); [b]U.S. Census Office, Eighth Census, *Statistics of the United States* (Washington, D.C., 1866); [c]U.S. Department of Agriculture, *Farm Wage Rates, Farm Employment and Related Data* (Washington, D.C., 1943).

Wage Rates, Farm Employment and Related Data permit us to estimate the length of employment over the year.[43] By dividing the average daily wage rate into the average annual earnings in 1866, we find that the period of employment varied from 186 days per year in Wisconsin to 211 days in New Hampshire and became higher the further east and south one travelled. These estimates of seven to eight months annual employment for agricultural labor are supported by independent evidence from farm records, which show few contracts of more than eight months, a median estimate of three months, and a mode of one month or less.[44]

Since the sample includes the data for all households within the township, we assume that it embraces the entire potential supply of agricultural labor. Among the nonfarm population, we assume that the agricultural work force comprises those reporting agriculturally related jobs–farmer, laborer, tenant, farmer with another occupation, and agriculturalist. The exclusion of males reporting no occupation reduces the supply of males by 10 percent or less, and these were primarily persons who probably would not have been in the labor force–young males of school age and those adults old enough to be retired from most heavy farm tasks. Persons residing in the sample township but working elsewhere are assumed to net out with those residing elsewhere yet working in that township. This potential labor supply was converted to "male equivalents" using the Battalio and Kagel estimates of equivalent average hand ratings that they developed from Conrad and Meyer's estimates for slave labor.[45] Children aged under 10 or adults older than 64 were excluded from the labor force; children 10–14 and adults 60–64 were rated at 25 percent; those aged between 15 and 19, and 55 and 59 at 75 percent; and adults 20–54 at 100 percent of the equivalent average field-hand rating. Women were rated at 50 percent of the equivalent male category, reflecting the difference in typical work tasks performed by each sex. This off-the-farm agricultural labor force was then allocated between township farms on the basis of improved acreage without regard to each farm's potential supply of on-farm labor.

The on-farm labor force was computed using the same adult-male equivalent ratings but applying these to everybody in the farm household who did not specifically report a nonfarm occupation. Those reporting no occupation were treated as farm workers. This labor is taken into consideration only in calculating the rate of return to farming in the next chapter.

Our estimates of per capita farm income by state, region, and tenancy for 1859–1860 are shown in Table 13.8. These were calculated by deduct-

TABLE 13.8. Estimated per Capita Farm Income by State and Tenancy, 1859–1860 ($)

State/Region	Tenants	Owner-Occupiers
Illinois	82	165
Indiana	58	113
Iowa	60	104
Kansas	52	120
Michigan	78	85
Minnesota	61	94
Missouri	21	68
Ohio	99	146
Wisconsin	73	96
Midwest	61	113
Connecticut	68	170
Maryland	19	88
New Hampshire	71	113
New Jersey	100	153
New York	133	221
Pennsylvania	76	128
Vermont	125	177
Northeast	78	174
Entire North	67	135

ing the cost of hired labor from outside the farm household and depreciation, plus rents if the farm operator was a tenant, from gross farm income and dividing by household size for each group. In the Midwest, tenant households tended to be smaller than those of the yeomanry. In the East, the reverse was true.

Per capita income of the yeomanry was substantially higher than that of tenants, and the differential both relative and absolute was larger in the Northeast than the Midwest. This differential reflects their asset holdings. There was also considerable state-to-state variation both within and between tenancy groups. Income was highest in New York, averaging $221 per capita for members of the yeomanry and $133 for tenants. It was lowest in the two slave states. In Maryland, per capita income for owner-occupiers was half the northeastern regional average and almost 25 percent lower than that earned by yeomen in the next poorest state in the region, New Hampshire. Similarly in Missouri, per capita income for the yeomanry was only one-half to two-thirds of its region's average and almost 30 percent below that of any other state.

Tenants typically earned about half as much as the yeomanry, although in Connecticut their earnings were only 40 percent those of owner-occupiers. Even more dramatic, however, is the situation facing the tenant farmer in the slave states. They earned only one-quarter to one-third of the regional averages for tenants and one-quarter to one-third as much as the yeomanry in those states. These are the "mean whites" who:

> are wholly neglected, and who suffer to while away in a state but one step in advance of the Indian of the forest . . . the thousands of poor, ignorant, degraded white people among us, who, in this land of plenty, live in comparative nakedness and starvation.[46]

They were the focus of Cairnes, Helper, and Olmstead.[47] However, even the yeomanry in these states, who were so vaunted by Owsley, Weaver, and others, fared poorly in comparison with their contemporaries elsewhere.[48]

Based on these income data, we have also made estimates of regional per capita farm income for 1859–1860. For the North as a whole, this was $124 per person. It was higher in the Northeast, $159, and lower in the Midwest, $105. If Maryland is excluded from the regional estimates then the average for the Northeast rises to $168 and that for the North to $126. Fogel and Engerman's independent estimates of per capita income for the whole population based upon Easterlin's regional relative per capita income figures and Gallman's constant dollar estimates of national income are 8–12 percent higher for the entire North and the Northeast, but our estimate of per capita farm income in the Midwest is 18 percent higher than theirs for the entire population in the region.[49] Conventional wisdom usually places agricultural income below that in manufacturing. Labor productivity in manufacturing, for example, is thought to have been almost double that in agriculture.[50] Whether or not this relation held true in a newly industrializing region is not known. Nevertheless since these estimates were arrived at by totally different means, Fogel and Engerman's from a macro standpoint and ours at the microlevel, and to the extent that they reflect two different populations, the degree of agreement between them is both noteworthy and corroborative of our estimation procedures.

Per capita farm income among tenants rose slowly with increasing farm size in the Midwest except between those farms with 161–320 acres and those with over 320 acres (Fig. 13.5). Tenants on midwestern farms of 1–10 acres earned $44 per person, those on 161- to 320-acre farms earned less than 50 percent more, $65. Tenants renting farms of over 320 acres, however, earned $115 per household member. In the Northeast, per capita income among the tenantry showed no trend. Household members on farms of 11–20 acres had an income of $100 each; those on farms of over 320 acres earned $101. For comparison with industrial employment, these per capita earnings may be more relevant than those of ten-

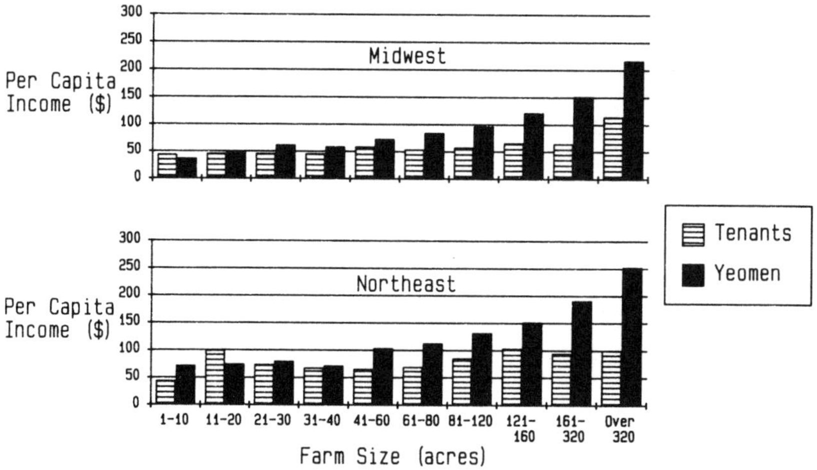

FIG. 13.5. Per capita farm income by region, farm size, and tenancy, 1859–1860.

ants and yeomanry combined in so far as they contain minimal income from property.

Per capita income in yeoman households increased quite rapidly with rising farm size in both the Midwest and the Northeast. It rose, however, more slowly than acreage. The different relationship of tenant and yeoman per capita income to farm size reflects the impact of rents that apparently captured most of the tenant income above opportunity cost. Comparing per capita income levels of owner-occupiers with the regional estimates of Fogel and Engerman shows that those with farms of 160 acres or more in the Northeast had above average incomes, while in the Midwest yeomen had income above average on farms of 80 acres or more.

Assuming that surpluses were sold, farming was capable of generating at least average income for many of its participants. Some earned substantially more. Even tenants whose income levels tended to be below average, had a degree of security not afforded those in other occupations. If prices were poor, they could survive on what they produced, especially if their landlord were understanding. Part of the income for both tenant and yeoman, however, was a return to capital and a reward for bearing risk and it is to these considerations that we now turn.

CHAPTER FOURTEEN

The Profitability of Northern Agriculture: Economic Survival and Resource Allocation

NORTHERN AGRICULTURE AT MIDCENTURY WAS PRODUCTIVE, characterized by relatively easy, unencumbered entry, and offered an appealing way of life as well as commercial potential. Was it also profitable? This question of profitability extends beyond farming, having broader implications for national resource allocation and economic development. Central to this issue is the level of, and relationship among, earned profit rates across sectors of economic activity and geographic regions. Empirical studies of profitability exist for southern agriculture, northern and southern manufacturing, and transportation.[1] The rate of return to agriculture in the northern United States traditionally was assumed to be a competitively determined level, which also served as a *numeraire* for all other sectoral profit estimates. In this chapter we offer new estimates of the northern agricultural profit rate for 1860 that are consistent in their assumptions and presentation with analyses in preceding chapters.[2] Our research includes revisions to previous farm-consumption and livestock-feed estimates, and the inclusion of data for the border slave states of Maryland and Missouri. We also examine the implications of these profit rates for sectoral resource allocation during the late antebellum period, their motivational role in the westward movement, and the "rationality" of northern farmers in selecting agriculture as the activity in which to invest their resources, including their own labor and entrepreneurial skills.

While we consider them to be the best estimates that we can produce, different perspectives and assumptions will lead to different conclusions. The basis for our assumptions has been developed in the preceding chapters. Here we examine the consequences of each assumption for our profit estimates by investigating the contribution of each of various cost and revenue assumptions to the estimated rate of profit.

Although many complex influences entered the farmer's decision whether to farm or seek alternate employment, this choice was not, and could not be, made without consideration of the agricultural rate of return. Interest in potential profits ran high and, according to some authorities, short-run profit maximization took precedence.[3] The contemporary literature abounded with glowing accounts of the profits to be made in farming, for farms of all sizes and in all price ranges, to whet the appetite of even the most jaded reader. Consider, for example, Frederick Gerhard's book, *Illinois as It Is*, which was a popular travelogue. He quotes Edward Bebb of Winnebago County as follows:[4]

In the summer of 1851, we had sixty-five acres of an eighty acre lot broken. In the spring of 1852, we fenced the whole eighty and sowed it with oats. The following is a statement of the crop:

80 acres of land, entered at $1.25 per acre	$100.00
Fencing 80 acres with post and board, (two boards only being put on)	320.00
Breaking 65 acres, at $2.00 per acre	130.00
Seed, 130 bushels, at 12 cents per bus., (oats being very cheap that spring)	15.65
Sowing and harrowing, at 37.5 cents per acre	24.37
5 acres mown and fed before harvest, no account kept. Reaping 60 acres, at 50 cents per acre	30.00
Binding 60 acres, at 75 cents per acre	45.00
Threshing	120.00
Total cost	$785.02
3000 bushels of oats, sold in January, at 30 cents per bushel	900.00
Balance in favor of crop	114.98

In the foregoing statement I made no mention of the straw, which being cut before it was dead ripe, and gotten up without any rain, wintered, with scarcely any other feed, 25 head of cattle.

A similar, but less sanguine estimate, quoted by Gerhard, was made by Joseph Reinhardt for Putnam County:[5]

80 acres prairie land, at $15	$1200.00
Breaking 70 at $2.50	175.00
320 rods fence (480 rods would have been necessary, but for 160 adjoining rods of the neighbor's fence), at $1	320.00
Second ploughing and harrowing at $1.50	105.00
Sowing 105 bushels of wheat, at $1.25	181.25
Harvesting, at $1 per acre 70.00 Threshing and transporting, at $1.80 per acre	126.00
Total cost	$2127.25
Assuming, at a moderate calculation, every acre to yield 20 bushels, we have 1400 bushels, at $1.25	1750.00
Hence, the 80 acres, after the first harvest, will cost only	$377.25

Relying on my own experience, I have based the above calculation upon the highest cost, an average price of wheat, and the low produce of 20 bushels per acre, although I myself have reaped 25 bushels, and many others from 30 to 35 bushels. I also assumed only 70 acres fit to be broken, as, among 80 acres of prairie lands, there are in most cases 10 acres of lowland, best fit for meadows. Every such acre may be safely supposed to yield 2 tons of hay, worth from $2 to $4 per ton, which amount does not form one of the items of my calculation.

Both sets of estimates make the mistake of including nonrecurring capital expenditures on land, sod breaking, and fencing as expenses, and neither allows for taxes, interest, livestock feed, and similar costs. Moreover, they fail to account for all of the expenses we might expect a functioning farm enterprise with a time horizon greater than one year to incur, such as interest costs, depreciation, and livestock feed. Furthermore, the yields per acre seem overly optimistic when compared with our estimates above and with more modern yields.

As a part of his first annual report, the Minnesota commissioner of statistics stressed the comparative profits to be made from Minnesota wheat farming. Comparing corn cultivation in Ohio with wheat farming in Minnesota, the commissioner offered the following figures:[6]

Ohio Corn		
One acre corn, thirty-three bushels, at forty cents		$13.20
Cost of production	$7.60	
Interest on cost of one acre, $21, at seven percent	1.47	9.07
		4.13
Minnesota Wheat		
One acre wheat, twenty bushels, at eighty-five cents		$17.00

Cost of production, at market price of labor	$6.75	
Interest on cost of one acre, at $5	.35	7.10
		$9.90
Difference in favor of Minnesota, in net value of product per acre,		$5.77

For wheat farming in each state the situation was said to be:[7]

Minnesota		
One acre wheat, twenty bushels, at $1		$20.00
Cost of production	$6.75	
Interest on cost of land, $5 per acre	.35	
Cost of transportation to Chicago, fifteen cents per bushel,	3.00	$10.10
Profit per acre in Minnesota,		$9.90
Ohio		
One acre wheat, thirteen bushels, at $1		$13.00
Cost of production,	$6.75	
Interest on cost of land, at $21 per acre.	1.47	8.22
Profit per acre in Ohio,		$4.78

This last quote is particularly interesting because of its explicit account of the costs of transporting the wheat to market and because the costs are treated in an "economic" manner.

Our estimates of the average return per dollar invested in northern agriculture (Table 14.1) are based upon the income estimates developed

TABLE 14.1. Northern Agricultural Profitability: The Return per Dollar Invested, 1859–1860 (percent)

State/Region	Rate of Return	State/Region	Rate of Return
Illinois	0.191	Connecticut	0.106
Indiana	0.104	Maryland	0.061
Iowa	0.111	New Hampshire	0.068
Kansas	0.100	New Jersey	0.100
Michigan	0.058	New York	0.173
Minnesota	0.088	Pennsylvania	0.101
Missouri	0.019	Vermont	0.122
Ohio	0.133		
Wisconsin	0.114	Northeast[a]	0.126
Midwest[a]	0.119	North[a]	0.121

[a]Weighted by farm capital in the population.

in Chapter 13 adjusted for farm family labor. No distinction here is made between tenants and yeomen since that is only a question of the distribution of benefits between landlords and tenants. The landlord received a part of the revenues that would otherwise go to the farm operator in the form of rents and capital gains on the land. The actual return received by a farmer, however, depended upon the size of farm being operated, as we shall discuss below. We have no evidence on the rate of return earned by the last dollar invested (except to the extent that frontier farms represented the "marginal" investment).

The traditionally assumed competitive approximation, 10 percent, seems to have been reasonably appropriate. Weighting our sample observations by the amount of capital invested in agriculture in each state, our best estimate of the average return per dollar invested in 1859 is about 12 percent. This rate is quite low relative to that available in such alternative fields as manufacturing or transportation. It is, however, close to that being earned by southern farmers at this time.[8] Yet in the border slave states, Maryland and Missouri, the rate was lower than the southern rate.[9]

While the figure on earned rate of return at the regional level is not out of line with expectations, those for the two subregions appear, at least at first glance, to be at variance with the traditional historical literature. The westward movement of northern agriculture, for example, frequently has been explained in terms of changing relative profit opportunities, yet our figures indicate a marginally higher return in the Northeast than in the West. Several possible explanations could make our estimates compatible with the traditional view. These are average figures that do not reveal the marginal rates. One could argue that the rate of return per dollar invested on the Kansas and Minnesota frontier represents the marginal western investments; if so, the earned rates were between 8.8 percent and 10 percent. This is virtually identical to those being earned on bonds at the time.[10] We have no comparable "frontier" figure for the Northeast. It is, nevertheless, entirely conceivable that at the margin, which would be the relevant consideration for those transferring their resources from one subregion to the other, the rate in the West exceeded that in the East. Lastly, even had the rate been low or negative, this need not imply that resources should not have been allocated to a particular state or region. On the contrary, those could be the areas where resources should have been allocated if indeed the rate prevailed in a locale in its early stages of settlement. During the initial investment period in pioneer farming, as in other economic activities, earned (but not expected long-run) rates of return are typically quite low, signaling not misallocation but merely the prevailing stage of investment. Similarly, our cross-sectional figures may be, and indeed probably are, capturing disequilibrium conditions in both regions, but particularly the West during this dynamic period of American development.

At the state level the highest rates of return were being earned by Illinois and New York farmers. To a large extent the high northeastern return is a result of the profitable farming in New York State, which accounts for more than one-third of the Northeast's sampled agriculture. The comparatively low western estimate is more heavily influenced by the lower returns in Michigan and Missouri than the northeastern estimates are by the modest rates in Maryland and New Hampshire. Within regions the ordinal rankings among states are consistent with historical evidence. Agriculture was most profitable in Illinois and New York, least so in Michigan and New Hampshire.

We believe that the estimates, mapped in Figure 14.1, accurately measure profitability at the nonurban township level and may indeed be generalized to the nonurban county level. These data show a fairly consistent and plausible gradation of profit rates from East to West and North to South. There were few sharp differences between adjacent townships. The highest profit rates were to be found in a band about 200 miles wide through northern New York State, southern Michigan and northern Indiana, and the northern half of Illinois into Iowa, with peaks in north-central New York and western Illinois. Rates of profit on the northern fringes of the United States, in Michigan, Wisconsin, and Minnesota, were negative, as they were on the southern edges of the westward expansion. Between adjacent townships where profit differentials did occur, some of the difference may be attributable to soil-type variations. In New Jersey's Union County as an example, Ochrepts predominated while the adjacent Middlesex County generally had Udult soils; in northwestern Indiana, Posey County was on Aqualls while the adjacent counties of Gibson and Warrick had Udalfs.

These profit estimates were derived using the following formula:

$$\begin{aligned}\text{RATE} = {} & [(\text{CROP} + \text{FGAIN} + \text{LGAIN} + \text{RENT}) \\ & - (\text{LABCOST} + \text{DEPRC} + \text{FEED} \\ & + \text{CONS})]/[\text{FARM} + \text{MACH} + \text{LIVE}\ (+\ \text{SVALUE})]\end{aligned}$$

where RATE = rate of return; CROP = (value of crops − seed requirement), where crops include the value of livestock slaughtered and home manufactures valued at farm gate prices (these are also corrected for those products omitted by the census); FGAIN = capital gain on land; LGAIN = capital gain on livestock; RENT = imputed gross rental value of farm dwelling; CONS = home consumption of farm products; LABCOST = cost of labor; DEPRC = depreciation on farm implements; FEED = livestock feed requirements; FARM = cash value of farm;

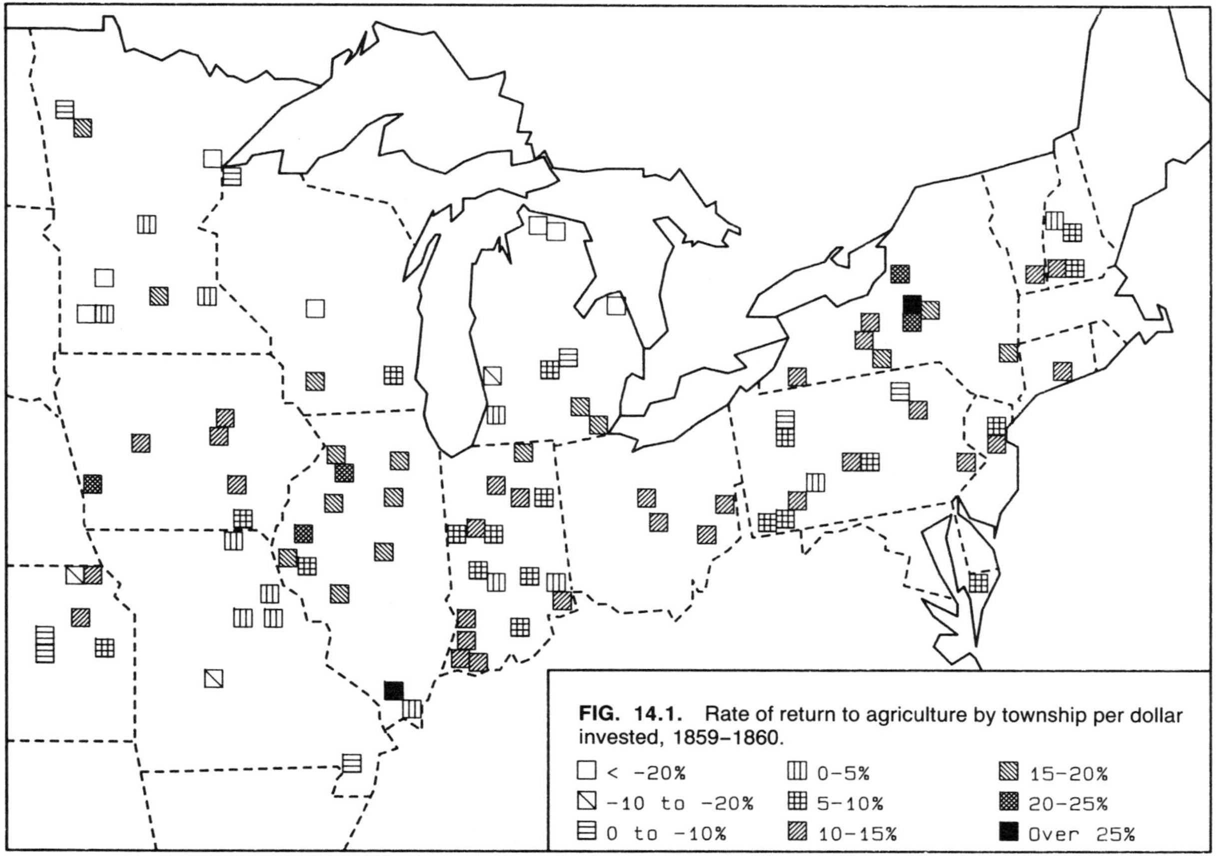

FIG. 14.1. Rate of return to agriculture by township per dollar invested, 1859–1860.

MACH = value of farm implements; LIVE = cash value of livestock inventory including poultry; SVALUE = approximate value of slaves held by farmer (estimated). Capital gains on land were excluded from tenant revenues and an allowance was made for rent in their costs in estimating individual farm returns. The value of their farms was not included in the denominator.

Except for slave values and the treatment of farm household labor, the assumptions underlying these various cost, revenue, and capital estimates have been discussed above. Slave values by age and sex are taken from Fogel and Engerman.[11] The farm family labor force consisted of all those in the household except those who reported nonfarm employment. They have been weighted by age and sex, using the Battalio and Kagel weights as described in Chapter 13. Whereas labor from off-the-farm was paid the without-board wage, farm family members were paid the with-board rates as the value of their consumption of farm products is treated separately.

The evidence that we have presented in Chapter 3 on male labor force participation rates by age suggests that by limiting employment to those under 65 we may be excluding some gainfully employed workers, but we believe that any such downward bias is small compared with the upward bias in the rating of adult equivalents and the assumption that all in the farm household were engaged in agricultural activities unless explicitly contradicted. The weights were originally derived for slaves, and it is unlikely that workers would freely supply more labor than they were compelled to under slavery. On balance, therefore, we feel that our figures will overstate the true size of the labor force.

To facilitate the direct evaluation of the appropriateness of the assumptions in calculating profitability rates, we provide the values needed to assess their individual influence upon the profit calculations (Table 14.2). To determine the effect of eliminating any specific variable or any combination of them, begin with the final profit estimate in the column labeled "Estimated Profit Rate" and subtract from it the figures contained in the columns lying to the right. The numbers at the top of the right-most ten columns are keyed to the variables appearing in the numerator of the profit calculation and variations thereon as indicated in the table footnote. Figures in these columns show the absolute numerical contribution to the final profit rate due to that variable. To illustrate, eliminating the contribution of the capital gains on land (variable 4) from the northern profit rate would reduce it from .121 to .080, or by a third; removing the contribution of our imputed gross rental value of farm dwellings (variable 6) would lower it from .121 to .101, or by 16 percent; eliminating the effects of both capital gains and gross rental value would reduce the northern rate to .060.

TABLE 14.2. The Contribution of Assumptions to the Estimated Rate of Profit per Dollar Invested in Northern Agriculture, 1859–1860

Region/State	Estimated Rate of Return	Contribution of Each Variable to the Estimated Profit Rate[a]									
		(1)	(2)	(3)	(4)	(5)	(6)	(7)	(8)	(9)	(10)
Midwest	0.119	0.003	0.026	0.012	0.055	0.006	0.016	0.029	–0.034	.002	–.004
Illinois	0.191	0.003	0.022	0.012	0.076	0.007	0.010	0.028	–0.032	.000	–.006
Indiana	0.104	0.003	0.012	0.012	0.062	0.004	0.015	0.016	–0.031	.000	–.004
Iowa	0.111	0.005	0.024	0.010	0.057	0.006	0.011	0.050	–0.042	.007	–.005
Kansas	0.100	0.004	0.030	0.019	0.082	0.008	0.009	0.048	–0.049	.018	–.006
Michigan	0.058	0.003	0.041	0.038	0.056	0.007	0.021	0.079	–0.065	.014	–.005
Minnesota	0.088	0.005	0.039	0.032	0.049	0.008	0.012	0.077	–0.092	.045	–.007
Missouri	0.019	0.004	0.016	0.011	0.037	0.010	0.012	0.032	–0.030	–.008	–.004
Ohio	0.133	0.003	0.029	0.006	0.045	0.005	0.020	0.017	–0.030	.001	–.003
Wisconsin	0.114	0.003	0.045	0.011	0.047	0.001	0.017	0.025	–0.054	.010	–.006
Northeast	0.126	0.004	0.036	0.008	0.028	0.003	0.024	0.019	–0.022	.003	–.004
Conneciticut	0.106	0.005	0.033	0.009	0.016	0.003	0.030	0.011	–.026	.006	–.003
Maryland	0.061	0.005	0.015	0.008	0.036	0.004	0.018	0.023	–.025	–.028	–.002
New Hampshire	0.068	0.006	0.047	0.015	0.012	0.003	0.025	0.020	–.043	.012	–.005
New Jersey	0.100	0.005	0.018	0.002	0.030	0.002	0.018	0.017	–.016	.008	–.005
New York	0.173	0.003	0.051	0.012	0.025	0.003	0.025	0.021	–.023	.004	–.004
Pennsylvania	0.101	0.003	0.030	0.004	0.031	0.003	0.026	0.015	–.019	.006	–.004
Vermont	0.122	0.003	0.026	0.005	0.031	0.002	0.026	0.027	–.028	.008	–.004
North	0.121	0.003	0.031	0.010	0.041	0.004	0.020	0.024	–.028	.003	–.004

[a]Key to number columns:
(1) Poultry and egg production
(2) Fluid milk not converted to butter or cheese
(3) Lumber production
(4) Capital gains on land
(5) Capital gains on livestock
(6) Rental value of farm dwelling
(7) Assuming 12-month employment for labor
(8) Paying farmer the same wage for the same time period as hired labor
(9) Substituting "without-board" wages for on-farm labor in place of home consumption plus "with-board" wages
(10) No depreciation on farm equipment

Not only do these figures reveal the absolute contribution of each component of the final profit estimate, they also demonstrate the relative importance of each to a state or a region (Table 14.3). The capital gain from increasing land values, for example, was more than twice as important to the western farmer as to the easterner. Similarly, although their contribution was numerically much smaller, livestock capital gains also favored westerners by a two to one margin. In the other direction, the contribution of dairy production in the Northeast was one-third greater than that in the Midwest, and a farmhouse was worth more as a residence in the East where rents were higher than in the West.

TABLE 14.3. Percentage Change in the Rate of Return per Dollar Invested in Agriculture in Midwest and Northeast due to Assumptions

	Midwest	Northeast
Base Rate	0.119	0.126
Percentage Reduction in Base Rate if:		
(a) No poultry or egg sales	2.5	3.2
(b) No fluid milk sold	21.8	28.6
(c) No wood cut and sold	10.1	6.3
(d) No capital gain on land	46.2	22.2
(e) No capital gain on livestock	5.0	2.4
(f) No family home on farm	13.4	19.0
(g) Labor employed year round	24.4	15.1
(h) Labor paid "without-board" wages but no home consumption	1.7	2.4
Percentage Increase in Base Rate if:		
(a) Farmer treated like other farm labor	28.6	17.5
(b) No depreciation charged on machinery	3.4	3.2

The rates of return discussed above represent the average return per dollar invested in agriculture in a randomly selected township. Farmers, however, invested in farms, not in farming. Their return depended critically upon the size farm they could afford to buy or rent. Similarly, the average farm rate of profit by state or region depends heavily upon the size distribution of farms. Bigger farms were more profitable per dollar invested than small. This coincides with our analysis of self-sufficiency, which demonstrated that 43 percent of farms under 40 acres could not feed their livestock and the farm population the recommended diet, whereas only 19 percent of those with more than 80 acres fell short of this standard.

The rate of return on yeoman farms in many states averaged between 6 and 9 percent (Table 14.4), though it ranged from as much as 18.5 percent in Illinois to −12.8 percent in Michigan. It was also negative in

TABLE 14.4. Mean Profitability of Owner-occupied Farms by State and Region, 1859–1860

State/Region	Rate of Return	State/Region	Rate of Return
Illinois	0.185	Connecticut	0.080
Indiana	0.061	Maryland	0.034
Iowa	0.069	New Hampshire	0.026
Kansas	0.090	New Jersey	0.086
Michigan	–0.128	New York	0.149
Minnesota	–0.007	Pennsylvania	0.065
Missouri	–0.046	Vermont	0.100
Ohio	0.120		
Wisconsin	0.077	Northeast	0.105
Midwest	0.050	North	0.071

Minnesota and Missouri and very low, though positive, in Maryland and New Hampshire. A rational farmer would have viewed starting farming in these states as a very dubious proposition if his time horizon were short.

Even in the states where they earned low returns, farmers who could afford a larger spread could still gain satisfactory rates of return equal to or greater than those offered by, as an example, bonds. Moreover they could live off their capital, investing time and energy in capital improvements that sooner or later would be rewarded either through higher productivity or enhanced land values. Thus, even in Michigan where the average "loss" for a farm under 40 acres was −21.6 percent, the farmer who could afford to buy a farm of 160 acres or larger could expect an average return of 11.5 percent.

Small western farms were much less profitable than comparably sized northeastern ones (Fig. 14.2), a reflection of regional differences in agriculture. For the West, the principal cash crop was wheat, which was best grown extensively. For the eastern producers, truck crops for urban markets and dairy products were important income sources. These activities could be conducted on a much smaller scale than grain farming. The most remarkable feature, however, is the marked relationship between farm size and profitability in each region. A similar systematic relationship between rate of return and scale existed in farming in every state covered in our sample.

When we considered the poor return per farm in Michigan, we deliberately placed quotation marks around "loss." While these farms were earning less than the opportunity cost of the labor and capital that they employed, it is unclear whether they incurred accounting losses as well. Our profitability calculation includes not only the wages of outside laborers as costs but also those imputed to farm household members at the with-board market rate for the same work year, and we assume that the

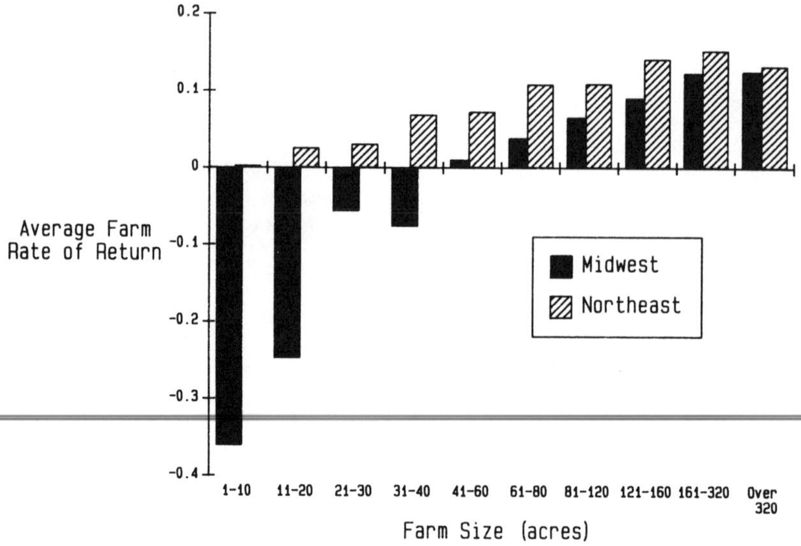

FIG. 14.2. Regional farm profitability by farm size, 1859–1860.

farmer was paid 125 percent of this prevailing agricultural wage for 12 months a year. These two assumptions regarding farm family labor had a large impact on the estimated rate of profit, especially in the West (see Table 14.3). If the without-board rate were substituted and no deduction made for home consumption, the effect on profits would have been minimal. This suggests that the difference between the with- and without-board rates is a very close approximation to the value of food consumed. We made no deduction for interest on the capital invested. Even the "unprofitable" farms could, however, probably meet out-of-pocket expenses.

We calculated the profit rates for tenants on the same basis, except that capital gains on land were disallowed, rents were included as a cost, and the value of the farm was not included in the denominator. The results were negative in all but five states – Illinois, Ohio, New Jersey, New York, and Vermont. They were also negative for each subregion and the North as a whole. Furthermore, not only were they negative, but the numbers were large. The average for eastern tenant farms, for example, was −26.3 percent. In the Midwest, it was −37.2 percent. These numbers are not only misleading, they are spurious.

They are misleading because the denominator in the profit calculation for tenant farmers was small, averaging perhaps one-sixth to one-eighth that for the yeomanry, so that for the same dollar of net revenue the profit or loss to a tenant will be four or five times that of the yeoman. In more concrete terms, what these figures mean is that the typical tenant farmer with $400–500 invested in livestock and implements made a loss of $100–200 when imputed labor costs are deducted. Even a simple change, such as making the wage imputed to the tenant farmer the same as that to other labor, has a dramatic effect on the profitability of tenancy, losses in both the East and West being cut 60 percent by such a change. In both regions too, the rental payments that we assume tenants made were equal to or greater than the losses. The capital gains they forfeited would have come close to making revenues cover costs.

The results are also misleading in that each tenant's profit rate counts equally in determining the mean. More tenants showed negative cash flows than positive ones under our assumptions. Nevertheless, aggregate gross revenues for tenants exceeded their aggregate total costs and therefore tenancy as an institution was viable. Indeed, we estimate that in the North tenants collectively earned 7.9 percent on their investment, which though lower than the return to owner-occupiers, was comparable to the return offered by many alternatives, such as bonds. If no deductions for rent and the loss of potential capital gains on land are made, then the return to landlords and tenants on their joint venture are indistinguishable from those accruing to owner-occupiers.

Our suggestion that the profit estimates for tenants are spurious reflects our view that the assumptions we have made assign too much labor to tenant farms. Tenants had less livestock, particularly milk cows, and therefore needed less labor on a day-to-day basis. Furthermore, we assumed that family labor not engaged in minor day-to-day chores or meeting peak labor demand at planting and harvest was engaged in farm making or improvement. Since the benefits of such labor would accrue principally to the landlord and might conceivably even result in higher rents for the tenants, it is unlikely that tenant labor was employed in this way. Tenants in settled areas may also have supplemented family incomes through part-time manufacturing work.

Profitability was also influenced by soil type, which affected yields and influenced what crops the farmer could best grow (Table 14.5). The most profitable soils were the Ochrepts and the Udolls. The former were generally confined to the eastern states where they were used for small grains and dairying in Pennsylvania and New York State (see Table 7.4). The Udolls, prairie soils found from western Indiana westward, were used primarily for wheat cultivation in the 1850s. Our analysis of yields

TABLE 14.5. Farm Profitability by Soil Type, 1859–1860

Soil Type	Rate of Return	Number of Farms	Number of Townships
Aqualf	0.105	244	4
Udalf	0.072	5038	35
Psamment	–0.130	44	2
Aquept	–1.406	6	1
Ochrept	0.115	2021	14
Aquall	0.087	186	2
Boroll	–0.139	21	2
Udoll	0.114	1447	24
Orthod	–0.100	713	8
Aquult	0.020	267	1
Udult	0.052	1126	9

by soil type suggest that wheat had a higher yield on this soil, so farmers were not only responding to the relatively favorable wheat prices but also grew the crop most heavily on the most suitable soil.

In a few instances a particular soil type was found in only one or two sample townships, limiting our ability to generalize from these observations. Profit estimates by soil type when the type was confined to a narrow geographic area should not command much attention. Too many purely local factors, besides soil, could influence the rate of profit in those localities. Psamments, for example, occurred in just two places – Benton County, Minnesota, and Juneau County, Wisconsin – while in our sample the Aquept soil subgroup was found only in Huron County, Michigan. Just one soil type, Udalf, was widely distributed in both regions. Its range stretched from northern New York State westward to Minnesota, Iowa, and Missouri. Other important soils such as Udults and Ochrepts were confined to specific regions.

Profitability as related to soil type and size of farm also suggests some significant differences between soil type and the minimum profitable farm size. On Udalf soils profitability rose steadily with increasing farm size, while on the Ochrepts there seems to have been little if any advantage in the earned rate of return to be gained from farming more than 120 acres. On Udult soils profits were virtually constant across farms of all sizes; on Udolls, farm size seems to have exerted little if any effect on profitability.

The historical and economic meaning of these profit rates can be assessed by comparing them with those being earned elsewhere in the economy at this time (Table 14.6). Consider first the rates that include all farms weighted equally in every sample township plus capital gains (A. Estimates). These are the relevant figures for individuals who are considering entering farming. The rate for the entire North would have been

TABLE 14.6. Mean Rates of Return by Sector and Region in the Antebellum Economy

Economic Activity	Mean Rate of Return (percent)	Standard Deviation	Coefficient of Variation
Agriculture:			
Northern			
A Estimates[a]			
Entire North	7.1	23.0	3.25
Northeast	10.5	16.4	1.56
Midwest	5.0	26.2	5.25
B Estimates[b]			
Entire North	12.1	n.a.	
Northeast	12.6	n.a.	
Midwest	12.1	n.a.	
C Estimates[c]			
Entire North	8.0	n.a.	
Northeast	9.8	n.a.	
Midwest	6.5	n.a.	
Southern			
Cotton (Fogel-Engerman)	10.0	7.9	0.79
Cotton (Vedder-Stockdale)	9.7	n.a.	
Land and Capital (Vedder-Stockdale)	10.6	n.a.	
Rice (Swan)	–3.8	n.a.	
Slave Hiring (Evans)	10.4	n.a.	
Manufacturing: (Bateman-Weiss)			
East, 1860	21.8	45.0	2.08
South, 1860	27.9	47.6	1.69
West, 1860	26.1	48.6	1.85
U.S., 1860	25.2	47.1	1.85
Transportation:			
Steamboats, 1850 (Atack et al.)			
Trunk River	8.5	5.5	0.65
Tributary River	24.1	13.7	0.57
Central Pacific RR (Mercer)			
Unaided Private Return	13.4	n.a.	
Aided Private Return	14.1	n.a.	

Sources: Robert Fogel and Stanley Engerman, *Time on the Cross* (Boston, 1974); Richard Vedder and David Stockdale, "The Profitability of Slavery Revisited," *Agricultural History* 49(1975):392–404; Dale Swan, "The Structure and Profitability of the American Rice Industry, 1859" (Ph.D. diss., Univ. of North Carolina, Chapel Hill, 1972); R. J. Evans, "The Economics of American Negro Slavery," in *Aspects of Labor Economics* (Princeton, 1962); Jeremy Atack et al., "The Profitability of Steamboating on the Western Rivers: 1850," *Business History Review* 49(1975):346–54; Lloyd Mercer, "Rates of Return for Land Grant Railroads: The Central Pacific System," *Journal of Economic History* 30(1970): 602–26; Fred Bateman and Thomas Weiss, *A Deplorable Scarcity* (Chapel Hill, 1981).

[a]Includes all townships in the sample. Owner-occupiers only; each farm weighted equally.

[b]Tenants and yeomen, weighted by capital. Frontier townships excluded (see text).

[c]Tenants and yeomen, weighted by capital. Excludes capital gains on land and excludes frontier townships.

about 7.1 percent, with 10.5 percent being earned by eastern farmers and 5.0 percent by westerners. Given the inclusion of capital gains on land in this return, the current rate of return would have been low, particularly for the westerner, in comparison with that of other investors in the economy. Eliminating the western and northern "frontier" townships (B. Estimates) and weighting by proportions of capital invested elevates the regional mean township rates of return and makes them virtually equal.[12] Computed this way, the rates of return represent the return per dollar invested in farming. They compare favorably with those earned by counterparts in the South. Farmers in neither northern region, however, were attaining the average rates of return being earned by manufacturing investors anywhere in the United States.

Perhaps the most relevant rates for comparative purposes are variations on the B. Estimates that exclude both the frontier townships and capital gains on land (C. Estimates), given that neither the existing estimates for cotton production nor those for industry include a capital gains component. By this standard, eastern producers were earning virtually the same return (10 percent) as southern cotton growers. Western farmers were not doing so well, getting only a 6.5 percentage return even in the settled, nonfrontier townships. This suggests the importance that farmers, particularly those already in the Midwest or considering migration there, attached to prospects for realizing capital gains on their land. In 1836, for example, an Albany, New York, farmer wrote in his local farm magazine, the Albany *Cultivator*, "That percentage [rate of capital gain] is sometimes very high, but in almost all cases, it adds materially to the profits of the investment . . . a tract of land, under judicious culture must be enhanced in value at least five percent per annum."[13] This has been a commonly expressed phenomenon among historians. Louis Stilwell argued that, "Vermonters' profits in the past [before 1860] were derived as much from increasing land values as they were from agriculture."[14] Similarly, Paul Gates has asserted that, "The pioneer farmer was well aware that in the end his profits would come largely from rising land values."[15] By the 1850s and 1860s, this source of return had diminished considerably in the East but was still important in the newer western states (see Table 14.3 and the B. Estimates in Table 14.6). Between 1850 and 1860 the cash value per acre of farmland in the eastern states grew an average of 2.8 percent, while in the West it rose 7.3 percent. But farmers were not the only beneficiaries of these returns. Manufacturers, for whom land often was a substantial component of their investment, particularly in urban areas and in choice locations for power generation, also stood to realize capital gains from their holdings.

Still, from the perspective of the national economy, the question remains why agricultural investors North or South would be satisfied to earn a relatively low rate of return when a considerably higher one was available in manufacturing, an activity open to even a small investor. First of all, as we have observed previously, farming represented more than a purely market investment; and presumably most individual western farmers at this time were still able to feed, shelter, and clothe their families despite their rather meager return on investment.

Nevertheless, even during the postbellum era, when satisfaction with mere survival would seem to have been disturbed by the presence of growing prosperity in the industrial sector, this behavior continued. "Perhaps no development of the nineteenth century," said Theodore Saloutos, "brought greater disappointment to the American farmers than did their failure to realize the prosperity that they had expected from industrialism."[16] Farmers, as we have seen, faced a difficult task in adapting to the realities of integrating into an industrialized system. Continued Saloutos, "Even before the wholesale transition from a subsistence to a commercialized status, the evidence was rather strong that the financial rewards of farming would be small."[17]

Although low, our estimates for rate of return excluding capital gains are clearly in accord with contemporary observations. If anything, they err on the high side. The wide variation between agricultural and industrial rates was also recognized. The secretary of the treasury reported in 1845, for example, that ". . . while the profit of agriculture varies from 1 to 8 percent, that of manufacturers is more than double."[18] In this same document reports of returns on agricultural investments of 3 to 6 percent were said to be typical for the 1830s and 1840s. Others throughout the period from 1830 until the end of the century report similarly low rates persistently recurring; "overproduction" is usually blamed. One additional comment from Saloutos in his review of this issue is pertinent:

> Certainly the period from the Civil War to 1897 was not profitable at least from the standpoint of remunerative farm operations. . . . Part of the answer for the unprofitableness of farming is to be found in the rapid territorial expansion—the land grant, immigration, and irrigation policies that encouraged people to take land without regard for the fact that they accelerated agricultural production beyond all reasonable market demands. . . . The capacity to produce foodstuffs, contrary to the predictions of Malthus greatly outstripped the capacities to consume them.[19]

Historical works contain numerous versions of this idea, which assumes some sort of agrarian bias among Americans that led them to become and remain farmers despite potentially better opportunities in nonfarm occupations. As we have seen, this is one of the most persistent themes in American economic and social history. Historians often refer to this preference pattern as irrationality when observed in southern farmers, but as a reflection of the Jeffersonian ideal, the "love of the land," or the desire to control one's economic destiny when applied to the northerner. Our estimates are consistent with this view of the economy during the latter part of the antebellum period: a wide disparity existed, and probably had long persisted, between rates of return in agriculture and other activities, particularly manufacturing. In economic terms, this can be seen as sectoral resource "stickiness"; in historical, it is a reflection of the persistence and attractiveness of the agrarian ideal.

There are a number of other possible economic justifications for the apparent tendency for Americans to become farmers despite better opportunities in nonfarm occupations. One major interpretive problem lies with our analysis' reliance on average rather than marginal rates of return. Were markets working perfectly, risk-adjusted rates of return on the marginal investment in any sector or region would have equalized over the long run, regardless of the levels of the average rates of return. There is an increasing body of evidence suggesting that antebellum manufacturing was characterized by significant elements of monopoly, particularly at the local level.[20] Under such circumstances, the establishment of one additional local manufacturing plant might be expected to shift the market supply curve outward, thereby lowering the product price. Consequently, the marginal return in manufacturing would lie below the average, possibly by a sizable amount. In agriculture, where market structure more closely approximated atomistic competition, entry of an additional producer would exert only a negligible effect on market price. Marginal and average returns thus would have been approximately equal.

Those entering or remaining in farming rather than in some alternative may also have been influenced by expectations of a higher long-term return. Thus the actual earned returns represented by our figures would not have been their sole, or perhaps even their primary, consideration. Farming perhaps was perceived by many farmers as a less risky venture than other pursuits. This is certainly Clarence Danhof's view when he argues that "if large capital gains were by no means assured, the risks of loss were relatively minor."[21] Starting a small manufacturing firm, a service establishment, or a transport enterprise might also have appeared beyond the financial or managerial capabilities of most individuals in this era before portfolio diversification was common or feasible. Or, after all, a substantial portion of the American population, native and immigrant alike, might indeed have possessed a single-minded ambition to become a farmer without much regard to unfettered economic rationality. If so, they would have considered the potential return from nonagricultural activities, however apparently remunerative, to be irrelevant to their menu of economic choices. Farming might indeed have been perceived as a way of life *nonpareil.* In fact, we think that these data can be interpreted as indicating that farmers behaved as satisficers within the constraint of bounded rationality and subject to the noneconomic appeal of agriculture as a way of life.

As we stated at the outset, we think it is misleading to view late antebellum agriculture in the northern United States within a purely market setting. Farming, as generations of historians have contended and as we have found, was considered a way of life—one in which a high rate of return was but one goal among many. Given the unique form of the labor supply, the nature of farm-formed capital, and appreciating land values, agriculture cannot be compared precisely with other economic activities. Farming as it existed in the antebellum North offered economic security, especially with regard to continuity of food supply, not available in most other places or occupations during the mid-nineteenth century. Farmers who wanted these and other benefits could remain undisturbed by even comparatively low financial returns provided that they could feed their families and meet fixed debt payments. They were, after all, earning for the most part positive rates of return on the purely economic aspects of their investments. And yet this was but one of their considerations. Even if the rate lay below some available alternative, a farmer might knowingly accept a lower return given the supplemental noneconomic benefits that he expected and valued. To an extent greater than their nonagricultural counterparts, they could indulge their preferences, allowing the noneconomic components of their utility functions to be influential in their economic decisions, even in the long run, because they could offset an explicit market loss, or even an implicit one arising from their failure to move to some higher-return alternative, in one area by gain in another. Over the short run they could even accept a negative market return while still surviving in a total economic-noneconomic context by continuing to feed themselves, to provide their housing, and to make their own clothing or other items of consumption; they could also build much of their own capital. As late as the beginning of the twentieth century scholars have observed that "for a large number of farmers, the production of agricultural commodities [was] not carried on as a means of making money, but rather as a mode of existence."[22] Industrial, service, or other nonfarm workers typically did not enjoy access to such an alternative. The farm of the American North was a multiproduct, multiple-objective enterprise, unlike most others of this era. Although markedly gaining in importance over the century, production destined for market constituted but a portion of most farmers' total output; maximization of current return on investment was but one of the farmers' objectives. This emerges as a major theme of our research. It is an aspect of farming that continued on a lesser scale to influence farmer behavior into the present century.

Nevertheless, from the national economic perspective, these estimates indicate that resources should have been reallocated from agriculture to alternative pursuits, more individuals should have selected other occupations, and more should have invested their capital elsewhere. Market signals alone would have dictated such resource shifting, but as of 1860 they seem to have been partially disregarded. Consequently the agricultural sector seemingly was becoming excessively endowed with resources even before the Civil War. The pressures of this endowment continued to haunt Americans periodically for decades to come in response to the fluctuations of the business cycle, the ebb and flow of immigration, the fortunes of foreign agricultural producers, tariff law changes, and similar events. Within the context of a developed, industrialized economy, the postbellum market would signal farmers that an acceptable level of product prices, input costs, and hence profit could not be achieved by a large number of existing producers given the level of demand. Frequently through the last third of the nineteenth century and into the twentieth, the signals became clear and unmistakable: supply was too great to provide the returns that a growing number of farmers thought appropriate. Although many chose to exit from farming or at least from the production of a specific crop, others elected to remain, fighting their problems through political action or simply by surviving with a marginal material welfare.

We perhaps have seen the roots of this economic and political behavior in the antebellum period. As the century wore on, American farmers may have become increasingly weary and impatient of anticipating earnings that were promises on the future or of earning less than their countrymen in the growing industrial sector. Nevertheless, as of 1860 the lure of the land and the traditional dream of agrarian paradise still seemed to be powerful enough to keep most Americans working with the soil and optimistic of their future as independent economic agents in a Jeffersonian agrarian economy.

CHAPTER FIFTEEN

To Their Own Soil

OURS HAS BEEN MORE than an investigation of an important historical experience in America's rural past. It was also an economic and historical test of the original American socioeconomic dream. The North, particularly the Middle West, provided the purest laboratory environment one could expect in the social sciences. The northern United States throughout most of the nineteenth century, with its peculiar notions of independence, mobility, equality, and agrarianism, was even perceived by contemporaries as an experiment. Yeoman agriculture represented the economic foundation for this ideal world whose success or failure largely depended upon how closely the agricultural ideal could be approached. Analytically, measuring the agricultural record indirectly assesses the success of this entire vision of democratic America. Fortunately those idealistic nineteenth-century experimenters also left us a rich legacy of information, none individually richer than the federal economic censuses, with which to evaluate their economic and historical achievement.

The clear recurrent theme that emerges throughout this study is the tension that existed between national pursuit of a new kind of social order characterized by individualism, independence, and self-containment founded upon a tightly knit family system, on the one side, and the drive for a market-oriented, capitalistic national economy in which farming assumed the trappings of a business enterprise, on the other. Conflict was inevitable. Ultimately, of course, the forces of market capitalism based upon an interdependent national economic system dominated in the North as well as the South, which had its own well-known tensions regarding the American Dream. The national split personality, though overwhelmed by the onrushing forces of the business system and corporate industrial enterprise, persisted into the twentieth century reappearing as periodic agrarian unrest even into the current decade.

If the Jeffersonian vision ever enjoyed an opportunity to flower as a rural economic system, however, it was during the antebellum era and across the northern states. Had the forces emanating from the Industrial Revolution not pushed it to one side, could an economy that was rural and agricultural, founded upon an independent, self-reliant yeomanry have emerged and succeeded? Or was it, after all, even in the absence of the industrial fever that swept through the nineteenth-century Western world, only a dream of the poets and political theorists that neither physical nor human resources could achieve and sustain? Perhaps the tension between sheltered self-reliance and market participation in pursuit of profit was endemic to the human mentality or at least to the American one. We can never be certain obviously about these counterfactuals that are so fundamental to historic American concerns about such gargantuan issues as equality, individualism, and self-reliance. What we have tried to do is to measure, within the constraints imposed by available data and analytical tools, how nearly achieved was the vision of a rural, agrarian economy during the time most favorable to its realization.

The rural household lay at the center of economic and noneconomic pursuits among farmers and those engaged in other occupations as well. While the agriculturalist was to be the foundation of the pastoral American society, even by 1860 one must be impressed by the great variety of occupations followed by rural residents, both East and West. Except on the most recently settled lands or the frontier did there not exist a substantial number of rural nonfarm workers by 1860. Local residentiary industry and service workers hinted at the demise of isolated self-sufficiency and of market disinterest that lay ahead. One must similarly be impressed by these people's continued working into their latter years, particularly in the Northeast.

While they shared the rural countryside, farmers and nonfarmers differed in significant respects. Farmers appeared to provide more education for their offspring, to marry later, and to produce larger families than their nonagricultural neighbors in their region. There were also notable regional differences in fertility, with midwestern farmers displaying higher fertility rates than northeastern farmers and midwestern nonfarm residents higher ones than their eastern counterparts.

Farm families were stable but not immobile. The agrarian dream, like the industrial one that succeeded it, demanded social and geographic mobility from those who wanted to reap the system's rewards. Geographically, native migrants tended to relocate generally over relatively small distances. In the great westward movement, immigrants with obviously fewer locational ties tended to move more frequently and over longer distances. Native and foreigner alike, however, sought familiar surroundings. It appears they did so not merely out of sentimentality, but also to maximize the potential return from their own human capital–such as their knowledge of farming techniques, or from the tools, seeds, and soils with which they had been familiar in their place of original residence. Substantial numbers of immigrants were particularly cautious in their migrational impulses, choosing to stay in or near those urban areas where they first entered the United States. From these various and complicated movements of people into and across the antebellum United States emerges a pattern of mobility accordant with the dreams of those who espoused settlement and creation of an agrarian-based economy. The rural population was remarkably diverse and heterogeneous as of 1860, but even then the seeds of urban settlement and concentration were being sown.

Social mobility among rural households was largely dependent upon the accumulation of wealth. In the antebellum rural paradise farmers were indeed wealthier than other residents, as might be expected in an economy where land was both a major productive input and a personal asset. With respect to wealth accumulation, individuals behaved in a predictable, almost surprisingly rational, manner. Additions to wealth beyond age fifty-five were minimal; wealth maximization typically was reached by one's midsixties. Age was, in fact, the single most important individual determinant of wealth. Although we do not have access to income estimates for a broad base in this population, we can surmise that it was reasonably closely related to wealth in this land-oriented economy.

Equality was a nineteenth-century American watchword. Nowhere were conditions riper for attaining the egalitarian ideal than in the antebellum rural North. Was it achieved? Probably. Although not perfect, compared with the South or the northern cities at that time wealth was diffused rather equally. Relative to the rest of the nation and perhaps to the world, this was an egalitarian society in terms of wealth holdings. Compared with the modern economy within these terms it would seem even more economically egalitarian than within its own temporal framework. This aspect of the Jeffersonian vision would appear to have been at least attainable in the rural areas of the 1850s and 1860s.

But comparative egalitarianism did not imply random access to wealth nor lack of discrimination among all groups in the rural economy. The ranks of the wealthiest held a disproportionate number of individuals who were male, native-born, white, literate, and middle-aged. The last is predictable, given the simple relationship between the passage of years and the building of wealth. While the others do not necessarily imply outright, deliberate discrimination, they are nevertheless more difficult to justify. Yet it was indeed a male- and white-dominated society in which new immigrants apparently had less access to education. All these attributes together would obviously tend to concentrate wealth into the hands of those who fit the profile indicated above. Thus, even the egalitarian economy had its blemishes. That should not detract from the basic reality, however, that the ideal was more nearly realized in the rural northern United States than elsewhere in human history about which we have substantial knowledge.

If farming was a basis for wealth, then establishing one's farm was a sine qua non for being wealthy. One's mobility geographically, where possible, could be thwarted if entry into farming by new producers was obstructed by prohibitive start-up costs. Could someone indeed go west to start a farm in the rural North? On the answer to that question hinged the pervasiveness of the success of an agrarian economy. Our evidence indicates that with some qualifications the answer was a positive one in the antebellum period. Based upon the investments of most farmers, the cost of forming a farm was not prohibitive in comparison with other small business ventures one could start. Moreover, tenancy offered a less costly, albeit less desirable, entry alternative. The issue was not usually framed in that context by contemporaries or later observers, however. In antebellum America the West represented an outlet, an escape from urban congestion into pastoral independence. Was this simply romantic folklore or indeed could the common man elect that alternative? Based upon our measurement of actual farm holdings it could have been an attainable objective for a substantial portion of the rural populace. While an urban manufacturing worker or craft apprentice may have lacked the needed financial capital to move directly to his own western farm, an established eastern farmer or manufacturer typically possessed the wherewithal to do so. Such resource mobility was encouraged by relative regional cost differentials. Expenses for land and buildings accounted for most of the locational variations in farm investment levels. A midwestern farmer in 1860 typically had an investment slightly more than one-half that of one in the East. A tenant had invested perhaps one-eighth to one-sixth as much as a yeoman. If willing to face the rigors of frontier life, an individual could initiate his agricultural enterprise at even lower cost. Like wealth, access to farm ownership was not randomly distributed or free of apparent discrimination. Native whites stood a far better chance of acquiring or establishing an independently owned farm than did a newly arrived immigrant, and even tenancy was beyond the financial resources of most free blacks. Anyone already owning an agricultural investment typically found westward movement more affordable than one who worked for someone else, but that, of course, was what the dream of independence was about: the individual farmer-landowner could afford mobility.

Once established, most farmers ultimately would face that common dilemma in antebellum American agriculture: the difficult choice between independence and self-containment, on one side, and market participation to gain a cash income, on the other. Architects of the pastoral ideal assumed the beauty and attractiveness of the former, but as some observers have noted, the farmer did not always see it that way. Says Richard Hofstadter, for example, "When the yeoman farmer practiced the self-sufficient economy expected of him, he usually did so not because he wanted to get into it. . . . Self-sufficiency was adopted for a time in order that it could eventually be unnecessary."[1] While such a broad generalization obviously has its exceptions, it strikes at the core of the agrarian dream. American farmers, even in the early part of the nineteenth century, wanted it both ways. They desired pastoral serenity, independent individualism, and psychic rewards, as well as a cash flow. They ultimately sought governmental support to help them maintain the best of both worlds. Before the Civil War, however, our evidence indicates they deliberately sought to produce for the market and to move away from the generalists' life of self-sufficiency toward specialization. Debts incurred to establish and maintain a farm often forced that choice upon them. They abandoned home manufacturing rather quickly in the North, and as a group they produced food products beyond mere family needs both in the East and West, but especially in the latter. Again, quoting Hofstadter: "The ideals of the agrarian myth were competing in his [the farmer's] breast, and gradually losing ground to another, ever stronger, ideal, the notion of opportunity, of career, of the self-made man."[2]

Except on the tiniest acreages, farmers in Illinois, Indiana, Iowa, and Kansas already grew substantial quantities of major crops beyond family needs. Most were located in townships that were 30–40 miles from a navigable river. They could sell locally, nationally, or even in international markets. The most commercially oriented, market-dependent producers were in Illinois and Iowa among western states and in Maryland and New Jersey in the East. Farmers from the rural West, however, were the prime sources of the grain crops on which the American diet was so heavily dependent. Surprisingly, the most surplus-prone units were not the largest acreages but the ones in middle-sized categories, those units favored by federal land policy.

Western farmers produced 50–100 percent more marketable output than did eastern ones, but their advantage was in the land-using production of field crops. Easterners, especially near cities, lacked that advantage; they compensated with production of market-garden crops and with animal products, especially those of the dairy. While dairy husbandry was a relatively neglected branch of agrarian industry, most northern farmers kept milk cows. Despite the comparative neglect nationally, the sale of butter and cheese produced a potentially lucrative income source for eastern agriculturalists. It was, in fact, for many their first entree into commercial involvement. Yields were reasonably high on eastern farms, and markets often readily accessible. Except on the smallest units, there was excess production of milk or dairy products. On holdings exceeding 80 acres in the eastern region, it offered a reasonably good supplement of cash or a means for barter to the rural farm family.

The per capita income from these activities compared favorably with that from the alternatives. That of family members on yeoman farms was equal to or greater than the regional average. Tenants' incomes were lower; so were their real asset holdings. Nevertheless, they typically earned at least half as much as the yeomanry, an amount comparable to that paid to factory workers. Tenancy in the sample slave states must have been much less attractive, but the tenant, like the yeoman, could always fall back on the security afforded by food production and the shelter provided by the farm.

In their quest to produce for the market, the farmers of the North revealed an acceptance of new techniques and practices that could raise yields or, particularly, increase labor productivity. Efforts to raise yields either for livestock or for field crops were hampered by the existing state of knowledge regarding plant and animal genetics, so individuals interested in raising yields sought other avenues. Dairy producers who were near good markets would better feed and care for their animals, for example, with a consequent improvement in yields even from nonspecialized or native stock animals. Among field crops, a major determinant of yield variation could be the type of soil a particular farmer's land offered. Although livestock and plant yields improved over the remainder of the century, partly as a consequence of educational efforts by the Department of Agriculture, not until the twentieth century did they do so substantially or as the result of systematic implementation of scientific techniques.

Within the land-abundant western family farming economy, however, labor constraints provided a more pressing problem. But raising labor productivity proved easier for the nineteenth-century producers. Even before the Civil War, mechanization played a primary role in increasing output per worker. By using animal-powered implements such as the reaper, farmers proved able to deal with the labor problems associated with American farming, particularly as practiced in the western region. They continued to make impressive gains in this direction during the postbellum years.

The dichotomy confronted by the American yeoman farmers of the North, as we have seen, was central to their everyday realities. In an analytical sense, nowhere is this better evident than in our profitability measures. Within the broad portfolio of economic choices, their behavior is consistent with that of the satisficer who is balancing psychic with monetary incentive, seeking satisfactory goals rather than economically optimal ones. Within this same framework it is consistent with risk averseness: individuals wishing to hold onto a base of security guaranteed by their farm's ability generally to feed the family even when markets turned sour but also desiring to enter markets for cash rewards when times were good. By selecting farming over a manufacturing or service occupation, individuals could hedge against market fluctuations, even if not against the whims of nature. If natural conditions cooperated, the family farm could earn at least a minimum real income. It could be a pleasant world, one combining the more poetical aspects of rustic living, such as individualism and independence, with the hard facts of economic security and of gaining outside monetary income.

Northern farmers were, after all, earning a rate of return comparable to that of their southern contemporaries, many of whom were also desirous of the "good life" of agrarianism. They could also anticipate capturing capital gains from their landholdings as independent owners. Nevertheless they were earning, by our estimates, a return well below that available in some other economic purusits. Thus, while as economic satisficers they may have been pleased with the situation, from the broader perspective of the national economy resources were being excessively allocated to agriculture even at this early date. Local manufacturing and such services as transportation, if the market signals are so interpreted, were being denied the resources for more rapid expansion. But, as we have seen, there are many possible quite understandable and rational reasons why this situation existed during the antebellum years. While not profit maximizers perhaps, these people were successfully straddling the fence between agriculture as a way of life and as a business enterprise like all others.

Tenants sacrificed some of the benefits that accrued to the yeomanry. Landlords seem to have been successful in eliminating any economic rents that might accrue to tenants. In truth, the tenants' position seems little different from that of wage laborers. They had little incentive to improve the land and farm except for their own comfort. Still, the tenant family that was frugal had an income level that offered the opportunity of saving to acquire its own farm. In the less densely settled areas this might have been possible within five to ten years, but it would have taken much longer elsewhere.

If we limit our purview to the time before the Civil War, how would we evaulate the economic status of northern farming in particular or its relationship to the broader agrarian ideal society in general? Clearly the success of the latter hinged upon that of the former; if the economic underpinning could not be made to work, then neither could the concept of a rural society of independent yeomen. By the standards that we have used, the northern rural economy was succeeding as a social, family, and economic unit. Jefferson could have been pleased. Had other things remained the same, perhaps it could have triumphed. Yet even by 1860 the basis for its demise already existed, both in the financial desires of the farmers themselves and in the emerging industrial-urban structures outside. Although it would be swept aside by these and other forces, as of the 1860s the dream of an American Eden still seemed within reach.

NOTES

CHAPTER ONE

1. U.S. Census Office, Eighth Census, *Manufactures of the United States in 1860* (Washington, D.C., 1864), especially 677–718.

2. U.S. Census Office, Twelfth Census, *Abstract of the Twelfth Census of the United States,* 3d. ed. (Washington, D.C., 1904), especially 300–301. Value-added data are from U.S. Department of Commerce, *Historical Statistics of the United States from Colonial Times to 1970* (Washington, D.C., 1975), Series F239 and F241.

3. U.S. Department of Commerce, *Historical Statistics*, Series A202–203.

4. Ibid., Series D170, D174.

5. Ibid., Series U214–18.

6. U.S. Census Office, Eighth Census, *Population of the United States in 1860* (Washington, D.C., 1864); U.S. Census Office, Eighth Census, *Agriculture of the United States in 1860* (Washington, D.C., 1864); U.S. Census Office, Eighth Census, *Manufactures*; U.S. Census Office, Eighth Census, *Statistics of the United States in 1860* (Washington, D.C., 1866).

7. Benjamin H. Hibbard, *A History of the Public Land Policies* (1924, reprinted Madison, 1965), 106.

8. U.S. Census Office, Eighth Census, *Agriculture*, 222.

9. The following model is taken from Robert W. Fogel and Jack Rutner, "The Efficiency Effects of Federal Land Policy, 1850–1900: A Report of Some Provisional Findings," in *The Dimension of Quantitative Research in History*, ed. William O. Aydelotte (Princeton, 1972), 390–418.

10. Because there is now more land of each degree of fertility for the existing stock of farmers to work. If the new land contained some of superior quality, then WY would lie above WX. If the best of the new land was inferior to the best of that already settled, then WX would be kinked at the point were there was now more land of equal quality.

11. Another implication of the Fogel-Rutner analysis is that inefficiencies resulting from land speculators were comparatively minor and that land was not made available "too rapidly" for economic efficiency. These conclusions, which differed from most older views, were challenged by R. Taylor Dennen, whose alternative model indicated a more significant distorting effect on resource allocation. His analysis also suggested resource overinvestment in agriculture at the end of the nineteenth century. See R. Taylor Dennen, "Some Efficiency Effects of Nineteenth-Century Federal Land Policy: A Dynamic Analysis," *Agricultural History* 51, 4(Oct. 1977):718–36.

12. U.S. Census Office, Eighth Census, *Agriculture*, 222.

13. See Ester Boserup, *The Conditions of Agricultural Growth* (London, 1965). Similar arguments have been made earlier by Johann H. Von Thunen, *The Isolated State* (1826 reprint, New York, 1966); A. V. Chayanov, *The Theory of the Peasant Economy* (Moscow, 1925), ed. D. Thorner et al. (Homewood, Ill., 1966); B. H. Slicher van Bath, *The Agrarian History of Western Europe, A.D. 500-1850* (London, 1963). See also Julian L. Simon, *The Economics of Population Growth* (Princeton, 1977); Ester Boserup, *Population and Technological Change* (Chicago, 1981).

PART ONE

1. Thomas Jefferson, *The Writings of Thomas Jefferson*, 20 vols. (Washington, D.C., 1903). This quote is from *Notes on Virginia*, in Jefferson, *Writings* 2:229.

2. Jefferson to John Jay, 23 Aug. 1785, *Writings* 5:93.

3. Ibid., 94.

4. Jefferson, *Notes,* in *Writings* 2:229.

5. Jefferson to William Short, 8 Sept. 1823, *Writings* 15:469.

CHAPTER TWO

1. See ARTICLE 1, SECTION 2, paragraph 3 of the *Constitution of the United States*. The requirement that the count be the basis for direct taxation was changed by the Sixteenth Amendment.

2. See Carroll D. Wright, *History and Growth of the United States Census* (Washington, D.C., 1900).

3. There were separate schedules for the free population, slaves, mortality, agriculture, manufacturing, and social statistics.

4. For a general description of census procedures and instructions, including those for specific years but not those for 1860, see Wright, *History and Growth,* 50–52, 154, and 236–37.

5. For a detailed discussion of the mechanics of mid-nineteenth-century census enumerations, see Carmen R. Delle Donne, "Federal Census Schedules, 1850–80: Primary Sources for Historical Research," National Archives and Record Service, *Reference Information Paper 67* (Washington, D.C., 1973). See also Wright, *History and Growth.*

6. Mr. Shriver, as we show in Part 2, appears in the agricultural census manuscripts as owner, agent, or manager of a 200-acre farm valued at $4,000, exactly what he reports on the population schedule as the value of his real estate.

7. See Wright, *History and Growth*, 166.

8. See U.S. Census Office, Eighth Census, *United States—1860. Act of Congress of twenty-third May 1850. Instruction to U.S. Marshals. Instructions to Assistants* (Washington, D.C., 1860). The instructions for the population and slave schedules are reproduced below in the App. to this chapter. Those for the agricultural schedules appear in the App. to Chap. 7.

9. State censuses for years between the decadal federal censuses were made by a number of states, among them Illinois, Iowa, Minnesota, and New York. These sources have been little used by quantitative economic historians.

10. See especially, U.S. Census Office, Eighth Census, *Population of the United States in 1860* (Washington, D.C., 1864). Some items such as the number of families and the tabulations of real and personal estates are summarized in U.S. Census Office, Eighth Census, *Statistics of the United States in 1860* (Washington, D.C., 1866), 340–51 and 296–319.

11. See Wright, *History and Growth*, 131.

12. Copies of the 1860 instructions have been found in the Library of Congress and the American Philosophical Library in Philadelphia. See U.S. Census Office, Eighth Census, *United States—1860.*

13. Compare, for example, Wright, *History and Growth*, 152, item 9, with item 14 in the App. to this chapter.

14. Fred Bateman and James D. Foust, *Agricultural and Demographic Records of 21,118 Rural Households Selected from the 1860 Manuscript Census*. This sample, available as a data tape from the authors at cost, was financed by the National Science Foundation under Grant GS-27143. A modified version of this data tape made by Richard Easterlin is on deposit with the Inter-University Consortium for Political and Social Research in Ann Arbor, Michigan. "Household" refers here to a sample observation, which may have been a farm that had no household associated with it.

15. See the various articles in William N. Parker, ed., *The Structure of the Cotton*

Economy of the Antebellum South (Washington, D.C., 1970), especially 58–61, 95–99 for descriptions of the Parker-Gallman sample.

16. Urban counties were defined as those in which at least 90 percent of the county's population lived in the largest city. This determination was based upon the published 1870 census volumes, which contain lists of townships and cities in each county. See U.S. Census Office, Ninth Census, *The Statistics of the Population of the United States* (Washington, D.C., 1872), 1:77–296.

17. The sparse settlement in four Minnesota counties (Cottonwood, Mahnomen, Murray, and Polk) led to the selection of the entire county as the sampling unit rather than an individual township within the county.

18. There were also 454 farms in the townships that were unmatched with population and an additional three observations that were in the sample contained no data beyond the name of the head of household and farm operator. Since names were not keypunched, these appear on the data tape as totally blank records.

19. One thousand and twenty-two of the households that were linked from the population schedules to the agricultural schedules using the name of the head of household and name of the farm operator as keys did not have any member of the household who reported his occupation as farmer. The Darrah household discussed in Chap. 7 is one such case.

20. See Richard A. Easterlin, George Alter, and Gretchen Condran, "Farm and Farm Families in Old and New Areas: The Northern States in 1860," in *Family and Population in Nineteenth Century America,* ed. Tamara Hareven and Maris Vinovskis (Princeton, 1978), 22–84.

21. See Richard A. Easterlin, "Population Change and Farm Settlement in the Northern United States," *Journal of Economic History* 37, 1(Mar. 1976):45–75; Richard A. Easterlin, "Factors in the Decline of Farm Family Fertility in the United States: Some Preliminary Results," *Journal of American History* 63, 3(Dec. 1976):600–614.

22. These age limits are deemed to represent the lower and upper bounds for female fertility.

CHAPTER THREE

1. The numbers of children aged less than 1, 1, 2, 3, or 4 showed some sharp, but different, fluctuations in both the East and West that seemed implausible. We therefore smoothed the age distribution of children for those 4 and under so that there were more infants than 1-year-olds, more 1-year-olds than 2-year-olds, and so on.

2. Nathan Keyfitz and Wilhelm Flieger, *World Population: An Analysis of Vital Data* (Chicago, 1968), 118.

3. The effects of "heaping," that is the observed propensity for older people to report age as a "nice" round number, have been minimized and the data smoothed by our choice of age intervals, 0–4, 5–9, and so forth.

4. See, for example, Lewis D. Stilwell, "Migration from Vermont, 1776–1860," *Proceedings of the Vermont Historical Society* 5(1937):63–245.

5. In the 25–29-year-old age cohort, for example, there were 1,598 males and 1,571 females, among those aged 55–59, 647 men to 626 women, and for the 65–69 age group there were 357 men and 354 women.

6. See Richard A. Easterlin, "Population Change and Farm Settlement in the Northern United States," *Journal of Economic History* 37, 1(Mar. 1976):45–75.

7. Merle Curti, *The Making of an American Community: A Case Study of Democracy in a Frontier County* (Stanford, 1959), especially 199ff. See also Paul W. Gates, *The Farmer's Age: Agriculture 1815-1860* (New York, 1960), 196–99.

8. Wisconsin spoils the pattern somewhat as there the ratio of "farmers without farms" to farms was only 37 percent.

9. See U.S. Census Office, Eighth Census, *United States—1860. Act of Congress of twenty-third May 1850. Instruction to U.S. Marshals. Instructions to Assistants* (Washington, D.C., 1860). See the App. to Chap. 2, Sec. 10.

CHAPTER FOUR

1. Ezra Seaman, *Essays on the Progress of Nations* (Detroit, 1846), especially 364–65.

2. See especially W. Thompson and P. Whelpton, *Population Trends in the United States* (New York, 1953); C. Taeuber and I. Taeuber, *Changing Population of the United States* (New York, 1958); Y. Yasuba, *Birth Rates of the White Population in the United States 1800–1860* (Baltimore, 1961); C. Forster and G. S. L. Tucker, *Economic Opportunity and White American Fertility Ratios 1800–1960* (New Haven, 1972). Work on the South has been done by Richard Steckel, but there is as yet no microlevel analysis of North-South differentials. See Richard H. Steckel, "Antebellum Southern White Fertility: A Demographic and Economic Analysis," *Journal of Economic History* 40, 2(June 1980):331–50.

3. See Donald Leet, "Human Fertility and Agricultural Opportunities in Ohio Counties: From Frontier to Maturity, 1810–60," in *Essays in Nineteenth Century Economic History*, ed. D. Klingaman and R. Vedder (Athens, 1975), 138–58; Donald Leet, "The Determinants of the Fertility Transition in Antebellum Ohio," *Journal of Economic History* 36, 2(June 1976):359–78; Richard Easterlin, "Population Change and Farm Settlement in the Northern United States," *Journal of Economic History* 37, 1(Mar. 1976):45–75; Richard Easterlin, "Factors in the Decline of Farm Family Fertility in the United States: Some Preliminary Research Results," *Journal of American History* 63, 3(Dec. 1976):600–14; Richard A. Easterlin, George Alter, and Gretchen Condran, "Farm and Farm Families in Old and New Areas: The Northern States in 1860," in *Family and Population in Nineteenth Century America*, ed. Tamara Hareven and Maris Vinovskis (Princeton, 1978),22–84.

4. In 1970, 44 percent of families were childless; 18 percent had one child, and less than 10 percent had four or more. See U.S. Department of Commerce, *Historical Statistics of the United States from Colonial Times to 1970* (Washington, D.C., 1975), Series A354–58.

5. The imperfections of this measure are obvious. Older children may have left the home or succumbed to mortality, and the number of people in progressively older age categories declines as a result of death. However, by examining the implicit age of marriage for a cohort, we can abstract from the differences in the age structures of the population. Further, we have selected that cohort of women for which the number of own children is a maximum, thereby minimizing any bias due to mortality or departure from the home.

6. Age-specific marital fertility rates calculated from the sample for women in their early 20s were 333 per 1,000. This fell to about 310 for women in their late 20s and to about 275 for the cohort of women in their early 30s.

7. Data have been smoothed. These rates, like all others quoted here, are for the white population only.

8. U.S. Department of Commerce, *Historical Statistics,* Series B6 and B148.

9. See, for example, Forster and Tucker, *Economic Opportunity,* and Steckel, "Antebellum Southern White Fertility."

10. Although there were about 3,500 infants in the sample, some of the cells for different groups were very small. For example, there were only 17 infants in the Vermont sample and 54 from New Jersey. An error, such as the omission of a single infant, could therefore have a substantial effect upon our estimate of fertility for groups within regions. By contrast, there were over 28,000 children under 10 in the entire sample.

11. These have not been standardized although Yasuba argues standardization is necessary because of childbearing mortality, higher fertility rates increasing the youthful proportion of the population, and the selectiveness of migration with respect to age (Yasuba, *Birth Rates,* 128–29). The procedure, however, is complicated because the amount of the correction depends upon the reference population – in our analysis, the North or the Northeast and Midwest. The correction factors at the state level for 1860 given by Yasuba are quite small. For the states in our sample they range from 0.966 (Indiana) to 1.086 (Kansas). Within a state, Leet concluded that "the effect of standardization was minor" (Leet, "Fertility Transition," 361). It therefore seems unlikely that our conclusions would be varied by standardization.

12. In order to maintain comparability with Yasuba's results and those of Forster and Tucker, we limit our attention to the white population. Sample sizes for blacks are small and therefore probably unreliable.

13. See especially Yasuba, *Birth Rates.*

14. Most of the studies dealing with fertility and economic opportunity have used aggregate rather than individual data such as we use here.

15. See, for example, the debate between the planter-dominance school represented by U. B. Phillips and Lewis C. Gray and the yeoman-democracy school of Clark, Owsley, and Weaver. To a lesser extent the argument is also implicit in the studies of the relative efficiency of plantation slavery. See U. B. Phillips, "The Origins and Growth of the Southern Black Belts," reprinted in *Ulrich B. Phillips: The Slave Economy of the Old South*, ed. Eugene Genovese (Baton Rouge, 1968); Lewis C. Gray, *History of Agriculture in the Southern United States to 1860* (Washington, D.C., 1933); Blanche Henry Clark, *The Tennessee Yeomen, 1840–1860* (Nashville, 1942); Frank W. Owsley, *Plain Folks of the Old South* (Baton Rouge, 1949); and Herbert Weaver, *Mississippi Farmers, 1850–1860* (Nashville, 1945). Also Robert W. Fogel and Stanley L. Engerman, "The Relative Efficiency of Slavery: A Comparison of Northern and Southern Agriculture in 1860," *Explorations in Economic History* 8, 2(1971):353–67.

16. See Easterlin, "Factors in the Decline of Farm Family Fertility" and "Population Change and Farm Settlement." See also R. M. McInnis, "Childbearing and Land Availability: Some Evidence from Individual Household Data," in *Population Patterns in the Past*, ed. Ronald Demos Lee (New York, 1977), 201–27, for an analysis of Canadian data that parallels ours.

17. See Lee Soltow, "Male Inheritance Expectations in the United States in 1870," *Review of Economics and Statistics* 64, 2(May 1982):252–60.

18. See Lee Soltow, "Land Fragmentation as an Index of History in the Virginia Military District of Ohio," *Explorations in Economic History* 20, 3(July 1983):263–73.

19. See Soltow, "Male Inheritance."

20. See Steckel, "Antebellum Southern White Fertility," 335–37.

21. For an alternate method of calculating the age at first birth see James Trussell and Richard Steckel, "The Age of Slaves at Menarche and Their First Birth," *Journal of Interdisciplinary History* 8, 3(1978):477–505.

22. See Chap. 3.

23. E. A. Wrigley, *Population and History* (New York, 1969), 92–94. See also R. G. Potter, "Birth Intervals: Structure and Change," *Population Studies* 17, 2(1963):156–66.

24. The percentage change in R and the relative importance of each component can be determined from the equation:

$$\frac{dR}{R} = \left(\frac{L}{L - F + S}\right)\frac{dL}{L} - \left(\frac{F}{L - F + S}\right)\frac{dF}{F} - \left(\frac{L - F}{L - F + S}\right)\frac{dS}{S} + \frac{d\beta}{\beta}$$

where R, L, F, S, and β are measured at the midpoint values. See Steckel, "Antebellum Southern White Fertility," 339.

25. No estimate was made for Maryland since there were no foreign-born in the sample township.

26. See Larry D. Neal and Paul J. Uselding, "Immigration: A Neglected Source of American Economic Growth, 1790–1912," *Oxford Economic Papers* 24, 1(Mar. 1972):68–88.

CHAPTER FIVE

1. Frederick Jackson Turner, *The Frontier in American History* (New York, 1920).

2. In 1860 there were 5.8 million native-born Americans also living in a state other than that of their birth. U.S. Census Office, Eighth Census, *Population of the United States in 1860* (Washington, D.C., 1864), 616–23.

3. See Carroll D. Wright, *History and Growth of the United States Census* (Washington, D.C., 1900), 92.

4. See U.S. Department of Commerce, *Historical Statistics of the United States from Colonial Times to 1970* (Washington, D.C., 1975), 97.

5. U.S. Census Office, Twelfth Census, *Twelfth Census of the United States: Population* (Washington, D.C., 1902), vol. 1, pt. 1, xxxvi.

6. See, for example, Edgar M. Hoover, "Interstate Redistribution of Population, 1850–1940," *Journal of Economic History* 1, 3(Nov. 1941):199–205; E. S. Lee, A. R. Miller, C. P. Brainerd, and R. A. Easterlin, *Population Redistribution and Economic Growth in the United States 1870–1950,* Vol. 1 (Philadelphia, 1957); Lowell Gallaway and Richard Vedder, "Mobility of Native Americans," *Journal of Economic History* 31, 3(Sept. 1971):613–49.

7. U.S. Census Office, Eighth Census, *Population*, xxxii, 345. Brooklyn had an additional 105,000 immigrants. Ibid., xxxi.

8. The Irish made up a half or more of the immigrant populations in most northeastern states. See U.S. Census Office, Eighth Census, *Population*, 621–23.

9. See Lowell E. Gallaway and Richard K. Vedder, "The Increasing Urbanization Thesis – Did 'New Immigrants' to the United States Have a Peculiar Fondness for Urban Life?" *Explorations in Economic History* 8, 2(1971):305–20, for evidence that immigrants did not follow the flight of the native population to the cities.

10. U.S. Census Office, Eighth Census, *Population*, xxxi–xxxii.

11. See also Lee et al., *Population*, especially 57–64, for a critique of the census place-of-birth data.

12. It may also be incidental, simply wherever the census enumerator happened to catch up with the family. The census tried to eliminate confusions of the latter sort by instructing enumerators to "insert the name of every free person in each family of every age, including the names of those temporarily absent on a journey, visit, or for the purposes of education, as well as those that were at home on that day" (see App. Chap. 2). This, however, leaves unclear what would happen in the event that the entire family were temporarily absent. Presumably they would not be counted anywhere. The numbers likely to be affected by this are small. Of much more importance is the issue of for whom is place of residence a discretionary variable.

13. Readers interested in at least a partial answer to that question could examine the 1850 census manuscripts for Illinois (and the 1855 Illinois state census returns) and the 1840 and 1830 census returns for New York state for records of the Bowman family.

14. On the Eastern Seaboard, the majority of household heads were born in the current state of residence; a majority in Ohio and Missouri came from just two states; three states or countries supplied a majority of the heads in Indiana, Iowa, Michigan, and Wisconsin, while five did so for Illinois, Kansas, and Minnesota. Quite a different picture emerges for the western states when children and other family members are included in the count as stayers. The 1860 Census estimated that the Illinois-born resident population was 41 percent of the state's total population, while in the more culturally homogeneous state of Michigan the percentage of Michigan-born Michigan residents was lower, 39 percent.

15. U.S. Census Office, Eighth Census, *Population*, 215.

16. St. Louis, for example, had 96,000 foreign-born in 1860. See U.S. Census Office, Eighth Census, *Population*, 300.

17. See, for example, Ray H. Billington, *Westward Expansion: A History of the American Frontier* (New York, 1967); Richard A. Easterlin, "Influences in European Overseas Emigration Before World War I," *Economic Development and Cultural Change* 9, 2(Apr. 1961):331–53; Walter Willcox, ed., *International Migrations* (New York, 1931), vol. 2, especially Chap. 2; Lowell E. Gallaway and Richard K. Vedder, "Emigration from the United Kingdom to the United States: 1860–1913," *Journal of Economic History* 31, 4(Dec. 1971):885–97; Marcus Hansen, *The Atlantic Migration, 1607–1860* (Cambridge, 1940); S. H. Holbrook, *The Yankee Exodus: An Account of Migration from New England* (New York, 1950); S. C. Johnson, *Emigration from the United Kingdom to North America, 1763–1912* (London, 1913); Richard Steckel, "The Economic Foundations of East-West Migration During the Nineteenth Century," *Explorations in Economic History* 20, 1(Jan. 1983):14–36; Lewis D. Stilwell, "Migration from Vermont, 1776–1860," *Proceedings of the Vermont Historical Society* 5(1937):63–245; Brinley Thomas, *Migration and Economic Growth*, 2d ed. (Cambridge, 1973); C. W. Thornthwaite, *Internal Migration in the United States* (Philadelphia, 1934); Maurice Wilkinson, "European Migration to the United States: An Econometric Analysis of Aggregate Labor Supply and Demand," *Review of Economics and Statistics* 52, 1(1970):272–79.

18. See Larry Neal, "Cross-Spectral Analysis of Long Swings in Atlantic Migration," *Research in Economic History* 1(1976):260–97.
19. See Turner, *Frontier*, 259.
20. Ibid., 21–22.
21. The critical value of the correlation coefficient in a one-tailed test at the 5 percent level is 0.16.
22. A simple model of current land sales as a function of past wheat prices, $L_t = a + P_{w[t-i]}$, displays rising *t*-values and improved fit as *i* increases from zero to 3 and the R^2 rises from 0.06 to 0.24. A distributed lag function has similar implications. See U.S. Department of Commerce, *Historical Statistics,* Series J20 and E123 for the data on land sales and wheat prices.
23. See Stilwell, "Migration."
24. See, for example, the recent analysis of this phenomenon by Steckel, "The Economic Foundations of East-West Migration," 14–36.
25. The experiment results are reported in Illinois Agricultural Experiment Station, "Field Experiments with Corn," *Illinois Agricultural Experiment Station Bulletins 4, 8, 13, 20, 25, 31,* (1889–1894).
26. Steckel, "The Economic Foundations of East-West Migration," 23.
27. David P. Davenport, "Population Persistence and Migration in Rural New York, 1853-1860," (Ph.D. diss., 1982), especially Fig. 5.3.
28. U.S. Census Office, Eighth Census, *Population,* 622.
29. Three hundred and sixty-five of the 368 households headed by Dutch immigrants in the sample lived in Holland Township in Ottawa County, Michigan, and they made up 87 percent of the households in the township. The existence of such ties may also explain why most of these families settled in Michigan directly from Holland as nearly as can be judged from the census data (see below). As a group, the Dutch immigrants averaged only 1.1 moves per family in reaching their destination. Similarly, in Wisconsin a group of ten German families settled therein with no detectable intermediate stopovers.
30. The early German settlers in Pennsylvania were called "Pennsylvania Dutch" as a corruption of Deutch.
31. See Gallaway and Vedder, "Mobility," for a discussion of the propensity for natives from the Northwest Central states (Minnesota, Iowa, Missouri, Kansas, Nebraska, and the Dakotas) to move back East later in the century.
32. The sample truncation attributable to requiring that a family have at least one child if we are to identify 2 moves, two children for 3 moves, and so on, does not appear to be too serious. Whereas about 86 percent of husband-wife households had at least one own child, only 13.4 percent made 2 or more moves. Similarly, while 61 percent of married couples had two or more surviving own children, only 2.2 percent made 3 or more moves.
33. One move is accounted for by a head-of-the-family birthplace other than the current state of residence. Additional moves are based upon the birthplaces of the children.
34. This table differs from Table 5.1 insofar as the percentage of families making at least 1 move is restricted to husband-wife headed households whereas the figures off the diagonal in Table 5.1 are for all households.

CHAPTER SIX

1. Alexis de Tocqueville, *Democracy in America,* vol. 1 (New York, 1946), 3.
2. The modern genesis of this debate is Edward Pessen, "The Egalitarian Myth and American Social Reality: Wealth, Mobility, and Equality in the 'Era of the Common Man,' " *American Historical Review* 76, 3(Oct. 1971):989–1034, and Edward Pessen, *Riches, Class and Power before the Civil War* (Lexington, Mass., 1973). For a critique of Pessen's argument and his responses see Robert E. Gallman, "Professor Pessen on the 'Egalitarian Myth,' " *Social Science History* 2, 1(1978):194–207; Edward Pessen, "On a Recent Cliometric Attempt to Resurrect the Myth of Antebellum Egalitarianism," *Social Science History* 3, 2(1979):208–27; Robert E. Gallman, "The 'Egalitarian Myth,' Once Again," *Social Science History* 5, 2(1981):223–34; Edward Pessen, "The Beleaguered Myth of Antebellum Egalitarianism," *Social Science History* 6, 1(1982):111–28.

3. See, for example, Pessen, "On a Recent Cliometric Attempt," 211, 213.

4. See, for example, Lee Soltow, *Patterns of Wealthholding in Wisconsin* (Madison, 1971); Gloria Main, "Inequality in Early America: The Evidence of Probate Records from Massachusetts and Maryland" (Paper presented to the Cliometrics Conference, Madison, Wis., 1976), mimeo.; William Newell, "The Sources of Increasing Wealth Inequality: A Study of Testators in Butler County, Ohio, 1803–65" (Paper presented at National Bureau of Economic Research Conference, Williamsburg, Va., 1977), mimeo.

5. Robert E. Gallman, "Trends in the Size Distribution of Wealth in the Nineteenth Century: Some Speculations," in *Six Papers on the Size Distribution of Wealth and Income*, ed. Lee Soltow, Studies in Income and Wealth 33 (New York, 1969), 1–25; Lee Soltow, *Men and Wealth in the United States, 1850–1870* (New Haven, 1975).

6. For 1945 Lampman estimated that the top 1 percent held 23.3 percent of the wealth, declining from a high of 36.3 percent in 1929. See Robert S. Lampman, *The Share of Top Wealth-Holders in National Wealth, 1922–1956* (New York, 1962). More recent estimates for 1962 and 1963 have been made by the Survey Research Center of the University of Michigan and the Federal Reserve Board respectively. See Survey Research Center, *1962 Survey of Consumer Finances, Monograph 32* (Ann Arbor, 1963), and Dorothy Projector and Gertrude S. Weiss, *Survey of Financial Characteristics of Consumers* (Washington, D.C., 1966).

7. Gavin Wright, "'Economic Democracy' and the Concentration of Agricultural Wealth in the Cotton South, 1850–1860," *Agricultural History* 44, 1(Jan. 1970):63–93, especially 85. In 1850 wealth refers only to real estate since personal estate was not recorded in the 1850 manuscripts. Because real estate was generally less equally distributed than personal estate, estimates of overall inequality in 1850 are biased upward.

8. For an analysis of the effects of this sample truncation see Donghyu Yang, "Notes on the Wealth Distribution of Farm Households in the United States, 1860: A New Look at Two Manuscript Census Samples," *Explorations in Economic History* 21, 1(Jan. 1984):88–102. The effects of truncation can be corrected if the fraction of propertyless households is known. The Gini for the entire population, G_p based on a sample in which 20 percent of the households were excluded would be $G_p = 0.20 + (1 - 0.20)G_s$ where G_s is the Gini index for the truncated sample. See Yang, "Notes on Wealth."

9. Randolph B. Campbell and Richard G. Lowe, *Wealth and Power in Antebellum Texas* (College Station, 1977).

10. Ibid.

11. See Soltow, *Wealthholding*, 5, 43. This figure is estimated from Soltow's Lorenz curve for Milwaukee.

12. Pessen, *Riches*.

13. The shares for Baltimore, New Orleans, and St. Louis in 1860 are estimated at 71.7, 71.6, and 67.7 percent respectively. See Gallman, "Trends."

14. The Gini for New Hampshire was almost as low as that found in Australia in the 1960s, which was the most egalitarian country for which there are reliable statistics. See N. Podder and N. C. Kakwoni, "The Distribution of Wealth in Australia," *Review of Income and Wealth* 22, 1(Mar. 1976):75–92.

15. Gallman, "Trends"; Soltow, *Men and Wealth*.

16. See Lampman, *Wealth-Holders*, and Lee Soltow, "The Census of Wealth of Men in Australia in 1915 and the United States in 1860 and 1870," *Australian Economic History Review* 12, 2(Sept. 1972):125–41.

17. See Walter G. Runciman, *Relative Deprivation and Social Justice* (Berkeley, 1966). Unfortunately, the hypothesis of relative deprivation does not lend itself to quantitative testing.

18. Only Michigan ($800) and Minnesota ($500) had median wealth levels below $1,000, Maryland excluded.

19. Clarence H. Danhof, "Farm-Making Costs and the 'Safety Valve': 1850–1860," *Journal of Political Economy* 49, 3(June 1941):317–59 and Chap. 8.

20. Over 6 percent of the households reported no wealth and hence the dependent variable is undefined for these observations. On the one hand, excluding them (the usual treatment in a log or semilog model) excludes an important segment of the population and

implicitly argues for a dichotomous model but results in there being no wealth variation to explain for one group. On the other hand, mimicking the behavior of the logarithmic function as wealth approaches zero by substituting a very large negative number gives undue weight to the group. Excluding the zero wealth holders results in much lower implicit accumulation rates, whereas substituting a large negative number results in much higher rates. On balance we felt that it was important to keep the very poor in the model and therefore we substituted $1 for zero wealth. As a result the dependent variable had a value of zero for these observations.

21. For example, the interest rate quotations given in Frederick R. Macaulay, *Some Theoretical Problems Suggested by the Movement of Interest Rates, Bond Yields and Stock Prices in the United States Since 1856* (New York, 1938), are in the range of 6 to 8 percent; the manufacturing profit rates given by Fred Bateman and Thomas Weiss, *A Deplorable Scarcity* (Chapel Hill, 1981), are about 20 percent. The accumulation rates implied by the regression coefficient of age should be realizable by anyone with a portfolio of these assets in the right proportions.

22. For discussion of the Life Cycle hypothesis see A. Ando and Franco Modigliani, "The Life Cycle Hypothesis of Saving: Aggregate Implications and Tests," *American Economic Review* 53, 1(Mar. 1963):55–84 and Franco Modigliani and Richard Brumberg, "Utility Analysis and the Consumption Function: An Interpretation of Cross-Section Data," in *Post-Keynesian Economics,* ed. K. Kurihara (New Brunswick, N.J., 1954).

23. The partial of the wealth equation with respect to age for the Midwest,

$$\partial \mathrm{WEALTH} / \partial \mathrm{AGE} = 213.87 - 3.38\mathrm{AGE},$$

reaches a maximum at age 63.

24. The potential for perpetuating wealth inequality through inheritance has been shown, for example, by Alan S. Blinder, "A Model of Inherited Wealth," *Quarterly Journal of Economics* 87, 4(Nov. 1973):608–26; J. E. Stiglitz, "Distribution of Income and Wealth Among Individuals," *Econometrica* 37, 3(July 1969):382–97; and John A. Brittain, *Inheritance and the Inequality of Material Wealth* (Washington, D.C., 1978).

25. The model could be extended to include daughters in the partitive inheritance scheme. The major effect would be the differential and higher rates of female mortality due to childbearing.

26. Lee Soltow, "Male Inheritance Expectations in the United States in 1870," *Review of Economics and Statistics* 64, 2(May 1982):252–60. See also Lee Soltow, "Land Fragmentation as an Index of History in the Virginia Military District of Ohio," *Explorations in Economic History* 20, 3(July 1983):263–73.

27. See Edgar Sydenstricker, *Health and Environment* (New York, 1933), 164. See also U.S. Department of Commerce, *Historical Statistics of the United States from Colonial Times to 1970* (Washington D.C., 1975), Series B128.

28. No person or group, of course, experienced the life cycles depicted here. Rather, in the presence of widely diffused economic growth, the decline in later years might be postponed indefinitely.

29. Robert Gallman, "Professor Pessen," 197. See also Gallman, "The 'Egalitarian Myth.' "

30. For women heads the average age was 49, while for nonfarm household heads the average age was 39. The hypothesis that the age structures were the same was not rejected only for white household heads compared with all household heads in 1860. Since most heads of household were white, this result is hardly surprising.

31. The methodology to accomplish this is given in Morton Paglin, "The Measurement and Trend of Inequality: A Basic Revision," *American Economic Review* 65, 3(Sept. 1975):598–609, and is corrected in Jeremy Atack and Fred Bateman, "The Measurement and Trend of Inequality: An Amendment to a Basic Revision," *Economic Letters* 4(Oct. 1979):389–93, and John P. Formby and Terry G. Seaks, "Paglin's Gini Measure of Inequality: A Modification," *American Economic Review* 70, 2(June 1980):479–82. The results of this procedure in the context of these data are described in Atack and Bateman, "The Measurement."

CHAPTER SEVEN

1. The actual number of farms for which data on acreage or values were recorded was 11,939, of which 454 were not matched with households. One thousand and twenty-two of those that were matched were linked to households in which no one reported their occupation as farmer. See Table 7.1 for a complete breakdown by state.

2. See Chap. 3.

3. A county history of Adams County notes Joel Darrah, M.D. as arriving in Honey Creek Township in the spring of 1840 as one of the earlier residents. See William H. Collins and C. F. Perry, *Past and Present of the City of Quincy and Adams County* (Chicago, 1905), 327.

4. Allan Bogue, *From Prairie to Corn Belt: Farming on the Illinois and Iowa Prairies in the Nineteenth Century* (Chicago, 1963), 63.

5. Ibid., 64.

6. D. L. Winters, *Farmers Without Farms: Agricultural Tenancy in Nineteenth Century Iowa* (Westport, Conn., 1978).

7. Donald E. Ginter, "A Critique of Landholding Variables in the 1860 Census and the Parker-Gallman Sample" (Paper presented at the 95th Annual Meeting of the American Historical Association, Washington, D.C., December 28–30, 1980).

8. U.S. Department of the Interior, Geological Survey, *The National Atlas of the United States of America* (Washington, D.C., 1970), Plates 86–87.

CHAPTER EIGHT

1. See, for example, Paul W. Gates, *History of Public Land Law Development* (Washington, D.C., 1968); Benjamin H. Hibbard, *A History of the Public Land Policies* (New York, 1924; reprint Madison, 1965); Roy M. Robbins, *Our Landed Heritage: The Public Domain 1776-1936* (Princeton, 1942, reprint Lincoln, 1962).

2. See Douglass C. North, *The Economic Growth of the United States 1790-1860* (New York, 1966), 136–37. North also includes corn, but most corn was consumed on the farm and is therefore not an index of commercial orientation.

3. The following analysis is developed from Robert W. Fogel and Jack L. Rutner, "The Efficiency Effects of Federal Land Policy, 1850–1900: A Report of Some Provisional Findings," in *The Dimensions of Quantitative Research in History,* ed. William O. Aydelotte (Princeton, 1972), 390–418, especially 411–15.

4. See, for example, the citations in Paul W. Gates, *The Farmer's Age: Agriculture 1815-1860* (New York, 1960), 85–89.

5. Nathan H. Parker, *The Iowa Handbook for 1856* (Boston, 1856), 18–19.

6. Ibid., 149.

7. Swierenga, in his study of speculators in Iowa, put the average fraction of public lands taken up by speculators at 32 percent. See Robert Swierenga, "Land Speculator 'Profits' Reconsidered: Central Iowa as a Test Case," *Journal of Economic History* 26 1(Mar. 1966):1–28; Robert Swierenga, *Pioneers and Profits: Land Speculation on the Iowa Frontier* (Ames, 1968). See also the profit estimates we present below.

8. Gates, *The Farmer's Age,* 399–400.

9. The following is based upon Jeremy Atack, "Farm and Farm-Making Costs Revisited," *Agricultural History* 56, 4(Oct. 1982):663–76.

10. Frederick Jackson Turner, *The Frontier in American History* (New York, 1920), 259.

11. Fred Gerhard, *Illinois as It Is* (Chicago, 1859), 289; Thomas H. Webb, *Information for Kansas Immigrants* (Boston, 1856), 21.

12. John Regan, *The Western Wilds of America, or, Backwoods and Prairies; and Scenes of the Valley of the Mississippi*, 2d ed. (Edinburgh, 1859), 353, 356–57. Regan gives a particularly detailed breakdown of the $550 expense: cost of 40 acres: $50; fencing with 8,000 rails: $100; log cabin: $20; house furniture: $50; two cows: $30; two heifers: $15; six sheep: $9; six pigs: $6; span of horses: $80; a wagon: $70; horse harness and chains: $23; plough: $10; harness (homemade): $2; spade, hoes, scythes, rakes, axe, and augers: $15; food for four in

family for six months: $50; seed corn, wheat, and sundries: $20. At the time Regan was writing, "wild lands" were still available in Illinois, for example, in Livingston County, which the earlier settlers had bypassed. Our sample includes a township from Livingston.

13. Gerhard, *Illinois*, 294–95.

14. J. B. Newhall, *A Glimpse of Iowa in 1846; or, The Emigrant's Guide, and State Directory; with a Description of the New Purchase: Embracing Much Practical Advice and Useful Information to Intending Emigrants,* 2d ed. (Burlington, Iowa, 1846), 59. Although this estimate is for 1846, prices appear little, if at all, different from those quoted ten years later.

15. Horace Greeley, *An Overland Journey from New York to San Francisco in the Summer of 1859* (New York, 1860), 68.

16. *Michigan Farmer* 8(1850):265.

17. Minnesota Commissioner of Statistics, *Minnesota: Its Place Among the States, Being the First Annual Report of the Commissioner of Statistics for the Year Ending January 1st, 1860* (Hartford, 1860), 88.

18. *Wisconsin Farmer* 8(1856):440.

19. *The Country Gentleman* 5(Apr. 1855):213–14.

20. Clarence H. Danhof, "Farm-Making Costs and the 'Safety Valve': 1850–1860," *Journal of Political Economy* 49(June 1941):318–59. See quotation, 354.

21. Ibid.

22. Robert E. Ankli, "Farm-Making Costs in the 1850's," *Agricultural History* 48, 1(Jan. 1974):51–70. See quotation, 70.

23. Judith L. V. Klein, "Farm-Making Costs in the 1850's: A Comment," *Agricultural History* 48 1(Jan. 1974):71–74.

24. Danhof, "Farm-Making Costs," 318.

25. The table is restricted to 160-acre farms because of the limited number of smaller tenant farms on the frontier.

26. See Robert E. Gallman, "Investment Flows and Capital Stocks: U.S. Experience in the Nineteenth Century," in *Quantity and Quiddity: Essays in U.S. Economic History in Honor of Stanley L. Lebergott*, ed. Peter Kilby (Middletown, Conn., forthcoming).

27. These values are consistent with the figures quoted by Danhof of $25 (for a log cabin) to $450 (for a four-room cottage) for the cost of housing. See Danhof, "Farm-Making Costs," 353–54. He notes that larger houses could cost as much as $1,000, or about the same as the constant term in the eastern regression for yeoman farms.

28. Alexander Campbell, *A Glance at Illinois* (La Salle, Ill., 1856), 7.

29. For example, "Oxen will work in the breaking team and grow fat on the grass they eat at night. They will work in the hottest weather, and they seldom or never loll as they do at the east" (Minnesota Commissioner of Statistics, *Annual Report*, 87).

30. In light of the Minnesota Commissioner of Statistics' comments that "(B)eyond all question, wool is the best crop to raise for export in Minnesota . . . freight on one hundred dollars worth of wool is not as much as on five dollars worth of wheat, and sheep do better here than in any other western state" (Ibid., 87) it is surprising that so few Minnesota farms had sheep in 1860.

31. See App., Chap. 7.

32. See U.S. Department of Agriculture, Division of Statistics, George K. Holmes, "The Course of Prices of Farm Implements and Machinery for a Series of Years," *Miscellaneous Bulletins* 18 (Washington, D.C., 1901), and the Bateman-Weiss samples from the manuscript censuses of manufacturing. Based on the Warren-Pearson price index, prices of metals and metal products changed little from the 1840s to the Civil War. See U.S. Department of Commerce, *Historical Statistics of the United States from Colonial Times to 1970* (Washington D.C., 1975), Series E58. This is also confirmed by the similarity between prices quoted by contemporary sources over the period 1846–1860.

33. Danhof, "Farm-Making Costs," 350–52. Compare with A. Cunynghame, *A Glimpse of the Great Western Republic* (London, 1851), 103; Regan, *Western Wilds of America*, 353; Minnesota Commissioner of Statistics, *Minnesota*, 87, which estimate that $50 would be adequate, while Newhall, *Glimpse of Iowa*, 59, put the figure at $75.

34. Danhof, "Farm-Making Costs," 349, assuming a 40-acre farm had 24–28 acres under

cultivation. *The Country Gentleman* 5, 14(Apr. 1855):213, set seed costs at $75 for 100 improved acres. Regan, *Western Wilds of America*, 353, set seed costs at $20 for a 40-acre farm, while for 10 acres of corn, 5 of wheat, and 5 of potatoes, turnips, and garden produce; Newhall, *Glimpse of Iowa*, 59, allowed $5.

35. See Danhof, "Farm-Making Costs," 327, and Minnesota Commissioner of Statistics, *Minnesota*, 87.

36. Fred A. Shannon, "The Homestead Act and the Labor Surplus," *American Historical Review* 41, 4(July, 1936):641.

CHAPTER NINE

1. For an elaboration, see Fred Bateman, "Improvement in American Dairy Farming, 1850-1910: A Quantitative Analysis," *Journal of Economic History* 28, 2(June 1968):255–73. The antebellum censuses provide neither direct nor indirect evidence on the care and attention received by farm livestock except for dairy cows. Even there, information is limited. All we have is a partial enumeration of the dairy inputs, cows, and the produce–butter and cheese. Missing is information on the labor inputs, feed and herd quality, and on the milk consumed or sold in fluid form. Nevertheless, the census data can be made to yield useful information on the status of this important industry, provided we are prepared to make a number of assumptions. We assume that preferences were homogeneous throughout the North with respect to fluid-milk consumption in the rural townships. After accounting for the milk used in butter and cheese making the residual differences per capita between production and consumption must be due to differences in the average herd quality or the amount of fluid milk marketed beyond the township boundaries. We will also assume that farm women or children supplied the bulk of the labor in the farm dairy. Although farmers increasingly came to realize the link between feed and yield and took better care of their animals, the typical practice was far from ideal.

2. J. Anderson, "On the Management of the Dairy," *American Farmer* 1, 18(July 1819):1.

3. *Journal of the New York Agricultural Society* 20(Mar. 1870):32.

4. Peter Collier, "How to Make Dairying More Profitable" (Address delivered before the Holstein-Friesian Association of America, 5th Annual Meeting, New York, 19 March 1890), 12.

5. Charles L. Flint, *Milch Cows and Dairy Farming* (Boston, 1871), 55.

6. Henry Stewart, *The Dairyman's Manual* (New York, 1888), 26.

7. U.S. Patent Office, *Report of the Commissioner of Patents, 1863. Part II, Agriculture,* 209–220, especially 210.

8. Milk which sold for $0.0083 a pound ($0.0166 a quart), for example, was more profitable than cheese selling for $0.08 a pound or butter selling for $0.18 a pound since at these prices the farmer's additional labor would not be compensated. The average on-farm butter price was below this ($0.15 a pound), the on-farm cheese price was somewhat above it ($0.10 a pound). Wholesale or retail sale, however, offered the chance of profit.

9. Paul W. Gates, *The Farmer's Age: Agriculture 1815-1860* (New York, 1960), 236, 241. According to the *Report of the Fifth Annual Meeting of the Ohio Dairyman's Association for 1899,* as early as 1811 cheese was being transported over relatively long distances into such port cities as New York and New Orleans. In 1848, according to an Ohio experiment station report, the Western Reserve counties exported more than 15,000,000 pounds of cheese, most of which went into eastern markets (*Ohio Agricultural Experiment Station Bulletin 326* [Wooster, Ohio, July 1918], 87).

10. The relationship between urban growth and dairy development in New York State is discussed in detail in Eric Brunger, "Dairying and Urban Development in New York State, 1850–1900," *Agricultural History* 29, 4(Oct. 1955):169–74.

11. Fluid milk was obviously less transportable than dairy products so that most cities drew their supplies from within a very small radius. Where conveyed by wagon, 15 miles usually defined the outer boundaries of a city's milkshed. The presence of rail facilities could extend this to as much as 150 miles. *The Report of the Commissioner of Patents for 1861* (U.S.

Patent Office, *Report, 1861. Part II, Agriculture*) claimed that about one-half of the milk consumed in New York City at that time came by wagon, with the remainder coming on such railroads as the Harlem, the Erie, and the Long Island, often from distances exceeding 100 miles. This report claims that most of the fluid-milk supply for Washington, however, came by wagon from producers located relatively close to the city. In the Midwest and South, urban milksheds were considerably smaller than New York's and were served by wagon deliveries. For specific discussion of this issue, see *Iowa Agricultural Experiment Station Bulletin 243* (Ames, 1928) and *New Hampshire Agricultural Experiment Station Bulletin 120* (Durham, 1905). Even by 1900, most fluid milk entered urban markets from fairly short distances, ranging from 20 to 30 miles for Detroit and Cincinnati to about 200 miles for New York City. See Edward G. Ward, "Milk Transportation: Freight Rates to the Fifteen Largest Cities in the United States," U.S. Department of Agriculture, Division of Statistics, *Bulletin 25* (Washington, D.C., 1903).

12. Gates, *The Farmer's Age*, 239–41. The Erie Railroad was extended into the Orange County dairy region of New York in 1842, shifting some of that region's butter and cheese producers to fluid-milk production.

13. See U.S. Census Office, Eighth Census, *Manufactures of the United States in 1860* (Washington, D.C., 1864), 735, 742.

14. The national average milk yield in 1860 was 2,585 pounds per milk cow; production per person was 714 pounds annually. In the Midwest, the milk production averaged 2,752 pounds per cow or 824 per person; the comparable figures for the Northeast were 4,125 and 959 respectively.

15. See Bateman, "Improvement," 255–73.

16. In the postbellum era, expansion of the milking season became an important step in promoting growth of annual yields per animal. During the second half of the century, the milking season was extended in most areas, as winter dairying became increasingly common and economically appealing in the North. See, for example, New York State Dairyman's Association, *Annual Report of the New York State Dairyman's Association for 1878* (Albany, N.Y., 1878); Wisconsin Dairymen's Association, *Fourteenth Annual Report of the Wisconsin Dairymen's Association, 1886,* (Madison, Wis., 1886), 135–39.

17. See Fred Bateman, "Labor Inputs and Productivity in American Dairy Agriculture, 1850–1910," *Journal of Economic History* 29, 2(June 1969):206–29. Said a USDA bulletin in 1907, "while no milking machine yet invented has shown its practical value in a way that has led to its general use . . . the prospect for the general introduction of milking machines appears to be so favorable that it was thought advisable by the Secretary of Agriculture to authorize an investigation of the fundamental problems involved in the use of such machines." The result was publication of a detailed 55-page bulletin by C. S. Lane and W. A. Stocking, "The Milking Machines as a Factor in Dairying: A Preliminary Report," U.S. Department of Agriculture, Bureau of Animal Industry, *Bulletin 92* (Washington, D.C., 1907). By 1910 there were approximately 12,000 machines of various designs in use on American farms; 55,000 by 1920 and 100,000 by 1930. Only during and after World War II did milking machines come into widespread use. See U.S. Department of Commerce, *Historical Statistics,* Series K189.

18. Dairying in the twentieth century consumed a sizable amount of farmers' time throughout the year. In 1937–1940, for example, farmers spent an estimated 3.3 billion manhours annually on milk cows alone, in addition to 3.6 billion hours for dairy calves, heifers, and bulls. This amount exceeded that spent on cotton, wheat, or oats during this period. Robert E. Elwood, Arthur A. Lewis, and Ronald A. Strubel, "Changes in Technology and Labor Requirements in Livestock Production: Dairying," in *Works Progress Administration, National Research Project, WPA Report A-14* (Washington, D.C., June 1941), v.

19. Clarence H. Danhof, *Change in Agriculture: The Northern United States, 1820–1870* (Cambridge, Mass., 1969), 21.

20. These are examined in more detail in Chap. 12. Also see Fred Bateman, "The 'Marketable Surplus' in Northern Dairy Farming: New Evidence by Size of Farm in 1860," *Agricultural History* 52, 3(July 1978):345–63.

21. Edgar W. Martin, *The Standard of Living in 1860* (Chicago, 1942), 23.

22. Richard O. Cummings, *The American and His Food* (Chicago, 1940), 236; U.S. De-

partment of Agriculture, *Statistical Bulletin 25* (Washington, D.C., 1929), 67.

23. U.S. Patent Office, *Report, 1861. Part II, Agriculture,* 216.

24. U.S. Department of Agriculture, *Yearbook of Agriculture, 1899* (Washington, D.C., 1900).

25. F. W. Woll, *Dairy Calendar for 1895* (New York, 1895).

26. T. R. Pirtle, *A Handbook of Dairy Statistics* (Washington, D.C., 1933), 64.

27. Merrill K. Bennett and Rosamond H. Peirce, "Changes in the American National Diet, 1879–1959," *Food Research Institute Studies* 2, 2(May 1961):95–119.

28. Loomis speculated in the *1861 Commissioner of Patents Report* (U.S. Patent Office, *Report, 1861. Part II, Agriculture,* 217) that average fluid-milk consumption in the thirteen states in his report was double that of New York City, but he fails to provide evidence in support of that contention.

29. John M. Cassels, *A Study of Fluid Milk Prices* (Cambridge, Mass., 1937), 93. Estimation of consumption remained difficult, according to Cassels, even with twentieth-century sources. Data on the market flow of milk and dairy products were imprecise, leading him to claim that the "uncritical use of receipts and population data as a means of estimating per capita consumption for an area has resulted in the publication of some figures which are manifestly absurd. . . ."

30. Use of the butter figures, which show a higher variation between these two groups than do the fluid-milk estimates, will also tend toward overstating consumption on the farm, thus leading to an understatement of the potential marketable surplus. Cassels does not estimate cheese consumption.

CHAPTER TEN

1. U.S. Patent Office, *Report of the Commissioner of Patents. Part II, Agriculture* (Washington, D.C., 1843–1855).

2. For example, William N. Parker and Judith L. V. Klein, "Productivity Growth in Grain Production in the United States, 1840–60 and 1900–10," in *Output, Employment and Productivity in the United States After 1800*, Studies in Income and Wealth 30 (Princeton, 1966), 523–82; Fred Bateman, "Improvement in American Dairy Farming 1850–1910: A Quantitative Analysis," *Journal of Economic History* 28, 2(June 1968):255–73; Fred Bateman, "Labor Inputs and Productivity in American Dairy Agriculture, 1850–1910," *Journal of Economic History* 29, 2(June 1969):206–29.

3. U.S. Patent Office, *Report, 1850. Part II, Agriculture,* 180, for Litchfield County, Connecticut.

4. Ibid., 244–46. For Adams County, Illinois.

5. Ibid., 222. For southern Indiana.

6. Ibid., 201–2. For Burlington County, New Jersey.

7. Ibid., 208–9. For Canandaigua, New York.

8. Ibid., 212. For Fayette County, Ohio.

9. Ibid., 212–13. For Westmoreland County, Pennsylvania.

10. U.S. Department of Agriculture, "Crop Yields and Weather," *Miscellaneous Publication 471* (Washington, D.C., 1942), 110–11.

11. For a discussion of land sales promotions by the Illinois Central Railroad, see Paul W. Gates, *The Illinois Central Railroad and Its Colonizing Work,* Harvard Economic Studies, vol. 42 (Cambridge, Mass., 1941).

12. Illinois Central Railroad Company, *The Illinois Central Railroad Company Offer for Sale over 2,400,000 Acres Selected Prairie, Farm and Woodland Tracts of Any Size . . . on Long Credits . . . Situated Each Side of their Railroad . . . from the Extreme North to the South of the State of Illinois* (New York, 1855), 19.

13. Ibid., 23.

14. Ibid., 21.

15. See, for example, Nathan H. Parker, *The Iowa Handbook for 1856* (Boston, 1856), 18, quoted in Chap. 7.

16. Frederick Gerhard, *Illinois as It Is* (Chicago, 1857), 290–91.

17. Ibid., 291.

18. Minnesota Commissioner of Statistics, *Minnesota: Its Place Among the States, Being the First Annual Report of the Commissioner of Statistics for the Year Ending January 1st, 1860* (Hartford, 1860), 89–96.

19. U.S. Census Office, Seventh Census, *Statistical View of the United States . . . Being a Compendium of the Seventh Census* (Washington, D.C., 1854), 176–77.

20. U.S. Department of Agriculture, "Crop Yields and Weather."

21. The technique was pioneered by Peter Passell and Gavin Wright in a paper presented at the Eighth Purdue Conference on the Application of Economic Theory and Quantitative Techniques to Problems in Economic History, February 1–3, 1968, but no results were published. A version of this equation was used by Robert Ankli, but his equations omitted many field crops and his yield estimates are therefore biased quite independently of the biases inherent in the methodology that we discuss below. See Robert Ankli, "Gross Farm Revenues in Pre-Civil War Illinois," (Ph.D. diss., 1969), 68–76. Peter Passell discusses the technique and different versions of the estimating equation in his thesis but presents no estimates derived from it and William Parker now notes that any estimates made have since been lost. See Peter Passell, *Essays in the Economics of Nineteenth Century Land Policy* (New York, 1975), and William N. Parker, "Labor Productivity in Cotton Farming: The History of a Research," *Agricultural History* 53, 1(Jan. 1979), 232–33.

22. For the most part we used a one-tailed test with a confidence interval of 95 percent. In a few instances we do report yields derived from regression coefficients that were only significantly different from zero at the 10 percent level. These will be clearly marked.

23. A weak case could be made that land on the frontier was freely (or at least cheaply) available so that a farmer made his production decisions and farmed sufficient acres to realize these goals. However, as we have already seen, even if not all potentially cultivable land were included in farms, the time and expense involved in transforming unimproved acres to improved acres make it far from a free good.

24. Even assuming zero covariance does not solve the problem but simply makes it less complicated.

25. Indeed, the published census reports only 12 tons of hay from the entire county in 1859. U.S. Census Office, Eighth Census, *Agriculture of the United States in 1860* (Washington, D.C., 1864), 72.

26. Parker and Klein, "Productivity Growth," 550–51.

27. Paul W. Gates, *The Farmer's Age: Agriculture 1815–1860* (New York, 1960), 173.

28. U.S. Census Office, Eighth Census, *Agriculture,* lxxv.

29. An extensive collection of quotes from contemporary sources for Illinois appears in Ankli, "Gross Farm Revenue," 340–43, 362–64.

30. *Prairie Farmer* 19, 8(24 Feb. 1859):120; Ibid., 19, 9(3 Mar. 1859):136.

31. Ibid., 19, 16(21 Apr. 1859):248.

32. Ibid.

33. See, for example, Ibid., 18 (30 June 1858):406, or Ohio Commissioner of Statistics, *Third Annual Report of the Commissioner of Statistics, 1859* (Columbus, 1860), 97–103.

34. Chicago Board of Trade, *Second Annual Statement of Trade and Commerce of Chicago* (Chicago, 1859), 18.

35. Chicago Board of Trade, *Third Annual Statement of Trade and Commerce of Chicago* (Chicago, 1861), vii.

36. Ohio Commissioner of Statistics, *Third Annual Report—1859,* 97–103.

37. Ibid., 98, 102.

38. Ibid., 99, 102.

39. Ibid.

40. This exceeded the capacity of SPSS v.8.3. All regressions were performed using this package on a CDC Cyber 175.

41. Five soil types were excluded from the regressions, Psamments, Aquepts, Borolls, Orthods, and Udults, because they lacked any significant interactions with the crops and because we could not discriminate between them.

42. Illinois State Auditor, *Biennial Report of the Auditor of Public Accounts of the State of Illinois to the Twenty-Third General Assembly* (Springfield, 1863), 51–52. Based on aggregate data the wheat yield for the state was 10.5 bushels per acre and the corn yield, 28.6 bushels.

43. Ohio Commissioner of Statistics, *Fourth Annual Report.*

44. Iowa Census Board, *The Census Returns of the Different Counties of the State of Iowa for 1859* (Des Moines, 1859). The returns are for the 1858 crop year.

45. See Ohio Commissioner of Statistics, *First Annual Report, 1857.*

46. U.S. Census Office, Seventh Census, *Statistical View of the United States,* 176.

47. U.S. Census Office, Tenth Census, *Report upon the Statistics of Agriculture Compiled from Returns Received at the Tenth Census* (Washington, D.C., 1883), 102.

48. See Fred Bateman, "Dairy Production, Yields, and Income: New Evidence on Distribution by Size of Farm in the Antebellum North" (Indiana Univ. paper, 1976). Mimeo.

49. U.S. Census Office, Seventh Census, *Statistical View of the United States,* 176.

50. Ibid.

51. Ibid.

52. Hay caused much of the problem. There is evidence that it may have been harvested from unimproved as well as improved acreage, while we assume it came only from improved meadow. New York State, for example, reported a hay crop of 3.5 million tons for which we estimate the yield was 1 ton per acre. This implies that about a quarter of the improved acreage in New York was in hay. In Missouri the problem was caused by a low corn yield (16.7 bushels per acre), which with a total crop of over 72 million bushels in 1859 accounts for over two-thirds of the cutlivable land in Missouri.

53. The range of estimates of wheat acreage reflects the range of yield estimates in Tables 10.5 and 10.8.

54. Clarence H. Danhof, *Change in Agriculture: The Northern United States, 1820–1870* (Cambridge, Mass., 1969), 21.

CHAPTER ELEVEN

1. U.S. Patent Office, *Report of the Commissioner of Patents, 1852. Part II, Agriculture* (Washington, D.C., 1852), 323.

2. William N. Parker, "Agriculture," in *American Economic Growth,* Lance E. Davis et al. (New York, 1972), 395.

3. William N. Parker and Judith L. V. Klein, "Productivity Growth in Grain Production in the United States, 1840–60 and 1900–10," in *Output, Employment and Productivity in the United States After 1800,* Studies in Income and Wealth 30 (Princeton, 1966), 523–82. These figures assume a 70-year interval between 1840–1860 and 1900–1910.

4. Ibid., 533.

5. See the Ohio Commissioner of Statistics, *Annual Report,* various years, and U.S. Department of Agriculture, "Crop Yields and Weather," *Miscellaneous Publication 471* (Washington, D.C., Feb. 1942).

6. On the other hand, if we view output as fixed and known, this is tantamount to overstating the acreage under cultivation and land in use was more likely to be taxed than land not under cultivation.

7. Robert E. Gallman, "Changes in Total U.S. Agricultural Factor Productivity in the Nineteenth Century," *Agricultural History* 46, 1(Jan. 1972):191–210. This issue was raised by Robert Fogel during the course of a workshop presentation at the University of Chicago.

8. Dividing both sides by L^α and noting that since $\alpha + \beta + \gamma = 1$, then $L^\alpha L^\beta L^\gamma = 1$.

9. Gallman, "Changes," Table 8, 208.

10. Stanley Lebergott, *Manpower in Economic Growth* (New York, 1964), 510.

11. See, for example, William T. Hutchinson, *Cyrus H. McCormick,* 2 vols. (New York, 1930); John F. Steward, *The Reaper* (New York, 1931); Leo Rogin, *The Introduction of Farm Machinery in its Relation to the Productivity of Labor in the Agriculture of the United States During the Nineteenth Century* (Berkeley, 1931).

12. Paul A. David, "The Mechanization of Reaping in the Antebellum Midwest," in *Industrialization in Two Systems,* ed. H. Rosovsky (New York, 1966), 3–28; Alan L. Olmstead, "The Mechanization of Reaping and Mowing in American Agriculture," *Journal of Economic History* 35, 3(June 1975):327–52; Robert E. Ankli, "The Coming of the Reaper," in *Business and Economic History: Papers Presented at the Twenty-Second Annual Meeting of the*

Business History Conference, ed. Paul A. Uselding (Urbana, 1976), 1–24.

13. Clarence H. Danhof, "Agriculture," in *The Growth of the American Economy,* ed. H. F. Williamson (New York, 1951), 146.

14. Rogin, *Farm Machinery,* 91.

15. Ibid., 69–72.

16. Steward, *Reaper,* 12.

17. David, "Mechanization of Reaping," 33.

18. It is necessary to return to the original source of David's figures–Rogin, *Farm Machinery*–to deduce the nature and basis of the labor savings.

19. Ibid., 126–32.

20. Ibid., 133–37.

21. David, "Mechanization of Reaping," 36–37.

22. David Schob, "Agricultural Labor in the Midwest, 1815–1860," (Ph.D. diss., 1970); David Schob, *Hired Hands and Plowboys* (Urbana, 1975). See also Ankli, "The Coming of the Reaper."

23. *Hunt's Merchants' Magazine* 41(Dec. 1859):758–61.

24. Ibid., 760.

25. Manuscript censuses of manufactures data.

26. Olmstead, "Mechanization of Reaping and Mowing," 331–32. The quote is from Illinois State Agricultural Society, *Transactions for 1856-57,* vol. 2 (Springfield, 1857), 120. Compare with David, "Mechanization of Reaping," 33.

27. See Hutchinson, *McCormick,* 323. Also David, "Mechanization of Reaping"; Olmstead, "Mechanization of Reaping and Mowing"; Ankli, "The Coming of the Reaper."

28. David, "Mechanization of Reaping," n. 57.

29. Assuming a weight of about 1,500 pounds and a ton-mile rate of $0.04/ton/mile using airline miles from the closest point of manufacture to the sample townships. Railroad rates in the 1850s averaged $0.023 to $0.035/ton/mile. See George Rogers Taylor, *The Transportation Revolution, 1815-1860* (New York, 1968), 442. The extra allowance is for wagon shipment from the railhead and extra distance involved in overland transport.

30. Olmstead, "Mechanization of Reaping and Mowing," 332–33.

31. Ibid.

32. Sidney Homer, *A History of Interest Rates* (New Brunswick, N.J., 1963), 316–26.

33. See David, "Mechanization of Reaping."

34. See U.S. Census Office, Eighth Census, *Agriculture of the United States in 1860* (Washington, D.C., 1864), 221.

35. Ibid., 222. In the South, reapers outside of Virginia were probably a rarity.

36. *Country Gentleman* 13(1859):259–60.

37. J. J. Thomas, *Farm Implements and Machinery* (New York, 1869), 8.

38. See Olmstead, "Mechanization of Reaping and Mowing," 337–38.

39. Ibid., 338–41.

40. Ibid., 337.

CHAPTER TWELVE

1. For a cogent discussion of the literature on this issue, see Winifred C. Rothenberg, "The Market and Massachusetts Farmers, 1750-1855," *Journal of Economic History* 41, 2(June 1981):283–314. See also James T. Lemon, "Comment of James A. Henretta's 'Families and Farms: *Mentalité* in Pre-Industrial America,'" *William and Mary Quarterly,* 3d ser., 37, 4(Oct. 1980):689–96; James T. Lemon, "Early Americans and their Social Environment," *Journal of Historical Geography* 6, 2(Apr. 1980):115–31.

2. James T. Lemon, *The Best Poor Man's Country* (Baltimore, 1972), 6.

3. James T. Lemon, "Household Consumption in Eighteenth-Century America and Its Relationship to Production and Trade: The Situation Among Farmers in Southeastern Pennsylvania," *Agricultural History* 41, 1(Jan. 1967):59–70.

4. James A. Henretta, "Families and Farms: *Mentalité* in Pre-Industrial America," *William and Mary Quarterly,* 3d ser., 35, 1(Jan. 1978):3–32; Lemon, *The Best Poor Man's Coun-*

try, 180; Clarence H. Danhof, "The Farm Enterprise: The Northern United States, 1820–1860s," *Research in Economic History* 4(1979):127–91, especially 131.

5. Lemon, "Comment"; Lemon, "Early Americans."

6. Alexis de Tocqueville, *Democracy in America* (New York, 1948), 2:136.

7. The 1820 figures are from Clarence H. Danhof, *Change in Agriculture: The Northern United States, 1820–1870* (Cambridge, Mass., 1969), 10. Figures for 1860 are from U.S. Department of Commerce, *Historical Statistics of the United States from Colonial Times to 1970* (Washington, D.C., 1975), Series A202–203. The figures for 1820 were 5.732 million total northern population, of which 0.589 million were urban, 4.081 million were farm, and 1.062 million were rural nonfarm. In 1860, population was 20.560 million, of which 5.374 million were classified as urban, 9.000 million as farm, and 6.186 million as rural nonfarm.

8. In the sample overall, 45.5 percent of households and 40.7 percent of the population residing in the townships did not have farms.

9. Rothenberg, "The Market," especially 291.

10. Alexander Campbell, *A Glance at Illinois* (La Salle, Ill., 1856).

11. New York State Agricultural Society, *Transactions* 12(1852):29. Cited by Danhof, *Change*, 16.

12. Ibid., 29. Cited by Danhof, *Change*, 21.

13. Douglass C. North, *The Economic Growth of the United States, 1790–1860* (Englewood Cliffs, N.J., 1961). The traditional version of North's thesis is given by Guy S. Callender, "The Early Transportation and Banking Enterprises of the States in Relation to the Growth of Corporations," *Quarterly Journal of Economics* 17(Nov. 1902):111–62; Louis B. Schmidt, "Internal Commerce and the Development of a National Economy Before 1860," *Journal of Political Economy* 47, 6(Dec. 1939):799–822.

14. Albert Fishlow, "Antebellum Interregional Trade Reconsidered," *American Economic Review* 54, 2(May 1961):352–64.

15. Diane Lindstrom, "Southern Dependence Upon Interregional Grain Supplies: A Review of the Trade Flows," *Agricultural History* 44, 1(Jan. 1970):101–14; Lawrence A. Herbst, "Interregional Commodity Trade from the North to the South, and American Economic Development in the Antebellum Period," *Journal of Economic History* 35, 2(Mar. 1975):264–70.

16. Robert E. Gallman, "Self-Sufficiency of the Cotton Economy of the Antebellum South," *Agricultural History* 44, 1(Jan. 1970):5–24; Raymond C. Battalio and John Kagel, "The Structure of Antebellum Southern Agriculture: South Carolina, A Case Study," *Agricultural History* 44, 1(Jan. 1970):25–37. See also Donald L. Kemmerer, "The Pre-Civil War South's Leading Crop, Corn," *Agricultural History* 23, 4(Oct. 1949):236–39.

17. William K. Hutchinson and Samuel H. Williamson, "The Self-Sufficiency of the Antebellum South: Estimates of the Food Supply," *Journal of Economic History* 31, 3(Sept. 1971):591–609.

18. Colleen M. Callahan and William K. Hutchinson, "Antebellum Interregional Trade in Agricultural Goods: Preliminary Results," *Journal of Economic History* 40, 2(Mar. 1980):25–31.

19. See Lemon, "Household Consumption," 60.

20. Rolla M. Tryon, *Household Manufacturers in the United States, 1640–1860* (Chicago, 1917), 376.

21. See, for example, *Plough, Loom and Anvil* 8(1858):438. Farms in Maryland reported the highest average value of home manufactures among the northeastern sample states, $5.12 per farm, compared with $4.34 in New York state and $3.25 in Pennsylvania. No home manufacturing was reported by sample farms in Connecticut or New Jersey.

22. Tryon, *Household Manufacturers.*

23. Fred Bateman and Thomas Weiss, *A Deplorable Scarcity* (Chapel Hill, 1981), 95–98.

24. Victor Clark, *History of Manufacturers in the United States* (New York, 1929), 1:318.

25. Farmers in the Far West produced 5 million and 1.5 million pounds of each, worth about $0.9 million.

26. U.S Department of Agriculture, *Report of the Commissioners of Agriculture for 1865* (Washington, D.C., 1866), 448. For an excellent description of most aspects of butter factories as they existed during the late 1860s, including the so-called associated dairy system,

see X. A. Willard, *A Treatise on American Butter Factories and Butter Manufacture* (Madison, 1871).

27. One dairy writer, T. R. Pirtle, indicates that the output of farm butter increased until about 1900. Farm cheese production, however, began to decline during the 1860s. See T. R. Pirtle, "Trend of the Butter Industry in the United States and Other Countries," in U.S. Department of Agriculture, *Circular 70* (Washington, D.C., 1919), especially 3–4. The income generated for farmers is discussed in Chaps. 9, 13, and 14.

28. Richard O. Cummings, *The American and His Food* (Chicago, 1940), 236.

29. Edgar W. Martin, *The Standard of Living in 1860* (Chicago, 1942), 45. According to U.S. Department of Commerce, *Historical Statistics,* Series G881, this level of meat consumption per capita was not exceeded until 1970.

30. See Martin, *The Standard of Living,* 50, for references to northern fisheries.

31. Merrill K. Bennett and Rosamond H. Peirce, "Changes in the American National Diet, 1879–1959," *Food Research Institute Studies* 2, 2(May 1961):95–119, especially 116–17.

32. J. V. G. A. Durbin and R. Passmore, *Energy, Work and Leisure* (London, 1967), 47. For moderate work loads they give a calorie consumption rate of 5–7.4 kcal/min/65kg, and 7.5–9.9 kcal/min/65kg for heavy work.

33. Lemon, "Household Consumption," Table 1, p. 62. Average 13.2 bushels of grain, with a mode of 12 bushels. Twelve bushels of wheat would yield about 500 pounds of flour. One cow would yield about 35 pounds of butter during the seven-month milking season. In meat, grains, and butter, these allotments would provide 3,500 calories a day.

34. Sarah F. McMahon, " 'Provisions Laid Up for the Family' Towards a History of Diet in New England, 1650–1850" (Brandeis Univ. paper, February 1980, mimeo.), especially Tables 3-B, 7, 9, 11, and 15. Indian corn and rye were substituted for in the Massachusetts diet. This is consistent with Cummings's observation. See Cummings, *American and His Food,* 14–15.

35. See Frederick Law Olmstead, *A Journey in the Seaboard Slave States* (New York, 1856), 698; Robert W. Fogel and Stanley L. Engerman, *Time on the Cross* (Boston, 1974), 1:109–15; Richard Sutch, "Care and Feeding of Slaves," in *Reckoning with Slavery,* ed. Paul A. David et al. (New York, 1976), especially 265–81.

36. Battalio and Kagel, "Antebellum Southern Agriculture," 30.

37. Fluid milk estimates are from Fred Bateman, "Dairy Production, Yields, and Income: New Evidence on Distribution by Size of Farm in the Antebellum North," (Indiana Univ. paper, 1976, mimeo.), Table 2, with allowance for reported butter and cheese production, and Fred Bateman, "The 'Marketable Surplus' in Northern Dairy Farming: New Evidence by Size of Farm," *Agricultural History* 52, 3(July 1978):345–63. Twenty-two pounds of milk was allowed per pound of butter and 10 pounds of milk for each pound of cheese. Meat estimates were obtained by dividing the reported value of livestock slaughtered by the average price per pound of undressed meat ($0.04) and multiplying by 0.76, this being the ratio of dressed carcass weight to live weight. See U.S.Department of Agriculture, "Conversion Factors and Weights and Measures for Agricultural Commodities and Their Products," *Statistical Bulletin 362* (Washington, D.C., 1965), and Gallman, "Self-Sufficiency," 18–19. All grains and root crops were converted to corn equivalents at the conversion rates given by Morrison. Potatoes were converted to corn at their calorie value. We allow corn equivalents to be substituted for some of the meat in the diet by assuming that the corn to hog conversion rate of 10 bushels of corn to 76 pounds of meat is reversible. See F. B. Morrison, *Feed and Feeding,* 20th ed. (Ithaca, N.Y., 1936). Battalio and Kagel allowed 4 bushels of sweet potatoes to 1 of corn; oats at 2:1; wheat, 1.3:1; rye, 2:1. See Battalio and Kagel, "Antebellum Southern Agriculture," 28. Henry and Wallace both give a conversion rate of 10 bushels of corn per 100 pounds of live-weight hog. Dressed to live-weight ratio is given by Gallman and the USDA. See W. A. Henry, *Feeds and Feeding* (Madison, Wis., 1901); Henry A. Wallace, *Agricultural Prices* (Des Moines, 1920), 30; Robert E. Gallman, "Self-Sufficiency," 15; U.S. Department of Agriculture, "Conversion Factors," 5–13. Also see United Nations Food and Agriculture Organization, *Technical Conversion Factors for Agricultural Commodities* (Rome, 1960), 315–30, for rates in less developed countries that may be comparable with nineteenth-century American rates. U.S. Department of Commerce, Bureau of Labor, *Eighteenth Annual Report of the Commissioner of Labor. 1903. Cost of Living and Retail Prices of Food*

(Washington, D.C., 1904), 102, provides adult equivalent consumption rates by age and sex. Males over 14 = 100%; females over 14 = 90%; children, 11–14 = 90%; children, 7–10 = 75%; children, 4–6 = 40%; and children under 4 = 15%.

38. Fogel and Engerman, *Time on the Cross,* 2:97.

39. Paul W. Gates, *The Farmer's Age: Agriculture 1815-1860* (New York, 1960), 201.

40. Except for the hog feed, these are the same as used in Fred Bateman and Jeremy Atack, "The Profitability of Northern Agriculture in 1860," *Research in Economic History* 4(1979):87–125, especially 110–14. We have drastically raised our hog feeding standard from 4 bushels based on a rereading of the commissioner of patents reports and the apparent sensitivity of an estimate to the magnitude of this item, particularly for East-West comparisons.

41. See Bateman, "Improvement."

42. New York State Agricultural Society, *Transactions* 5(1845):59, quoted in Percy W. Bidwell and J. I. Falconer, *History of Agriculture in the Northern United States, 1620–1860* (reprinted New York, 1941), 427.

43. U.S. Patent Office, *Report of the Commissioner of Patents, 1855. Part II, Agriculture* (Washington, D.C., 1857), 22–23, 24.

44. Ibid., 12, 13.

45. Bidwell and Falconer, *History of Agriculture,* 392.

46. U.S. Patent Office, *Report, 1854. Part II, Agriculture,* 57.

47. See, for example, Ezra Seaman, *Essays on the Progress of Nations* (Detroit, 1846. New ed. 1852), 353; U.S. Census Office, Eighth Census, *Agriculture of the United States in 1860* (Washington, D.C., 1864), cxxvi; U.S. Patent Office, *Report, 1853. Part II, Agriculture,* 50–51; *Report, 1855,* 61, etc.

48. U.S. Patent Office, *Report, 1853. Part II, Agriculture,* 51–58; *Report, 1855. Part II, Agriculture,* 61, etc.; Thomas S. Berry, *Western Prices Before 1861* (Cambridge, Mass., 1943), 230–31. See also Callahan and Hutchinson, "Antebellum Regional Trade," 30.

49. U.S. Patent Office, *Report, 1852. Part II, Agriculture,* 137; U.S. Patent Office, *Report, 1855. Part II, Agriculture,* 51; U.S. Patent Office, *Report, 1850. Part II, Agriculture,* 473.

50. Most of the cost estimates are those for raising to age 3 at a cost of from $30 to $60 or more and include feed, labor, and all other related expenses. We assume, like Battalio and Kagel, that these nonfeed expenses just compensated for the lower feed requirement during the first year of life.

51. Battalio and Kagel, "Antebellum Southern Agriculture," 29–30.

52. The allocation of two-thirds the horse diet for mules and oxen is based on the lower body weight of mules and the contemporary assertions that oxen required less feed than horses.

53. U.S. Census Office, Twelfth Census, *Agriculture, Part I. Farms, Livestock and Animal Products* (Washington, D.C., 1902).

54. In addition to the corn equivalent rations discussed above, we allowed half a ton of hay per horse, mule, ox, milk cow, and steer, and 100 pounds of hay per sheep.

55. Credit for the first solution is usually given to L. V. Kantorovitch in 1939, though it was also developed independently by George B. Dantzig, who published in 1947.

56. Henry, *Feeds.*

57. Morrison, *Feed.*

58. Chicago Board of Trade, *Third Annual Report.*

59. See, for example, W. P. Mortenson, H. H. Erdman, and J. H. Draxler, "Wisconsin Farm Prices–1841 to 1933," *Agricultural Experiment Station of the University of Wisconsin Research Bulletin 119* (Nov. 1933); F. Strauss and L. H. Bean, "Gross Farm Income and Indices of Farm Production and Prices in the United States 1869–1937," *USDA Technical Bulletin 703* (Washington, D.C., 1940); and M. W. Towne and W. D. Rasmussen, "Gross Farm Product and Gross Investment in the Nineteenth Century," in *Trends in the American Economy of the Nineteenth Century,* Studies in Income and Wealth 24, (Princeton, 1960), 255–312.

60. U.S. Patent Office, *Annual Reports, 1844–56. Part II, Agriculture.*

61. Jeremy Atack and Fred Bateman, "Mid-Nineteenth Century Crop Yields and Labor

Productivity Growth in American Agriculture," in *Technique, Spirit, and Form in the Making of the Modern Economies: Essays in Honor of William N. Parker,* eds. Gary Saxenhouse and Gavin Wright, *Research in Economic History,* suppl. 3(1985):215–42.

62. See Bateman and Atack, "Profitability."

63. Bateman, "Dairy Production."

CHAPTER THIRTEEN

1. See Table 12.5.

2. This is, of course, the conclusion of other studies such as Colleen Callahan and William K. Hutchinson, "Antebellum Interregional Trade in Agricultural Goods: Preliminary Results," *Journal of Economic History* 40, 1(Mar. 1980):25–31.

3. See, for example, Albert Fishlow, *American Railroads and the Transformation of the Ante-Bellum Economy* (Cambridge, Mass., 1965), 163–204; Douglass C. North, *The Economic Growth of the United States, 1790–1860* (Englewood Cliffs, N.J., 1961), 146–53.

4. Paul W. Gates, *The Farmer's Age: Agriculture 1815–1860* (New York, 1960), 159–63.

5. F. Strauss and L. H. Bean, "Gross Farm Income and Indices of Farm Production and Prices in the United States 1869–1937," *USDA Technical Bulletin 703* (Washington, D.C., 1940).

6. See data on prices contained in text above. The range of quoted prices per pound was $0.053 in Illinois; $0.04 in Indiana; $0.061 in Wisconsin; $0.077 in New York.

7. Merrill K. Bennett and Rosamond H. Peirce. "Changes in the American National Diet, 1879–1959," *Food Research Institute Studies* 2, 2(May 1961):95–119.

8. U.S. Census Office, Twelfth Census, *Agriculture, Part I. Farms, Livestock and Animal Products* (Washington, D.C., 1902), 372–89.

9. Strauss and Bean, "Gross Farm Income."

10. Fred Bateman, "The 'Marketable Surplus' in Northern Dairy Farming: New Evidence by Size of Farm in 1860," *Agricultural History* 52, 3(July 1978):345–63; Strauss and Bean, "Gross Farm Income"; E. P. Vial, "Production and Consumption of Dairy Products," *USDA Technical Bulletin 722* (Washington, D.C., 1940).

11. U.S. Census Office, Tenth Census, *Report upon the Statistics of Agriculture Compiled from Returns Received at the Tenth Census* (Washington, D.C., 1883).

12. Robert E. Gallman, "Commodity Output, 1839–1899," in *Trends in the American Economy in the Nineteenth Century,* Studies in Income and Wealth 24, (Princeton, 1960); M. W. Towne and W. D. Rasmussen, "Gross Farm Product and Gross Investment in the Nineteenth Century," in *Trends in the American Economy,* 255–312.

13. U.S. Census Office, Tenth Census, *Report upon the Statistics of Agriculture.*

14. See data on prices cited below, especially those for Illinois, New York, and Wisconsin. The range of quoted prices for one dozen eggs was: Illinois, $0.08; New York, $0.15; Wisconsin, $0.103.

15. Illinois: L. J. Norton and B. B. Wilson, "Prices of Illinois Farm Products from 1866 to 1929," *University of Illinois Agricultural Experiment Station, Urbana, Bulletin 351* (July 1930); Indiana: Howard J. Houk, "A Century of Indiana Farm Prices, 1841–1941," *Purdue University Agricultural Experiment Station Bulletin 476* (Jan. 1943); Iowa: Norman V. Strand, "Prices of Farm Products in Iowa, 1851–1940," *Iowa State College Agricultural Experiment Station Research Bulletin 303* (May 1942); Maryland: R. F. Hale, "Price Paid Producers for Maryland Farm Products, 1851–1927," *University of Maryland Agricultural Experiment Station Bulletin 321* (Sept. 1930); New York: S. E. Ronk, "Prices of Farm Products in New York State, 1841 to 1935," *Cornell University Agricultural Experiment Station Bulletin 643* (Mar. 1936); Wisconsin: W. P. Mortenson, H. H. Erdman, and J. H. Draxler, "Wisconsin Farm Prices–1841 to 1933," *Agricultural Experiment Station of the University of Wisconsin Research Bulletin 119* (Nov. 1933).

16. The Indiana figures are the monthly averages of Friday prices. See Houk, "Indiana Farm Prices."

17. Chicago Board of Trade, *Annual Statement of the Trade and Commerce of Chicago for the Year Ending . . .* (Chicago, 1860, 1861).

18. Milwaukee Chamber of Commerce, *Second Annual Statement of the Trade, Commerce and General Business of the City of Milwaukee for the Year 1859* (Milwaukee, 1860).

19. New York State Chamber of Commerce, *Annual Report of the Chamber of Commerce of the State of New York for the Year 1859–60* (New York, 1860).

20. Winifred C. Rothenberg, "A Price Index for Rural Massachusetts, 1750–1855," *Journal of Economic History* 39, 4(Dec. 1980):975–1001.

21. Thomas S. Berry, *Western Prices Before 1861* (Cambridge, Mass., 1943).

22. The Warren and Pearson price index for farm products is 95 in 1859 (1900–1914 = 100), 92 in 1860, and 89 in 1861. See U.S. Department of Commerce, *Historical Statistics of the United States from Colonial Times to 1970* (Washington D.C., 1975), Series 52.

23. Anne Bezanson, *Wholesale Prices in Philadelphia, 1852–1896* (Philadelphia, 1954).

24. Samples gathered by Fred Bateman and Thomas Weiss from the manuscripts of the United States Census, 1850–1870, under National Science Foundation sponsorship. For elaboration on these samples, see Fred Bateman and Thomas Weiss, *A Deplorable Scarcity* (Chapel Hill, 1981).

25. F. Strauss and Bean, "Gross Farm Income."

26. U.S. Census Office, Eighth Census, *Agriculture of the United States in 1860* (Washington, D.C., 1864).

27. Ibid.

28. Gates, *The Farmer's Age,* 398–99.

29. Towne and Rasmussen, "Gross Farm Product."

30. U.S. Census Office, Fifteenth Census, *Agriculture, Volume II, Part I—The Northern States* (Washington, D.C., 1932).

31. U.S. Census Office, Tenth Census, *Report on the Statistics of Wages . . . , supplement to the Tenth Census,* vol. 20 (Washington, D.C., 1886).

32. In the Midwest, only tenant farmers in Minnesota earned less than those in Missouri. No yeoman farms averaged less in the region. In the East, Maryland tenants earned the least by a considerable margin.

33. There were 1,366,340 farms in the region and we assume that 83.6 percent were operated by owner-occupiers.

34. The increase in farm size from 61–80 to 121–160 acres produced a gain of 55 percent.

35. That is, we assume an average seven-year life expectancy on farm implements and machinery. Some, such as wagons, probably served longer; others, such as reapers, may have served less.

36. See Gates, *The Farmer's Age,* 97. See also Allan G. Bogue, *From Prairie to Corn Belt: Farming on the Illinois and Iowa Prairies in the Nineteenth Century* (Chicago, 1963), 61.

37. Massachusetts Bureau of Statistics of Labor, *Sixteenth Annual Report* (Boston, 1885).

38. U.S. Department of Agriculture, "Wages of Farm Labor in the United States," *Division of Statistics, Miscellaneous Series Report 4* (Washington, D.C., 1892).

39. U.S. Census Office, Eighth Census, *Statistics of the United States in 1860* (Washington, D.C., 1866), 512.

40. Ibid.

41. U.S. Department of Agriculture, "Wages of Farm Labor."

42. Ibid.; U. S. Department of Agriculture, Bureau of Agricultural Economics, *Farm Wage Rates, Farm Employment and Related Data* (Washington, D.C., 1943).

43. U.S. Department of Agriculture, *Farm Wage Rates.*

44. U.S. Department of Agriculture, "Wages of Farm Labor"; Luther Huston, "Business Records and Account Ledger, 1845–1861," MSS, Illinois Historical Survey of the University of Illinois Library, Urbana.

45. Raymond C. Battalio and John Kagel, "The Structure of Antebellum Southern Agriculture: South Carolina, a Case Study," *Agricultural History* 44, 1(Jan. 1970):25–37; Alfred H. Conrad and John R. Meyer, "The Economics of Slavery in the Antebellum South," *Journal of Political Economy* 66, 2(Apr. 1958):95–122.

46. Hinton R. Helper, *The Impending Crisis in the South* (New York, 1860), 377.

47. See J. E. Cairnes, *The Slave Power* (Cambridge and London, 1863); Helper, *Impend-*

ing Crisis; Frederick Law Olmstead, *A Journey in the Seaboard Slave States* (New York, 1856).

48. See, for example, Frank L. Owsley, *Plain Folk of the Old South* (Baton Rouge, 1949); Herbert Weaver, *Mississippi Farmers, 1850–1860* (Nashville, 1945); and Blanche Henry Clark, *The Tennessee Yeomen, 1840–1860* (Nashville, 1942).

49. See Robert W. Fogel and Stanley L. Engerman, *Time on the Cross* (Boston, 1974), 1:248, 2:App. B, 162–63, for their estimates and a discussion of methodology. Their comparable estimates were $141 for the North, $181 in the Northeast, and $89 in the Midwest. The underlying data were from Richard A. Easterlin, "Interregional Differences in Per Capita Income, Population, and Total Income, 1840–1950," in Conference on Research in Income and Wealth, *Trends in the American Economy in the Nineteenth Century,* 73–140; also Richard A. Easterlin, "Regional Income Trends, 1840–1950," in *American Economic History,* ed. Seymour Harris (New York, 1961), 525–47; Robert E. Gallman, "Gross National Product in the United States, 1834–1909," in Conference on Research in Income and Wealth, *Output, Employment, and Productivity in the United States After 1800,* Studies in Income and Wealth 30 (New York, 1966), 3–76.

50. See, for example, Paul A. David, "The Growth of Real Product in the United States Before 1840: New Evidence, Controlled Conjectures," *Journal of Economic History* 27, 2(July 1967):151–97.

CHAPTER FOURTEEN

1. For example, on southern agriculture, see Alfred H. Conrad and John R. Meyer, "The Economics of Slavery in the Antebellum South," *Journal of Political Economy* 66, 2(Apr. 1958):95–122; Robert J. Evans, "The Economics of American Negro Slavery," in *Aspects of Labor Economics* (Princeton, 1962), 185–243; Richard Vedder, David Klingaman, and Lowell Gallaway, "The Profitability of Ante-Bellum Agriculture in the Cotton Belt: Some New Evidence," *Atlantic Economic Journal* 2, 2(1974):30–47; Richard Vedder and David Stockdale, "The Profitability of Slavery Revisited: A Different Approach," *Agricultural History* 49, 2(Apr. 1975):392–404; Robert W. Fogel and Stanley L. Engerman, *Time on the Cross,* 2 vols. (Boston, 1974); on manufacturing, Fred Bateman, James Foust, and Thomas Weiss, "Profitability in Southern Manufacturing: Estimates for 1860," *Explorations in Economic History* 12, 3(1975):211–31; Fred Bateman and Thomas Weiss, "Manufacturing in the Antebellum South," *Research in Economic History* 1(1976):1–44; Fred Bateman and Thomas Weiss, *A Deplorable Scarcity* (Chapel Hill, 1981); on transportation, Lloyd J. Mercer, "Rates of Return for Land Grant Railroads: the Central Pacific System," *Journal of Economic History* 30, 3(Sept. 1970):602–26; Jeremy Atack, Erik F. Haites, James Mak, and Gary Walton, "The Profitability of Steamboating on the Western Rivers: 1850," *Business History Review* 49, 3(1975):346–54.

2. These estimates revise our earlier, preliminary ones presented in Fred Bateman and Jeremy Atack, "The Profitability of Northern Agriculture in 1860," *Research in Economic History* 4(1979):87–125.

3. See, for example, Paul W. Gates, *The Farmer's Age: Agriculture 1815–1860* (New York, 1960), 399–400.

4. Frederick Gerhard, *Illinois as It Is* (Chicago, 1856), 293–94.

5. Ibid., 295.

6. Minnesota Commissioner of Statistics, *Minnesota: Its Place Among the States Being the First Annual Report of the Commissioner of Statistics for the Year Ending January 1st, 1860,* (Hartford, 1860), 85–87.

7. Ibid.

8. See Conrad and Meyer, "The Economics of Slavery"; Evans, "The Economics of American Negro Slavery"; Vedder, Klingaman, and Galloway, "The Profitability of Ante-Bellum Agriculture"; Vedder and Stockdale, "The Profitability of Slavery Revisited"; Fogel and Engerman, *Time on the Cross.*

9. Two reasons largely account for this result. First, although gross farm income in both states was lower than elsewhere, income was further reduced by the large off-the-farm agricultural labor force. Despite (or maybe because of) the existence of slaves, these com-

munities generally had more wage labor per improved acre than most others. Net income was therefore driven down, but at the same time the inclusion of slaves in the denominator of the profit expression reduced the rate for any given level of net revenue.

10. See Frederick R. Macaulay, *Some Theoretical Problems Suggested by the Movement of Interest Rates, Bond Yields and Stock Prices in the United States Since 1856* (New York, 1938).

11. Fogel and Engerman, *Time on the Cross,* 1:76, Fig. 18.

12. The western- and northern-most townships in the Midwest were excluded. They were Pottawatomie County in Iowa on the Nebraska border; Chase, Morris, and Nemeha counties in Kansas; Cheboygan, Emmett, and Huron counties of Michigan in the northern half of the Lower Peninsula; Cottonwood, Mahnomen, Murray, Polk, Renville, and St. Louis counties in northern and western Minnesota; and Douglas County, Wisconsin, at the northern tip of Lake Superior. See Fig. 2.2 for the locations.

13. Quoted by Gates, *The Farmer's Age*, 403.

14. Lewis D. Stilwell, "Migration from Vermont, 1776–1860," *Proceedings of the Vermont Historical Society* 5(1937):232.

15. Gates, *The Farmer's Age*, 399.

16. Theordore Saloutos, "The Agricultural Problem and Nineteenth-Century Industrialism," *Agricultural History* 22, 3(1948):156.

17. Ibid., 159.

18. *Report from the Secretary of the Treasury, on the State of the Finances, December 3, 1845,* 29th Cong., 1st sess., 1846, Sen. Doc. 2, ser. 1, pp. 12, 245–46, 249, 339. Also see Saloutos, "The Agricultural Problem."

19. Saloutos, "The Agricultural Problem,", 161, 162, 163.

20. Bateman and Weiss, *A Deplorable Scarcity,* 143–56.

21. Clarence H. Danhof, *Change in Agriculture: The Northern United States, 1820–1870* (Cambridge, Mass., 1969), 104.

22. Harold Barger and Hans Landsberg, *American Agriculture 1899–1939* (New York, 1942), 6.

CHAPTER FIFTEEN

1. Richard Hofstadter, "The Myth of the Happy Yeoman," in *A Treasury of American Heritage* (New York, 1960), 264.

2. Ibid.

BIBLIOGRAPHY

Anderson, J. "On the Management of the Dairy." *American Farmer* 1, 18(30 July 1819):1.

Ando, A., and Franco Modigliani. "The Life Cycle Hypothesis of Saving: Aggregate Implications and Tests." *American Economic Review* 53, 1(Mar. 1963):55–84.

Ankli, Robert E. "Gross Farm Revenues in Pre-Civil War Illinois." Ph.D. diss., Univ. of Illinois, 1969.

______. "Farm-Making Costs in the 1850's." *Agricultural History* 48, 1(Jan. 1974):51–70.

______. "The Coming of the Reaper." In *Business and Economic History: Papers Presented at the Twenty-Second Annual Meeting of the Business History Conference*, ed. Paul A. Uselding. Urbana: Univ. of Illinois, 1976, 1–24.

Atack, Jeremy. "Farm and Farm-Making Costs Revisited." *Agricultural History* 56, 3(Oct. 1982):663–76.

Atack, Jeremy, and Fred Bateman. "The Measurement and Trend of Inequality: An Amendment to a Basic Revision." *Economic Letters* 4(Oct. 1979):389–93.

______. "The 'Egalitarian Ideal' and the Distribution of Wealth in the Northern Agricultural Community: A Backward Look." *Review of Economics and Statistics* 63, 1(Feb. 1981):124–29.

______. "Self-Sufficiency and the Marketable Surplus in the Rural North, 1860." *Agricultural History* 58, 3(July 1984):296–313.

______. "Mid-Nineteenth Century Crop Yields and Labor Productivity Growth in American Agriculture." In *Technique, Spirit and Form in the Making of the Modern Economies: Essays in Honor of William N. Parker*, ed. Gary Saxenhouse and Gavin Wright. *Research in Economic History,* suppl. 3(1984): 215–42.

______. "Marketable Farm Surpluses: Northeastern and Midwestern United States, 1859 and 1860." *Social Science History* 8, 4(Fall 1984):371–93.

Atack, Jeremy, Erik F. Haites, James Mak, and Gary Walton. "The Profitability of Steamboating on the Western Rivers: 1850." *Business History Review* 49, 3(1975):346–54.

Barger, Hal, and Hans Lundsberg. *American Agriculture 1899–1939.* New York: NBER, 1942.

For a bibliographic essay on research in the area of northern agriculture, the reader should consult Fred Bateman, "Research Developments in American Agricultural History Since 1960: The Northern Farm Economy," *Agricultural History Review* 31, 2(1983):132–48. This piece also references the many additional bibliographies available.

Bateman, Fred. "Improvement in American Dairy Farming 1850–1910: A Quantitative Analysis." *Journal of Economic History* 28, 2(June 1968):255–73.

______. "Labor Inputs and Productivity in American Dairy Agriculture, 1850–1910." *Journal of Economic History* 29, 2(June 1969):206–29.

______. "Dairy Production, Yields, and Income: New Evidence on Distribution by Size of Farm in the Antebellum North." Indiana Univ. paper, 1976. Mimeo.

______. "The 'Marketable Surplus' in Northern Dairy Farming: New Evidence by Size of Farm." *Agricultural History* 52, 3(July 1978):345–63.

Bateman, Fred, and Jeremy Atack. "The Profitability of Northern Agriculture in 1860." *Research in Economic History* 4(1979):87–125.

Bateman, Fred, and James Foust. *Agricultural and Demographic Records of 21,118 Rural Households Selected from the 1860 Manuscript Censuses.* Indiana Univ. data tape, 1973.

______. "A Sample of Rural Households Selected from the 1860 Manuscript Censuses." *Agricultural History* 48, 1(Jan. 1974):75–93.

Bateman, Fred, and Thomas Weiss. "Manufacturing in the Antebellum South." *Research in Economic History* 1(1976):1–44.

______. *A Deplorable Scarcity.* Chapel Hill: Univ. of North Carolina Press, 1981.

Bateman, Fred, James Foust, and Thomas Weiss. "Profitability in Southern Manufacturing: Estimates for 1860." *Explorations in Economic History* 12, 3(1975):211–31.

Battalio, Raymond C., and John Kagel. "The Structure of Antebellum Southern Agriculture: South Carolina, a Case Study." *Agricultural History* 44, 1(Jan. 1970):25–37.

Bennett, Merrill K., and Rosamond H. Peirce. "Changes in the American National Diet, 1879–1959." *Food Research Institute Studies* 2, 2(May 1961):95–119.

Berry, Thomas S. *Western Prices Before 1861.* Cambridge: Harvard Univ. Press, 1943.

Bezanson, Anne. *Wholesale Prices in Philadelphia, 1852–1896.* Philadelphia: Univ. of Pennsylvania Press, 1954.

Bidwell, Percy W., and John I. Falconer. *History of Agriculture in the Northern United States 1620–1860.* Washington, D.C.: Carnegie Institution, 1925.

Billington, Ray H. *Westward Expansion: A History of the American Frontier.* New York: Macmillan, 1967.

Blinder, Alan S. "A Model of Inherited Wealth." *Quarterly Journal of Economics* 87, 4(Nov. 1973):608–26.

Bogue, Allan G. *From Prairie to Corn Belt: Farming on the Illinois and Iowa Prairies in the Nineteenth Century.* Chicago: Univ. of Chicago Press, 1963.

Boserup, Ester. *The Conditions of Agricultural Growth.* London: George Allen & Unwin, 1965.

______. *Population and Technological Change.* Chicago: Univ. of Chicago Press, 1981.

Brittain, John A. *Inheritance and the Inequality of Material Wealth.* Washington, D.C.: Brookings Institution, 1978.

Brunger, Eric. "Dairying and Urban Development in New York State, 1850–1900." *Agricultural History* 29, 4(Oct. 1955):169–74.

Caird, James. *Prairie Farming in America.* London: Longman, Brown, Green, Longman, and Roberts, 1859.

Cairnes, J. E. *The Slave Power.* 2d ed. London and Cambridge: Macmillan, 1863.

Callahan, Colleen, and William K. Hutchinson. "Antebellum Interregional Trade in Agricultural Goods: Preliminary Results." *Journal of Economic History* 40, 1(Mar. 1980):25–31.

Callender, Guy S. "The Early Transportation and Banking Enterprises of the States in Relation to the Growth of the Corporation." *Quarterly Journal of Economics* 17(Nov. 1902):111–62.

Campbell, Alexander. *A Glance at Illinois.* La Salle, Ill.: C. Boynton, 1856.

Campbell, Randolph B., and Richard G. Lowe. *Wealth and Power in Antebellum Texas.* College Station: Texas A&M Univ. Press, 1977.

Cassels, John M. *A Study of Fluid Milk Prices.* Cambridge: Harvard Univ. Press, 1937.

Chayanov, A. V. *The Theory of the Peasant Economy,* ed. D. Thorner, et al., Homewood, Ill.: Richard D. Irwin, 1966 (first published *Organizatsiia Krestianskogo Khozizstvo,* Moscow: Koop Izdatelstvo, 1925).

Chicago Board of Trade. *Annual Statement of Trade and Commerce of Chicago.* Chicago: various publishers, 1859, 1860, and 1861.

Clark, Blanche Henry. *The Tennessee Yeomen, 1840–1860.* Nashville: Vanderbilt Univ. Press, 1942.

Clark, Victor. *History of Manufactures in the United States.* 3 vols. New York: McGraw-Hill, 1929.

Collier, Peter. "How to Make Dairying More Profitable." Address delivered before the Holstein-Friesian Association of America, 5th Annual Meeting, New York, 19 March, 1890.

Collins, William H., and C. F. Perry. *Past and Present of the City of Quincy and Adams County.* Chicago: S. J. Clarke, 1905.

Connecticut Valley Farmer and Mechanic 1(1854).

Conrad, Alfred H., and John R. Meyer. "The Economics of Slavery in the Antebellum South." *Journal of Political Economy* 66, 2(Apr. 1958):95–122.

Country Gentleman (various issues).

Cummings, Richard O. *The American and His Food.* Chicago: Univ. of Chicago Press, 1940.

Cunynghame, A. *A Glimpse of the Great Western Republic.* London: Richard Bentley, 1851.

Curti, Merle. *The Making of an American Community: A Case Study of Democracy in a Frontier County.* Stanford: Stanford Univ. Press, 1959.

Danhof, Clarence H. "Farm-Making Costs and the 'Safety Valve': 1850–1860." *Journal of Political Economy* 49, 3(June 1941):317–59.

______. *Change in Agriculture: The Northern United States, 1820–1870.* Cambridge: Harvard Univ. Press, 1969.

______. "The Farm Enterprise: The Northern United States, 1820–1860s." *Research in Economic History* 4(1979):127–91.

Davenport, David P. "Population Persistence and Migration in Rural New York, 1853–1860." Ph.D. diss., Univ. of Illinois, 1982.

David, Paul A. "The Mechanization of Reaping in the Antebellum Midwest." In *Industrialization in Two Systems,* ed. H. Rosovsky. New York: John Wiley, 1966, 3–28.

______. "The Growth of Real Product in the United States Before 1840: New Evidence, Controlled Conjectures." *Journal of Economic History* 27, 2(July 1967):151–97.

Davis, Lance E., et al. *American Economic Growth.* New York: Harper & Row, 1972.

Dennen, R. Taylor. "Some Efficiency Effects of Nineteenth-Century Federal Land

Policy: A Dynamic Analysis." *Agricultural History* 51, 4(Oct. 1977):718–36.

Donne, Carmen R. Delle. "Federal Census Schedules, 1850–80: Primary Sources for Historical Research." National Archives and Record Service, *Reference Information Paper 67.* Washington, D.C.: General Services Administration, 1973.

Durbin, J. V. G. A., and R. Passmore. *Energy, Work and Leisure.* London: Heinemann Educational Books, 1967.

Easterlin, Richard A. "Interregional Differences in Per Capita Income, Population, and Total Income, 1840–1950." In Conference on Research in Income and Wealth, *Trends in the American Economy in the Nineteenth Century,* Studies in Income and Wealth 24. Princeton: Princeton Univ. Press (1960):73–140.

______. "Influences in European Overseas Emigration Before World War I." *Economic Development and Cultural Change* 9, 2(Apr. 1961):331–53.

______. "Regional Income Trends 1840–1950." In *American Economic History,* ed. Seymour Harris. New York: McGraw-Hill, 1961, 525–47.

______. "Population Change and Farm Settlement in the Northern United States." *Journal of Economic History* 37, 1(Mar. 1976):45–75.

______. "Factors in the Decline of Farm Family Fertility in the United States: Some Preliminary Research Results." *Journal of American History* 63, 3(Dec. 1976):600–14.

Easterlin, Richard A., George Alter, and Gretchen Condran. "Farm and Farm Families in Old and New Areas: The Northern States in 1860." In *Family and Population in Nineteenth Century America,* ed. Tamara Hareven and Maris Vinovskis. Princeton: Princeton Univ. Press, 1978, 22–84.

Elwood, Robert E., Arthur A. Lewis, and Ronald A. Strubel. "Changes in Technology and Labor Requirements in Livestock Production: Dairying." In *Works Progress Administration, National Research Project, WPA Report A-14.* Washington, D.C., June 1941.

Evans, Robert J. "The Economics of American Negro Slavery." In Universities–NBER, *Aspects of Labor Economics.* Princeton: Princeton Univ. Press, 1962, 185–243.

Ferenczi, Irme, and Walter Willcox. *International Migrations.* 2 vols. New York: NBER, 1929.

Fishlow, Albert. "Antebellum Interregional Trade Reconsidered." *American Economic Review* 54, 2(May 1961):352–64.

______. *American Railroads and the Transformation of the Antebellum Economy.* Cambridge: Harvard Univ. Press, 1965.

Flint, Charles L. *Milk Cows and Dairy Farming.* Boston: J. E. Tilton, 1871.

Fogel, Robert W., and Stanley L. Engerman. "The Relative Efficiency of Slavery: A Comparison of Northern and Southern Agriculture in 1860." *Explorations in Economic History* 8, 2(1971):353–67.

______. *Time on the Cross.* 2 vols. Boston: Little, Brown, 1974.

Fogel, Robert W., and Jack Rutner. "The Efficiency Effects of Federal Land Policy, 1850–1900: A Report of Some Provisional Findings." In *The Dimension of Quantitative Research in History,* ed. William O. Aydelotte. Princeton: Princeton Univ. Press, 1972, 390–418.

Formby, John P., and Terry G. Seaks. "Paglin's Gini Measure of Inequality: A Modification." *American Economic Review* 70, 2(June 1980):479–82.

Forster, C., and G. S. L. Tucker. *Economic Opportunity and White American Fertility Ratios 1800–1960.* New Haven: Yale Univ. Press, 1972.

Gallaway, Lowell E., and Richard K. Vedder. "The Increasing Urbanization Thesis – Did 'New Immigrants' to the United States Have a Peculiar Fondness for Urban Life?" *Explorations in Economic History* 8, 2(1971):305–20.

______. "Mobility of Native Americans." *Journal of Economic History* 31, 3(Sept. 1971):613–49.

______. "Emigration from the United Kingdom to the United States: 1860–1913." *Journal of Economic History* 31, 4(Dec. 1971):885–97.

Gallman, Robert E. "Commodity Output, 1839–1899." In Conference on Research in Income and Wealth, *Trends in the American Economy in the Nineteenth Century,* Studies in Income and Wealth 24. Princeton: Princeton Univ. Press, 1960, 13–67.

______. "Gross National Product in the United States, 1834–1909." In Conference on Research in Income and Wealth, *Output, Employment, and Productivity in the United States After 1800,* Studies in Income and Wealth 30. New York: Columbia Univ. Press, 1966, 3–76.

______. "Trends in the Size Distribution of Wealth in the Nineteenth Century: Some Speculations." In Conference on Research in Income and Wealth, *Six Papers on the Size Distribution of Wealth and Income,* ed. Lee Soltow. Studies in Income and Wealth 33. New York: Columbia Univ. Press, 1969, 1–25.

______. "Self-Sufficiency of the Cotton Economy of the Antebellum South." *Agricultural History* 44, 1(Jan. 1970):5–24.

______. "Changes in Total U.S. Agricultural Factor Productivity in the Nineteenth Century." *Agricultural History* 46, 1(Jan. 1972):191–210.

______. "Professor Pessen on the 'Egalitarian Myth.'" *Social Sciences History* 2, 2(1978):194–207 .

______. "The 'Egalitarian Myth,' Once Again." *Social Science History* 5, 2(1981):223–34.

______. "Investment Flows and Capital Stocks: U.S. Experience in the Nineteenth Century." In *Quantity and Quiddity: Essays in U.S. Economic History in Honor of Stanley L. Lebergott,* ed. Peter Kilby. Middletown, Conn.:Wesleyan Univ. Press, forthcoming.

Gates, Paul W. *The Illinois Central Railroad and Its Colonizing Work.* Harvard Economic Studies 42. Cambridge: Harvard Univ. Press, 1941.

______. *The Farmer's Age: Agriculture 1815-1860.* New York: Holt, Rinehart and Winston, 1960.

______. *History of Public Land Law Development.* Washington, D.C.: GPO, 1968.

Genovese, Eugene, ed. *Ulrich B. Phillips: The Slave Economy of the Old South.* Baton Rouge: Louisiana State Univ. Press, 1968.

Gerhard, Fred. *Illinois as It Is.* Chicago: Keen and Lee, 1857.

Ginter, Donald E. "A Critique of Landholding Variables in the 1860 Census and the Parker-Gallman Sample." Paper presented at the 95th Annual Meeting of the American Historical Association, Washington, D.C., December 28–30, 1980.

Gray, Lewis C. *History of Agriculture in the Southern United States to 1860.* Washington, D.C.: Carnegie Institution, 1933.

Greeley, Horace. *An Overland Journey from New York to San Francisco in the Summer of 1859.* New York: C. M. Saxton, Barker, 1860.

Hale, R. F. "Price Paid Producers for Maryland Farm Products, 1851–1927." *University of Maryland Agricultural Experiment Station Bulletin 321.* Sept. 1930.

Hansen, Marcus. *The Atlantic Migration, 1607-1860.* Cambridge: Harvard Univ. Press, 1940.

Helper, Hinton Rowan. *The Impending Crisis of the South.* New York: A. B. Burdick, 1860.

Henretta, James A. "Families and Farms: *Mentalité* in Pre-Industrial America." *William and Mary Quarterly,* 3d ser., 35, 1(Jan. 1978):3–32.

Henry, W. A. *Feeds and Feeding.* Madison, Wis.: by author, 1901.

Herbst, Lawrence A. "Interregional Commodity Trade from the North to the South and American Economic Development in the Antebellum Period." *Journal of Economic History* 35, 1(Mar. 1975):264–70.

Hibbard, Benjamin H. *A History of the Public Land Policies.* New York, 1924. Reprinted Madison: Univ. of Wisconsin Press, 1965.

Hofstader, Richard. "The Myth of the Happy Yeoman." In *A Treasury of American Heritage.* New York: Simon and Schuster, 1960.

Holbrook, S. H. *The Yankee Exodus: An Account of Migration from New England.* New York: Macmillan, 1950.

Homer, Sidney. *A History of Interest Rates.* New Brunswick, N.J.: Rutgers Univ. Press, 1963.

Hoover, Edgar M. "Interstate Redistribution of Population, 1850–1940." *Journal of Economic History* 1, 3(Nov. 1941):199–205.

Houk, Howard J. "A Century of Indiana Farm Prices, 1841–1941." *Purdue University Agricultural Experiment Station Bulletin 476.* Jan. 1943.

Hunt's Merchants' Magazine and Commercial Review (various issues).

Huston, Luther. "Business Records and Account Ledger, 1845–1861." MSS, Illinois Historical Survey of the University of Illinois Library, Urbana.

Hutchinson, William K., and Samuel H. Williamson. "The Self-Sufficiency of the Antebellum South: Estimate of the Food Supply." *Journal of Economic History* 31, 3(Sept. 1971):591–609.

Hutchinson, William T. *Cyrus H. McCormick.* 2 vols. New York: Century, 1930.

Illinois Agricultural Experiment Station. "Field Experiments with Corn." *Illinois Agricultural Experiment Station Bulletins 4, 8, 13, 20, 25, 31* (1889–1894).

Illinois Central Railroad Company. *The Illinois Central Railroad Company Offer for Sale over 2,400,000 Acres Selected Prairie, Farm and Woodland Tracts of Any Size . . . on Long Credits . . . Situated Each Side of their Railroad . . . from the Extreme North to the South of the State of Illinois.* New York: John W. Amerman, 1855.

The Illinois Farmer (various issues).

Illinois State Agricultural Society. *Transactions for 1856–57.* Vol. 2. Springfield: Lamphier and Walker, 1857.

Illinois State Auditor. *Biennial Report of the Auditor of Public Accounts of the State of Illinois to the Twenty-Third General Assembly.* Springfield: Baker and Phillips, 1863.

Iowa Agricultural Experiment Station. *Bulletin 243.* Ames: Iowa State Univ., 1928.

Iowa Census Board. *The Census Returns of the Different Counties of the State of Iowa for 1859.* Des Moines: John Teesdale, 1859.

Iowa Farmer and Horticulturalist 5(1857).

Jefferson, Thomas. *Notes on the state of Virginia; written in the year 1781, somewhat corrected and enlarged in the winter of 1782, for the use of a foreigner of distinction in answer to certain queries proposed by him . . . 1782.* Paris: printed 1784-85.

______. *The Writings of Thomas Jefferson.* 20 vols, ed. Andrew A. Lipscomb. Washington, D.C.: Thomas Jefferson Memorial Association of the United States, 1903.

Johnson, S. C. *Emigration from the United Kingdom to North America, 1763–1912.* London: Frank Cass, 1913.

Kemmerer, Donald L. "The Pre-Civil War South's Leading Crop, Corn." *Agricultural History* 23, 4(Oct. 1949):236–39.

Keyfitz, Nathan, and Wilhelm Flieger. *World Population: An Analysis of Vital Data.* Chicago: Univ. of Chicago Press, 1968.

Klein, Judith L. V. "Farm-Making Costs in the 1850's: A Comment." *Agricultural History* 48, 1(Jan. 1974):71–74.

Lampman, Robert S. *The Share of Top Wealth-Holders in National Wealth, 1922–1956.* New York: NBER, 1962.

Lane, C. S., and W. A. Stocking. "The Milking Machine as a Factor in Dairying: A Preliminary Report." U.S. Department of Agriculture, Bureau of Animal Industry, *Bulletin 92.* Washington, D.C.: GPO, 1907.

Lebergott, Stanley. *Manpower in Economic Growth.* New York: McGraw-Hill, 1964.

Lee, E. S., A. R. Miller, C. P. Brainerd, and R. A. Easterlin. *Population Redistribution and Economic Growth in the United States 1870–1950. Volume 1: Methodological Considerations and Reference Tables.* Philadelphia: American Philosophical Society, 1957.

Leet, Donald. "Human Fertility and Agricultural Opportunities in Ohio Counties: From Frontier to Maturity, 1810–60." In *Essays in Nineteenth Century Economic History,* ed. D. Klingaman and R. Vedder. Athens: Ohio Univ. Press, 1975, 138–58.

______. "The Determinants of the Fertility Transition in Antebellum Ohio." *Journal of Economic History* 36, 2(June 1976):359–78.

Lemon, James T. "Household Consumption in Eighteenth-Century America and Its Relationship to Production and Trade: The Situation Among Farmers in Southeastern Pennsylvania." *Agricultural History* 41, 1(Jan. 1967):59–70.

______. *The Best Poor Man's Country.* Baltimore: The Johns Hopkins Univ. Press, 1972.

______. "Early Americans and their Social Environment." *Journal of Historical Geography* 6, 2(Apr. 1980):115–31.

______. "Comment on James A. Henretta's 'Families and Farms: *Mentalité* in Pre-Industrial America.'" *William and Mary Quarterly,* 3d ser., 37, 4(Oct. 1980):688–96.

Linden, Fabien. "Economic Democracy in the Slave South: An Appraisal of Some Recent Views." *Journal of Negro History* 31, 2(Apr. 1946):140–89.

Lindert, Peter, and Jeffrey Williamson. "Three Centuries of American Inequality." *Research in Economic History* 1(1976):69–123.

Lindstrom, Diane. "Southern Dependence Upon Interregional Grain Supplies: A Review of the Trade Flows." *Agricultural History* 44, 1(Jan. 1970):101–14.

Loehr, Rodney. "Self-Sufficiency on the Farm." *Agricultural History* 26, 2(Apr. 1962):37–41.

Macaulay, Frederick R. *Some Theoretical Problems Suggested by the Movement of Interest Rates, Bond Yields and Stock Prices in the United States Since 1856.* New York: NBER, 1938.

McInnis, R. M. "Childbearing and Land Availability: Some Evidence from Individual Household Data." In *Population Patterns in the Past,* ed. Ronald Demos Lee. New York: Academic Press, 1977, 201–27.

McMahon, Sarah F. "'Provisions Laid Up for the Family' Towards a History of Diet in New England, 1650–1850." Brandeis Univ. paper, February 1980. Mimeo.

Main, Gloria. "Inequality in Early America: The Evidence of Probate Records from Massachusetts and Maryland." Paper presented to the Cliometrics Conference, Madison, Wisconsin, 1976. Mimeo.

Marshall, Josiah T. *The Farmer's and Emigrant's Hand-Book.* Boston: H. Wentworth, 1852.

Martin, Edgar W. *The Standard of Living in 1860.* Chicago: Univ. of Chicago Press, 1942.

Massachusetts Bureau of Statistics of Labor. *Sixteenth Annual Report.* Boston: Massachusetts Bureau of Labor, 1885.

Mercer, Lloyd J. "Rates of Return for Land Grant Railroads: The Central Pacific System." *Journal of Economic History* 30, 3(Sept. 1970):602–26.

Michigan Farmer 8(1850).

Milwaukee Chamber of Commerce. *Second Annual Statement of the Trade, Commerce and General Business of the City of Milwaukee for the Year 1859.* Milwaukee: Crouse and Thomson, 1860.

Minnesota Commissioner of Statistics. *Minnesota: Its Place Among the States Being the First Annual Report of the Commissioner of Statistics for the Year Ending January 1st, 1860.* Hartford: Press of Case, Lockwood, 1860.

Missouri. State Board of Agriculture. *Twenty-Eighth Annual Report of the Missouri State Board of Agriculture.* Jefferson City, Mo.: State Printers, 1895.

Modigliani, Franco, and Richard Brumberg. "Utility Analysis and the Consumption Function: An Interpretation of Cross-Section Data." In *Post-Keynesian Economics,* ed. K. Kurihara. New Brunswick, N.J.: Rutgers Univ. Press, 1954.

Morrison, F. B. *Feed and Feeding.* 20th ed. Ithaca, N.Y.: Morrison, 1936.

Mortenson, W. P., H. H. Erdman, and J. H. Draxler. "Wisconsin Farm Prices–1841 to 1933." *Agricultural Experiment Station of the University of Wisconsin Research Bulletin 119,* Nov. 1933.

Neal, Larry D. "Cross-Spectral Analysis of Long Swings in Atlantic Migration." *Research in Economic History* 1(1976):260–97.

Neal, Larry D., and Paul J. Uselding. "Immigration: A Neglected Source of American Economic Growth, 1790–1912." *Oxford Economic Papers* 24, 1(Mar. 1972):68–88.

Newell, William. "The Sources of Increasing Wealth Inequality: A Study of Testators in Butler County, Ohio, 1803–65." Paper presented at National Bureau of Economic Research Conference, Williamsburg, Va., 1977.

Newhall, J. B. *A Glimpse of Iowa in 1846; or, The Emigrant's Guide, and State Directory; with a Description of the New Purchase: Embracing Much Practical Advice and Useful Information to Intending Emigrants.* 2d ed. Burlington, Iowa: W. D. Skillman, 1846.

New Hampshire Agricultural Experiment Station. *Bulletin 120.* Durham: Univ. of New Hampshire, 1905.

New Hampshire Journal of Agriculture, 14 Apr. 1859.

New York State Agricultural Society. *Journal* (various issues).

______. *Transactions* 8(1845).

New York State Dairymen's Association. *Annual Report of the New York State Dairymen's Association for 1878.* Albany, N.Y., 1878.

New York State Chamber of Commerce. *Annual Report of the Chamber of Commerce of the State of New York for the Year 1859–60.* New York: John W. Amerman, 1860.

North, Douglass C. *The Economic Growth of the United States, 1790-1860.* Englewood Cliffs, N.J.: Prentice Hall, 1961.
Northern Farmer 1(1854).
Norton, L. J., and B. B. Wilson. "Prices of Illinois Farm Products from 1866 to 1929." *University of Illinois Agricultural Experiment Station Bulletin 351,* July 1930.
Ohio Agricultural Experiment Station. *Bulletin 326.* Wooster, Ohio: Experiment Station Press, July 1918.
Ohio Commissioner of Statistics. *Annual Report.* Columbus (various issues).
Ohio Dairyman's Association. *Report of the Fifth Annual Meeting for 1899.* Columbus, Ohio, 1900.
Olmstead, Alan L. "The Mechanization of Reaping and Mowing in American Agriculture." *Journal of Economic History* 35, 2(June 1975):327-52.
Olmstead, Frederick Law. *A Journey in the Seaboard Slave States.* New York: Dix and Edwards, 1856.
Owsley, Frank W. *Plain Folks of the Old South.* Baton Rouge: Louisiana State Univ. Press, 1949.
Paglin, Morton. "The Measurement and Trend of Inequality: A Basic Revision." *American Economic Review* 65, 3(Sept. 1975):598-609.
Parker, Nathan H. *The Iowa Handbook for 1856.* Boston: John P. Jewett, 1856.
Parker, William N., ed. *The Structure of the Cotton Economy of the Antebellum South.* Washington, D.C.: Agricultural History Society, 1970.
______. "Labor Productivity in Cotton Farming: The History of a Research." *Agricultural History* 53, 1(Jan. 1979):228-44.
Parker, William N., and Judith L. V. Klein. "Productivity Growth in Grain Production in the United States, 1840-60 and 1900-10." In Conference on Research in Income and Wealth, *Output, Employment and Productivity in the United States After 1800,* Studies in Income and Wealth 30. Princeton: Princeton Univ. Press, 1966, 523-82.
Passell, Peter. *Essays in the Economics of Nineteenth Century Land Policy.* New York: Arno Press, 1975.
Peet, Richard. "The Spatial Dynamics of Commercial Agriculture in the Nineteenth-Century: A Von Thunen Approach." *Economic Geography* 45, 4(Oct. 1969):283-301.
Pessen, Edward. "The Egalitarian Myth and American Social Reality: Wealth, Mobility, and Equality in the 'Era of the Common Man,' " *American Historical Review* 76, 3(Oct. 1971):989-1034.
______. *Riches, Class and Power before the Civil War.* Lexington, Mass.: D. C. Heath, 1973.
______. "On a Recent Cliometric Attempt to Resurrect the Myth of Antebellum Egalitarianism." *Social Science History* 3, 2(1979):208-27.
______. "The Beleaguered Myth of Antebellum Egalitarianism." *Social Science History* 6, 1(1982):111-28.
Phillips, Ulrich B. "The Origin and Growth of the Southern Black Belts." *American Historical Review* 11, 9(July 1906):798-816.
Pirtle, T. R. "Trend of the Butter Industry in the United States and Other Countries." U.S. Department of Agriculture, *Circular 70.* Washington, D.C.: GPO, 1919.
______. *A Handbook of Dairy Statistics.* Washington, D.C.: GPO, 1933.
Plough, Loom and Anvil 8(1858):438.

Podder, N., and N. C. Kakwoni. "The Distribution of Wealth in Australia." *Review of Income and Wealth* 22, 1(Mar. 1976):75–92.

Potter, R. G. "Birth Intervals: Structure and Change." *Population Studies* 17, 2(1963):156–66.

Prairie Farmer (various issues).

Projector, Dorothy, and Gertrude S. Weiss. *Survey of Financial Characteristics of Consumers.* Washington, D.C.: Federal Reserve Board, 1966.

Regan, John. *The Western Wilds of America, or, Backwoods and Prairies; and Scenes of the Valley of the Mississippi.* 2d ed. Edinburgh: John Menzies, 1859. Also published under the title *The Emigrant's Guide to the Western States of America.*

Robbins, Roy M. *Our Landed Heritage: The Public Domain 1776–1936.* Princeton: 1942. Reprinted Lincoln: Univ. of Nebraska Press, 1962.

Rogin, Leo. *The Introduction of Farm Machinery in its Relation to the Productivity of Labor in the Agriculture of the United States during the Nineteenth Century.* Berkeley: Univ. of California Press, 1931.

Ronk, S. E. "Prices of Farm Products in New York State, 1841 to 1935." *Cornell University Agricultural Experiment Station Bulletin 643.* Mar. 1936.

Rothenberg, Winifred C. "A Price Index for Rural Massachusetts, 1750–1855." *Journal of Economic History* 39, 4(Dec. 1980):975–1001.

______. "The Market and Massachusetts Farmers, 1750–1855." *Journal of Economic History* 41, 2(June 1981):283–314.

Runciman, Walter G. *Relative Deprivation and Social Justice.* Berkeley: Univ. of California Press, 1966.

Saloutos, Theodore. "The Agricultural Problem and Nineteenth-Century Industrialism." *Agricultural History* 22, 3(1948):156–74.

Schmidt, Louis B. "Internal Commerce and the Development of a National Economy Before 1860." *Journal of Political Economy* 47, 6(Dec. 1939):798–822.

Schob, David. "Agricultural Labor in the Midwest, 1815–1860." Ph.D. diss., Univ. of Illinois, 1970.

______. *Hired Hands and Plowboys.* Urbana: Univ. of Illinois Press, 1975.

Seaman, Ezra. *Essays on the Progress of Nations.* Detroit: M. Geiger, 1846.

Shannon, Fred A. "The Homestead Act and the Labor Surplus." *American Historical Review* 41, 4(July 1936):631–51.

Simon, Julian L. *The Economics of Population Growth.* Princeton: Princeton Univ. Press, 1977.

Slicher van Bath, B. H. *The Agrarian History of Western Europe, A.D. 500–1850.* London: Arnold, 1963.

Smith, Sidney. *The Settler's New Home.* London: J. Hendrick, 1849.

Soltow, Lee. *Patterns of Wealthholding in Wisconsin Since 1850.* Madison, Wis.: Univ. of Wisconsin Press, 1971.

______. "The Census of Wealth of Men in Australia in 1915 and the United States in 1860 and 1870." *Australian Economic History Review* 12, 2(Sept. 1972):125–41.

______. *Men and Wealth in the United States, 1850–1870.* New Haven: Yale Univ. Press, 1975.

______. "Male Inheritance Expectations in the United States in 1870." *Review of Economics and Statistics* 64, 2(May 1982):252–60.

______. "Land Fragmentation as an Index of History in the Virginia Military

District of Ohio." *Explorations in Economic History* 20, 3(July 1983):263–73.

Steckel, Richard H. "Antebellum Southern White Fertility: A Demographic and Economic Analysis." *Journal of Economic History* 40, 2(June 1980):331–50.

______. "The Economic Foundations of East-West Migration During the Nineteenth Century." *Explorations in Economic History* 20, 1(Jan. 1983):14–36.

Stewart, Henry. *The Dairyman's Manual.* New York: Orange Judd, 1888.

Steward, John F. *The Reaper.* New York: Greenberg, 1931.

Stiglitz, J. E. "Distribution of Income and Wealth Among Individuals." *Econometrica* 37, 3(July 1969):382–97.

Stilwell, Lewis D. "Migration from Vermont, 1776–1860." *Proceedings of the Vermont Historical Society* 5(1937):63–245.

Strand, Norman V. "Prices of Farm Products in Iowa, 1851–1940." *Iowa State College Agricultural Experiment Station Research Bulletin 303.* May 1942.

Strauss, F., and L. H. Bean. "Gross Farm Income and Indices of Farm Production and Prices in the United States 1869–1937." *USDA Technical Bulletin 703.* Washington, D.C.: U.S. Department of Agriculture, 1940.

Survey Research Center. *1962 Survey of Consumer Finances, Monograph 32.* Survey Research Center of the Univ. of Michigan, Ann Arbor, 1963.

Sutch, Richard. "Care and Feeding of Slaves." In *Reckoning With Slavery,* ed. Paul A. David et al. New York: Oxford Univ. Press, 1976.

Swan, Dale. The Structure and Profitability of the American Rice Industry, 1859. Ph.D. diss., Univ. of North Carolina, Chapel Hill, 1972.

Swierenga, Robert P. "Land Speculator 'Profits' Reconsidered: Central Iowa as a Test Case." *Journal of Economic History* 26, 1(Mar. 1966):1–28.

______. *Pioneers and Profits: Land Speculation on the Iowa Frontier.* Ames: Iowa State Univ. Press, 1968.

Sydenstricker, Edgar. *Health and Environment.* New York: McGraw-Hill, 1933.

Taeuber, C., and I. Taeuber. *Changing Population of the United States.* New York: John Wiley, 1958.

Taylor, George Rogers. *The Transportation Revolution, 1815–1860.* New York: Harper and Row, 1968.

Thomas, Brinley. *Migration and Economic Growth.* 2d ed. Cambridge: Cambridge Univ. Press, 1973.

Thomas, J. J. *Farm Implements and Farm Machinery.* New York: Orange Judd, 1869.

Thompson, W., and P. Whelpton. *Population Trends in the United States.* New York: McGraw-Hill, 1953.

Thornthwaite, C. W. *Internal Migration in the United States.* Philadelphia: Univ. of Pennsylvania Press, 1934.

The (London) *Times,* September 28, 1968.

Tocqueville, Alexis de. *Democracy in America.* 2 vols. New York: Alfred Knopf, 1946 (first published in French in 1835 and in English as translated by Henry Reeve in 1838. This translation is a revision of the Reeve and Bowen translations by Phillip Bradley).

Towne, M. W., and W. D. Rasmussen. "Gross Farm Product and Gross Investment in the Nineteenth Century." In Conference on Research in Income and Wealth, *Trends in the American Economy of the Nineteenth Century,* Studies in Income and Wealth 24. Princeton: Princeton Univ. Press, 1960, 255–312.

Trussell, James, and Richard Steckel. "The Age of Slaves at Menarche and Their First Birth." *Journal of Interdisciplinary History* 8, 3(1978):477–505.

Tryon, Rolla M. *Household Manufacturers in the United States, 1640–1860.* Chicago: Univ. of Chicago Press, 1917.

Turner, Frederick Jackson. *The Frontier in American History.* New York: Henry Holt, 1920.

United Nations. Food and Agriculture Organization. *Technical Conversion Factors for Agricultural Commodities.* Rome: FAO, 1960.

U.S. Census Office. Seventh Census. *Statistical View of the United States . . . Being a Compendium of the Seventh Census.* Washington, D.C.: A. O. P. Nicholson, 1854.

U.S. Census Office. Eighth Census. *United States—1860. Act of Congress of twenty-third May 1850. Instruction to U.S. Marshals. Instructions to Assistants.* Washington, D.C.: G. W. Bowman, 1860.

______. *Agriculture of the United States in 1860.* Washington, D.C.: GPO, 1864.

______. *Manufactures of the United States in 1860.* Washington, D.C.: GPO, 1864.

______. *Population of the United States in 1860.* Washington, D.C.: GPO, 1864.

______. *Statistics of the United States in 1860.* Washington, D.C.: GPO, 1866.

U.S. Census Office. Ninth Census. *The Statistics of the Population of the United States.* Washington, D.C.: GPO, 1872.

U.S. Census Office. Tenth Census. *Report upon the Statistics of Agriculture Compiled from Returns Received at the Tenth Census.* Washington, D.C.: GPO, 1883.

______. *Report on the Statistics of Wages . . ., supplement to the Tenth Census.* Vol. 20. Washington, D.C.: GPO, 1886.

U.S. Census Office. Twelfth Census. *Agriculture, Part I. Farms, Livestock and Animal Products.* Washington, D.C.: GPO, 1902.

______. *Twelfth Census of the United States: Population.* Vol. 1. Washington, D.C.: GPO, 1902.

______. *Abstract of the Twelfth Census of the United States.* 3d ed. Washington, D.C.: GPO, 1904.

U.S. Census Office. Fifteenth Census. *Agriculture, Volume II. Part 1—The Northern States.* Washington, D.C.: GPO, 1932.

U.S. Congress. *Report from the Secretary of the Treasury, on the State of the Finances, Dec. 3, 1845.* 29th Cong., 1st sess., 1846. Sen. Doc. 2.

U.S. Department of Agriculture. *Report of the Commissioners of Agriculture for 1865.* Washington, D.C.: GPO, 1866.

______. Division of Statistics. "Wages of Farm Labor in the United States." *Miscellaneous Series Report 4.* Washington, D.C.: GPO, 1892.

______. Bureau of Animal Industry. *Sixteenth Annual Report of the Bureau of Animal Industry.* Washington, D.C.: GPO, 1899.

______. *Yearbook of Agriculture, 1899.* Washington, D.C.: GPO, 1900.

______. Division of Statistics. George K. Holmes. "The Course of Prices of Farm Implements and Machinery for a Series of Years." *Miscellaneous Bulletin 18.* Washington, D.C.: GPO, 1901.

______. Division of Statistics. *Bulletin 25.* Washington, D.C.: GPO, 1903.

______. Bureau of Animal Industry. *Bulletin 169.* Washington, D.C.: GPO, 1913.

______. *Statistical Bulletin 25.* Washington, D.C.: GPO, 1929.

______. "Crop Yields and Weather." *Miscellaneous Publication 471.* Washington, D. C.: GPO, Feb. 1942.

______. *Farm Wage Rates, Farm Employment, and Related Data.* Washington, D.C.: Bureau of Agricultural Economics, 1943.

______. "Conversion Factors and Weights and Measures for Agricultural Commodities and Their Products." *USDA Statistical Bulletin 362.* Washington, D.C.: GPO, 1965.
U.S. Department of Commerce. Bureau of Labor. *Eighteenth Annual Report of the Commissioner of Labor. 1903. Cost of Living and Retail Prices of Food.* Washington, D.C.: GPO, 1904.
______. *Historical Statistics of the United States from Colonial Times to 1970.* Washington, D.C.: GPO, 1975. Series A202–203.
U.S. Department of the Interior. Geological Survey. *The National Atlas of the United States of America.* Washington, D.C.: GPO, 1970.
U.S. Patent Office. *Report of the Commissioner of Patents. Part II, Agriculture.* Washington, D.C., various issues, 1844–1860.
Vedder, Richard K., and David Stockdale. "The Profitability of Slavery Revisited: A Different Approach." *Agricultural History* 49, 2(Apr. 1975), 392–404.
Vedder, Richard K., David Klingaman, and Lowell Galloway. "The Profitability of Ante-Bellum Agriculture in the Cotton Belt: Some New Evidence." *Atlantic Economic Journal* 2, 2(1974):30–47.
Vial, E. P. "Production and Consumption of Dairy Products." *USDA Technical Bulletin 722.* Washington, D.C.: GPO, 1940.
Von Thunen, Johann H. *The Isolated State.* 1826. Reprinted New York: Pergamon Press, 1966.
Wallace, Henry A. *Agricultural Prices.* Des Moines, Iowa: Wallace Publishing, 1920.
Ward, Edward G. "Milk Transportation: Freight Rates to the Fifteen Largest Cities in the United States." U.S. Department of Agriculture, Division of Statistics, *Bulletin 25.* Washington, D.C.: GPO, 1903.
Weaver, Herbert. *Mississippi Farmers, 1850–1860.* Nashville: Vanderbilt Univ. Press, 1945.
Webb, Thomas H. *Information for Kansas Immigrants.* Boston: New England Emigrant Aid Co., 1856.
Wilkinson, Maurice. "European Migration to the United States: An Econometric Analysis of Aggregate Labor Supply and Demand." *Review of Economics and Statistics* 52, 1(Jan. 1970):272–79.
Willard, X. A. *A Treatise on American Butter Factories and Butter Manufacture.* Madison, Wis.: Wisconsin State Agricultural Society, 1871.
Willcox, Walter, ed. *International Migrations.* Vol. 2. New York: NBER, 1931.
Williamson, H. F., ed. *The Growth of the American Economy.* New York: Prentice-Hall, 1951.
Winters, D. L. *Farmers Without Farms: Agricultural Tenancy in Nineteenth Century Iowa.* Westport, Conn.: Greenwood Press, 1978.
Wisconsin Dairymen's Association. *Fourteenth Annual Report of the Wisconsin Dairymen's Association.* Madison, Wis., 1886.
Wisconsin Farmer 8(1856).
Wisconsin State Agricultural Society. *Transactions of the Wisconsin State Agricultural Society 1883-84.* Madison, Wis.: State Printer, 1883, 1884.
Woll, F. W. *Dairy Calendar for 1895.* New York: John Wiley, 1895.
Working Farmer 2(1850).
Wright, Carroll D. *History and Growth of the United States Census.* Washington, D.C.: GPO, 1900.
Wright, Gavin. " 'Economic Democracy' and the Concentration of Agricultural

Wealth in the Cotton South, 1850–1860." *Agricultural History* 44, 1(Jan. 1970):63–93. Reprinted in William N. Parker, ed. *The Cotton Economy and the Structure of the Antebellum South.* Washington, D.C.: Agricultural History Society, 1970, 63–93.

Wrigley, E. A. *Population and History.* New York: McGraw-Hill, 1969.

Yang, Donghyu. "Notes on the Wealth Distribution of Farm Households in the United States, 1860: A New Look at Two Manuscript Census Samples." *Explorations in Economic History* 21, 1(Jan. 1984):88–102.

Yasuba, Y. *Birth Rates of the White Population in the United States 1800–1860.* Baltimore: Johns Hopkins Univ. Press, 1961.

INDEX